NOT BY FACT ALONE

Essays on the Writing and Reading of History

John Clive was born in Berlin in 1924 and educated in Germany, England and the United States, graduating from the University of North Carolina in 1943. He served in the US Army during World War Two, then obtained his doctorate from Harvard University in 1952 and taught history there until 1960. After a spell in the History Department of the University of Chicago, he returned to Harvard in 1965 as Professor of History and Literature. In 1978 he became William R. Kenan, Jr., Professor of History and Literature at Harvard.

He has served as general editor of the University of Chicago Press series "Classics of British Historical Literature". His own publications include *Scotch Reviewers* (1957), an edition of Carlyle's *History of Frederick the Great* and (with Thomas Pinney) of Macaulay's *Selected Writings*. His *Macaulay: The Shaping of the Historian* (1973) won the National Book Award in 1974 and the Robert Livingston Schuyler Prize of the American Historical Association in 1976.

John Clive

NOT BY FACT
ALONE

*Essays on the Writing and
Reading of History*

COLLINS HARVILL
8 Grafton Street, London W1
1990

COLLINS HARVILL
William Collins Sons & Co. Ltd
London · Glasgow · Sydney · Auckland
Toronto · Johannesburg

100890178

Grateful acknowledgment is made to the following, who printed or broadcast the original versions of the essays: *The American Scholar*; Australian Broadcasting Corporation; Australian Historical Association *Bulletin*; *Critical Review*; *Daedalus*; Gerald Duckworth & Co., Ltd.; Edinburgh University Press; *Harvard English Studies*; *Harvard Magazine*; *History & Theory*; *History Today*; *The Nation*; *New Republic*; *New York Times*; *Partisan Review*; Massachusetts Historical Society *Proceedings*; *Review of English Literature*; *Times Literary Supplement*; University of Chicago Press; *University Publishing*; *Victorian Studies*.

BRITISH LIBRARY CATALOGUING IN PUBLICATION DATA

Clive, John, *1924*–
Not by fact alone: essays on the writing and reading of history
1. Historiography
I. Title
907'.2

ISBN 0-00-272060-4

Published in the United States by Alfred A. Knopf Inc. 1989
First published in Great Britain by Collins Harvill 1989
This edition first published by Collins Harvill 1990

© 1989 by John Clive

Printed and bound in Great Britain by
Hartnolls Limited, Bodmin, Cornwall

To
Charles and Hanna Gray
Wallace MacCaffrey
and to
the memory of
Isabel MacCaffrey

Contents

Preface

One can learn from the great historians: first of all, about the nature of genius. Reading masterpieces like Gibbon's *Decline and Fall of the Roman Empire* or Burckhardt's *Renaissance in Italy*, one encounters that mixture of learning, personal voice, view of the world and human nature, and knowledge of the past filtered through mind and art out of which great history emerges. But one can acquire more than a general sense of awe in the face of greatness. One can observe how at times works of history are cast in certain molds, e.g., how those historians writing in the tradition of the "Whig Interpretation of History" in England tend to shape their works within the given context of a continuous pattern of uninterrupted, glorious constitutional progress through the ages. The mold is both flexible and resilient, but it naturally shapes the structure of the matter it contains. And one need not go all the way with the historiographer and critic Hayden White, who advocates approaching written history as if it were simply another genre of literature, like the novel or poetry, to agree with him that there are indeed literary as well as substantive molds, that as alert readers we should be on the lookout for "modes," such as irony, comedy, or tragedy. But beyond these larger shaping forces there are the tricks of the trade. Each historian possesses and uses a bagful of them, and we are in the fortunate position of being able to watch them fish the appropriate trick out of the bag.

Take transitions, for instance, something that Macaulay considered to be the hardest and at the same time the most essential part of effective historical writing. As a reading of the famous third chapter of his *History* demonstrates in particularly striking fashion, he made himself a master in the use of transitions; leading his readers in seemingly inevitable fashion from one subject to the next. As another example of a trick of the trade, take the creation of suspense, the art of not revealing one's "thesis" or interpretation at the start, but rather taking the reader along as a companion in an apparently gradual and arduous search for what the writer or guide certainly already knows when he starts out on his final (written) journey. Here Elie Halévy is the great master, and we have much to learn from him. One of the essays in this volume deals with the use of the personal pronoun by certain historians. That, too, may be regarded as an occasionally effective trick of the trade.

I am not maintaining that the study of such matters will necessarily make us, as readers, into great historians. Listening to records of great piano playing will not make us into great pianists, either. But it gives us some sense of the difficulties and the particular skills involved; and who knows, once in a while, it might even improve an amateur performance. The same is true when we read the great historians with the intention of learning from them.

Their use of wit and humor—ever since Herodotus, some of the great historians have employed one or both—is something else to watch out for. In my essay on Gibbon's wit I try to show not only that he was one of the most amusing writers of the eighteenth century, but also that his wit served a more serious purpose in the *Decline and Fall*; that it underlined his conviction that enthusiasm and attempted denials of the earthbound realities of human nature were bound to be delusive, and therefore fit to be laughed out of court. Gibbon's wit derives in great part from that conviction—as does his treatment of the early Christians.

The most important, but perhaps at the same time the most evanescent and hard-to-catch of a great historian's skills is the way in which he uses his historical imagination. I have attempted, in the case of Macaulay, to define his own particular brand of that indispensable skill, and have used the word "propulsive" to characterize it. I have also tried to link it to his personal propensity for daydreaming, which he himself maintained—in paradoxical fashion—was a prerequisite for his devotion to accuracy in historical writing. I hope, of course, that

I am right in what I say. But this sort of thing is hard to prove. There is still plenty of room for students of the great historians from this angle of vision. What is vital is that all readers should be aware of the crucial role played by the historical imagination in the writings of the great historians.

LIVES AND VARIETY

Is there a special "historical personality" that lends itself in particular to the writing of history? Are similar motives at work, impelling historians to write? I take up these questions in some detail in the essay on cliographers. But there are no short and easy answers to them, mainly because the variety of personalities involved is so great: Carlyle, driven to history by urgent needs related to that strange amalgam of diluted Calvinism and German idealism that had replaced orthodox Christianity in his life; Gibbon, attracted to his mighty theme by that fateful conjunction of Christian triumph and Roman decline that first captured his imagination (so he tells us) on October 15, 1764, as he sat musing amidst the ruins of the Capitol, "while the barefooted fryars were singing Vespers in the temple of Jupiter." Macaulay, that lifelong epitome of the precocious child, imbued by his stern Evangelical father, Zachary, the antislavist, with that combination of moral conviction and public service that marked his political career as well as his writings; Jacob Burckhardt, the Swiss clergyman's son, led to the study of history in general, and that of the Italian Renaissance in particular, by his consuming interest in German medieval architecture; Tocqueville, proud scion of generations of Norman nobility, attempting to cope through history with the double traumas of revolution and democracy; his countryman Jules Michelet, printer's son and celebrant of the great French Revolution, obsessed by Gnostic notions about the conjunction of opposites, determined to erase the border between the worlds of history and nature—the list could go on and on, and variety would remain its essence.

And the variety of factors conducive to historical writing would have to take account of institutional as well as personal and intellectual ones. Thus I have tried to show, for instance, in my essay on "The Social Background of the Scottish Renaissance," that it was no accident that the teaching of history at Scottish universities in the late seventeenth century was fostered by the prevalence in Scotland at that time of "civil," i.e., Roman, law, which, so to speak, had built-in historical dimensions. But even though, over the last three centuries, universities have become ever more important in their capacity to form a matrix for historical studies and the writing of history, one should not forget that museums, monuments, traditions, pageantry, and ceremonial, as well as the very streets and buildings of ancient towns and cities, have also played their part in turning the minds of future historians towards the exploration of the past.

Variety, by the way, need not only be sought among universally acknowledged "great" historians. There are others who, by virtue of their special roles, contribute to it. Take, as an example, Lytton Strachey, the quintessential product of Bloomsbury, to whom some would deny the very name of historian because his respect for historical fact does not always meet the minimum standards expected from practitioners of the art of history. Nonetheless, his *Eminent Victorians* (1918), a slashing attack by way of four biographical essays on some hypocritical and self-righteous aspects of the Victorian age, will endure as an iconoclastic masterpiece, and not only because it impelled a civil servant named G. M. Young—later an essayist and historian—who considered it a "preposterous misreading of the age," to write his own, masterly *Victorian England: Portrait of an Age* (first published in 1934). Here is evidence that anger and polemics, however "bad" in themselves, can and do serve to advance the cause of getting at historical truth.

Very different from either Strachey or Young, but nonetheless entitled to attention as an extraordinary writer of history in fictional form, is Flora Thompson, who in the guise of Laura, the stonemason's daughter, has given us in *Lark Rise to Candleford* (first published in 1945), a truly remarkable evocation of Oxfordshire village and small-town life at the turn of the nineteenth century; probing profoundly into *mentalités* before that concept had even been invented, and depicting unforgettably how an organic society, with its special customs and ways of expression, yielded to the new economic and cultural forces of modernity. If the definition of greatness on the part of historians includes durability, then Flora Thompson, more widely read now than ever before, certainly qualifies, along with seemingly more exalted figures in the pantheon.

COMPARISONS

The great historians did not write in isolation from one another. For one thing, those writing in modern times have been well aware that they are standing on the shoulders of formidable predecessors. Macaulay—in his private journal—used to compare his own achievement with that of Thucydides; and, judging himself by that standard, more than once expressed his chagrin at not being able to match the great Athenian. Henry Adams passionately admired Tocqueville, and modeled his own chapters on "The United States in 1800" on Macaulay's third chapter in *The History of England*, in which he surveys English society in 1685. But, as I have pointed out in one or two essays, the connections between great historians from various countries, writing in the nineteenth century, go considerably beyond their constituting a mutual admiration society, and deserve to be further explored. After all, many of them were subject to strains and stresses arising from broad general trends that had an impact on them all—democratization, secularization, various ways in which the advent of modernity made itself felt—and those trends and their reaction to them could not but be reflected in their historical work. That reflection manifests itself not only in statements, at times explicit, at other times implicit, in which they express their concern about contemporary problems. It also becomes apparent in the way in which they emphasize certain historical questions, for example the role of collectivities, whether classes or groups, or of figures representative of these collective bodies. It is by making such comparisons that we can get a sense of the manner in which changes in historical method may be linked to more general patterns of social and ideological change, and in which historians very different in their political views and preoccupations yet find themselves confronted in their historical writing by similar problems and challenges. The distance between Macaulay's archetypical country gentleman mocked and bespattered by the London crowd, and Burckhardt's attempt to distill and to define a particular Renaissance personality may seem very long. But comparison between historians shows that the length may well be deceptive.

Indeed, one of the chief pleasures of reading historians comparatively is to come across the unexpected. This can happen either when, as I recount in the essay called "Peter and the Wallah," it turns out that two series of pseudonymous letters published by two different British authors more than forty years apart—one dealing with the Edinburgh cultural scene in the early nineteenth century, the other with some of the more unsavory aspects of the British *Raj* in the 1860s—surprise the reader by some common assumptions underlying very different preoccupations. It can also happen when, as I point out in "Looking over a Four-Leaf Clover," one suddenly finds oneself admiring well-known historians for reasons not usually adduced in the textbooks: Marx for his literary skill, Tocqueville for his mixture of mordancy and mystery. It is my hope that these and the other essays might persuade some readers to turn to the historians themselves, and to find out what instruction and enjoyment *they* are able to derive from them.

Two things are worth pointing out in conclusion: Historians, unlike poets and novelists, must try to get their facts right. But fact alone, even when aided and abetted by the most sophisticated cliometrics, will never be sufficient to cast that spell that lingers in the memory and is conducive not just to reading, but to rereading. Which explains the title of this book.

Apart from corrections of printing errors, and a few very minor stylistic changes, the essays in this volume appear as originally published.

I should like to express special thanks to two old friends, Bernard Bailyn and Jane Garrett, for their good advice and their steadfast encouragement.

CAMBRIDGE, MASSACHUSETTS
JUNE 1988

I

INTRODUCTION

The Use of the Past

Some uses of history are both personal and practical. I am writing what I hope will eventually turn out to be this talk standing up—my sheets of paper resting on a lectern kindly lent me by a colleague at the Australian National University. I have assumed this unaccustomed position because of a sore neck that makes writing in any other position painful, and concentration almost impossible. Needless to say, I feel sorry for myself. But there is some comfort. As a historian of nineteenth-century England, I am familiar with the Rev. Robert Malthus's great and gloomy essay on population. And I recall that one of the ways in which Malthus effectively demolishes William Godwin's contention that it ought to be possible for mankind eventually to place all bodily functions under the control of reason is by remarking that in the very act of writing his essay he finds himself afflicted by a toothache so virulent that, try as he might, it keeps his mind off the subject.

I am not remotely comparing myself with a thinker of genius like Malthus. But I am beginning this talk with a personal anecdote because some knowledge of history—in this instance the history of ideas—enables me to solace myself with the reflection that others before me

Broadcast Talk, Australian Broadcasting Corporation, April 30, 1984 tried to work while in pain, failed for a while, but in the end managed to finish the task at hand.

Not exactly a noble use of the past? Too egocentric? I plead guilty on both counts. Perhaps it would have been more apposite to begin by quoting Burckhardt to the effect that history teaches wisdom forever, or Thucydides on the instructive benefits to be derived by future readers—in particular, statesmen in quest of avoiding mistakes—from his account of the Peloponnesian War; an account, he hoped, that would prove to be a possession for all time.

But I happen to believe that the use of the past is a very personal matter; almost, to use a variant of the Malthusian *Leitmotiv,* like the use of a toothbrush. For the historian, as for everyone else, it is bound to involve one's own past; one's professional preoccupations; and one's predilections, be they loves or hatreds, likes or dislikes, opinions or prejudices. Let me take up each of these in turn; remaining frankly subjective rather than attempting to assume a tone that might sound either oracular or didactic.

I grew up in Berlin, the son of middle-class German Jewish parents who were so "assimilated" that they couldn't believe that the Nazis would retain power for more than a few years, or were really serious about their anti-Semitic slogans; until shop windows were smashed, synagogues burned, and lawyers, doctors, and businessmen carted off by the thousands to concentration camps during and after the "Crystal Night" of November 1938.

Assimilated they may have believed themselves to be, yet at the same time no less proud of being Jewish. One image that sticks in my mind is that of my father, himself a lawyer, walking to Jewish High Holy Day services in formal attire, top hat and all, carrying his prayer book in his right hand, for all to see; the iron cross "first class," which he had won in the First World War, pinned to his frock coat. "They wouldn't dare lay a hand on me," he used to say. He turned out to be one of the lucky ones. He was arrested; then released, on condition that he and my mother and brother get out of Germany at once, leaving all their money and possessions behind.

By that time I had already been sent away to boarding school in England, a decision taken by my parents when the secondary school I attended in Berlin, the Französische Gymnasium (traditionally under French influence and supposedly immune from anti-Jewish manifestations), forbade all "non-Aryan" boys and girls to join the annual school outing, a boating party on the river Spree. *That* had been too much for my mother, whose great pride and joy was that I, then a twelve-year-old, had indubitably earned the coveted privilege of entertaining cruise passengers on my concertina, or, as it was (for this occasion aptly) called, my *Schifferklavier.*

I conjure up these two vignettes—my father en route to the synagogue, myself in tears as the school's *Direktor* made the announcement that barred me from the boating party—not in order to lay claim to extraordinary scars and sufferings that taught me the real meaning of tyranny and persecution, but merely to state that this early part of my past left me with an insight I have found useful, both as a historian and as a human being: there *are* evil people who won't be deterred from their nefarious doings by what might be considered by the self-deceived as special circumstances. His iron cross, first class and all, did not save my father from arrest. The fact that my school had close links with France did not prevent it from getting rid of its Jewish students.

I must, however, supplement that insight with another, which may appear to be in conflict with it, but which simply reinforces that portion of it which tells us to take nothing for granted, especially when it comes to the judgment of human character. One of the mathematics teachers at the Französische Gymnasium was a marvelously good-humored and civilized Jewish gentleman called Dr. L. I remember him singing the role of Doctor Bartolo in a resonant bass voice at a school performance of *The Barber of Seville,* and doing so with irresistible comic gusto. The general assumption among former students of his was that since he had been unable to emigrate, he must have perished in a concentration camp. To the surprise of all of us, he survived World War II and was able to live to a ripe old age. The seemingly incredible, but actually true, explanation was that for a number of years Dr. L. had been hidden, at incalculable risk to his benefactor's own life, in the house belonging to a fellow teacher who, often jack-booted and swaggering about in his Brown Shirt uniform, had generally been considered by far the most brutal and relentless Nazi on the school staff.

I think I have said enough to indicate that one's own personal history can prove to be useful; and that by no means all the lessons the past has to teach us must derive from public events such as wars, international crises, or the lives and careers of the great and powerful.

But, of course, as a professional historian, one is bound to have a special interest in the whole problem of the use of the past, an interest going beyond one's personal experiences. From this professional point of view, I have been fortunate in the subjects that have preoccupied

me: the Victorian age in England and, more specifically, the life and
works of perhaps the most famous English nineteenth-century historian, Thomas Babington Macaulay.

All ages can, in some sense, be called transitional; but the Victorian
age, in particular, lends itself to that hackneyed description. Iron and
steel were coming into their own. A largely agricultural society of
villages and small towns was giving way to an urban one in which
cities and factories came to play the predominant role. The old hierarchical class structure, dominated by the aristocracy, was being
both questioned and threatened from below, as prosperous middle-
class merchants and factory owners gradually managed to gain the
political power they still lacked at the start of the nineteenth century,
and as an ever more restless (and numerous) working class made it
clear, at times by means of violent action, that it could not be expected
to bear appalling living conditions and deprivations of every kind in
acquiescent silence. Socialism, Biblical criticism, Darwinism, agnosticism—new and shocking ideas—made themselves felt and posed a
danger to traditional values and opinions. Orthodoxies, whether political, economic, or religious, were increasingly open to argument
and question. Doubt was everywhere.

In such an age, when established institutions and verities were laid
under considerable stress, the past—or, rather, selected views of selected portions of the past—had many uses: as yardstick and example,
source of comfort or retreat, object of attack. Certainly, spokesmen
for various political creeds fully exploited those possibilities. You
might reasonably ask: How were they able to do so with impunity?
Didn't the historians correct them when they went wrong? Well, first
of all, even the professional historians of our own day—like other
people—have views about politics and do not always make an effort
to keep those views out of their histories. And this was even more
the case at a time before professional history had come into its own.
Indeed, the spokesmen for the various political creeds often *included*
historians.

Radicals argued that Anglo-Saxon England had been a truly free
country with democratic institutions, and that it was the Normans
who had subverted those institutions by imposing a royal and aristocratic "yoke." Whigs and Liberals, in their turn, argued that it was
the revolutions of the seventeenth century, particularly the bloodless
"glorious" revolution of 1688 (which brought William and Mary to
the throne) that had put an end to the despotism of the Tudors and
Stuarts, and had laid the foundations of English stability and pros-

perity. Romantic Tories, like Disraeli, maintained that the real harm had been done by the Reformation—in particular, the dissolution of the monasteries—which had put an end to that natural alliance between crown, church, and people that had marked England before Henry the Eighth broke with Rome.

All three positions contained sufficient truth to make them palatable even to educated men and women. But all were really using—or, rather, abusing—the past, always a patient and pliable victim, in order to make points about the present. The radicals wanted to get rid of the aristocracy, to give power to the people at large, and to make England into a real democracy. The Liberals were frightened of both the people at large *and* democracy, and wished to keep the governance of England in the safely respectable hands of the middle class. Disraelian Tories despised the Philistine and money-grubbing middle classes and, far from being terrified by the working class, envisioned a nation in which patriotic workingmen, duly provided with their social needs by a benevolent state, would loyally support monarch and aristocracy.

Let us then come to a preliminary finding, to the effect that the past lends itself all too readily to use by those who have a political axe to grind. Nothing works better to further a cause—good or bad—than to lend it legitimacy by supplying it with a long heritage. That is true just as much in our own day as it was true in Victorian England. And not necessarily undesirable. No American who has observed the progress made within the span of just a couple of decades by women and blacks can be altogether cynical or dismissive about the role that the search for a usable past has played in those causes. The historian ought always to be on the lookout for distortion, fantasy, and misrepresentation. Myths die hard, and he or she probably won't be able to find universal acceptance for corrections. But the historian should— at least in retrospect—be able to tell us *why* certain people came to believe certain things about the past.

That sounds eminently reasonable. But it isn't as easy as it sounds. Take, for example, Victorian medievalism, the cult of the middle ages so congenial to some nineteenth-century minds. For many years most historians assumed that a nostalgic return to the middle ages in quest of inspiration and instruction was bound to represent a reactionary, a regressive strategy, employed by those Victorians who, appalled by the ugliness of industrialism, the heartlessness of laissez-faire, and the leveling tendencies of radical democracy, found refuge and surcease in the dreaming spires and hierarchical social arrangements of medieval

Europe. There is, to be sure, plenty of evidence for that point of view. Those intrepid gentlemen in authentic armor who jousted in proper fashion—and in pouring rain—at the Eglinton Tournament for the delectation of a sodden assemblage of lords and ladies (in 1838) were no more advocates of political, economic, or democratic progress than that architect of genius, Welby Pugin, who, in a series of drawings entitled *Contrasts* (1836), set side by side medieval townscapes dominated by Gothic churches and statues and generously flowing water fountains, and their nineteenth-century equivalents, full of prisons, workhouses, and gasworks; or than Thomas Carlyle who, in his *Past and Present* (1843), looked back with affection and admiration to the time when a strong-minded leader like Abbot Samson could give his monastery that fatherly guidance and direction which the parliamentary "talking-shop" of Carlyle's own day had shown itself incapable of exerting.

Yet what are we to make of the neo-Gothic splendors of St. Pancras Station? Or of those Lancashire and North Country merchants and manufacturers who, in their public buildings, their town and trade halls, harked back to the days of the guilds and the Hanseatic League? Or of William Morris, one of the last and greatest of Victorian prophets, whose socialism caught fire from his devotion to medieval art and poetry? It is now quite apparent that nineteenth-century medievalism was not a purely reactionary phenomenon; but, rather, a congeries of ideas, an approach, an outlook that could also be used to lend respectability and grandeur to the new, whether in the form of railway stations or free trade halls, and to inspire those like Morris who wished to change rather than to preserve the society of their day.

If, then, as a historian interested in the Victorians, I became increasingly aware of the fact that the use of the past is a matter of some complexity, that awareness was considerably heightened by my familiarity with the life and works of Macaulay, a familiarity I had to acquire in the process of writing a book about him. Macaulay ought to appear in the *Guinness Book of Records* as perhaps the most precocious child of all time—"Thank you, madam, the agony is abated," he replied, aged four, to the solicitous Lady Waldegrave who, her maid having spilled some hot tea over him, inquired as to how he was feeling. It wasn't *that* many years later that he began to carve out for himself a dazzling career both as a parliamentary orator on the side of the Whigs, and then, after a stint in India, as the author of a *History of England* which, when it began to appear in 1848, became one of the great best sellers of the age. In the first of those roles he participated memorably in the debates on the great Reform Bill of 1832, which enfranchised and gave parliamentary representation to the English middle class and thereby put an end to the favorite nightmare of the aristocracy, a revolutionary alliance between workers and *bourgeoisie,* directed against itself.

One of Macaulay's chief arguments in favor of reform was based on a historical precedent very much present in the minds of his auditors in the House of Commons, the French Revolution of 1789. (There had been another French Revolution in 1830, and that made the exemplary use of the first more frequent in the Reform Bill debates.) It was because the French nobility had not yielded with a good grace, and in good time, to the just demands of the French people in 1789 that there had followed bloodshed, the execution of the king, and eventually the Terror. This is what Macaulay said, on September 20, 1831, to those Members of Parliament who wanted the House of Lords to reject the Reform Bill:

Have they never heard what effects counsels like their own, when too faithfully followed, have produced? Have they never visited that neighboring country, which still presents to the eye, even of a passing stranger, the signs of a great dissolution and renovation of society? Have they never walked by those stately mansions, now sinking into decay, and portioned out into lodging rooms, which line the silent streets of the Faubourg St. Germain? Have they never seen the ruins of those castles whose terraces and gardens overhang the Loire? Have they never heard that from those magnificent hotels, from those ancient castles, an aristocracy as splendid, as brave, as proud, as accomplished as ever Europe saw, was driven forth to exile and beggary, to implore the charity of hostile governments and hostile creeds, to cut wood in the back settlements of America, or to teach French in the schoolrooms of London? And why were those haughty nobles destroyed with that utter destruction? Why were they scattered over the face of the earth, their titles abolished, their escutcheons defaced, their parks wasted, their palaces dismantled, their heritage given to strangers? Because they had no sympathy with the people, no discernment of the signs of their time; because, in the pride and narrowness of their hearts, they called those whose warnings might have saved them theorists and speculators; because they refused all concessions till the time had arrived when no concessions would avail.

Not all those present concurred in Macaulay's line of thought. Some Tories argued that it was, in fact, because the French nobles had been too supine, the king too feeble, that the French Revolution took the bloody course it took. And some historians today are still bringing forward similar arguments. But my point now is not so much to endorse Macaulay's historical analysis—though I happen to believe it was correct; but that, for a gifted orator like himself, who could deliver a great speech in the House of Commons when it was needed, the use of the past lay to hand as a weapon that could be effectively deployed. It would, of course, be difficult to prove that it was Macaulay's speeches rather than some very practical and hard-headed considerations on the part of the English aristocracy that turned the tide in favor of the Reform Bill of 1832. It would be even harder to prove that those speeches did not at least play some role in that turning of the tide. Which is not to leave you with the reflection that today's historians—myself, in this instance—should leave previous uses of the past unexamined because they were couched in persuasive rhetoric. It is, rather, to admit that one of the things I learned from my work on Macaulay is that, for better or worse, eloquence and fervor are very much part of an effective use of the past.

I shall proceed even further along this admittedly dangerous path to maintain, still using Macaulay as an example, that the mere fact that someone uses the past for purposes not strictly or exclusively historical, in the professional sense, does not necessarily mean that the result cannot constitute a major contribution to historiography. I have in mind Macaulay's great third chapter of his *History of England*. Written in 1848, the year of European revolutions, it explicitly celebrates the fact that, unlike the continent, England remained free from major violence and bloodshed and in what must be called, by friend or foe, a pioneering piece of social history, cites chapter and verse to show that the English people in 1848 were much better off in every respect than their ancestors in 1685. Thus, so Macaulay implies, there really was no reason for discontent or uprising. The chapter ends with a ringing assertion of progress since the age of the later Stuarts:

> It is now the fashion to place the golden age of England in times when noblemen were destitute of comforts the want of which would be intolerable to a modern footman, when farmers and shopkeepers breakfasted on loaves the very sight of which would raise a riot in a modern workhouse, when to have a clean shirt once a week was a privilege reserved for the higher class of gen-

try, when men died faster in the purest country air than they now die in the most pestilential lanes of our towns, and when men died faster in the lanes of our towns, than they now die on the coast of Guiana. We too shall, in our turn be outstripped, and in our turn be envied. It may well be, in the twentieth century, that the peasant of Dorsetshire may think himself miserably paid with twenty shillings a week; that the carpenter at Greenwich may receive ten shillings a day; that laboring men may be as little used to dine without meat as they now are to eat rye bread; that sanitary police and medical discoveries may have added several more years to the average length of human life; that numerous comforts and luxuries which are now unknown, or confined to a few, may be within the reach of every diligent and thrifty working man. And yet it may then be the mode to assert that the increase of wealth and the progress of science have benefited the few at the expense of the many, and to talk of the reign of Queen Victoria as the time when England was truly merry England, when all classes were bound together by brotherly sympathy, when the rich did not grind the faces of the poor, and when the poor did not envy the splendor of the rich.

Now, you may well respond that one of Macaulay's motives for writing that famous third chapter was to shore up English society, to celebrate English immunity from major disturbances—a misuse of the past. You may say that a historian should never, under any circumstances, be driven by such impure motives. He should only seek the truth, with no ulterior purpose in mind. Yet Macaulay produced in that chapter a major contribution to the writing of history. Who are we to quarrel with the way in which that came about?

I said that I would end these reflections by touching on my own predilections and prejudices which, along with my life history and my professional concerns, have had some bearing on my views about the use of the past. I possess an ironical temper. I love music. My ironical temper drove me to Gibbon, who taught me that an ironical view of the foibles of mankind need not be fatal to historical writing. My love of music drove me to Mozart, who taught me that irony may be compatible with the expression of the very deepest of human emotions. I like surprises and unexpected happenings, preferably pleasant ones. And that has made me suspicious of people who think that they can formulate historical laws, thereby eliminating the unique, the contingent, the unforeseen. Perhaps that is why I get annoyed when historians are classed among social scientists; even though my present sojourn in Australia, a country I have come to love, is due to the Research School of Social Sciences at the Australian National University. Finally, I dislike illness and physical discomfort. That is why I am happy to report that in the course of composing this talk, my neck has improved sufficiently for me to conclude writing it in a seated position. The past may not always be of use; but for me, at least, it is no longer a pain in the neck.

II

WHY
READ THE
GREAT
HISTORIANS?

Majestic Histories

No one ever questions the desirability of, or the need for, rereading *Pride and Prejudice,* attending yet another performance of *The Marriage of Figaro,* or watching *Hamlet* and *The Tempest* once again. These are, after all, richly textured works of genius yielding new meanings, insights, and pleasures each time one returns to them.

But does the same apply to the great historians?

Mozart and Shakespeare are neither right nor wrong; their works possess a truth that does not belong to the realm of verifiable fact. But historians deal with evidence, and even the very greatest are not immune from being proved wrong. New documents, new methods of research, new facts may come to light and shed doubt on, or make obsolete, the conclusions even of giants like Edward Gibbon, author of *The History of the Decline and Fall of the Roman Empire,* and Thucydides.

Unlike poetry and music, the 'art of history is cumulative—that is to say its most recent practitioners tend to know more about events and problems of the past than their predecessors, however exalted. One would not, in the first instance, recommend Thomas Babington Macaulay to a student who wants to know something about the "Glorious" Revolution of 1688 or Alexis de Tocqueville to someone cu-

From the *New York Times,* August 27, 1974

rious about the old regime in France. Why, then, bother at all with historians in large part superseded and out of date?

One obvious answer involves style. To read Francis Parkman on the discovery of the Mississippi or Macaulay on the siege of Londonderry is to encounter literary artistry of a kind not inferior to that of the great novelists.

Gibbon's irony, at once grave and playful, does more than epitomize his century. It shows a master of the art at work and it will never cease to give pleasure and to amuse. Indeed, to amuse and to entertain was not the least aim of the great historians.

Another of their aims has usually been to instruct, either by pointing out lessons from the past that would enable posterity to benefit from previous errors, or by depicting historical actors in moral terms, as exemplars of virtue to be imitated or embodiments of vice to be condemned and eschewed. No timelier injunction against imperialist adventures may be found outside the pages of Thucydides; no weightier warnings against concessions "too late and too little" to unjustly treated groups of individuals outside those of Tocqueville.

Yet an entertaining style and the inculcation of moral lessons would not alone suffice to keep alive works of history shown to have been wholly or partly wrong in detail. The great historians still deserve to be read because they mediate a view of the world, one that transcends particular lessons, warnings, and injunctions.

To reread Jules Michelet or Jacob Burckhardt is not only to encounter the events and personalities of the French Revolution and the Italian Renaissance, but to enter the mental and moral universe of two extraordinarily sensitive and gifted men whose attitudes and predilections inform their writings and give them special power and resonance. Neither Michelet nor Burckhardt set out to be "objective," and neither asked to be judged by that yardstick. Both created their own worlds.

Entertainment, moral lessons, views of the world—doesn't that take us a long way from history? After all, we could read fiction, sermons, and philosophical treatises to supply those needs, while relying on the very latest scholarship to keep us abreast of what are now the most accurate interpretations of the past.

But there is at least one other, and unique, reward to be gained from the great historians, and that consists of being witness to their pioneering efforts to expand both the scope of historical knowledge and the means used to obtain it.

To read Gibbon's fifteenth and sixteenth chapters, where the subject of Christianity and its growth is for the first time subjected to a purely secular approach; the third chapter of Macaulay's *History of England,* a brilliant survey of English society in 1685 showing possibilities lying open to the social historian; or Karl Marx's "The Eighteenth Brumaire of Louis Bonaparte," which demonstrates in every line how men's economic circumstances are linked to what they believe and what they say, is to marvel at the true originality of these few historians of genius who, regardless of later corrections and emendations, will continue to delight and instruct the amateur, and fill with envy as well as inspire the professional historian.

Transitions and Suspense: Some Practical Hints from the Great Historians

TO THE MEMORY OF JIM MAIN

Historiography has become a somewhat unfashionable subject in American universities. One or two "great historians"—more often than not, excerpts from Thucydides and Gibbon—are occasionally given to freshmen to read in general education courses. Graduate students are sometimes required to take a "methods" course, in which matters such as causation and objectivity are discussed, with the aid of a few examples; along with advice on how to take notes and compile a bibliography. And, thanks to the current vogue for semiology, some work is being done on modes of narrative and literary structure in historical writing.

But the sort of course on "The Great Historians" which all undergraduate honors students in history had to take when I started to give tutorials at Harvard almost forty years ago—in which the sophomores made their way from the Greeks via Augustine and Machiavelli toward Voltaire and Gibbon, Marx, Tocqueville, and Carlyle—has given way to sessions on "revolutions," "restorations," "bureaucracies," and "*mentalités*." Social history reigns supreme. And the devil take Herodotus!

I suppose all of this is inevitable, given the intellectual fashions of our times. And in this brief essay I shall not attempt to argue for the

From the *Australian Historical Association Bulletin*, March 1985 return of university courses on historiography, whether designed with the intention of illustrating the literary beauties of various great works of history, or that of demonstrating the manner in which each historian in turn set out to deal with particular problems. I want, instead, to make the case for reading some of the great historians from a very pragmatic point of view: because they can teach our students, as well as ourselves, some tricks of the trade that might be of use in the actual writing of history, even in an age of computers and word processors. I shall confine myself here to two examples—Thomas Babington Macaulay and Elie Halévy—in the hope that readers will think of others. In what I shall be pointing out, I lay claim to no originality; except that of calling attention to some nowadays neglected aspects of the originality of two of our great predecessors.

Let me make it clear that I am far from advocating imitation of the great historians, literary imitation in particular. Macaulay himself remarked more than once that while he was tolerably proud of his historical style, those who would try to imitate it would certainly come to grief. How right he was! Even today we can still read some of his purple passages, such as that on the trial of Hastings or that on the cruel antics of Judge Jeffreys or that on the New Zealander sketching the ruins of St. Paul's, with a tingling of the spine. But any historian who had the gall to write prose in a similar fashion would, quite rightly, be laughed out of court.

Nor, to stay with Macaulay for the moment, do I wish to propose that today's aspiring historians should be advised to employ historical methods based to the letter on those pioneered by the great historians of the past. Thus the third chapter of Macaulay's *History of England,* that marvelous description of English society in 1685, remains a milestone in the writing of social history, the portrayal within a brief compass of the population, geography, class divisions, institutions, and modes of thought and feeling of an entire nation. No less a historian than Henry Adams had that chapter very much in mind when he composed his own description of the United States in 1800 at the start of his *History of the United States of America during the First Administration of Thomas Jefferson;* and there have surely been many other historians who have found both inspiration and example in the famous "chapter 3."

But the writing of social history has made enormous strides since Macaulay, whether in terms of demographic and statistical techniques, approaches to urban and rural history, sociology of knowledge, or economic analysis. Furthermore, there is doubtless some justice—

though not as much as Macaulay's severest critics appear to believe—
in the often reiterated point that by "isolating" his social history into
a single chapter, however brilliant, Macaulay failed to depict throughout his *History* as a whole that constant interplay between social, political, and cultural factors which comes closest to the actual historical
process as it occurs through time. Certainly students should read Macaulay's third chapter. But there are many other books and articles a
young historian ought to read first, if, for example, he wishes to
produce a chapter-length survey of Australia in 1885.

In what sense, then, *do* I believe that, quite apart from admiring
and rereading the great historians, we ourselves, as well as our students, can actually derive specific help from them, help that will prove
to be of use in our own historical endeavors? The answer varies from
one historian to the next, of course. But, as far as Macaulay is concerned, it seems to me that it can be summed up in four words: "the
art of transition." He himself once called it the hardest part of writing
history; and we know that he took infinite pains over it. We also
know—or perhaps I should modify that statement so that it reads "I
happen to know"—that transition is an art almost totally unknown
to students of history today. "One thing after another" best sums up
the arrangement of their essays and theses. Sometimes, if he is lucky,
the reader is told that subject "A" will come first, to be followed in
turn by subjects "B" and "C." He will then be informed that subjects
"B" and "C" have indeed followed subject "A," as previously an-
nounced—a veritable triumph, he is made to feel, of planning and
foresight on the part of the writer. At other times not even those
elementary courtesies are extended to the reader, and he must battle
his way through a succession of topics bound together by nothing
more than the author's laudable desire somehow to cover them.

How refreshingly different Macaulay is in this regard! With what
subtlety and care does he manage his transitions in the third chapter!
We move naturally from the subject of the difficulty of traveling in
late-seventeenth-century England, which resulted in making the fusion of the different elements in society so imperfect, to the subject
of the badness of the roads. For it was, of course, by road that both
travelers and goods generally passed from place to place. Why were
the roads in such a wretched condition? One major reason was the
defective state of the law. And that brings Macaulay to the first of
the turnpike acts and its results. How did the different classes accomplish their travel? We are told about private coaches-and-six, public
carriages, and the persistence of travel on horseback for men not en-

cumbered by too much baggage. What risks were travelers exposed to en route? Highwaymen, of course, and darkness. Inns, then, were a necessity. What were they like? And why had not the improvement of inns kept up with that of roads and conveyances?

And that leads the historian, as if inevitably—I write "as if" because the inevitability is of the historian's making—to the mode in which correspondence was carried on in 1685, and thus to the operations of the post office—its revenues, the frequency and speed of its service, its monopoly of post horses. Those horses carried not just personal letters, but also conveyed news. And that introduces the subject of newspapers and advertisements, whether issued by the government or by private persons. But the postbags also carried books. What sort of books? Well, that depended on the degree of education of the recipients. Female education, even in the upper classes, was then at a very low ebb. And why? Here Macaulay begins his denunciation of the Restoration as a period of licentiousness.

I could go on with my summary. But there is a much better way of making the point I am trying to make; and that is simply to recommend reading and rereading Macaulay to all who, on the one hand, wish to obtain some sense of his mastery of the art of transition in historical writing, and, on the other, wish themselves to begin to master that art.

My second exemplar, the great French historian Elie Halévy, teaches a different, though by no means less important lesson: how to create suspense and curiosity on the part of the reader by means of narrative structure. Nothing can induce tedium and indifference on the reader's part more rapidly than a historian's advance summary of his conclusions. One's natural reaction to such summaries may well be: "Why, then, should I bother to read this book, or thesis, or essay; when, after all, I know what the author is going to tell me?" I exaggerate, of course. Virtuous souls surely exist who will take nothing on trust, and who wish to examine evidence before agreeing with any sort of conclusion. (If those souls are *truly* virtuous, they should by rights pursue their quest for truth to the archives!) There are others for whom reading history is not so much a matter of "conclusions," one way or the other; but, at the lowest level, getting their money's worth, or, at the highest, sheer joy in the telling. Still, is it merely poetic license to claim that history stories are mystery stories? I think not. In one of his roles, the historian is, after all, the skilled detective who asks questions, locates and follows clues, and must not reveal the solution until the tale is told.

If one takes that view of the historian's task, then there can be no doubt about the fact that Halévy is one of the truly great masters of performing it to perfection. *England in 1815,* the first volume of his *History of the English People in the Nineteenth Century,* begins with a question: Why did England have no "French" revolution? Why was she able to preserve political and social continuity without major violence? Was it because her economic organization and her political institutions were inherently stable? Or is it necessary to look for other explanatory factors? Halévy does not reveal the answer in his preface. Instead, he proceeds to take the reader through a lengthy and meticulous analysis of English political and economic structures at the start of the nineteenth century. It is only *after* he has concluded that neither of those structures possessed the needed stability for the prevention of revolution that he turns to the realm of religion and culture, and finds his answer there.

This is not the place to weigh the merits of that answer, the famous "Halévy thesis," which maintained that Methodism and Evangelicalism were the chief stabilizing forces in English society at the turn of the eighteenth century. But, whatever view we may take of Halévy's thesis, we can learn from the manner in which he has structured his book how the historian can effectively create tension and suspense for the benefit of his readers.

That useful lesson is brought home even more strikingly in Halévy's *Birth of Methodism* (University of Chicago Press, 1971), a translation by Bernard Semmel of two articles which the French historian first published in 1906. Here Halévy begins by noting that historians tended often to explain the success of the Methodist revival in England too simplistically; attributing it to a few individuals with a genius for leadership and organization. How can one say, Halévy asks, "that a movement which has absorbed so many millions of men would not have come to pass if two clergymen, John Wesley and George Whitefield, had not lived?"

He was, of course, aware of how he would answer his own question when he put it to his readers. But, rather than sharing that knowledge with them at the start, he takes them, instead, through the same course of inquiry and reasoning which he himself had to pursue in search of his conclusion; and, once again, but in an even more riveting way than in *England in 1815,* he engages his readers' interest by means similar to those employed by a writer of mystery stories.

Halévy's argument proceeds as follows: To begin with, don't exaggerate what most historians were taking for granted, the decline of the religious spirit in the Church of England during the first half of the eighteenth century. There were, after all, a number of religious societies—John Wesley's own Oxford society (1729) was one of them—that kept alive devotion and observances, even in the shallow days of latitudinarianism. But those societies usually adhered to the high church; which, at that time, was for many synonymous with Jacobitism. Before they could appeal to a wider audience, both Wesley and Whitefield had to be "Puritanized." That was accomplished by the Moravian Brethren, disciples of Count Zinzendorf, who had come to England as missionaries for a more emotional religion of experience than that offered by contemporary Anglicanism. It was their preaching of justification by faith, in particular by Peter Boehler, who entered the lives of both John and Charles Wesley, which led to John's own conversion experience at Aldersgate chapel in 1738.

But a change in doctrinal emphasis was not sufficient to start a popular movement. The new message had to be brought to the people who thirsted for it. How could that be accomplished, in an age of church pews and social stratification? The answer came not from Wesley or Whitefield, but from Wales, where two Anglican clergymen, Griffith Jones and Howell Harris, had traveled far and wide, preaching in Welsh to all who would listen, outdoors if necessary. It was Harris who invited Whitefield to come and help him in his ministry; and it was Whitefield, in turn, who persuaded John Wesley to join him in Bristol in March 1739. It was then and there that English Methodism as a popular movement had its start.

One question remained to be asked. What in particular accounted for the explosive force that drew immense crowds to hear Whitefield's and Wesley's outdoor sermons in Gloucestershire and Somersetshire? Halévy's answer is that the same overproduction crisis of 1738 that ultimately led to the fall of Sir Robert Walpole caused dislocations in the woolen and coal industries, which threw thousands out of work and into suffering and starvation. It was, to a large extent, those weavers and colliers who, in 1739, ensured the sensational success of the Methodist movement. Fully granting the genius of both Wesley and Whitefield, without the religious societies, without the Moravian Brethren, without the Welsh example, and without the economic crisis of 1738, that success would not have been possible.

Here is a second Halévy thesis that remains controversial and that is by no means universally accepted by historians. (For a recent estimate, see John D. Walsh, "Elie Halévy and the Birth of Methodism," *Transactions of the Royal Historical Society,* 5th Series, 1975.) But, here again, my purpose is not so much to argue in favor of Halévy's thesis as it is to praise his mastery of narrative structure, the fruit of his conviction—to my mind, both correct and instructive—that readers of history find it both enjoyable and beneficial to be enticed by mystery and suspense. What I say to my students is "do ye likewise."

Macaulay and Halévy are by no means the only great historians of the past who can teach us lessons about the writing of history. Other great historians teach different lessons. But if we, and our students, wish to learn those lessons, we've got to keep reading and rereading those historians. I hope we shall.

The Most Disgusting
of Pronouns

"Thucydides, an Athenian, wrote the war of the Peloponnesians and the Athenians as they warred against each other, beginning to write as soon as the war was on foot, with expectation it should prove a great one and most worthy the relation of all that had been before it." So reads the opening sentence of *The Peloponnesian War,* austerely cast in the third person. On the whole, twentieth-century historians have tended to range themselves in this Olympian tradition. To be sure, they do not customarily refer to themselves by name in the third person, in the manner of Thucydides and Julius Caesar. But they generally avoid what Edward Gibbon once called "the most disgusting of the pronouns." They use the editorial "we," or, less frequently, they adopt the chaste disguise of "the writer" or "the historian." The reasons lie partly in modesty, partly in the assumption that the ever-beckoning, though illusory, goal of "objectivity" is somehow fostered by an impersonal mode of writing—perhaps mainly in the conviction that good taste dictates distance between author and reader.

One is certainly startled, in reading Elie Halévy's great *History of the English People in the Nineteenth Century,* to find him suddenly—and very briefly—deserting the impersonal mode as he comes to deal with the effect on Londoners of the news of the unexpected reverses

From *The American Scholar,* Winter 1976–77

suffered by British troops during the opening phases of the Boer War
(1899):

> I was in London. I remember seeing the troops on their way to
> the front marching through the streets amid the cheers of the
> crowd. I remember a few days later watching in the halls of clubs
> and in hotels the tape unroll its tidings of defeat. I can still see
> the old gentleman—obviously a retired army officer of superior
> rank—who threw himself on me, while I was reading the news,
> to ask in anxious tones "Have they come to blows?" And in the
> porch of the old War Office in Pall Mall I remember the little
> group whose composition was continually renewed, standing in
> front of the official list of dead and wounded. One evening when
> I was there it divided to let a carriage pass, at the back of which
> we caught a glimpse of Balfour, wearing a look of profound
> dejection; he was coming, like everyone else, in search of news.

An autobiographical intrusion of this sort is both unexpected and
moving, and leads to reflections about the different ways in which
some of the great historians since the eighteenth century have brought
themselves explicitly into their histories. Gibbon is a case in point. It
is in his footnotes, of course, that he lets his personality emerge in
the most uninhibited manner. There we encounter an author who tells
us that "I am not fond of repeating words like a parrot," and who
does not hesitate to confide in us that "the portrait of Athanasius is
one of the passages of my history with which I am the least dissatisfied." It is in a footnote that Gibbon, commenting on the report that
Saint Bernard had piously closed his eyes to avoid looking at Lake
Geneva, remarks: "To admire or despise St. Bernard as he ought, the
reader, like myself, should have before the windows of his library the
beauties of that incomparable landscape." And it is a footnote that
contains what is probably the most self-revelatory passage in *The
Decline and Fall*. Abdalrahman, a caliph of Spain, had found only fourteen days of happiness during his reign of more than half a century.
Gibbon's comment on this runs as follows: "If I may speak of myself
(the only person of whom I can speak with certainty), *my* happy hours
have far exceeded, and far exceed, the scanty numbers of the caliph
of Spain; and I shall not scruple to add, that many of them are due
to the pleasing labor of the present composition." In yet another footnote the historian bids his memorable farewell to that heroically in-
dustrious critic and compiler of classical and ecclesiastical sources,

Sébastien Le Nain de Tillemont, on whom he has leaned for so long: "And here I must take leave for ever of that incomparable guide, whose bigotry is overbalanced by the merits of erudition, diligence, veracity, and scrupulous minuteness."

But Gibbon's use of the personal pronoun is by no means confined to his footnotes. He employs it not infrequently in the text itself to express his attitude toward the subject in hand. Thus: "I am impatient to pursue the final ruin of that Kingdom [of Burgundy]." "I have descanted with pleasure on the fortunate condition of Italy." "I enter with just diffidence on the subject of civil law." Furthermore, he unhesitatingly passes moral judgments in the first person: "Hypocrisy I shall never justify or palliate; but I will dare to observe that the odious vice of avarice is of all others most hastily arraigned, and most unmercifully condemned." As *The Decline and Fall* nears its end, Gibbon rightly assumes that his readers have by now become thoroughly familiar with his personality and his outlook on the world. Hence he can afford to mock himself—at one point expressing the far from pious hope that "I shall not, I trust, be accused of superstition"; at another, after recounting the feudal knight's pledge to spread truth as the champion of God and the ladies, adding the mock-apologetic phrase "I blush to write such discordant names." We are not surprised, then, that the majestic work ends on a personal note: "It was among the ruins of the Capitol that I first conceived the idea of a work which has amused and exercised near twenty years of my life, and which, however inadequate to my own wishes, I finally deliver to the curiosity and candor of the public."

If Gibbon ended his masterwork in the first person, Macaulay began his in the same way: "I propose to write the history of England from the accession of King James the Second down to a time which is within the memory of men still living." But, apart from occasional guidepost sentences such as that at the opening of the famous third chapter— "I intend, in this chapter, to give a description of the state in which England was at the time when the Crown passed from Charles the Second to his brother"—he confined his explicitly personal remarks to the footnotes. Sir Walter Scott and the Romantic movement intervened between Gibbon and Macaulay. And Macaulay's comments in the first person serve a purpose different from any of Gibbon's— a purpose tied closely not only to the historian's pride in having personally visited and explored the locales of his history, but also to his desire to convey to his readers the sense of immediacy derived from oral tradition. Thus Macaulay's description of Monmouth's Rebellion includes the information that old persons related "very recently" that as children they were accustomed to play a war game of a fight between King James's and King Monmouth's men, and that the latter always raised the cry of "Soho!" Macaulay's footnote reads: "I learned these things from persons living close to Sedgemoor." It is Monmouth's burial place, Saint Peter's Chapel in the Tower of London, that draws another, closely related kind of personal expression from Macaulay—outright anger at the desecration of historical landmarks. "I cannot refrain," he writes in a footnote, "from expressing my disgust at the barbarous stupidity which has transformed this most interesting little church into the likeness of a meeting house in a manufacturing town."

Francis Parkman, another master of historical narrative, who also wrote under the impact of the Romantic movement but a generation later and in America, was more exercised over the spoliation of the natural American landscape than over the loss of historical monuments. But he shared Macaulay's obsession with place and local color. From his early youth he had traveled in the footsteps of the settlers and explorers of the New World, and his writings explicitly convey the message "I was there." Footnoting his description of the change that has occurred in the Illinois prairie landscape—from the dull green boundless pasture of buffalo and deer to yellow wheatfields dotted with the roofs of a "hardy and valiant yeomanry"—Parkman reports that "in 1840, a friend of mine shot a deer from the window of a farmhouse, near the present town of La Salle." Another footnote, this one accompanying the depiction of a battle between Iroquois and Illinois in 1860, reads in part: "Being once in an encampment of Sioux when a quarrel broke out, and the adverse factions raised the war-whoop and began to fire at each other, I had a good, though for the moment a rather dangerous, opportunity of seeing the demeanor of Indians at the beginning of a fight."

Macaulay and Parkman, then, made use of the first person singular to persuade their readers that they had done their homework on the spot. Their personal testimony was intended to enliven and authenticate their historical narratives. Thomas Carlyle, often linked to them as yet another Romantic historian, went much further than that. The relation that he established between himself and his readers cast him not merely as a tourist guide, but in the combined role of instructor, preacher, and brother. "Ill stands it with me if I have spoken falsely," he wrote at the conclusion of *The French Revolution;* "thine also it was to hear truly. Farewell." And the *History of Frederick the Great* ends, "Adieu, good readers; bad also, adieu." With the historian playing such an explicitly pedagogical role, it should not occasion surprise to find Carlyle uninhibitedly personal in the expression of his views. "To me the Eighteenth Century has nothing grand about it," he announces right at the start of *Frederick,* "except that grand universal Suicide, named French Revolution, by which it terminated its otherwise most worthless existence with at least one worthy act;—setting fire to its old house and self, and going up in flames and volcanic explosions, in a truly memorable important manner. A very fit termination, as I thankfully feel, for such a Century."

Carlyle even goes so far as to address his subject, as well as his readers, personally. Writing of the siege of Weinsberg—from which the besieged wives emerged, according to the terms of capitulation, with their "most valuable property," each carrying her husband on her back—the historian breezily interjects, as if in conversation: "a Hohenzollern ancestor of yours, I think I have heard, was of the besieging party." But the most interesting and most novel aspect of Carlyle's self-intrusion into his work has to do with the way in which he takes the reader into his workshop, where he lets him not only watch but participate in the historian's struggle with his sources, and in the resulting frustrations, defeats, and triumphs. Thus he describes the products of the Prussian Dryasdust school of historians:

> I have often sorrowfully felt as if there were not in Nature, for darkness, dreariness, immethodic platitude, anything comparable to him [the Prussian Dryasdust]. He writes big Books wanting in almost every quality; and does not even give an *Index* to them. He has made of Friedrich's History a wide-spread, inorganic, trackless matter, dismal to your mind, and barren as a continent of Brandenburg sand!—Enough, he could do no other: I have striven to forgive him. Let the reader now forgive me; and think sometimes what probably my raw-material was!

Upon that raw material Carlyle freely passes strictures in the first person whenever he deems that necessary. Thus: "Of this respectable Madame de Roucoulles, I have read, at least seven times, what the Prussian Books say of her by way of Biography; but it is always given in their dull tombstone style: it has moreover next to no importance; and I, alas, I do not yet too well remember it!" There is something uniquely instructive in being allowed to watch the historian labor with his raw materials in this fashion. There is also, as with so much else in Carlyle, something very modern about it. One of the predominant trends of our own times is that increasingly spectators, listeners, and readers expect to be more than passive observers of works of art and literature. If they cannot themselves participate in them, they want at the very least to be privy to the effects and methods that went into the making of those works. Carlyle deliberately accorded his readers that privilege.

In his *Old Régime and the French Revolution,* Tocqueville, too, takes the reader into his personal confidence as he adverts on occasion to his encounters with archival sources; more especially to those encounters that served to overturn his preconceptions. "I well remember my surprise," he reports, "when I was for the first time examining the records of an intendancy with a view to finding out how a parish was administered under the old order." Tocqueville was surprised because he had, up to that point, been convinced that the mode of local government of American rural townships was peculiar to the New World. Now he found those same features in the French parishes of the Old Régime—and for good reason, since the original model for both had been the rural parish of the Middle Ages. In similar fashion, he tells us that "I was almost startled"—a mind as sovereign as Tocqueville's was never startled without qualification—to find eighteenth-century bishops and abbots engaged in planning the construction of roads and canals; and that, in studying the *cahiers* drawn up by the three orders before the meeting of the Estates General, "I realized with something like consternation that what was being asked for was nothing short of the systematic, simultaneous abolition of *all* existing French laws and customs."

Rarely has a great historian been able to communicate so vividly the personal drama sometimes involved in historical research, and there is no doubt that Tocqueville's use of the first person singular enhances the dramatic quality of his account. His rigorously analytical mind and austere temperament make his personal interventions in the text all the more effective; the more so upon the occasions when he gives vent to his patriotic feelings. These feelings about the greatness of France and about certain elements in the French national character are far from uncritical, but no less charged with deep and genuine emotion. Perhaps his most moving tribute of this kind is one that this acute and profound critic of the French Revolution and its effects pays to the unselfish idealism of those who made that revolution in the first place. "Much of my life," Tocqueville writes, "has been devoted to the study of history and I have no hesitation in affirming that never in the course of my studies have I discovered a revolution in which, anyhow to begin with, so many men displayed a patriotism so intense, such unselfishness, such real greatness of mind." Looking at the French Revolution not as an isolated phenomenon but in the light of the events preceding it, and keeping in mind the peculiarities of the Old Régime and of the French temperament, Tocqueville declares at the end of his book: "I find the nation itself far more remarkable than any of the events in its long history. It hardly seems possible that there can ever have existed any other people so full of contrasts and so extreme in all their doings, so much guided by their emotions and so little by fixed principles, always behaving better, or worse, than one expected of them."

Such fervent patriotic sentiments inevitably remind us of another historian of the French Revolution, a fellow countryman and contemporary of Tocqueville's—Jules Michelet. Like Tocqueville, who found in the French revolutionaries the sort of civic virtue not much in evidence in France at the time of his writing (1856), Michelet, in his *History of the French Revolution* (1847), contrasts the Frenchmen of his day with those of the early revolutionary period: "When I think of the times that followed, of our own time, so listless and self-seeking, I cannot help wondering that extreme misery did not in the least dispirit this people, nor drew from them one regret for their ancient slavery." But if Michelet resembles Tocqueville in this respect, he goes considerably further than the latter—or, indeed, than any other great historian—in the explicit linkage he constructs between his own personal history and the historical period about which he is writing.

One gets an immediate sense of how closely bound up history and autobiography were in Michelet's work in the preface to his *French Revolution,* where he tells us that his father died just as he, the son, was attempting to depict the fall of the Bastille: "When that blow fell upon me, I was lost in contemplation. I was elsewhere, hastily realizing this work, so long the object of my meditation. I was at the foot of the Bastille, taking that fortress, and planting our immortal banner upon its towers. That blow came upon me, unforeseen, like a shot from the Bastille." Analogies between Michelet's intimate personal life and his historical writing are by no means confined to the prefatory pages of his work. If they were, they would resemble the approach of many other historians, past and present, who, while keeping their principal text impersonal, are willing to put themselves more directly into their introductory remarks. But that is hardly the way of this historian, who said of himself, "I move across history like the Greek actor who, when playing Electra, bore the funeral urn of his son." The past offers personal solace, inspiration, a guide to action: "Whilst I have been writing these lines [on the prisoners in the Bastille] a mountain, a Bastille has been crushing my breast. Alas! Why stay so long talking of dilapidated prisons, and wretches whom death has delivered? The world is covered with prisons, from Spielberg to Siberia, from Spandau to Mont-St.-Michel. The world is a prison!"

Michelet would have shaken his head in wonderment at our current discussions as to whether the past is or is not "usable." As far as he was concerned, the whole point of writing history was to re-create a past that not only could, but must, be used—eventually by the historian's readers, but in the first place by the historian himself—to satisfy his own psychic and spiritual needs, and to inspire him both to bear witness to past virtues and to do his share in the rooting out of present evils. For Michelet, writing history is tantamount to self-expression, to total commitment at the most personal level. When he has finished describing the pure patriotic fervor that marked the festival of village federations celebrating the first anniversary of the fall of the Bastille, Michelet gives vent to his feelings in the very words used on that occasion by the members of one such federation: "Thus ended the happiest day of our life." That sentence, the historian tells us, "I was very near writing myself in concluding this chapter. It is ended, and nothing like it is in store for me. I leave here an irreparable moment of my life, a part of myself, which, I plainly feel, will remain here and accompany me no more: I seem to depart poor and needy."

Enough has been said to show that twentieth-century historians too timid to introduce themselves into their histories need have no qualms about a lack of less timid but nonetheless distinguished predecessors. One who has had no such qualms is Martin Duberman, whose recent history of Black Mountain College exemplifies his conviction that "when a historian allows more of himself to show—his feelings, fantasies and needs, not merely his skills at information-retrieval, organization, and analysis—he is *less* likely to contaminate the data, simply because there is less pretense that he and it are one." By no means would all of his colleagues agree with that view. But it would be difficult to argue that the insertion of self on the part of some of the great historians of the modern period has harmed, rather than enhanced, the worth or reputation of their works. For his part, the author of this essay—or, I suppose I should now say I myself—will certainly think twice henceforth before preaching the virtue of never employing "the most disgusting of the pronouns" to students of history and historical writing.

Why Read the
Great Nineteenth-Century
Historians?

A short answer to the question posed by my title might be: "Because they wrote well; because they may be said to have reinterpreted aspects of the past in fundamental ways; because they saw themselves as prophets as well as historians, firmly believing that their role carried with it the obligation to say what they thought about the society and politics of the present and the future as well as of the past; because they usually said this with a confidence made evident in the cadence of their prose; because, along with the specific view of that segment of the past with which each of them was concerned, they also communicated a general view of the world." But a short answer of this sort calls for qualification and elaboration.

Style alone will not insure the durability of historical works. Great history can indeed be great literature at the same time—one need do no more than mention the name of Gibbon. But, as V. S. Pritchett has put it, unlike the novelist and the poet, the historian can never be the absolute ruler of an imaginary kingdom. For, however skillful he may be, he cannot invent his facts. That is why some critics—most recently a number of structuralists—seem to me to be on the wrong track when they treat historians and histories primarily as employers and examples of literary forms. The old battle against those who

From *The American Scholar* 48, no. 1 (Winter, 1978–1979)

wished to make history a science has been fought and won. A new battle may be shaping up, against those who wish to make it into pure literature. If one does not, then, return to the great historians for their literary artistry alone, does one do so mainly for their message, their philosophy, their *Weltanschauung?* Here I think Geoffrey Elton is right when he warns against reducing the historian's function in society to that of a preacher. To be sure, that was a role many of them assumed in the nineteenth century. But while by no means unconnected with their survival, that role alone does not seem to me their sole claim to durability. Finally, what of innovations and new approaches to old subjects? Those certainly supply one motive for a reader's return to the great historians—to observe and admire once again how they were able to reinterpret historical events, institutions, and personalities from a new angle or from a fresh point of view. But innovations and new points of view are soon absorbed into the canon of historical knowledge, and usually superseded within not too long a period of time. One does not, in the first instance, turn to Carlyle or Michelet for light on the French Revolution, or to Macaulay for the latest word on Restoration politics.

Why, then, are the great nineteenth-century historians still worth reading? Or are they? The only way to find out is to reread them, if possible with a minimum of preconceptions and anticipations. Thus, what follows is an account of what struck me most forcibly in the course of a recent rereading of five great works of history: a very brief report on four of them—Marx's *Eighteenth Brumaire,* Tocqueville's *Old Régime,* Carlyle's *French Revolution,* and Burckhardt's *Renaissance*—and a somewhat lengthier report on the fifth: Macaulay's *History of England.* Inevitably I am recording a personal reaction. Other readers will no doubt react very differently, and that is as it should be. For part of the continuing power of masterpieces, in history as well as in other arts, resides in the variegated nature of their appeal.

The detailed sequence of events that led to Louis Napoleon's coup d'état in 1851 is so complex, and demands such a degree of familiarity with a plethora of groups, factions, and individuals, that I am bound to confess that a good many rereadings of Marx's *Eighteenth Brumaire* still leave me, to some extent, puzzled and perplexed. However, what I do find more gripping and effective with each reading is the masterful manner in which Marx reinforces his initial epigram, derived in part from Hegel: all facts and personages of great importance in world history occur twice, the first time as tragedy, the second time as farce. Having begun with this image from the world of the theater, he continues throughout his brilliant essay to come back time and again, in a variety of ways, to the contrast between the world of reality—the class struggle in France—and that realm of shadow and illusion in which the actors fancy that their posturings and speeches make a difference to the process of history. Edmund Wilson, in *To the Finland Station,* has memorably described the intellectual excitement felt by the reader as he follows Marx in penetrating to the class interests actually involved in the shaping of historical events. But worth adding, perhaps, is that what sustains that excitement is a marvelously skillful use of language and imagery. Specters walk about; masquerades are performed; curtains are drawn; cardsharpers do their conjuring tricks; objects change their shape—shoulders turn into bayonets, veils into iron masks, eagles into vultures; night watchmen are unable to see; canes fail to stop rapiers; bubbles are pricked; actors come offstage to don their workaday clothes behind the scenes; people get lost in blind alleys; marionettes and dummies entertain; ostriches hide their heads in the sand. And, everywhere, shadows and ghosts and dreams and riddles abound, while Marx, the puppet master, puts his creatures through their paces.

What I have described is Marx's literary skill. He loved Shakespeare and the drama, and was thus perhaps particularly drawn to the imagery of illusion. But the spellbinding power of the imagery is directly related to the spell-banishing power of the historian. Marx's metaphors and similes exert such great effect because they reflect and reinforce his conviction that the realities of class and economic forces underlie a make-believe world of paper slogans and ideological foam.

What draws one back to the *Eighteenth Brumaire* is, at least to some degree, its literary quality. What draws one back to Tocqueville's *Old Régime* is something quite different—not, at least for this reader, its famous thesis about the continuity of centralization in French history, but rather something that one might call its unique conjunction of mystery and mordancy. On the one hand, Tocqueville, by his own description, is the anatomist who dissects the body politic in search of its laws of life. But, curiously enough, what seems most moving and instructive about his book is not its author's pioneering use of the methods of historical sociology, but the sense that the ultimate currents running deep below the surface of the lives of states and societies will not yield to scientific analysis, but will remain forever mysterious. In all human institutions, as in the human body, Tocqueville notes, "there is a hidden source of energy, the life principle itself, independent of the organs which perform the various functions needed for survival; once this vital flame burns low, the whole organism languishes and wastes away, and though the organs seem to function as before, they serve no useful purpose." It is not that Tocqueville begins by throwing up his hands in the face of what he calls "the slow persistent action of our institutions," or the seemingly ineluctable manner in which the "id" of equality tends so often to defeat the "ego" of freedom. On the contrary. Rarely has any historian applied his mind more vigorously to the detection of those ultimate forces. But he leaves us with the sense that, in the end, the body politic, like the human body, possesses mysteries it will not yield up. At the same time he displays a very unmystical awareness of the shortcomings of the France of his own day, of a time marked by "discreet, well-regulated sensualism," a time when a man no longer, as in the old days, pays hard cash for an official post, but goes one better and sells himself; a time, like previous times in history, when those who destroy men's freedom begin by trying to retain its forms. For me the power of *The Old Régime* lies in its tone of voice—the combination of the historian who recognizes the limits of the sociological, the scientific approach to history, even as he pioneers its use, and the patriotic and freedom-loving Frenchman, the author of *Democracy in America,* who is never less than frank about the fact that it is his disillusionment with, and his fears for, the future of the society of his own time that have helped both to inspire and to direct his quest for the laws of political and social life.

It may sound paradoxical to call a clearheaded analytical historian rereadable because he communicates a sense of mystery, while calling a mystically inclined narrative historian rereadable because he constantly directs attention to one of the unsolved technical problems of writing any sort of history, narrative or analytical. But that is what I have done and am about to do. Rereading Carlyle can be a daunting task, especially when it involves works of such monstrous size as *Frederick the Great.* But *The French Revolution* is another story. Even here one may tire of the style, one may bridle at the philosophy. But one cannot help being captivated by Carlyle's attempts to put to the test of actual historical writing the dictum in his essay "On History" (1830): "Narrative is *linear,* Action is *solid.*" Again and again Carlyle tries to capture the flow of historical action in time by crowding into his paragraphs contemporaneous happenings; some feeling about the lives of the participants before and after as well as during those events; a sense of place in historical as well as geographical terms; and, with all that, the truth that, however dramatic and violent the events he is

describing, ordinary life goes on: people eat and work and love and
hate, the sun rises, the earth revolves. It seems to me that whether or
not he always succeeds in meeting it, Carlyle continually tries to face
the challenge of reproducing both the solid texture and the continual
ebb and flow of the past. It is, of course, an impossibly difficult challenge. But historians today are still trying to meet it. For me, watching
Carlyle's heroic attempts to do so is the chief reward for returning to
his historical writings. What it is important to remember is that for
Carlyle this way of writing history was far from merely a technical
device. It formed, rather, an integral part of some of his most deeply
held beliefs: earthly time as the mere vesture of eternal time; time
perpetually rushing on, the mysterious River of Existence; time's do-
minion over us, a destiny whose edicts of oblivion could only be
revoked by books like Boswell's *Johnson*—"a little row of Naphtha-
lamps, with its line of Naphtha-light, burn[ing] clear and holy through
the dead Night of the Past."

I suppose that some specialists in the history of early modern Europe
still approach Burckhardt's *Civilization of the Renaissance in Italy* with
a view to testing, questioning, or endorsing his thesis about the birth
of individualism in the Italian city-states of the fifteenth century. For
other readers—and, of course, I speak only for myself here—the continuing greatness of Burckhardt's work lies in a different sphere. No
other historian raised so forcefully the problem of the inevitable
intermixture of good and evil in history, the problem he defines when
he comes to judge the morality of the Italian people during the period
he has dealt with: "The ultimate truth with respect to the character,
the conscience, and the guilt of a people remains forever a secret; if
only for the reason that its defects have another side, where they appear
as peculiarities or even as virtues." Good and evil, Burckhardt writes,
lay strangely mixed in fifteenth-century Italy. Ambition, self-asser-
tion, the quest for fame, the pursuit of greatness—all modern qualities,
for the modern Italian spirit was destined to serve as model and ideal
for the entire Western world—may be praised as "good." But, on
the other hand, "the curtain is now and then drawn aside, and we see
with frightful evidence a boundless ambition and thirst after greatness,
independent of all means and consequences." The question Burckhardt raises so insistently is whether it is possible for one set of qualities
to exist without the other, in view of his conclusion that excessive
individualism, the fundamental vice of the Italian character, was at
the same time a condition of its greatness. The immorality of that age
might well make one shudder. But the most ferocious internecine

battles in Perugia supplied the young Raphael with impressions he later made use of in some of his greatest paintings, and Lodovico il Moro—who, as the perfect type of despot of the age, "almost disarms our moral judgment"—attracted Leonardo to his court. We know that Burckhardt regarded his own time as one lacking in spontaneity and increasingly marked by mediocrity, materialism, and philistinism. Even the sense of "honor" that in the Renaissance had provided the strongest bulwark against evil seemed to be losing its power. Given that apparently unique conjunction of national spirit with antiquity which had constituted the Italian revival, was another Renaissance possible? And even if it was, was the moral price worth paying? For Burckhardt, these were intensely personal questions.

One thing emerges, then, from a rereading of Marx, Tocqueville, Carlyle, and Burckhardt—that the quality of their writing, which turns out to exert the greatest power over us (and that may be an unexpected quality), is intimately related to each historian's chief intellectual or personal concerns. It is never merely stylistic, merely methodological, or merely didactic. Marx's use of literary devices reflected his view of history as class struggle; Tocqueville's quest for the laws of social life derived in great part from his French and American political experience; Carlyle's obsession with a new method of writing history was closely related to his metaphysics; Burckhardt's view of the moral ambivalence to be found in fifteenth-century Italy was colored by his own pessimism about the fate of nineteenth-century Europe.

What of Macaulay, the historian with whom, having written an account of his early life, I was most familiar when I began rereading? In *The History of England* I certainly encountered once again those qualities that even his most severe critics have granted him: his narrative skill, more especially his mastery of transitions; the clarity of his style, which enables him to make even unpromising subjects, such as the founding of the Bank of England or the recoinage, palatable to the inexpert reader; his sense of the human drama of history that emerges in particular in his great set pieces, such as the siege of Londonderry or the landing of William; his feeling for local color and his use of popular and ephemeral literature as source material; his pioneering survey of English society in 1685 in his third chapter; his well-nigh infallible judgment of the various alternatives presented by important political and constitutional situations—something that S. R. Gardiner singled out as Macaulay's greatest achievement as a historian. At the same time, I was struck by other, less attractive qualities:

his tendency to view historical characters one-dimensionally, as heroes
or villains; the unquestioning solidity of his belief in progress, which
makes him conjure up, often with gratuitous frequency and with possibly excessive satisfaction, the wonders of peeping villas, gay shrubberies, and busy streets and shops; his apparent conviction, recently
much questioned, that the Revolution of 1688 was a foreordained
happy event bringing only beneficial effects in its train; his strong
biases and prejudices, by no means always on the Whig side; his
schoolmasterly and frequently simplistic moral judgments; his occasional tendency to slip from drama into melodrama; and, finally, his
habit of too readily intruding himself into his *History*. One may not
entirely agree with Lord Acton that "the business of historians is to
get out of the way, and, like the man who plays Punch, to concentrate
attention on their personages." But one must certainly agree when he
says that no one did this less than did Macaulay.

What struck me most forcibly in a recent rereading of Macaulay's
History was how much of it had little or nothing to do with any
of the things I have just mentioned, but was centered on public
opinion, public feelings, what Macaulay liked to call the public mind.
One need do no more than plunge into the second chapter (the first
having transported the reader rapidly from the Romans to the Restoration) in order to verify this emphasis—quite apart from the fact
that the words "feeling" and "public mind" occur no less than thirty-
five times in its course. Cromwell's military tyranny "had left deep
and enduring traces in the public mind"; hostile "feelings" about a
standing army were stronger among the Cavaliers than among the
Roundheads; the "feelings" of the Cavaliers about indemnities and
royal favors differed from those of the Roundheads; it was "generally
felt" that the certificates issued to holders of benefices by Cromwell's
triers saved the country from being overrun by ignorant and drunken
reprobates; the "feelings" of those royalists who had loved the Church
because she was the enemy of their enemies were blamable but not
wholly inexcusable; the Puritan opposition to bearbaiting had nothing
to do with the humane "feelings" of the nineteenth century: the Puritan "hated bearbaiting, not because it gave pain to the bear, but
because it gave pleasure to the spectators." Quakers were "popularly
regarded" as the most despicable of fanatics, and wrongly confounded
by the public with the Puritans—whatever was ridiculous or odious
in either increased the scorn and aversion which the multitude "felt"
for both. In any event, the theology, the manners, the dialect of the

Puritan were associated "in the public mind" with the darkest and meanest vices. But after the court showed the extent to which it abused its victory, by its cruel treatment of the nonconformists, they became objects of pity and respect to well-constituted "minds," and these "feelings" became stronger when it was noised abroad that the court was less severe with Papists than with Presbyterians. The "minds of men" were now in such a "temper" that every public act "excited discontent." There were "murmurs" about Charles's marriage to Catherine. "General indignation" followed the sale of Dunkirk, and "public discontent" resulted from the retention of Tangiers. But the "murmurs" excited by those events were faint when compared with the "clamors" that soon broke out. Hyde's fall in some degree took the edge off "the public appetite for revenge." But "public feeling" was alarmed by the growing power of France. Between the "public mind" of England and the "public mind" of France, there was a great gulf. As for the Country party's views of France, it was riven by "two strong feelings" in opposite directions. By 1678 "the public mind" was once again in the state it had been in when the Long Parliament met. Historical memories, the Gunpowder Plot above all, had left "in the minds of the vulgar a deep and bitter feeling." Juries partook of "the feelings then common throughout the nation," and were encouraged by the Church to indulge "these feelings." I shall cite no further examples from this chapter—lest I expose myself to what Macaulay himself considered the only important criticism he heard of his *History:* repetitiousness—*except* to note that toward the end of the chapter he calls May 26, 1679, the day Charles prorogued Parliament, a great one in British history, not only because on that day the Habeas Corpus Act received the royal assent, but because the Licensing Act expired with the royal dismissal of the two houses.

It was characteristic of Macaulay that he should attach so much significance to this event. He was certainly one of the first to have been fully cognizant of the importance of news and its dissemination as a subject for the political and social historian. Here was one of those "noiseless revolutions" which previous historians had all but ignored and to which Macaulay delighted in drawing attention. In fact, of course, it was a noiseless revolution that produced quite a lot of noise. One need only recollect those memorable passages in the third chapter in which Macaulay first brings to life Whitehall as the chief staple of news and rumors—"Had Halifax got the better of Rochester?" "Was the Duke of York really going to Scotland?" "Had Monmouth really been sent for to the Hague?"—and then goes on to describe in detail the function of coffeehouses as the chief means by which London public opinion found an outlet. In 1685 nothing like a daily national newspaper existed. The provinces were dependent on newsletters from London, the product of news writers who "rambled from coffee room to coffee room collecting reports, squeezed [themselves] into the Sessions House at the Old Bailey, if there was an interesting trial, nay, perhaps obtained admission to the gallery of Whitehall, and noticed how the king and duke looked." The Licensing Act, renewed in 1685, expired once again in 1693 and was duly renewed—"not however without an opposition, which . . . proved that the public mind was beginning dimly to perceive how closely civil freedom and freedom of conscience are connected with freedom of discussion." Macaulay goes on to comment that no preceding writer had thought it worthwhile to expend care or labor on the history of that act. "Yet," he continues, "surely the events which led to the establishment of the liberty of the press in England, and in all the countries peopled by the English race, may be thought to have as much interest for the present generation as any of those battles and sieges of which the most minute details have been carefully recorded."

Macaulay pays due attention first to the history of licensing and then to the appearance of newspapers in London in 1695—a "great experiment," a "great revolution," something "which no preceding historian had condescended to mention but which [was] of far greater importance than the achievements of William's army or of Russell's fleet." But his interest in the public mind went far beyond an interest in the formal or informal means of communication: newspapers, gazettes, broadsides, pamphlets, coffeehouses. Like his fellow Victorians, he was persuaded of the importance of rational argument in forming opinions—a persuasion that found expression in *The History,* not only in those abstracts of parliamentary debates which he himself called "a new, and, I hope, a striking feature in the book," but also in the technical device he invented as a modern substitute for the ancient historians' "speeches": the "declamatory disquisition" in which he summarized, in indirect discourse, arguments that would have been brought forward and questions that would have been raised about important issues by various groups, parties, and factions in church and state. The historian's task was to show what people thought and how people felt, to depict the pride and prejudice of the English country squire, to point out the difference in attitude and mental habits between the Roman Catholic courtier and the Roman Catholic country gentleman, to describe the feelings of those exiled Whigs who, toward the end of Charles II's reign, had sought asylum in the Low Countries.

For the historian who wished to do this, squibs and ballads were just as important as more formal and official sources. In 1688, as Macaulay points out, "public feeling" did not manifest itself by large meetings and vehement harangues. But it found a vent through satirical ballads like "Lillibullero," whose success, to be sure, was "the effect, and not the cause, of that excited state of public feeling which produced the revolution." Legends and rumors were equally grist for the historian's mill. Such was the devotion of the people to Monmouth, for instance, that "in the face of the strongest evidence of which the fact of a death was ever verified, many continued to hope he was still alive and would again appear in arms." And it was "a whisper which swelled fast into a fearful clamor," to the effect that the Irish were marching on London and massacring every man, woman, and child on the road that (at the end of 1688) set off "Irish night" in London, "the strangest and most terrible that England had ever seen."

An attempt to represent the thoughts and feelings of various groups and classes at times of crisis seems to me to lie at the heart of Macaulay's historical endeavor, and may well be what he had in mind when he noted in his journal in December 1849: "There is merit, no doubt, in Hume, Robertson, Voltaire, and Gibbon. Yet it is not the thing. I have a conception of history more just, I am confident, than theirs." His narrative technique in *The History* was closely tied to that conception:

> Wise men began to perceive that
> It was even whispered that
> It was remarked that
> Those who remembered
> It was observed that
> The traveler saw that
> Nor did men omit to remark
> It was apprehended that

Time and again the reader receives the impression—as was, of course, Macaulay's intention—that various views and feelings about events

reach him directly from historical spectators, observers, and participants. The public mind itself is heard to speak.

And the state of that public mind was crucial. In 1686 William was
aware, quite correctly, that "the public mind of England, though
heated by grievances, was by no means ripe for revolution." Two
years later, the prosecution of the bishops and the birth of the Prince
of Wales had produced that "great revolution in the feelings of many
Tories" which helped to bring success to William's cause. But did
Macaulay regard his task as chronicler of feeling and opinion as merely
descriptive? After all, the question arises at once as to the nature of
the dynamic factors that cause changes and revolutions in public opinion and in the feelings of various groups in the nation. Here one must
beware of making too large a claim for him. But two things may be
said, beyond reiterating his general belief that out of the clash of opposing opinions, truth and progress were bound irresistibly to emerge.
One is to remind ourselves of his conviction that "the history of England during the seventeenth century is the history of the transformation of a limited monarchy, constituted after the fashion of the
middle ages, into a limited monarchy suited to that more advanced
state of society in which the public defense can no longer be intrusted
to a feudal militia." A more advanced state of society inevitably
brought with it more advanced views and opinions. The other thing
worth recalling is Macaulay's habitual linkage of feelings to situation.
Why were Presbyterian ministers not unanimous in wishing for the
passage of a Comprehension Bill in 1689? Because, since the Declaration of Indulgence, the "situation" of the ablest and most eloquent
preachers was "such as the great majority of the divines of the Established Church might well envy." Why were the politicians of the
Restoration period generally corrupt and unprincipled by nineteenth-
century standards? Because their characters had been formed amid
frequent and violent revolutions and counterrevolutions. "Their situation naturally developed in them to the highest degree a peculiar
class of abilities and a peculiar mass of vices." Why did the Country
party in the 1670s on the one hand call for a war against France but,
as soon as recruiting commenced, refuse supplies? Because they were
"in the embarrassing situation of subjects who have reason to believe
that their prince is conspiring with a foreign and hostile power against
their liberties." To give him military resources might only be to arm
him against the state. Why did the Tories in 1691 take the view that
laws against treason should provide legal privileges for the accused?
Because

in the days when none but Roundheads and Nonconformists were accused of treason, even the most humane and upright Cavaliers were disposed to think that the laws which were the safeguard of the throne could hardly be too severe. But, as soon as loyal Tory gentlemen and venerable fathers of the Church were in danger of being called in question for corresponding with St. Germains, a new light flashed on many understandings which had been unable to discover the smallest injustice in the proceedings against Algernon Sidney or Alice Lisle.

Macaulay was certainly not the first historian to have noticed the relationship between people's circumstances and their thoughts and feelings, or to have conceived of the ineluctable progress of society as taking place by stages. One need only mention Montesquieu and Gibbon as preceding him in the first endeavor and the Scottish historical school as preceding him in the second. But, as Professor Trevor-Roper has pointed out, Macaulay went beyond Hume in showing that the progress of society was not distinct from politics, but connected with it, because it could be fostered by enlightened, liberal, and rational reform. Such reform, I would add, could only be accomplished when the public mind demanded and endorsed it, when the feelings and opinions of the nation at large were attuned to it.

That phrase, "the nation at large," should be regarded in the context of Macaulay's general views about society. Within his limits, Macaulay was indeed a pioneering historian of the public mind. But the limits were there. He remained the Whig of 1832 whose great fear, then and throughout his life, was that, as he put it in his account of Irish night in London, "the human vermin which, neglected by ministers of state and ministers of religion, barbarous in the midst of civilization, heathen in the midst of Christianity, burrows among all physical and all moral pollution, in the cellars and garrets of great cities, will at once rise into terrible importance."

Eighteen thirty-two, in fact, is more than a measure of Macaulay's limits as a social historian. To my mind it provides the answer to the question that remains to be asked: If the secret of the continuing survival of Marx, Tocqueville, Burckhardt, and Carlyle lies mainly in the intimate connection that exists between those features of their historical writing which most powerfully attract us as readers and their own most deeply held feelings about the world and their place in it, is Macaulay's "public mind in history" related to his innermost preoccupations, and if so, how? For the answer to that question we must look back from Macaulay the historian to Macaulay the politician. In 1828 he had ended his essay on Hallam's *Constitutional History* by stressing what he called "the revolution of public feeling" that had led to general dissatisfaction with the state of the representation in England. He who, not so many years later, was himself to play a major role in instituting freedom of the press in India, now pointed out that "the gallery in which the reporters sit [in Parliament] [had] become a fourth estate of the realm." (He was, by the way, the first to have applied that term to the press in general.) But at a time when public opinion had become more important than it ever was, the House of Commons was "far from being an express image of the general feeling. . . . Instead of outrunning the public mind, as before the Revolution it frequently did, it now follows with slow steps and at a wide distance." Reform was necessary. As we know, Macaulay's own speeches played some part in bringing it about. And it is in those speeches that we find him, again and again, involving the public mind and public feelings as crucial determining factors:

March 2, 1831: "Who flatters himself how he can turn this feeling back?"

July 5, 1831: "Woe to the Government which thinks that a great, a steady, a long continued movement of the public mind is to be stopped like a street riot!"

September 20, 1831: Public feeling about reform commenced far back in British history. During the last seventy years that feeling has had a great influence on "the public mind."

October 10, 1831: There are only two ways in which societies can normally be governed—by "public opinion" and by the sword. The law is nothing but a piece of paper printed by the king's printer, with the king's arms at the top, "till 'public opinion' breathes the breath of life into the dead letter."

December 16, 1831: There had been no change in the government for the worse but, rather, a change in the "public mind" that produced exactly the same effect that would be produced by a change in the government for the worse. "Agitations of the public mind, so deep and so long continued as those which we have witnessed, do not end in nothing."

It was no accident, then, that in *The History* Macaulay occupied himself to the extent that he did with the formation and influence on affairs of state of what he called the "public mind." *The History* has often been called politically biased in various Whiggish ways. There is some of that, though less than one might expect. If one is going to make a case for the political coloring of *The History,* then, it appears to me, that case must be made in the terms I have set out. Having celebrated the power of the public mind as the major factor in the greatest political battle of his generation—a battle that also marked the scene of his greatest personal triumph—Macaulay made its study and exploration a paramount theme of his *History.* It is in great part because preoccupation with the "public mind" had been and remained so vital a part of his personal and political concerns that when he came to focus on it as a historian, he produced history not merely original but readable beyond its own time. He and the other great nineteenth-century historians are still worth reading because we can still feel the powerful impact of that encounter between personal commitment and scholarly curiosity which lies at the heart of all great history, from the Greeks to the present.

The Rise and Ascent of the
Decline and Fall . . .

The sky over London was gloomy and overcast as the jumbo jet, bound for Bombay and Hong Kong via Rome, lifted off from Heathrow Airport. For someone en route to a conference commemorating the two-hundredth anniversary of the publication of Volume I of *The Decline and Fall of the Roman Empire,* London meant the place where Gibbon had written that volume in his elegant house on Bentinck Street; where for eight sessions he had sat—silently—in Parliament, that "school of civil prudence, the first and most essential virtue of an historian"; and where he had died in 1794, aged fifty-seven. As a boy, sickly and precocious, he had attended Westminster School here for two years (1749–1750), residing in a boardinghouse near the school kept by his beloved aunt Catherine Porten, "the true mother of my mind as well as of my health." It was to her kind lessons that he was to ascribe in his *Memoirs* "my early and invincible love of reading, which I would not exchange for the treasure of India."

Edward Gibbon's health was not up to the rigors of a public school. His aunt took him to Bath, where it was hoped that the waters would cure his complaints. "It might be apprehended," the historian later recalled, "that I should continue for life an illiterate cripple." Had this happened, history and literature would have been robbed of one of

From *Harvard Magazine,* March 1976

their few undisputed works of genius. Fortunately, the young Gibbon suddenly (and mysteriously) regained his health; and at the age of fifteen he arrived at Oxford, "with a stock of erudition that might have puzzled a doctor and a degree of ignorance of which a schoolboy would have been ashamed."

It was at Oxford (in 1753) that, to the horror of his father, he was converted to Roman Catholicism by a reading of Bossuet. ("I surely fell by a noble hand.") The elder Gibbon packed him off to Lausanne and put him under the charge of a Calvinist minister, Daniel Pavillard, whose unenviable task it was to argue the determined youth out of his new-won faith. Pavillard later recalled the astonishment with which he gazed on his pupil, "a thin little figure with a large head, disputing and urging, with the greatest ability, all the best arguments that had ever been used in favor of popery." By the end of 1754, Gibbon was again, as he put it in a letter to his aunt, "good Protestant and extremely glad of it." And he never ceased to be grateful for the "fortunate shipwreck" that had brought him to the shores of Lake Geneva, which—*"This is your captain speaking"*—was soon to be coming into view for those lucky passengers sitting on the left side of the aircraft.

"If," Gibbon wrote late in life, "my childish revolt against the Religion of my country had not stripped me in time of my Academic gown, the five important years, so liberally improved in the studies and conversation of Lausanne, would have been steeped in port and prejudice among the monks of Oxford." Instead, Gibbon lost his insularity and was able to absorb the culture of the European Enlightenment amidst surroundings so beautiful that when he came to write in his history about St. Bernard's piously veiling his eyes when he passed Lake Geneva, he expressed the wish that the reader, before deciding whether to admire or to despise the saint, [should] "like myself . . . have before the windows of his library the beauties of that incomparable landscape." It was in Lausanne—in a letter of 1785 Gibbon speaks of his passion for "my wife or mistress (Fanny Lausanne)"—that he wrote the concluding volumes of *The Decline and Fall*. And it was from Lausanne, more than twenty years earlier, that he had set out on that Italian journey in the course of which he was inspired to write his great work.

We were flying over the Alps now, at thirty-five thousand feet. We had left the gloom of England far behind us, and the mountain peaks below were white and sparkling in the sun. Modes of transport had

changed since 1764. The future historian of the Roman Empire had
been carried across Mont Cenis by four porters, taking turns. "I
mounted a mule," his traveling companion reported at the time, "and
my Friend Gibbon got into a chaire. This chair is made of a kind of
rushes, and is only a seat between two long poles. Your legs are
supported by a cord and a piece of wood fastend across the poles to
prevent their hanging down; and their is a low back and arms to the
chair: nothing can be better contrived for the lightness or convenience
of carriing." Gibbon himself did not like to be carried in this fashion
by his fellow human beings. But repugnance yielded to necessity.

Our captain was speaking to us again in those reassuringly clipped
accents in which British Airways seems to specialize: Turin, then
Rome. Gibbon had taken the same route. In Turin he had met the
king's daughters: "I chatted for about a quarter of an hour with them,
talked about Lausanne, and grew so very free and easy that I drew
out my snuff box, rapped it, took snuff twice (a crime never known
before in the presence chamber) and continued my discourse, in my
usual attitude of my body bent forward and my forefinger out."

We had landed in Rome. For a while it appeared that all the baggage
was going on to Bombay; and I thought of Gibbon, who upon his
own arrival in Rome (on October 2, 1764), was rudely awakened from
his "dream of antiquity" by "those very modern figures, the customs
officials." The next day, after a sleepless night, he was once again free
to immerse himself in the past, already so familiar to him through his
prodigious reading. "I trod with a lofty step the ruins of the Forum;
each memorable spot where Romulus *stood,* or Tully spoke, or Caesar
fell was at once present to my eye and several days of intoxication
were lost or enjoyed before I could descend to a cool and minute
investigation." But the great and decisive moment was yet to come:
"It was at Rome, on the fifteenth of October 1764, as I sat musing
amidst the ruins of the Capitol, while the barefooted fryars were singing Vespers in the temple of Jupiter, that the idea of writing the decline
and fall of the City first started to my mind."

From that moment was to emerge far more than the history of a
city. Beginning with a description of the extent and military power
of the Roman Empire in the happy days of the Antonines (A.D. 98–
180), Gibbon pursued its subsequent misfortunes for thirteen centuries, down to that day in 1430 when the learned humanist Poggio and
a friend "ascended the Capitoline hill, reposed themselves among the
ruins of columns and temples, and viewed from that commanding
spot the wide and various prospect of desolation."

In the course of six volumes (published between 1776 and 1788) and more than three thousand pages, the historian, combining the learning of the seventeenth century with the philosophical approach of the eighteenth, traced in masterly fashion the complex history of the Western and Eastern Empires—keeping always in view the character and influence of the leading actors, brilliantly portrayed, while at the same time paying close attention to those impersonal forces that transcend, and often frustrate, the desires and efforts of individuals.

Here is no mere narrative of events, but a history also of institutions, of currents of thought and feeling, of the multifarious societies whose contacts and clashes dominate so much of the story of Rome's decline. There are marvelous set pieces on the rise and progress of Christianity, the foundation of Constantinople, the barbarian invasions, the habits of pastoral nations, the Trinitarian controversy, monasticism, the Moguls and their conquests. And there are unforgettable portraits—of Constantine, Julian the Apostate, Athanasius, Justinian, Attila, and Mohammed, to name but a few. All is filtered through Gibbon's searching and powerful mind, and presented in a style whose orderly and elaborate periods, shot through with grave irony, seem to create elegance and harmony out of chaos and confusion.

The footnotes must not be forgotten. Not only do they reveal an erudition so enormous and accurate that even today it is foolhardy to challenge it. They contain those flashes of wit and humor that help to ease the reader's long trek through the centuries, from the reference to the Abbé le Boeuf, "an antiquarian, whose name was happily expressive of his talents," to the comment on the learned Origen, who, eager for perpetual chastity, thought fit to castrate himself ("to disarm the tempter," in Gibbon's phrase). "As it was his general practise to allegorise Scripture, it seems unfortunate that, in this instance only, he should have adopted the literal sense."

When the first volume of *The Decline and Fall* appeared, on February 17, 1776, in an edition of a thousand copies, it was received with an almost universal chorus of praise. Except for a few clergymen who were offended by Gibbon's disrespectful treatment of the early Christians, readers and reviewers tended to agree with Horace Walpole, who wrote the historian that he had unexpectedly given the world a classic history. Posterity has seen no reason to repudiate that judgment. That was why a score of scholars from as many universities in Europe and the United States had gathered in Rome to commemorate the Gibbonian bicentennial. The papers they had written—ranging in subject matter from "Gibbon and the History of Art" to "Gibbon on Civilization and Barbarism"—had been circulated in advance; so that for three solid days there was a chance to raise and discuss questions. Had Gibbon read Vico? Why didn't he idealize Venice? What about Montesquieu's influence? Why was Gibbon more sympathetic to Arabia than to Byzantium? What special meaning did the word "effeminacy" have for him? Was he a skeptic or a theologian *manqué?* Or both? Did he set out to refute Rousseau's idea of the noble savage in one of his chapters? Did he understand the role of the irrational? Did he distinguish between wickedness and sin? What did he really mean when he ascribed the decline of Rome to barbarism and religion? And so on.

The first session was held on the Campidoglio, within sight of those steps of the church of S. Maria in Ara Coeli where Gibbon had sat and heard the friars chanting their vespers. A century later, a bemused Henry Adams had sat on those same steps, in search of wisdom. Now, somewhat self-consciously, the members of the conference could not resist the chance of posing on them for the photographer. The weather was balmy. There was a general strike. The Italian government was once again about to fall. But the dome of St. Peter's, serene and beautiful, floated above the city in the gentle light of an Italian afternoon. It was so warm, even in early January, that in the intervals of the conference it was possible to sit in an open-air café, to enjoy one's *gelato misto,* and to read in the Paris *Tribune* that in a new thriller that had just opened on the London stage, the heroine made it a habit to hide her gin bottles behind two volumes of *The Decline and Fall.* But one really did not require that piece of news in order to assure oneself of Gibbon's continuing vitality. As the discussions went on, day after day; as more and more questions were raised and debated; as the extent and variety of Gibbon's achievement became ever more manifest, one increasingly got the sense that *The Decline and Fall* was a classic that was two hundred years young, one that had barely begun its majestic and assured journey into immortality.

III

AMUSEMENT
AND
INSTRUCTION

Gibbon's Humor

Oliphant Smeaton, editor of the "Everyman" *Decline and Fall,* speaks of "those silly witticisms as pointless as they are puerile in which Gibbon at times indulges."[1] How would the great historian have dealt with that comment and its author? The latter's name, though the mere act of pronouncing it may even now raise a smile, would not have lent itself to punning—unlike that of the Abbé le Boeuf, "an antiquarian, whose name was happily expressive of his talents."[2] But his censorious remark might have moved Gibbon to credit him with "that naïveté, that unconscious simplicity, which always constitutes genuine humor."[3]

To take issue with Oliphant Smeaton is neither to deny that any historian who admits the comic spirit to his pages puts strict historical truth at risk, nor to maintain that Gibbon's humor demands to be treated with reverence and awe. To be sure, he had learned from Pascal the art of wielding "grave and temperate irony" in a great cause. But it did not require the excesses of the early Christians to set free his sense of farce and his ability to indulge in what, writing of Bayle, he referred to as "wicked wit."[4] Delinquent authors sufficed. For evidence one need look no higher than his footnotes, which in themselves constitute a veritable academy of raillery and humor. Voltaire is a

From *Daedalus,* July 1976

favorite target, casting, as he does, "a keen and lively glance over the surface of history."[5] Thus, "unsupported by either fact or probability, [he] has generously bestowed the Canary Islands on the Roman empire."[6] As a Gibbonian victim, the Patriarch of Ferney duly takes his place alongside Ammianus Marcellinus, whose bad taste is such "that it is not easy to distinguish his facts from his metaphors"; Salmasius, who "too often involves himself in the maze of his disorderly erudition"; St. Augustine, "[whose] learning is too often borrowed, and . . . [whose] arguments are too often his own"; and Corneille, whose tragedy of Heraclius "requires more than one representation to be clearly understood; and . . . after an interval of some years, is said to have puzzled the author himself."[7]

Sex and Christianity are conventionally mentioned as two of the principal arenas in which Gibbon's wit disported itself to the fullest, and there is little reason to dispute that judgment. Like Theodora's murmurs, pleasures, and arts, some of Gibbon's anecdotes involving sexual matters "must be veiled in the obscurity of a learned language."[8] And so we hear of Lycopolis, the modern Siut, or Osiot, which has a very convenient fountain, *cujus potû signa virginitatis eripiuntur.*[9] At other times, a learned language is not required; for instance, when Gibbon describes Claudius as the only one of the first fifteen Roman emperors "whose taste in love was entirely correct"; or when he reports that Arius reckoned among his immediate followers "two bishops of Egypt, seven presbyters, twelve deacons, and (what may appear almost incredible) seven hundred virgins."[10] No essay about Gibbon's humor may omit the younger Gordian: "Twenty-two acknowledged concubines, and a library of sixty-two thousand volumes, attested the variety of his inclinations, and from the productions which he left behind him, it appears that the former as well as the latter were designed for use rather than ostentation." The footnote reads: "By each of his concubines, the younger Gordian left three or four children. His literary productions were by no means contemptible."[11]

The combination of sex and Christianity seems to be particularly effective in triggering Gibbon's risibilities. When he describes those nuns of Constantinople who were torn from the altar by the conquering Turks, "with naked bosoms, outstretched hands, and disheveled hair," he cannot refrain from commenting that "we should piously believe that few could be tempted to prefer the vigils of the harem to those of the monastery."[12] When he recalls that he has somewhere heard or read the frank confession of a Benedictine abbot—

"My vow of poverty has given me an hundred thousand crowns a year; my vow of obedience has raised me to the rank of a sovereign prince"—he cannot stop there, but must add: "I forget the consequences of his vow of chastity."[13]

It is, of course, no accident that Gibbon's wit is so frequently directed at Christianity and its adherents. The same "arms of ridicule and *comic* raillery"[14] which Constantine employed against the heretics, Gibbon employed against the Christians. One of his aims in *The Decline and Fall* was to capture the territory of early church history for the secular historian. In order to accomplish that aim, it was not enough—at least it was not enough for Gibbon—to put fact in place of fancy. The miraculous had to be ridiculed as well as questioned. And this he proceeded to do, with a mastery of literary devices designed both to infuriate the orthodox and to delight and titillate his fellow skeptics.

C'est le ton qui fait la musique. By no means the least effective of those devices was the tone of mock seriousness that Gibbon was able to assume at will when he dealt with sacred matters. From the beginning of chapter 15, when he complains about "the melancholy duty" imposed on the historian who "must discover the inevitable mixture of error and corruption which [religion] contracted in a long residence upon earth," to its end, when he records in a matter-of-fact manner that during the age of Christ, his apostles, and their first disciples, "the lame walked, the blind saw, the sick were healed, the dead were raised, demons were expelled, and the laws of Nature were frequently suspended for the benefit of the Church,"[15] that tone reinforces the secular implications of the five "secondary causes" for the rapid growth of Christianity. The Old Testament is not immune. After quoting from Numbers 14:11—"How long will this people provoke me? and how long will it be ere they *believe* me, for all the *signs* which I have shown among them?"—Gibbon assures his readers that it would be easy, "but it would be unbecoming," to justify the complaint of the Deity from the whole tenor of the Mosaic history. After noting that there exist some objections against the authority of Moses and the prophets that too readily present themselves to the skeptical mind, he feels bound to add that these "can only be derived from our ignorance of remote antiquity, and from our incapacity to form an adequate judgment of the Divine economy."[16]

That tone of voice is not confined to chapter 15. It reappears at the conclusion of the second of the "Christian" chapters, where the observation that the Christians in the course of their intestine dissensions

have inflicted far graver severities on each other than they have experienced from the zeal of the infidels is called "a melancholy truth
which obtrudes itself on the reluctant mind";[17] and, later, in Gibbon's
account of the monastic saints: "They familiarly accosted, or impe-
riously commanded, the lions and serpents of the desert; infused veg-
etation into a sapless trunk; suspended iron on the surface of the water;
passed the Nile on the back of a crocodile; and refreshed themselves
in a fiery furnace."[18] More difficult feats, certainly, than those of the
Empress Eudocia. All *she* did was to enjoy the conscious satisfaction
of returning to Constantinople "with the chains of St. Peter, the right
arm of St. Stephen, and an undoubted picture of the Virgin painted
by St. Luke."[19] Hardly ever can a "melancholy duty" have been performed in a more sprightly fashion.

Part of the humor all along resides in the sort of persona that Gibbon
presents to his readers, in the disjunction between the skeptical man
of the world and the mask of credulity and devotion which he so
readily assumes. Throughout *The Decline and Fall,* there is carried on
a benevolent conspiracy between the reader and the historian, carefully
engineered by the latter, who uses it to entertain his audience as well
as to take it into camp. Gibbon is ever present. "Before we enter upon
the memorable reign of that prince [Diocletian]," he writes, "it will
be proper to punish and dismiss the unworthy brother of Numer-
ian."[20] Later, he confesses that "I have neither power nor inclination
to follow the Hungarians beyond the Rhine."[21] Concluding his sketch
of Muhammad's life, he admits how difficult it is to decide whether
to call him an enthusiast or an impostor: "At the distance of twelve
centuries I darkly contemplate his shade through a cloud of religious
incense."[22]

As the history draws to a close, the historian increasingly mocks
himself. The feudal knight, he tells us, devoted himself to speaking
the truth as the champion of God and the ladies—and adds, paren-
thetically, that "I blush to write such discordant names."[23] Before
remarking that even in this world the natural order of events sometimes affords strong appearances of moral retribution, he solemnly
announces: "I shall not, I trust, be accused of superstition."[24] And,
as he takes leave of the papacy in the sixteenth century, he has some
praise even for the temporal government of that institution. "For myself," he movingly declares, "it is my wish to depart in charity with
all mankind, nor am I willing, in these last moments, to offend even
the Pope and clergy of Rome."[25]

The reader acts throughout as the historian's good-humored accomplice—civilized, impatient of too much detail, and not averse to a little mockery of himself. "In the course of this history," Gibbon writes, "the most voracious appetite for war will be abundantly satiated."[26] But that is not *really* what the reader wants. For after quoting the stern Tertullian on what will happen at the Last Judgment—"so many sage philosophers blushing in red-hot flames with their deluded scholars; so many celebrated poets trembling before the tribunal, not of Minos, but of Christ; so many tragedians, more tuneful in the expression of their own sufferings; so many dancers—" Here the historian breaks off in mid-passage, in the belief that "the humanity of the reader will permit me to draw a veil over the rest of this infernal description, which the zealous African pursues in a long variety of affected and unfeeling witticisms."[27] Gibbon's readers are generous as well as humane. If, in his *Anecdotes,* Procopius insinuates that "the fame and even the virtue of Belisarius were polluted by the lust and cruelty of his wife," and that the hero deserved "an appellation which may not drop from the pen of the decent historian," that is something which "the generous reader" will confess only reluctantly, having cast away the libel and been persuaded only by the evidence of the facts.[28] The reader's attention is apt to wander, especially when it comes to the deliberations of Church councils. In the treaty between the Greek and the Latin churches, "it was agreed," so Gibbon writes, "that the Holy Ghost proceeds from the Father *and* the Son, as from one principle and one substance; that he proceeds *by* the Son, being of the same nature and substance; and that he proceeds from the Father *and* the Son, by one *spiration,* and production." After the word "agreed," the historian felt it incumbent upon him to insert the phrase, "I must entreat the attention of the reader."[29] Faced with such an entreaty, few of his readers would be so hardhearted as to withhold their attention, and few would fail to forgive Gibbon for using his appeal to them for his own sly ends.

But where his humor is concerned, one must not make too much of Gibbon's polemical intentions, sly or otherwise. His irony, it has been pointed out, could serve many purposes: it could be used as a weapon; it could provide the requisite distance between himself and his subject matter, and thus lend the appearance of Olympian detachment to his history; it could act as a useful protective device in an age when explicit attacks on the essentials of Christian faith and doctrine still held a certain amount of danger; it could help to mediate an amused and objective view of human nature in all its (sometimes paradoxical) variety; it could also help the historian to evade judgments where he did not wish to make them. Gibbon's sneer was not always good-humored, and has even been seen by some as an outlet for his aggressions. But, granted all that, it is still worth remarking that there is in him a playfulness, a gaiety, a delight in wit for its own sake, that bubbles up time and again, irrepressibly. Like Julian, he "could not always restrain the levity of his temper."[30] Take the Armoricans, for instance. Armorica was the Roman name for the maritime counties of Gaul between the Seine and the Loire; whenever he comes to deal with the inhabitants of that region, Gibbon cannot resist verbal allusions to events taking place in his own time in certain other provinces. And so we hear of the Armoricans "in a state of disorderly independence"; of "the slight foundations of the *Armorican* republic"; of the Bretons of Armorica refusing their customary tribute; and of liberty peopling "the morasses of Armorica."[31]

Other forms of verbal wit abound in *The Decline and Fall,* some taken over from his sources, some of his own making: "A swarm of monks" issues from the desert; Julian's beard, louse-infested, earns the right to be called "populous"; pursuit of religious controversy affords a new occupation to "the busy idleness" of Constantinople; Roman senators complete their ruin "by an expensive effort to disguise their poverty"; Simeon Stylites spends thirty years on his column, "this last and lofty station."[32] Boswell had found spring guns and man-traps in Gibbon's garden of flowery eloquence. How the historian must have enjoyed setting them! Here is one: " 'May those who divide Christ be divided with the sword, may they be hewn in pieces, may they be burned alive!' were the charitable wishes of a Christian synod."[33] Here is another: "He [Justinian] piously labored to establish with fire and sword the unity of the Christian faith."[34] And here is a third: The Syracusans had held out for more than twenty days against the Arab besiegers; "and the place might have been relieved, if the mariners of the Imperial fleet had not been detained at Constantinople in building a church to the Virgin Mary."[35]

It may be argued, of course, that the last three examples combine high spirits with the censure of Christian hypocrisy. That particular form of censure could not be passed by Gibbon, or anyone else, upon the learned Origen, who, eager for perpetual chastity, "judged it the most prudent to disarm the tempter." Here the historian's gloss is sympathetic rather than critical: "As it was his general practise to allegorise Scripture, it seems unfortunate that, in this instance only, he should have adopted the literal sense."[36] Gibbon's wit was not tied to his polemical sallies, even when it accompanied them. When he remarks, "But there *is* a Providence (such at least was the opinion of the historian Procopius) that watches over innocence and folly,"[37] he is less concerned with disabusing his readers of a providential interpretation of history than with making a good joke. And the same sense of mischievous fun impels him to quote Malaterra to the effect that the bite of the tarantula "provokes a windy disposition, quae per anum inhoneste crepitando emergit—a symptom most ridiculously felt by the whole Norman army in their camp near Palermo."[38]

Is that, then, all there is to Gibbon's humor—footnoted reprimands for delinquent authors, sexual innuendo, solemn sneers at religion, amusing games played with his readers, and, throughout, an irrepressible element of playfulness and sheer high spirits? Let us look at a few more examples, and try to establish what, besides possibly exhibiting one or the other of the qualities already adverted to, they may have in common:

Their peaceful inhabitants enjoyed and abused the advantages of wealth and luxury.[39]

Such folly was disdained and indulged by the wisest princes.[40]

Strangers and pilgrims who already felt the strong intoxication of fanaticism, and, perhaps, of wine.[41]

. . . the sacred but licentious crowd of priests, of inferior ministers, and of female dancers.[42]

. . . some resemblance may be found in the situation of two princes who conquered France by their valor, their policy, and the merits of a seasonable conversion.[43]

. . . the Romans invited the Huns to a splendid, or, at least, a plentiful supper.[44]

By the repetition of a sentence and the loss of a foreskin, the subject or the slave, the captive or the criminal, arose in a moment the free and equal companions of the victorious Moslems.[45]

In these examples the humor arises in large part from Gibbon's undercutting the abstract, the spiritual, the unworldly, the formal, the pompous, the pretentious, the merely verbal, with the concrete, the mundane, the down-to-earth, the reality as he sees it. That same attitude characterizes a good many of his epigrams:

It is easier to deplore the fate, than to describe the actual condition, of Corsica.[46]

Corruption, the most infallible symptom of constitutional liberty . . .[47]

It is much easier to ascertain the appetites of a quadruped than the speculations of a philosopher.[48]

What is involved, of course, is a particular view of human existence—cynical, realistic, disdainful of cant and hypocrisy. It assumes that human beings everywhere and at all times share a desire for power, for material gain, and for pleasure, a desire they might be able to control to a certain extent by exercising a rational prudence, but which resists idealistic or suprarational efforts (however well intentioned) to extirpate it. One is reminded of La Rochefoucauld's maxim: *"Les vertus se perdent dans l'intérêt comme les fleuves se perdent dans la mer."* True wisdom resides in those who can rebuff or rid themselves of chimerical dreams and are able to adopt instead an unvarnished view of human character and a utilitarian view of social and political institutions. Those who refuse to do this, who let themselves be misled by the idle speculations of poets or priests, or chastise themselves in the vain hope of denying their natural proclivities, become the object of Gibbon's amusement as well as of his censure.

Thus Julian "gradually acquired for his troops the imaginary protection of the gods, and for himself the firm and effective support of the Roman legions."[49] Thus the attachment of the Roman soldiers to their standards was inspired to some extent by the united influence of religion and honor. But "these motives, which derived their strength from the imagination, were enforced by fears and hopes of a more substantial kind."[50] Two adverse choirs chanted the Trisagion in the cathedral of Constantinople; "and, when their lungs were exhausted, they had recourse to the more solid arguments of sticks and stones."[51] After the failure of the line of Alaric, royal dignity was still limited to the pure and noble blood of the Goths: "The clergy, who anointed their lawful prince, always recommended, and sometimes practised, the duty of allegiance."[52] "The various modes of worship, which prevailed in the Roman world, were all considered by the people as equally true; by the philosopher, as equally false; and by the magistrate, as equally useful."[53]

Gibbon's sympathies clearly lie with the magistrate. He would surely have agreed with Lord Melbourne's complaint that things had come to a pretty pass when religion was allowed to invade private life, though he might have added, "and to evade public life." It was, after all, the withdrawal of the early Christians from civic duty and responsibility that contributed to Rome's fall. This is one serious message of the Christian chapters. As we have observed, their comic effect lies, in part, in the mock solemnity of the author's tone. But only in part. For the same view of human nature that informs the work as a whole informs these chapters as well, and it is there, as elsewhere, integrally related to Gibbon's center of levity:

> Disdaining an ignominious flight, the virgins of the warm climate of Africa encountered the enemy in the closest engagement: they permitted priests and deacons to share their beds, and gloried amidst the flames in their unsullied purity. But insulted Nature sometimes vindicated her rights, and this new species of martyrdom served only to introduce a new scandal into the church.[54]

"Insulted nature" here represents the sexual passion which will not let itself be entirely repressed. Elsewhere, it is the desire for pecuniary gain that resists curbing: "Even the reverses of the Greek and Roman coins were frequently of an idolatrous nature. Here, indeed, the scruples of the Christian were suspended by a stronger passion."[55] Men, in Gibbon's view, crave material rewards, and those who claim to despise these more likely than not are able to make that claim because they cannot, in fact, obtain them: "It is always easy, as well as agreeable, for the inferior ranks of mankind to claim a merit from the contempt of the pomp and pleasure which fortune has placed beyond their reach."[56] Cyprian "had renounced those temporal honors which it is probable he would never have obtained."[57]

In these examples the humor arises from a tacitly assumed agreement between the historian and his reader that there must be something irrational, something almost demented, certainly something comical, about a religion that expected men to renounce carnal desires and worldly success. As for miraculous intervention, one story told by Gibbon and his comment on it can stand for many others of a similar kind:

> The victorious king of the Franks [Clovis] proceeded without delay to the siege of Angoulême. At the sound of his trumpets the walls of the city imitated the example of Jericho, and instantly fell to the ground; a splendid miracle, which may be reduced to

the supposition that some clerical engineers had secretly under-
mined the foundations of the rampart.[58]

Here, as elsewhere, practical common sense triumphs over the miraculous; the engineer (even if, this time, he be a *clerical* engineer) over
the priest. And the reader is meant to smile. But what Gibbon has in
mind is more than mere entertainment, more, even, than yet another
lighthearted blow at the truth or efficacy of Christian miracles. The
ground bass of practicality and common sense that resounds in so
much of his humor both echoes and sustains one of the major themes
of *The Decline and Fall:* that the past and future progress of civilization
rest not on the unbridled abstractions of speculators or the vain in-
cantations of priests and poets, but rather on the slow and steady
conquests of science and the practical arts.

That theme is to be found throughout the work. But it is in the
"General Observations on the Fall of the Roman Empire in the
West"[59] that Gibbon proclaims it with the greatest eloquence. Here
he ascribes the end of the barbarian incursions, "the long repose," not
to a decrease of population, but to the progress of arts and agriculture.
From an abject condition of savagery—naked in both mind and body,
destitute of laws, arts, ideas, and almost of language, man has gradually arisen to command the animals, to fertilize the earth, to traverse
the ocean, and to measure the heavens. It may safely be presumed
that no people, unless the face of nature is changed, will relapse into
their original barbarism.

Gibbon then proceeds to view the improvements of society under
a threefold aspect: poets and philosophers first—but their superior
powers of reason or fancy are rare and spontaneous productions. The
benefits of law and policy, trade and manufactures, arts and sciences
come second—but that complex machinery may be decayed by time,
or injured by violence. But, fortunately for mankind, the more useful,
or at least the more necessary, arts are in no such danger.

Each village, each family, each individual, must always possess
both ability and inclination to perpetuate the use of fire and of
metals; the propagation and service of domestic animals; the
methods of hunting and fishing; the rudiments of navigation;
the imperfect cultivation of corn or other nutritive grain; and the
simple practice of the mechanic trades. Private genius and public
industry may be extirpated; but these hardy plants survive the

tempest, and strike an everlasting root into the most unfavorable soil.[60]

It is true, as Gibbon goes on to point out, that since these practical arts were first discovered, religious zeal, as well as war and commerce, has helped to diffuse them among the savages of the Old and the New World. But they are more than the sum of those agents of diffusion. They are nothing less than the bedrock of civilization. Useful and practical, they stand in no need of elaborate speculations and feverish imaginings. They correspond in their steady and constant operation to the happy mean of human nature, free from extremes of virtue and vice, solidly based on a recognition of reality. That is one of the great lessons of *The Decline and Fall*. And when the reader laughs and smiles with the historian at the excesses and absurdities of misguided men and women, be they pagan, Christian, or Muslim, he shows that he has learned his lesson. By his laughter and his smile he is helping to support the foundations of Gibbon's own rampart.

Macaulay's Historical Imagination

In reading the opening chapters of *The Decline and Fall* one finds that Gibbon often constructs his paragraphs in such a way that the first half of the paragraph consists of a series of statements describing an *apparent* situation, character, or sequence of events; while the second half, usually beginning with a qualifying conjunction such as "but" or "however," reveals the *real* forces or motives operating underneath the appearance. This is Gibbon's way of unfolding the narrative while at the same time commenting on it from his vantage point of omniscience after the event. But, more than that, this method of paragraph construction means that each such paragraph mirrors the historian's general theme of *actual* decay hidden under *apparent* peace and prosperity.

Is such conscious or unconscious elective affinity between style and subject to be found in Macaulay? Taine was perhaps the first to draw attention to the manner in which Macaulay in his *History* used apparently random anecdotes, illustrations, and allusions to reinforce his major themes. The French critic chose the example of James II's arrival in Ireland in 1689 to make his point: "No horses to be found at Cork, the country a desert, the peasants marauders and butchers." All this adds up to more than some random observations on social history.

x

From *Review of English Literature*, October 1960

For from this description it becomes clear what will happen when William and the Protestants face the Irish Catholic forces at the Boyne: "The history of manners is thus seen to be involved in the history of events; the one is the cause of the other, and the description explains the narrative." One might go further than this and point out that Macaulay's habit of constructing his paragraphs by rounding off a tattoo of short, breathless sentences with a resolving period is more than what Sir Richard Jebb called it—a trick of oratory, the surging and subsidence of thought and feeling in the orator's mind. Does not this stylistically reiterated sequence of tension and crisis leading to climactic resolution reflect the critical and tense sequence of events that found a happy issue in the Glorious Revolution; or, in a larger context, Macaulay's general theme of *per aspera ad astra?*

This aspect of the relationship between style and content—the possibility of an affinity between the subject chosen by the historian and his manner of expression (which is, of course, in turn an aspect of his personality)—must inevitably remain in the realm of speculation. But there is no doubt at all that Macaulay was very conscious of less intangible matters pertaining to arrangement and structure in historical writing. He wanted to make his *History* instructive, entertaining, and universally intelligible; and he rewrote and polished endlessly to achieve these goals. One need only reread chapter 3 on the state of England in 1685 to find instances of masterfully planned transitions—logical, easy, and seemingly inevitable—and to discount his own modest statement confided to his journal in 1854 that "arrangement and transition are arts which I value much, but which I do not flatter myself that I have attained." He was very much aware of how the great historians of the past had dealt with problems of presenting and arranging narrative history; Thucydides and Herodotus remained yardsticks for his own performance. When he devised as a means of exposition the declamatory disquisition, a summary of the arguments that might have been used by various parties to sustain their feelings at critical junctures, he did so because he felt he needed to have an equivalent for the speeches employed by the ancient historians.

Not only was Macaulay very conscious, then, of the importance of scaffolding in historical writing—but he was indeed a consummate master of the art of draping his narrative around that scaffolding in such a way that the latter remained for the most part invisible. He has also, in his personal papers and in reports of his conversation, left some revealing glimpses of the extent to which he was generally familiar with the workings of his historical imagination. His method in *The History of England,* as he wrote in his journal on March 3, 1853, was to get as fast as he could over what was dull, and to dwell as long as he could on what could be made picturesque and dramatic. One way of making history "picturesque" was to give the reader a vivid sense of place; and Macaulay's travels to the scenes of the events he was describing helped him collect, as he wrote after his trip to Ireland in 1849, "a large store of images and thoughts"—images which his photographic memory retained, so to speak, as negative film to be developed into positives when he came to write. Sometimes a more complex process occurred. A vivid contemporary image totally unrelated to his subject became the means of enhancing his depiction of past events. Thus he notes in his journal on May 19, 1851, that the sight of the Great Exhibition has made him feel a flow of eloquence or something like it; and that it has made him think of some touches which would greatly improve his description of the battle of Steinkirk.

Finally, and this is perhaps the most interesting aspect of the problem of the relation of Macaulay's imaginative powers to his historical writing, there is the historian's consciousness of the connection between his fantasy life and his written history. In the verses he wrote after being defeated at the Edinburgh election of 1847 he consoled himself with the comforting reflection that:

> *Mine is the world of thought, the world of dream*
> *Mine all the past, and all the future mine*

And these lines merely give poetic expression to the importance for his work of a linkage between thought and dream upon which he often commented less formally. To his sister Margaret (who noted the remark in her journal on March 30, 1831) he once said that his factual accuracy was due to his love of castle-building. From childhood on he had retained the habit of constructing the past into a romance. As soon as he found himself in the streets he imagined himself in Greece, in Rome, in the midst of the French Revolution. And in these daydreams, in the course of which he composed conversations between the great people of the time in the style of Sir Walter Scott, precision in dates, the day or hour in which a man was born, was of crucial importance. In a letter written to Margaret some time later he referred to his "power of forgetting what surrounds me, and of living with the past, the future, the distant, and the unreal." In 1857, while engaged on what were to be the last chapters of his *History,* he confides to his journal that if he lives long enough he will one day write a disquisition on the strange habit of daydreaming to which he imputes a great part of his literary success.

He did not, as he half-suspected, live to write this disquisition. But not long before his death, during a trip to Weybridge with the Trevelyans and their children, he and his sister Hannah (Lady Trevelyan) fell to talking about the habit of building castles in the air—"a habit in which Lady Trevelyan and I indulge beyond any people that I ever knew. I mentioned to George [his nephew, later his biographer] what, as far as I know, no critic has observed, that the Greeks called this habit κενὴ μακαρία [empty happiness]. Alice [his niece] who was some way off and did not hear distinctly, said 'Kenneth Macaulay! What did the Greeks say about Kenneth Macaulay?' I shall always call the unreal world in which I pass a large part of my life Kenneth Macaulay."

"The unreal world in which I pass a large part of my life"—the statement jibes with what we know of Macaulay's love of fiction and drama and of his own considerable histrionic abilities. This is the Macaulay who, in his boyhood, addressed a letter to "one of the high and mighty triumvirate of girls, member of the most Honourable Committee for Circulating the Bride of Abydos"—in short, his sister; who years later delighted the Trevelyans by acting out an old clothesman and by romancing about a secret embassy to America on which he pretended he had been sent twenty years before; and who, in an April Fool's Day letter to his sister Hannah, informed her that Mrs. Beecher Stowe had invited herself to dinner, bringing along a Negro parson named Caesar Ugbark. In what ways, for better or for worse, did the historian's strongly developed visual and dramatic imagination and his equally strongly developed fantasy life influence his historical writing?

I should like to suggest that on the positive side this imaginative capacity contributed in great measure to two important qualities that helped to lend The History of England its never-ending fascination: a strongly developed sense of the concrete in pictorial form and the capacity to animate into forward motion in time motives, characters and situations—a capacity which at the same time that it benefited the style and general structure of The History also contributed to the strong sense of linkage between past and present that pervades it. This sense of linkage we have come to recognize, perhaps a little too readily, as characteristic of the "Whig interpretation of history."

In his essay entitled "History" Macaulay demanded that the perfect historian must indicate changes of manners not merely by a few general phrases, or in extracts from statistics, but by appropriate images presented in every line. When he came to write his *History* many years later, Macaulay followed his own prescription, always making explicit through concrete and familiar images what would otherwise have stood in danger of remaining distant and dull.

Here he is on the tenets of the Puritans: "It was a sin to hang garlands on a Maypole, to drink a friend's health, to fly a hawk, to hunt a stag, to play at chess, to wear lovelocks, to put starch into a ruff, to touch the virginals, to read the *Faerie Queene*." Here he is describing the Princess Mary skating on the Dutch canals, "poised on one leg, and clad in petticoats shorter than are generally worn by ladies so strictly decorous." And here on the profound submission and obedience of the Jesuit "whether he should live under the arctic circle or under the equator, whether he should pass his life in arranging gems and collating manuscripts at the Vatican or in persuading naked barbarians under the Southern Cross not to eat each other." Here on the country squires hurrying to London early in 1690 to oppose the Corporation Bill, which they interpreted as a retrospective penal law against the entire Tory party: "A hundred knights and squires left their halls hung with mistletoe and holly, and their boards groaning with brawn and plum porridge, and rode up post to town, cursing the short days, the cold weather, the miry road, and the villainous Whigs."

These examples could be multiplied indefinitely; and there is no need to comment on their visual and dramatic impact. What *is* worth noting is how often the historian's visual imagination is reinforced by what might be called his propulsive imagination. In other words, he demonstrates an instinctive ability to propel inert facts into motion— an ability closely akin to his private daydreaming and fantasy life in which he was able to propel *himself* into imaginary situations. At its simplest level this capacity means that when confronted with the statement "The rain in Spain stays mainly in the plain," one at once visualizes the Spanish plain as soggy. The original statement describes only the process, leaving the effects to the imagination. The transition, once made, seems natural, logical, and obvious. But the ability to make it, regularly and as a matter of course, is rare and not to be despised. At a more complex level, it is this same capacity which enabled Macaulay to propel the lord of the manor of the late seventeenth century to London, and to see him there jostled by bullies, splashed by hackney coachmen, victimized by pickpockets and shopkeepers, and derided by fops; or to describe the effect on Englishmen of all ranks of the possible closing of hundreds of houses of entertainment and public resort:

> Men of fashion would have missed the chocolate house in Saint James's Street, and men of business the coffee pot, round which they were accustomed to smoke and talk politics, in Change Alley. Half the clubs would have been wandering in search of shelter. The traveller at nightfall would have found the inn where he had expected to sup and lodge deserted. The clown would have regretted the hedge alehouse, where he had been accustomed to take his pot on the bench before the door in summer, and at the chimney corner in winter.

His propulsive imagination enabled Macaulay to set in motion what for most other historians would have remained stationary puppets, to exploit to the full the dynamic potential of what in other hands would have been merely a static situation or social setting.

It is this same propulsive imagination that helped make Macaulay such a master of the art of transition, an art which in its essence is after all nothing more than the orderly linkage of one paragraph or section of writing to the next, in a seemingly ineluctable propulsion, conceived in terms of the author's total vision and cemented by means of linguistic or logical association. In this way his particular gift of imagination supplemented effectively his concern for the technical structure of historical writing.

Macaulay's personal fantasy life oscillated naturally between present and past. The streets of London and Paris evoked vivid historical associations for him. His thoughts for weeks on end, we are told by his biographer, dwelt more in Latium and Attica than in Middlesex. Cicero and Curio were to him as real as Peel and Stanley. When he helped to carry the Great Reform Bill the drama of the parliamentary scene turned his thoughts at once to Caesar stabbed in the Senate House and to Cromwell taking the mace from the table. And it is this close personal involvement with the great events and the great men preceding those of his own time, as much as any theory of progress, that becomes transformed into that contrapuntal interweaving of past and present which runs through and dominates *The History* at every turn. Here subjective imagination and philosophy of history blend into one.

If, then, Macaulay's powerful imagination, nurtured on his inner life of daydreams and fantasy, exerted itself in his historical writing in all these ways, what was it that led Sir Charles Firth to remark that the historian "had little insight into men's motives and very little sympathy or imagination"? And why does Professor Geyl call Macaulay a man in whom the intellect is far more developed than the imagination, a man who does not express a feeling of awe before the mystery of the past? The answer, as even a cursory reading of Macaulay is sufficient to show, is, of course, that he did not possess the all-embracing sympathy, the capacity for *Einfühlung,* that would have enabled him to treat all personages, parties, and ideas in history with equal respect and understanding. This lack was due, in part, to the fact that when all is said and done, and when the simplistic interpretation of Macaulay as merely a Whig historian has been properly modified, he was undeniably a person of strong prejudices and, on occasion, of unfair bias. The charges so brilliantly brought forward in Paget's *New Examen* have never been satisfactorily refuted. One does not go to Macaulay for an impartial view of English history.

I should like to suggest that, even discounting prejudice and *parti pris,* it was the particular quality of Macaulay's imagination itself that militated against the sort of all-inclusive sympathy which he is justly accused of having lacked. As one reads the historian's letters and journals one is struck again and again by his express intention to make his historical writing lively, amusing and dramatic. Steeped from childhood in the English novel—to the point where he and his sisters would discuss household affairs and family gossip in the language of Austen's Mr. Woodhouse and Mrs. Elton—an avid admirer of Scott's fictional historical reconstructions, Macaulay set himself the task of making his own *History* as vivid and as entertaining as the latest work of fiction. In this he succeeded. Yet the very harping on the necessity for making history lively, the self-conscious sense of literary artifice, and of what he himself called the need for purple patches, these traits— admirable as they are—may also have acted as impediments to the genuine historical imagination which is more concerned with the un- varnished truth than with enlivening it.

After rereading Defoe, Macaulay once remarked that the novelist had a knack of making fiction look like truth . . . "but is such a knack much to be admired?" One might turn the question around, and ask whether Macaulay's own knack of making truth look like fiction or romance did not itself hold certain dangers, did not, for instance, produce the kind of artificial heightening for effect that made William III into a saint and Marlborough into a villain. And here the historian's fantasy life, so fruitful for his historical writing in other respects, tended to let him down. Not only, as Sir Charles Firth has pointed out, did his castle-building lead to inaccuracies and errors because it made him form all too vivid and clear conceptions of the chief figures in his story before he undertook a systematic examination of all the accessible evidence. The propulsive capacity of his imagination, beneficial to *The History* in so many ways, was strong but solipsistic. It was always *he* who talked to the great figures of the past, he who saw *himself* in various imaginary situations. His daydreams were at once product and enhancement of his inborn sense of histrionics. They added immeasurably to the color and the drama of his great work. But, self-centered as they were, they did not really enable him, in fact, they made it very difficult for him to project himself into the hearts and minds of the men and women of the past; especially those against whom he was inclined by temperament or politics. The propulsion remained external. There was no internal projection—for he never left his own skin. It is singularly fitting that, in jokingly christening his fantasy life "Kenneth Macaulay," he should have chosen to dub it with his own name.

Amusement and Instruction:
Gibbon and Macaulay

On April 18, 1775, Dr. Johnson remarked to Boswell, "We must consider how very little authentic history there is. We can depend on as true that certain kings reigned, that certain battles were fought. But all the coloring, all the philosophy of history is conjecture." Boswell replied, "Then, sir, you would reduce all history to no better than an almanack, or mere chronological series of events." Gibbon, who was present, said nothing. He was writing history, not talking about it, and, less than a year later, published a book to prove it. Perhaps I should follow his example. But that would bring this lecture to a premature close.

We can't have Gibbon on Macaulay, but we can have Macaulay on Gibbon. "I read a good deal of Gibbon," Macaulay recorded in his journal in 1838. "He is grossly partial to the pagan persecutors; quite offensively so. His opinion of the Christian fathers is very little removed from me; but his excuses for the tyranny of their oppressors give to his book the character which Porson describes." (Porson had written that Gibbon "often makes when he cannot readily find an occasion to insult our religion which he hates so cordially that he might seem to revenge some personal injury.") Some years later, after conceding that *The Decline and Fall* could be justly criticized, Macaulay

From Massachusetts Historical Society *Proceedings* 87 (1975)

added, "Still the book, with all its great faults of substance and style, retains, and will retain, its place in our literature, and this though it is offensive to the religious feeling of the country, and really most unfair where religion is concerned." And, finally, we have an extended comment by Macaulay on the subject of Gibbon's "indecency." It occurs in a letter of 1849 to an unknown correspondent who had complained about what he considered to be this defect in Macaulay's own work. Macaulay replied:

> I am grateful for your suggestions, though I am not convinced that I ought to adopt them. If I were conscious of having any-where disgraced myself by trying to gratify prurient imagina-tions with licentious descriptions, I should, I hope, with shame and sorrow, hasten to repair so great an offense. I have always thought the indelicacy of Gibbon's great work a more serious blemish than even his uncandid hostility to the Christian religion. But I cannot admit that a book like mine is to be regarded as written for female boarding schools. I open a school for men: I teach the causes of national prosperity and decay; and the par-ticular time about which I write is a time when profligacy, having been compelled during some years to wear the mask of hypoc-risy, has just thrown that mask away, and stood forth with a brazen impudence of which there is scarcely another example in any modern society. How is it possible to treat a subject like mine without inserting a few paragraphs,—perhaps there may be, in my two thick volumes, two pages,—which it would be better that a young lady should not read aloud? How many of the most instructive chapters in the Bible, chapters of the highest value as illustrating the frailty of human nature, the tendency of crime to draw on crime, and the frightful effect of private vices on public affairs, are such as no parent would desire his daughter to read aloud? I am not aware that there is a single line in my work which can sully the imagination of anybody who is in the habit of listening to the morning and evening lessons at church.

What is interesting about this letter is not only that Macaulay (who found it hard to shake off his Puritan heritage completely) regarded Gibbon's "indelicacy" as a major blemish, but that he defends his own admitted straying from the paths of decency and morality in terms of *raison d'histoire,* of the historian's duty not to falsify the past by omit-ting in his account possibly offensive aspects that were a part of that past. How different is Gibbon's view, where gaiety and humor were reason enough for leaving the high road of sober seriousness. Thus, on the emperor Gordianus, "Twenty-two acknowledged concubines, and a library of sixty-two thousand volumes, attested the variety of his inclinations, and from the productions which he left behind him, it appears that the former as well as the latter were designed for use rather than ostentation." And the footnote reads, "By each of his concubines, the younger Gordian left three or four children. His literary productions were by no means contemptible." In another footnote Gibbon reports that he has somewhere heard or read the frank confession of a Benedictine abbot: "My vow of poverty has given me an hundred thousand crowns a year; my vow of obedience has raised me to the rank of a sovereign prince." Then he adds his own comment, "I forget the consequences of his vow of chastity." The playful tone, the tongue-in-cheek mischievousness, the Voltairean anticlerical note of scoffing and ridicule—all these things are miles away from Macaulay's generally straitlaced approach.

The two historians certainly differed, then, in their attitude to indecency. In what were they alike? Both were said by contemporaries to have been ugly. Dr. Johnson remarked about Gibbon, "He is an ugly, affected, disgusting fellow, and poisons our literary club to me." And when Sydney Smith advised Lady Holland not to visit the Netherlands, one reason he gave was that all the people there were uglier than Macaulay. Both were fat. Gibbon was known to some as "Monsieur Pomme de Terre." His corpulence was even commemorated in verse:

> *His person looked so funnily obese*
> *As if a pagod, growing large as man,*
> *Had rashly waddled off its chimney-piece,*
> *To visit a Chinese upon a fan.*

In 1831 Lady Lyndhurst remarked to Macaulay, "You are quite different to what I expected. I thought I should find you dark and thin, but you are fair and, really, Mr. Macaulay, you are quite fat." Their voices seem to have been alike. We are told that Gibbon's was normally shrill—though at the least contradiction it could swell to a "manly bass." Macaulay's was shrill and hissing when he spoke in the House of Commons.

Both historians remained unmarried; and, as it happened, rejected the prospect of marriage early in life in almost identical terms. Thus

Gibbon's comment about a certain Fanny Page, whom some people spoke of as a possible spouse for him, ran, "I must have a wife I can speak to." And Macaulay's about his cousin, Mary Babington, with whom he fancied himself half in love during his Cambridge years, went, "Her conversation soon healed the wound made by her eyes." Both historians found it difficult to maintain harmonious relations with their fathers. Gibbon's father, who squandered his son's wealth, "probably caused him more anguish than any other individual during the course of his life." And what was crucial for Macaulay's character and outlook was the conflict between his father's stern Evangelicalism and his own more sanguine and less disciplined temperament. Both Gibbon and Macaulay made their way in society by means of the brilliance of their writings, the former from a solid but unfashionable county background, the latter from the middle-class atmosphere of the Clapham Sect. Both were men of action as well as scholars and writers. Gibbon never forgot how useful his years in the Hampshire Militia had been to him as a historian. At one point he referred to Salmasius, Casaubon, and Lipsius as "mere scholars who perhaps had never seen a battalion under arms." He also sat in Parliament, an experience he came to regard as the most valuable school of civil prudence. Macaulay, of course, not only sat in the House of Commons, where he played an important and memorable role in the Reform Bill debates, but then proceeded to India in the capacity of legal member of the Governor's Council and there made significant contributions to educational and legal policies by his minute on the necessity for the employment of English in Indian education and by his authorship of a new penal code for India, which in its essentials is still in force today.

Both Gibbon and Macaulay (to our wonderment) thought they had a propensity to indolence. Both, from early youth, were more attracted to urban than to rustic scenes and surroundings. Both shared what Gibbon called an "invincible love of reading." Both believed in progress. Both wrote memorably about Rome, one in prose, the other in verse. Both had the knack of being able to enliven dull subjects in their histories, Gibbon the trinitarian controversies and Roman law, Macaulay the bank of England and recoinage. Both were, on the whole, pleased with their fate. Thus Gibbon remarks in his memoirs that "my lot might have been that of a slave, a savage or a peasant; nor can I reflect without pleasure on the bounty of nature, which cast my birth in a free and civilised country, in an age of science and philosophy, in a family of honourable rank and decently endowed with the gifts of fortune." And Macaulay, in a letter to Edward Everett, expresses a very similar sort of self-satisfaction. The first volumes of his *History* had just appeared (1849) and had scored a resounding success. "I have done with politics," he writes. "I have competence, liberty, leisure, tolerable health, very dear and affectionate relations. The serious business of the rest of my life will be my history, and that business will be a pleasure. I am one of the few people to whom Horace's 'qui fit Maecenas' is inapplicable. For . . . if I had to choose my own lot in life, I should carefully pick out from the whole vast heap the precise ticket which has fallen to my share."

But, of course, one must not overemphasize the similarities between the two historians. One must try to go beneath the surface, and the first question one must ask concerns their respective views of history. Both made programmatic statements about that subject early in their careers. Gibbon's *Essai sur la Littérature* is a defense of scholarship against the sort of *philosophe* approach exemplified by Voltaire's calling details "vermin." Not that Gibbon had anything against the *philosophes'* desire to see history as more than a dry-as-dust account of battles and political intrigues. He shared their broader vision, but he wanted to combine it with respect for fact and learning. In his discussion of writing history in the *Essai* he celebrates the *esprit philosophique,* i.e., getting at first principles, seeing things as a whole from a great height, attempting to construct a science of human nature. The rarest facts, Gibbon writes, are those that move the springs of human action—and it is rarer still to find those spirits who can discover them. It is desirable, he points out, that historians should always be *philosophes;* though it has been noted that for Gibbon this meant not so much "philosophy" or even being a *philosophe* in the manner of Voltaire as it did the adaptation of Renaissance humanism to the Enlightenment. Tacitus, Gibbon writes, was a greater historian than Livy because he did more than take us into the midst of past events. He saw structural connections, such as those between the laws of the Roman republic and the genius of the Romans. It is in this sense that in 1783, seven years after the appearance of the first two volumes of *The Decline and Fall,* Gibbon still refers to himself as "philosophe et historien."

Macaulay stated *his* historiographical credo in 1828, in his essay on "History." There he accused modern historians of having gone too far in their efforts to deduce general principles from facts, so that (and here he mentions Gibbon along with Hume and Mitford) they tended to distort facts to suit general principles. What had suffered most in all this was the art of narration, "interesting the affections and presenting pictures to the imagination." He wanted the historian to become the bard or poet of the age, reconciling reason and imagination. History was a branch of literature. Historians were to learn from novelists. And their subject matter ought to be social history in the broadest sense; emphasizing changes in manners and morals, from power to wealth, and from ignorance to knowledge. Thus, unlike Gibbon, who called for respect for scholarship and who wanted his ideal historian to help in the construction of a science of human nature, Macaulay stressed narrative art and a new kind of social history.

What sort of *persona* did these two historians present to the world? Gibbon referred to himself on different occasions as man of letters, philosopher, and historian of the Roman Empire; more informally, writing to friends as "the Gib" and "the Gibbon." Thus, addressing Holroyd in 1775, he remarks that "I think that through the dark and doubtful mist of futurity, I can discern some faint probability that the Gibbon and his aunt will arrive at Sheffield Place before the sun or rather the earth has accomplished eight diurnal revolutions." How does he appear to his readers in his *History?* In an early work he had written that "every man of genius who writes history infuses into it, perhaps unconsciously, the character of his own spirit. His characters, despite their extensive variety of passion and situation, seem to have only one manner of thinking and feeling, and that is the manner of the author." In *The Decline and Fall* his own role is mostly that of the philosopher who wants to engage the minds of his readers, so that with him they might apply human reason to an understanding of the world, to enlarge, as he often put it, the circle of their ideas. The philosophic historian imposes order on history as he writes it, and makes its crimes, follies, and misfortunes subject to reason in the process of chronicling them. Thus, after describing a quick succession of Byzantine royal intrigues, murders, and conspiracies, Gibbon comments:

A being of the nature of man, endowed with the same faculties, but with a longer measure of existence, would cast down a smile of pity and contempt on the crimes and follies of human ambition, so eager, in a narrow span, to grasp at a precarious and short-lived enjoyment. It is thus that the experience of history exalts and enlarges the horizon of our intellectual view. In a composition of some days, in a perusal of some hours,

six hundred years have rolled away, and the duration of a
life or reign is contracted to a fleeting moment: the grave
is ever beside the throne; the success of a criminal is almost in-
stantly followed by the loss of his prize; and our immortal reason survives and disdains the sixty phantoms of kings
who have passed before our eyes, and faintly dwell on our
remembrance.

The philosophical historian reflects on events, and attempts to judge
them in their broadest context, which may include explicit points of
reference to his own time. Thus this footnote of Gibbon's:

> *Within the ancient walls of Vindonissa, the castle of Hapsburg, the abbey
> of Koenigsfeld, and the town of Bruck have successively arisen. The
> philosophic traveler may compare the monuments of Roman conquest,
> of feudal or Austrian tyranny, of monkish superstition, and of industrious
> freedom. If he be truly a philosopher, he will applaud the happiness of
> his own time.*

If Gibbon exalts the reason of the historian (and of the presumably
like-minded reader) as they together examine and smile at the crimes,
follies, and misfortunes of mankind, Macaulay is more openly hor-
tatory and pedagogical. He, too, praises reason wherever he finds it;
but it is reason as displayed by historical actors in past events and
situations rather than the reason of the historian and his readers. Recall
his phrase in the letter cited above: "I open a school for men." He is
a teacher and a kind of secular preacher, the sort of teacher who is
successful because he makes his students believe that they themselves
have reached the conclusions to which they have, in fact, been led by
him. If Gibbon is a *cicerone,* Macaulay is a tour director. His principal
aim is to make the past tangible to his readers; for that is the prerequisite for any lessons that might be drawn from it. Thus in a letter
to Lady Holland he writes:

> I have got the household books of an old Leicestershire family
> with which I am connected [the Babingtons], and here I find full
> accounts of their income, their expenses, what they gave Lord
> Rutland's cook when they dined at Belvoir, what the son at Cam-
> bridge and the son at Westminster cost them and so forth. . . .
> These are in my opinion the real materials of history. . . . I shall

do my best to place my readers in the England of the seventeenth century.

Gibbon would have been less interested in placing his readers in the past than in enabling them to judge and survey it.

For Macaulay as for Gibbon the purpose of written history was certainly, in part, to amuse. Thus Macaulay in 1841, as he was beginning to work on his *History,* "The materials for an amusing narrative are immense." And thus Gibbon in 1783, "There is some philosophical amusement in tracing the birth of progress and error." The emphasis is different, but amusement is a common aim. For Gibbon, amusement for its own sake, for the delectation of the reader, is a desideratum. Instruction is another. They exist side by side, not necessarily connected. For Macaulay clarity of style, readability, and entertainment were prime virtues; but they were means to an end, and that end was instruction.

Both historians wanted to teach as well as to amuse. Gibbon's idol Tacitus had been as much moralist as historian. There is a general message in *The Decline and Fall,* concerned with the worth of freedom and the idealization of the Roman republic. Furthermore, Gibbon has no doubts about ethical standards of conduct and behavior, singling out, for instance, the love of pleasure and the love of action as essential components of normal human nature. Some attempts have been made to trace Gibbon's politics specifically through his *History,* but these have failed to reveal a simple pattern. His instruction has more to do with the principles of human nature and character. If there is any general lesson beyond that, it takes (as L. P. Curtis has observed) the form of a memorial oration to the governing classes on the subject of wisdom, virtue, and power. But Gibbon was too cynical to have had much faith in the effects of instruction, though that did not prevent him from making it part of his historical writing. The experience of past faults, he pointed out, was seldom profitable to the successive generations of mankind. In this respect, Macaulay's *History* is very different.

As our previous speaker, Professor Trevor-Roper, has pointed out, Macaulay shows that (*pace* Hume) the progress of society is not distinct from politics but connected with it, because it may be fostered by enlightened, liberal, and rational reform. One of the main themes of his *History* is that of demonstrating how people thought, felt, and acted when crucial political and moral decisions had to be taken. There was no doubt in Macaulay's mind about the fact that knowledge of the past could be of great use for the future. The principal political lesson of the *History* is probably less a Whiggish one than one of judicious trimming between two extremes. But there are more specific references to current politics. Macaulay rejoices that England has not seen the equivalent of the revolutions of 1848 on the continent of Europe and, when he deals with the siege of Londonderry, does not fail to remark that the animosities of the valiant defenders had descended along with their glory. It is significant that while Gibbon in his "General Observations" on the fall of Rome feared new external barbarians, Macaulay feared a new sort of internal barbarism, i.e., democracy. Gibbon admitted that he did not understand the French Revolution; it was something entirely novel as far as he was concerned. But, as I have argued elsewhere, Macaulay may be said to have employed social history as social anodyne. Placing really important historical changes into the context of a general moral atmosphere rather than into one of politics and public affairs tended to diminish, or blur over, the significance of contemporary confrontations of rich and poor, progress and reaction, in the political sphere.

Two examples will illustrate the different ways of teaching used by our two historians. Gibbon comments that the Attacotti, a valiant Caledonian tribe, are said to have attacked shepherds rather than their flocks, selecting the most delicate and brawny parts of males and females for their horrid repasts. He continues, "If in the neighborhood of the commercial and literary town of Glasgow a race of cannibals has really existed, we may contemplate in the period of Scottish history the opposite extremes of savage and civilized life. Such reflections tend to enlarge the circle of our ideas, and to encourage the pleasing hope that New Zealand may produce in some future age the Hume of the Southern hemisphere." Macaulay justifies the study of early English history in this way: "Then it was that the great English people was formed. . . . Then first appeared with distinctness that constitution which has ever since, through all changes, preserved its identity; that constitution of which all the other free constitutions in the world are copies, and which, in spite of some defects, deserves to be regarded as the best under which any great society has ever yet existed during many ages."

Between those two quotations lie the Romantic Movement and the novels of Scott. National history, less cosmopolitan, less philosophical, was in process of replacing the kind of history written during the Enlightenment. Macaulay was very much aware of this change. Thus he was genuinely puzzled by the enormous success of his *History* in the United States. "For," he writes to Edward Everett in 1849, "the book is quite insular in spirit. There is nothing cosmopolitan about it. I can well understand that it might have an interest for a few highly educated men in your country. But I do not at all understand how it should be acceptable to the body of a people who have no king, no lords, no knights, no established church, no Tories, nay, I might say, no Whigs in the English sense of the word."

One major reason for the phenomenal success of *The History* in America was, of course, its style—plain, straightforward, pellucid. All this was the result of much effort and art. But it was an artfulness very different from Gibbon's, that master of irony and the periodic sentence. One mustn't believe him when he writes to Lady Elizabeth Foster in 1792, "I am a mere narrator of matter of fact." Where Macaulay hurled artillery shells, Gibbon worked with depth bombs and mines. Great prose writers, when read aloud, reveal different rhythms and "tunes." If you try the experiment of reading almost any passage of Gibbon and Macaulay aloud in succession, you will, I think, be struck by the complex "singsong" movement of the former and the constant forward thrust of the latter. I have argued before that the difference here is more than merely stylistic; that Gibbon's reservations and qualifications, his "buts," and "yets," and "howevers," reflect and reinforce his theme of the appearance of prosperity covering the reality of decay; while Macaulay's steadily advancing prose reflects his theme of advance and success after setbacks and disasters. If we imagine each historian addressing his readers implicitly between the lines, we might hear Gibbon say: "We, men and women of the world, are quite aware of the fact that we encounter masks and disguises in history. Let us amuse and instruct ourselves by penetrating them." Macaulay, on the other hand, might be heard remarking: "It may appear strange to you that these things happened. But when I have informed you of the circumstances and the context, then what seemed at first odd and extraordinary will turn out to have been entirely natural and predictable."

The two historians were, of course, writing for different audiences. Gibbon wrote for a like-minded circle of relatives and friends, for the fashionable world of London salons and coffeehouses. It is not without significance that in reporting the initial reception of *The Decline and Fall* he first mentions the praise of fashionable women, especially the young and beautiful ones, for whom ancient history had become like the latest novel of the day, and only then reports the praise of Hume and Robertson. Macaulay, too, writing to a friend about the hopes he had for his *History*, remarked that he would not be satisfied "unless I produce something which shall for a few days supersede the last fashionable novel on the tables of young ladies." But the young ladies he had in mind were very different from Gibbon's, more like his sisters than the *grandes dames* of Whig society. He thought of himself as a popular writer, and the clarity of his style was designed to make his *History* accessible to the wider and more heterogeneous reading public that had come into being since Gibbon's day. We are told that a Manchester gentleman invited his poorer neighbors to come every evening so that he could read Macaulay's *History* aloud to them. At the close of the last meeting, one listener moved a vote of thanks to Mr. Macaulay "for having written a history which working men can understand." We are a long way from Gibbon's remark in 1776 that the historian was crowned by the taste or fashion of the day.

Both historians attained quick and lasting fame. Both deprecated it, even while reporting it. Thus Gibbon in his *Autobiography,* "Upon the whole, *The Decline and Fall* seems to have struck root both at home and abroad, and may perhaps a hundred years hence continue to be abused." And thus Macaulay in his journal,

> At last I have attained true glory. As I walked through Fleet Street the day before yesterday, I saw a copy of Hume at a bookseller's window with the following label: 'Only £2 2s. Hume's History of England in eight volumes, highly valuable as an introduction to Macaulay.' I laughed so convulsively that the other people who were staring at the books took me for a poor demented gentleman. Alas for poor David!

But in neither case was the deprecatory stance entirely genuine. When in 1792 Lord Sheffield wrote to Gibbon suggesting that he leave his personal library as a public trust, to be known as "the Gibbonian Collection," the historian replied, "I am not flattered by the Gibbonian collection, and I shall own my presumptuous belief that six quarto volumes may be sufficient for the preservation of that name." And, in reading Macaulay's journals, one can see how he constantly encouraged himself with the prospect that his *History* would be read many years hence. Thus he noted once, "Corraggio! And think of

2850! Where will the Carlyles and Emersons be then? But Herodotus will still be read." (And, presumably, Macaulay as well.) Certainly, neither historian would have been in the least surprised upon being told that the Massachusetts Historical Society would devote an evening to him in 1975.

Carlyle's
Frederick the Great

In April 1945, in the fastness of the *Führerbunker* in the Reich chancellery in Berlin, Goebbels read aloud to Hitler from the latter's favorite book, Carlyle's *Frederick the Great*. What he read were those pages dealing with the desperate and, apparently, hopeless posture of the Prussian king toward the end of the Seven Years' War, just before the sudden and unexpected death of the Czarina Elizabeth which resulted in the elimination of Russia from the alliance against Frederick, and thus his seemingly miraculous salvation. Goebbels reported that "tears stood in the Führer's eyes" during this reading. When Franklin D. Roosevelt died, a few days later, Hitler thought that another, similar miracle was about to occur. But the analogy proved to be inexact. By the end of April both Hitler and Goebbels were dead, and the thousand-year Reich had collapsed.[1]

It would be of little avail to attempt to use this true story as evidence for yet another vain attempt to document Carlyle's "fascism." Let it stand, rather, as testimony to the continuing power and influence of this particular work of his. It is, of course, idle to deny the presence in this book, as well as in much of the rest of Carlyle's later writings,

---

From the "Editor's Introduction," Thomas Carlyle's *History of Frederick the Great* (Chicago, 1969)

of certain elements which might be expected to appeal to twentieth-century dictators. The exaltation of personal government (with the express corollary that it was superior to the ballot box), of military prowess in war, and above all, of stubborn heroism in the face of all odds—all that is not incompatible with authoritarian regimes of this or of any other time. But it is a long way from Victorian anti-democratic currents of thought to the horrors of Germany under Hitler. In order properly to understand the less palatable aspects of Carlyle's thought, one must try to see them in the context of the nineteenth rather than of the twentieth century.

That context has been nowhere better delineated than in Walter Houghton's *Victorian Frame of Mind.*[2] Houghton devotes an entire section of his book to an analysis of the enormous vogue of hero worship in the Victorian age. That period witnessed a partial merging of the Romantic cult of genius with the Calvinist creed of the elect, still a very powerful concept in nineteenth-century England. It must be kept in mind, furthermore, that the Victorian age was, par excellence, an age of intellectual doubt and spiritual uncertainty. Apparently established truths were challenged; belief in God and Revelation was questioned. In such a time people tend to turn to great men as sources of comfort, instruction, and example. Carlyle's obsession with Frederick the Great must be seen within this general context; not forgetting, besides, that the Prussian monarch had been one of the heroes of John Stuart Mill's youth, and that Macaulay had written one of his most celebrated essays about him several years before Carlyle's work began to take shape.

More important, the answer to the question of how Carlyle came to write *Frederick the Great* lies in his personal history as much as it lies in the intellectual history of the age. For the first thing to be remembered in any discussion of Carlyle's historical writings is that he was not primarily a historian at all, but, rather, a self-appointed prophet and sage whose entire life work was an expression of his fundamental beliefs. Those beliefs owed a great deal to his origins. He was born in 1795 in the Scottish village of Ecclefechan. His father was a stonemason by trade. Both parents were rigid and devout Scottish Calvinists, and Carlyle's family background was one of extreme poverty. In 1809 the boy walked the hundred miles from his home to Edinburgh in order to enter the university as a theological student. He spent the period from 1809 to 1814 at Edinburgh, but in the event neither took his degree nor became a minister of the Scottish kirk.

Rather, he taught school for some years, first at Annan Academy (where he himself had received part of his education), then, from 1816 to 1818, at Kirkcaldy.

It was in the course of these years that his faith in orthodox Christianity, already impaired (as evidenced by his abandonment of the ministry as a vocation), was further shaken by his reading of Gibbon, whose "winged sarcasms, so quiet and yet so conclusively transpiercing, and killing dead" had the effect of "extirpating from his mind the last remnant that had been left in it of the orthodox belief in miracles."[3] He recalled much later that it was then that he first clearly saw that Christianity was not true. In 1818, tired of teaching, Carlyle returned to Edinburgh, and after a brief period of legal studies decided to make his career as a man of letters. It was now that he began the study of German. And it was in Edinburgh, either in 1821 or 1822, that he underwent the spiritual crisis so vividly described by him in *Sartor Resartus* (1833). The crisis was resolved, for a time at least, by his finding new resources of strength within himself to work actively in a world that belonged to God, not to the orthodox God of Christian Revelation, but to a God who was present in all things. A commission to write an article on Friedrich Schiller for the *London Magazine* initiated his role as the chief interpreter of German thought and literature for the educated British reading public. And it is hard to overestimate the influence upon him of certain German writers and thinkers of the Romantic period.

Here is an area where one must tread carefully. On the one hand, there is no doubt whatever that Carlyle learned much from the Germans, above all from Goethe, Fichte, and Schiller. From Goethe, whom he was to single out on many occasions as his favorite teacher and master, whose *Wilhelm Meister* he translated in a version so felicitous that it was reissued in our time, he learned above all the spiritually therapeutic value of action and activity as against idle metaphysical speculation. Goethe also taught Carlyle the necessity for renunciation (*Entsagen*) for those who wanted to gain happiness in this world. In Fichte's works, Carlyle found expounded the spiritual nature of all existence, the immanence of the divine in the actual, the alternation in history of periods of belief with periods of unbelief, and the exalted mission of the hero-thinker, the poet, the prophet, and the king. And Schiller's *Revolt of the Netherlands* showed him how the poet could find the highest historical reality in the original sources of history. He sympathized with the German thinkers' distrust of the primacy assigned to reason and the senses by the eighteenth-century Enlightenment, and he shared their conviction that feeling, intuition, and emotion must play a predominant role in human affairs. More specifically, as far as the writing of history was concerned, he derived from them a sense of the past not as the record of human beings, alike in all periods and countries, acting out their affairs upon a stage where only the scenery was shifted to denote the passage of time; but as a vital and constantly developing process carried on by a rich variety of men and women who could not easily be fitted into neat a priori categories.

All this is true enough. But it is risky to try to determine exactly what specific ideas Carlyle took from particular German authors. In fact, as René Wellek has pointed out, there is some question as to whether he even completely understood the philosophical system of someone like Fichte. And, according to Ernst Cassirer, he interpreted Goethe's thought very much in his own fashion.[4] But that is just the point. Carlyle took what he needed from the great German poets and thinkers; and what he needed was reassurance that the skeptics and rationalists, the Gibbons of the eighteenth century, were wrong after all; and that human beings were more than machines, mechanical toys put together, wound up, and taken apart at will.

The German writers supplied Carlyle with consolation. Nature was not a machine set in motion by a remote clockmaker but, rather, a constant process of change and becoming, working itself out in mysteriously predestined fashion through the ages. Neither nature nor history was in itself ultimate reality. Both were no more than emblems of spiritual and divine truth. And "reason" as it was used by the *philosophes* of the eighteenth century was not sufficient to enable one to gain knowledge of this ultimately real spiritual realm. That required a faculty superior to the mere "understanding" of the Enlightment, a largely subjective faculty in some ways closer to intuitive insight than to ratiocination.

It is striking how well many of these ideas meshed with some of the basic tenets of the Calvinism which had dominated Carlyle's childhood and youth and which continued to hold sway over him for the rest of his life, though it suffered many "a sea-change into something rich and strange." To emphasize work, activity, and renunciation rather than personal happiness as the final end of existence, to see things earthly as mere shadows of a higher spiritual reality, to regard history as predestined, to single out certain heroic figures as elected above all others to be bearers and conveyors of truth—all this must have appeared congenial to a youth who had temporarily lost his spiritual bearings, but who carried the stern imperatives of the Calvinist faith in his blood.

Above all, then, the young Carlyle found in Germany the answer to what he was to call Gibbon's detached and deadly irony. "Deadly," because the eighteenth century had been literally moribund in its endorsement of head over heart, of the material over the spiritual. Encouraged by the answer he had found, Carlyle made his life work, his vocation, in large part a refutation of eighteenth-century attitudes and errors. In the realm of historiography this meant, as he pointed out in his essay on "History" (1830), that historians should no longer concentrate their efforts on courts and politics and wars, but should instead attempt to deal with the lives and achievements of ordinary men and women. "Which was the greatest innovator, which was the more important personage in man's history, he who first led armies over the Alps, and gained the victories of Cannae and Thrasymene; or the homeless boor who first hammered out for himself an iron spade?"[5] To study the life of a society in the past was to study the aggregate of all the individual lives which constituted that society. Thus, in a famous phrase, Carlyle dubbed history the essence of innumerable biographies.

The historian who set about to retrieve those lives from the obscurity of the past must possess a sense of wonder and mystery as he went about his business. History was not a mere merchant's ledger. Writing a century before computers began to threaten to replace the historian, Carlyle aimed his sarcasm at those cause-and-effect speculators "with whom no wonder would remain wonderful, but all things in Heaven and Earth must be computed and 'accounted for.' "[6] For Carlyle the past itself, the very knowledge on our part that someone long since dead had once lived out his life on this earth, was matter for wonder and awe. History, as he put it in his essay on Boswell (1832), was the new poetry. The reality of the past, if rightly interpreted, was grander than fiction. And the right interpretation of reality and of history *was,* in fact, genuine poetry.

In his advocacy of social rather than political history and of a poetic view of the past Carlyle was, of course, by no means alone, even in Britain. Sir Walter Scott's historical novels had struck a responsive chord in all of the Romantic generation, including Macaulay as well as Carlyle. Nor was Carlyle the only English man of letters to uphold an organic rather than a mechanistic view of nature and the universe. The names of Burke and Coleridge at once come to mind as the founders of a tradition that was to find distinguished disciples in Ruskin and Morris. But there is no doubt at all that Carlyle must occupy a central place in that tradition. In his great essay "Signs of the Times" (1829), a marvelously perceptive analysis of the effects of industrialism on English society, he warned of the deleterious consequences that would ensue if the mechanical principle were to be allowed to run on unchecked. In his autobiographical confession of faith lost and regained, *Sartor Resartus* (1833), he spelled out in full his "German" view of the world as nothing but the vesture of the divine. Upon his readers as upon himself he urged work and discipline rather than idle complainings and self-pity: "Close thy Byron. Open thy Goethe."

Carlyle wrote *Sartor* amid the loneliness of the Scottish moors, at Craigenputtock, where he and his wife, Jane Welsh (whom he had married in 1826), spent the years from 1828 until 1834. Whether the writing of *Sartor* finally resolved the spiritual crisis it was intended to chronicle and to illuminate remains doubtful. It has often been pointed out that the "work ethic" so urgently preached in that book and so strenuously pursued for the rest of his life by Carlyle himself can also be seen as an "escape-from-doubt" ethic. For Carlyle, as for other troubled Victorians, the plunge into frantic activity provided relief from morbid speculation. In any event, having (so to speak) worked out his salvation in the wilderness, Carlyle thereafter settled in London with his wife in 1834; and it was here that he pursued the remainder of his career as a man of letters.

The keynote of "Signs of the Times" as well as of *Sartor* had been antimechanism. This, on the part of Carlyle, was not merely an abstract philosophical attitude, but one intimately linked to his view of politics and history. For, in Carlyle's mind, there existed a very close connection between the mechanical principle and the doctrines of the laissez-faire economists, dominant in utilitarian thought and in the social policies of early-nineteenth-century England. Both erred in exalting the operation of mechanical laws to the detriment of the soul of man, just as the eighteenth-century historians had erred in deluding themselves into thinking that they could compress the often chaotic and irrational processes of human history into the narrow confines of ordinary laws of cause and effect. In his *French Revolution* (1837), probably his greatest historical work, he showed that the historian, if he wished to re-create the reality of such a conflagration, had to become a sort of prose poet. For Carlyle, the Revolution was indeed a conflagration, a roaring fire set by destiny to consume the shams and quackery of a so-called enlightened age. Such a holocaust, in which men's passions become inflamed, in which fanaticism, violence, and unreason rule supreme, cannot be described in the coldly elegant periods of a Gibbon or a William Robertson. It must be literally reproduced on the printed page, in all its chaotic fury. And this Carlyle succeeded in doing.

By the time he came to write *Sartor,* he had deliberately discarded the classical style of the Augustans in which the great eighteenth-century British historians had composed their works. In 1835 he wrote to John Sterling that this was not a time for purism of style: "With whole ragged battalions of Scott's-Novel Scotch, with Irish, German, French, and even Newspaper Cockney . . . storming in on us, and the whole structure of our Johnsonian English breaking up from its foundations—revolution there as visible as anywhere else!"[7] John Stuart Mill pointed out in his review of the *French Revolution* that Carlyle was the first to show that all that was done for history by the best historical playwright, Schiller, for example, could also be done by the apt selection and judicious grouping of authentic facts. And Carlyle's facts were as authentic as the sources available to him could insure.

The French Revolution itself Carlyle regarded as a divine judgment upon the century that had, in his view, exchanged reality for formulas. Sansculottism, the uprising of the poor against their masters, he considered to have been a force of nature, a "fact" one was free to like or dislike, but which had henceforth to be reckoned with, not only in French but also in world history. How close to home the principles of the French Revolution were manifesting themselves Carlyle made evident in his tract entitled *Chartism* (1839), where he depicted the protests and violence of the English working class as part of a phenomenon which Europe had witnessed since 1789—an inexorable struggle between the lower and the upper classes. It was in this tract that Carlyle fulminated against laissez-faire and the cash nexus, and declared that "a government of the under classes by the upper on a principle of *Let-alone* is no longer possible in England in these days." The meaning of all the popular commotions of the century added up to the inarticulate prayer: "Guide me, govern me! I am mad and miserable, and cannot guide myself!"[8]

For Carlyle the answer to this prayer was not democracy, not debating and voting in Parliament, but government of the masses by the wisest, by a genuine aristocracy. At this point it becomes clear that if Carlyle's social criticism and his historical thought were bound together methodologically by the antimechanical principle, they were bound together substantively by the search for great men, for heroes, for clearsighted individuals able to see through the shams to the realities of their time, and to act accordingly.

The single figure of potentially heroic proportions in the *French Revolution* had been Mirabeau; and he had died before he could become effective. If that work could be said to have had a hero, it was the French people as a whole. But as Carlyle became more and more deeply persuaded that the social dislocation in his own country—both consequence and manifestation of the French Revolution—showed the need for wise leadership by the few, his own historical work increasingly became a search for exemplary heroic figures in the past. Universal history, Carlyle told his fashionable audiences in his course of lectures *On Heroes and Hero Worship* (1840), was at bottom the history of great men. The real purpose of all social procedure in the world ought to be to find the ablest man, the true king, and to have him invested with the symbols of his ability. If only such a man could be found, and if all men then acknowledged his divine right—"this is precisely the healing which a sick world is everywhere, in these ages, seeking after!"⁹ But how to find him?

In the twelfth century the monks of St. Edmundsbury seemed to have had the answer. As their abbot they chose, without benefit of the ballot, Samson, who governed them with a judicious mixture of fatherly sternness and solicitude. How he managed to do so, and how medieval England supplied an example of a sensible social policy toward the poor not emulated in the age of laissez-faire, Carlyle described in his next tract for the times, *Past and Present* (1843). In writing this book, he leaned heavily on the authentic chronicle of a monk of St. Edmundsbury, Jocelin of Brakelond. Here, as in his favorite Boswell's *Life of Johnson,* was the actual past, fortunately available for the edification and use of posterity. Indeed, Carlyle referred to Brakelond as "Bozzy" Jocelin. His obsession with the actual sources of history found expression in his next major work, *Cromwell's Letters and Speeches* (1845), which was above all else a source book—the story of the great Civil War and the early years of the Commonwealth told through Cromwell's actual letters and speeches, with Carlyle supplying an extended commentary by means of lengthy annotations.

Cromwell was one of the heroes Carlyle had celebrated in his lectures on hero worship. There he had defended him against still widely current imputations that he had been a traitor as well as hypocrite; and he had praised his "practical eye," his contempt for shams, and his genuine insight into what was fact. Now he lauded him as a defender of order who knew how to rule in the face of leveling threats

from below. Three years later, in the course of the revolutions of
1848, Europe's kings showed that they apparently did not possess a
similar capacity. They were, Carlyle pointed out in his *Latter-Day
Pamphlets* (1850), "Sham-Kings, playacting as at Drury Lane."[10] And
the millions under them were dupes in a universe of imposture. What
was needed was not democracy, but wise guidance. England, not yet
sunk into open anarchy, must set an example for other nations by
summoning forth its "Kings," men foreordained to command, men
who knew "the divine appointment of this universe, the Eternal Laws
ordained by God the Maker," and could govern by those laws. Perhaps some of them were to be found among the "Captains of Industry." In any event, it was they who had to bring the poor under
their due captaincy. Else all was lost.

It was just a few months after he made this appeal for new kings
that Carlyle wrote to a German friend, in October 1851: "If I were a
brave Prussian, I believe I should forthwith attempt some picture of
Friedrich the Great, the *last* real *king* that we have had in Europe—a
long time till the *next,* I fear—and nothing but sordid anarchy *till* the
next."[11] It is quite evident that in eventually picking that subject himself, Carlyle had in mind much more than making a contribution to
historiography. He was continuing his search for a hero and a true
king who could serve as example and inspiration for the England of
his own day.

At first glance there appears to be something almost bizarre about
this self-appointed sage, this son of a pious Scottish peasant, this declared enemy of the Enlightenment, deciding to spend a major portion
of his life in celebrating the achievements of an eighteenth-century
enlightened and cynical despot in order to furnish an example of moral
heroism for the Victorian middle classes. It should be added at once
that Carlyle was, from the very beginning, not totally happy about
his own choice of subject. He had considered William the Conqueror
and Luther as alternative candidates; and even after he had determined
to write about Frederick he found it hard to develop much affection
for him. In the summer of 1852 he wrote to Ralph Waldo Emerson:
"The man looks brilliant and noble to me; but how *love* him, or the
sad wreck he lived and worked in? I do not even yet *see* him clearly;
and to try making others see him?" But, he added, Frederick and
Voltaire constituted the one "celestial" element of "the poor Eighteenth Century." And the Prussian soldiers were perhaps the real
priests and virtuous martyrs of "that loud-babbling rotten generation!"[12]

It is as if Carlyle, up in arms against the quackeries of his own age, went back to the period that for most of his life had represented for him an age of sham par excellence, and asked: What was worth saving from *that* age? Was there *anything* worthwhile in what he referred to as "the putrid Eighteenth Century"? For, as he put it, "Frederick's century did nothing I approve except *cut its own throat, and so* end its dishonest nonsenses, in the French Revolution!"[13] At the end of August 1852, Carlyle left for Germany in order to inspect the chief scenes of Frederick's life and activities. In Berlin he found no great enthusiasm for his project. He recoiled, too, at the sight of "actual Germany, with its flat-soled puddlings in the slough of nonsense."[14]

His hesitations continued throughout the dozen years of his life that was to be devoted to what he came to call "the valley of the shadow of Frederick"; from the summer of 1853, when he finally made the decision to go ahead with the project, to the late winter of 1865, when he completed it. The book became a sort of extended torture for him; in part because of the immense accumulation of sources he had to plow through in order to write it, even though he had the help of two assistants, one in London and one in Germany; in part because these same sources did not confirm the picture of true kingship that Carlyle had conjured up in his own mind. It became increasingly harder for him to defend Frederick's wars and diplomacy as quintessential truth, when the documents gave evidence of chicanery and duplicity. That these were common practices in eighteenth-century Europe did not entirely exculpate someone like Frederick, who in the eyes of Carlyle was supposed to represent the superhuman and the heroic. With her customary acerbity Mrs. Carlyle remarked that her husband came to realize that he was trying to make a silk purse out of a sow's ear.

There were other troubles, of a more personal and practical nature, that made the writing of *Frederick* difficult for Carlyle. His own dyspepsia and extreme sensitivity to noise—he had a special sound-proof study built, so that he could work undisturbed; his wife's ill health; above all, the sheer labor involved, which seemed endless. The first two volumes were completed in 1858, and like their successors, were received with considerable enthusiasm. That autumn Carlyle undertook another tour of Germany, this time principally to visit the battlefields he was about to describe in Volumes III (1862) and IV (1864). "God help me to get through this Book *in opposition to the whole World and the Devil to back, as it often seems to me,*" was his *cri de coeur* to his German assistant, Neuberg, in the latter year.[15] A few months later he had indeed "got through"; and the final two volumes made their appearance.

The long years of work on *Frederick* Carlyle described in his reminiscences as "to me a desperate dead-lift pull at that time; my whole strength devoted to it; alone, withdrawn from all the world . . . , all the world withdrawing from me; I desperate of ever *getting through* (not to speak of 'succeeding'); left solitary 'with the nightmares' (as I sometimes expressed it), 'hugging unclean creatures' (Prussian Blockheadisms) 'to my bosom, trying to caress and flatter their secret out of them!' "[16] During the last seven years of his "nightmare," Carlyle recalled that he did not write the smallest message to friends or undertake the least business, except upon plain compulsion of necessity.

It has been argued that Carlyle's struggle with *Frederick* parallels the Prussian king's own struggle against adversity, as depicted in the book. Alternatively, that there exists some analogy between the running battle fought between Voltaire and Frederick, and Carlyle's literary efforts to master the king. Be that as it may, certainly some process of identification took place between the Prussian king, beset by enemies and almost at bay on several occasions, and the sage of Chelsea, pursuing his monumental task in the face of ill health and exhaustion. "The truth is," Carlyle wrote to Emerson in 1867, "I was nearly killed by that hideous Book on Friedrich—twelve years in continuous wrestle with the nightmare and the subterranean hydras."[17]

The result of Carlyle's struggles, the *History of Frederick the Great,* is a curious book. Like all of Carlyle's historical works it differs greatly from a conventional history. It is in the first place a very personal book, undertaken as much to bring solace to the author as to illuminate the past. Carlyle, though increasingly lionized in aristocratic and literary circles, had come to regard himself more and more as a prophet without honor in his own country. His warnings, his injunctions seemed to have fallen on deaf ears. The mechanical principle had not retreated, debates in Parliament had not become less interminable, great new leaders had not come forward. What was Carlyle to do? The answer was: what he had done before—to look for an exemplar in the past and to contrast his virtues with the vices of the present day; and to identify himself and his own heroic struggles against falsehood and sham with those of his protagonist.

The particular choice of Frederick the Great as his subject is a good indication of the extent to which the conservative elements in Carlyle's thought had come to predominate over the radical elements. In *The*

French Revolution his sympathies had lain, on the whole, with the revolutionaries, since they were putting an end to what had become fraudulent as well as moribund. In *Past and Present,* Abbot Samson, to be sure, represented leadership and rule; but emphasis fell just as much on his social benevolence as on his authority. Carlyle's Cromwell is depicted as the foe of the Levellers rather than as the rebel. But the historical movement led by Cromwell was, after all, the Puritan Revolution. Frederick the Great, in contrast, had nothing revolutionary about him. To Carlyle he represented, in essence, the ruler beset by enemies who triumphed through sheer will and fortitude; and, unlike Samson or Cromwell, without benefit of Christian faith. Frederick's strength of spirit owed more to the Stoics than to Christ. It is well to remember, however, that, like Carlyle himself, Frederick grew up in an atmosphere suffused with powerful Calvinist currents; and that one of the things that most offended his father, Frederick William, was the youth's predestinarianism. In the thought of the Prussian king, as well as in that of the Scottish stonemason's son, fate and destiny continued to exert their power, even after faith in a Christian revelation had foundered.

This is not the place for a detailed analysis of the historiographical weaknesses of *Frederick the Great.* But some of them may be briefly noted. Carlyle's most glaring omission is his failure to do justice to Frederick's domestic policies and achievements, particularly his crucial historical role in forging an alliance between aristocracy and monarchy within the framework of the bureaucratic state. In spite of Carlyle's youthful pleas for social rather than political history, he concentrated in these volumes almost entirely on Frederick's diplomacy and wars; though, to be sure, he never lost sight of his hero's character and personality. He was, of course, dependent upon the sources as they existed in his day. And if one now wanted to obtain an accurate version of, say, the origins of the Seven Years' War, one would not and should not in the first place turn to Carlyle who, it appears, leaned far too heavily on Frederick's own account of the matter.

In the realm of intellectual history, too, Carlyle is deficient. One need only look at Friedrich Meinecke's brilliant discussion of Frederick's *Anti-Machiavel,* with its subtle appraisal of the Prussian king caught up in the dualism that existed between the needs of a power state on the one hand, and the demand of the Enlightenment for a humanitarian cosmopolitanism on the other, in order to become aware of how thin and unsatisfactory Carlyle's treatment is.[18] As for his manner of expression, it was vulnerable to criticism from the time these volumes first appeared. Thomas Babington Macaulay noted in his journal in September 1858 that he had never seen a worse book— "the philosophy nonsense and the style gibberish." When Queen Victoria asked him a few months later what he thought of it, he quickly changed the subject to Prescott, whom he could praise in good conscience.[19] Acton's judgment was similarly severe: "A history made up of eccentricities."[20] In our century Harold Laski probably spoke for many when he wrote to Holmes that "I couldn't do more than read the first volume. The manner drove me wild."[21]

In fact, a case could probably be made for *Frederick* as a handbook for students, teaching them how *not* to write history! In making such a case, one could legitimately argue that Carlyle spends far too much time in relating anecdotes about courts and courtiers, and in describing battles at length, time that could have been better spent in analyzing the institutional structure of the Prussian state. That his philosophy of history and destiny, whatever one may think of its merits, plays an undue role, both obfuscatory and intrusive. That his constant juggling of the time dimension and his hop-skip-and-jump method of narration confuses rather than enlightens the reader. That his perpetually inserting himself and his views of the present ills of England and mankind into the history is both irrelevant and supererogatory. And, above all, that there exists a lack of proportion and proper arrangement in the totality of the work and the multiplicity of its themes which is irritating at best, and at worst highly inimical to the reader's enjoyment of the book.

Not that Carlyle had any *intention* of ignoring his readers. In a sense it could be argued that his *Frederick* is, in the final analysis, only incidentally about the Prussian king; and that it is as much, if not more, concerned with the education of the reader as it is with the historical account of the subject. Just as there are *Bildungsromane* (novels of apprenticeship) in which the hero gains self-knowledge and insight by means of undergoing a variety of experiences, so there may be said to be *Bildungsgeschichte*—history addressed primarily to the reader in order to teach him valuable lessons. It is not just that the reader of Carlyle's book is supposed to absorb the explicit lessons for contemporary England which the author derives from the life of Frederick. By continually associating the reader with him in the historical enterprise; by making him, so to speak, a collaborator, encountering the same difficulties with the sources, scoring the same triumphs of insight into character and circumstances, making him feel at all times part of a long and arduous expedition which must reach its goal in the end—

Carlyle intends to do something far more fundamental than merely draw a few moral lessons from the past. His implicit aim is to make the reader more than a passive observer of the passing show. It is nothing less than to make him a disciple.

Carlyle accomplishes this by his style. Again and again, it is the reader and he who together (as "we") proceed to some new source or event. And the historian's repeated exposure of his sources, the revelation of the scaffolding beneath the narrative, turns the reader into an active participant. *Frederick,* in fact, proceeds simultaneously at three levels: There is, first, the level of description of events and personalities. There is, second, the level of Carlyle's didactic and personal concerns. And there is also the level of the reader's active passage through a pedagogical experience that should, ideally, take him into camp—Carlyle's as much as Frederick's.

What binds all these levels together is the human factor. For Carlyle, all history that did not place primary emphasis upon the human aspect of things was nothing but the ill-conceived product of "Dryasdusts," people who had no notion of what, in the past, was truly significant. Unfortunately, many of these "Dryasdusts" seemed to be German scholars who had devoted themselves to the subject in which Carlyle was now primarily interested—"pedants and tenebrific persons . . . dwelling not on things, but, at endless length, on the outer husks of things"; authors of confused and confusing books, "opulent in nugatory pedantism and learned marine-stores," in which all that was human remained distressingly obscure.[22] Why did previous histories of Frederick, mainly of German origin, make such dreary reading? The answer, according to "Smelfungus," one of the various *personae* employed by Carlyle throughout these volumes, was that those histories had been written not by poets or men of true human genius, but by Dryasdusts. Carlyle writes in a passage not included in the present selection that had the poets and the geniuses attended to their primary task, that of interpreting human heroisms, "of painfully extricating, and extorting from the circumambient chaos of muddy babble, rumor and mendacity, some not inconceivable human and divine Image" of those heroisms, then by now the world would have had an entirely different picture of Frederick.[23] As it was, it was left to Carlyle to present the true picture of the Prussian monarch.

To write the sort of history that could result in such a picture one must be able to love the past and everything human that has survived from it. Carlyle, here as elsewhere in his work, demonstrates this romantic view of the past—sometimes in commenting regretfully on not being able to recapture it for lack of sources. Over Frederick William's contemporaries, the "grim semi-articulate Prussian men," the "strange blond-complexioned, not un-beautiful Prussian honorable women," he exclaims: "*Ach Gott,* they too are gone; and their musical talk, in the French or German language, that also is gone; and the hollow Eternities have swallowed it."[24] But just as he regrets the inevitable extinction of some aspects of the past, so also does he welcome the survival of any evidence that illuminates for a brief moment what would otherwise have disappeared—"wastepaper spill (so to speak) . . . which you can *kindle;* and, by the brief flame of it, bid a reader look with his own eyes!"[25]

This last comment was à propos a journal providing a glimpse of Louis XV holding his levée at Versailles: "Historical Figure's very self, in his work-day attitude; eating his victuals; writing, receiving letters, talking to his fellow creatures; unaware that Posterity, miraculously . . . has got its eye upon him!"[26] But it is not just glimpses of high life that Carlyle treasures in this way. Just as, in *The French Revolution,* he called attention time and again to the ordinary men and women living through that period, so here, too, like the epic poets, like Shakespeare, he does not let the reader entirely forget that history is not *all* kings and queens and princes—though his theme forces him to concentrate upon them. Thus of the Prussian march on Glogau, through flooded territory, in 1740, it was reported that there was only one casualty, the wife of a soldier. But she, too, was part of history. Carlyle comments: "Poor Soldier's Wife, she is not named to me at all; and has no history since this, 'and that she was of the regiment Bredow.' But I perceive she washed herself away in a World-Transaction; and there was one rough Bredower, who probably sat sad that night on getting to quarters."[27]

Moments in time past, then, may be recaptured by often fortuitous flashes of illumination of this sort. But time never stands still; and something that Carlyle tries to do throughout his histories is to communicate a sense of flux, of constant motion. Thus when in 1730 the young crown prince, detected in his attempted flight from the tyranny of his father, travels under guard from Darmstadt to Frankfurt, Carlyle cannot resist pointing out that the party passes the site of a battle not to be fought for another three years, "an obscure village called *Dettingen,* not yet become famous in the Newspapers of an idle world; of an England surely very idle to go thither seeking quarrels!"[28] (Note the ex post facto irony here. All those scenes in Hollywood movies

in which the apparently run-of-the-mill young officer identifies himself as Horatio Nelson or Bonaparte and is then told by a superior
that he will go far someday owe something to Carlyle.)

When the same party arrives in Frankfurt, Carlyle must immediately point out that the golden weathervane on the bridge across the
Main was the same that Goethe would one day be looking at, "in the
next generation."[29] What does the historian accomplish by these apparently irrelevant interpolations? They serve, in the first place, to
make past history more vivid to the reader by associating it with places
and names more immediately familiar to him. In the second place—
and this is even more important—the linkage of events and personalities from different periods succeeds in communicating both a sense
of the constantly moving historical process and of inexorable fate. An
obscure village becomes the scene of a great battle. An illustrious poet,
as yet unborn, will one day view the same sights as Carlyle's hero.
And it need hardly be pointed out that the poet in question was to
become the historian's own chief spiritual mentor, and that in evoking
him Carlyle reinforces the linkage between himself and his subject.
"God moves in a mysterious way, His wonders to perform."

There are, of course, more obvious ways in which past and present
are connected in Carlyle's *Frederick*. Like the rest of his historical works
it is as much a tract for the times as it is a history; and its pages abound
with Carlyle's social and political concerns. In 1854 he had written to
Emerson that Frederick should not be left to lie in an ocean of sordid
nothingness, shams, and scandalous hypocrisies, "if any use is ever
to be had of him."[30] And it soon becomes apparent what Carlyle
meant by "use." He can never resist the exemplary use of Prussian
history and the life of Frederick to strike more blows against ballot
boxes and parliamentary eloquence, philanthropic societies, unlimited
freedom of the press, "Mammon worship," and current misguided
ideas about educating the young. The austere and Spartan regimen of
Frederick William, the stern and singleminded devotion to duty of
the Prussian soldiers, Frederick's own invincible heroism in the face
of misfortune—in all of this there are to be found lessons for an England where self-indulgence and cant appeared to be in the saddle.

Presentism, the use of the past to teach lessons about contemporary
politics and society, is perhaps the most obvious way in which Carlyle
intrudes his own prejudices and predilections into *Frederick*. But it is
by no means the only way. The book serves as a vehicle, not only
for the expression of his social and political views, but also for his
general philosophy. We encounter the familiar themes: of the contin-

ual battle between truth and falsehood, which had first found expression in modern history in the Protestant Reformation; of certain "life-elements," such as the figure of Frederick himself, which are to be discovered in even the most egregious periods of sham and falsehood, such as the eighteenth century; above all, of a just destiny, divinely directed, working itself out in time. Carlyle, like the German historians writing in the historicist tradition, held the sometimes dangerous doctrine that what occurs in history occurs justly. Thus, by the end of the Seven Years' War, Frederick (Carlyle believes) had carried out what was required of him in world history—to have made Prussia into a nation to be reckoned with. And his claims on Silesia, dubious at best, were "allowed by the Destinies."

High destiny is always in command. The Anglo-French wars of the mid-eighteenth century, in which neither nation at first sight seemed to have any real business, resulted in France lying down "to rot into grand Spontaneous-Combustion, Apotheosis of Sansculottism," and thus the French Revolution; as well as in the triumph of England as a great overseas commercial empire. "The Eternal Providences," Carlyle comments, "little as poor Dryasdust now knows of it, mumbling and maundering that sad stuff of his—do rule; and the great soul of the world, I assure you once more, is *just*."[31] One is reminded not only of Hegel, but also of Ranke's essay on "The Great Powers," in which he sees the great nations of Europe working out their destinies (sometimes at the expense of their neighbors) in such a way that no one of them ever becomes permanently predominant.

It was Frederick's destiny, then, according to Carlyle, to forge Prussia into a nation. Unlike Macaulay in his essay on the Prussian king, Carlyle does not dwell on the historical irony in a sequence of events that made Frederick, whose literary and artistic tastes were almost wholly oriented toward France, and who spoke French rather than German by preference, into an instrument of revival for German culture and the German national spirit. Instead, he emphasizes Frederick's grasp of "reality" through his superior "eyesight." To Carlyle, Frederick stands as the champion of fact, the enemy of falsehood and fraud. "Facts are a kind of divine thing to Friedrich," Carlyle writes; "much more so than to common men! this is essentially what Religion I have found in Friedrich."[32] Thus it is Frederick the Great's realism, as well as his lack of pomp, his courage, and his perseverance that Carlyle stresses in his portrait of the king. It has often been pointed out that in some ways Frederick's father, who built up the army his son was to use to such effect, was fundamentally closer to Carlyle's heart than

Frederick himself, with whose aesthetic tastes and accomplishments Carlyle had little sympathy. Certainly, in his hero worship of the son he fastens on that element which came closest to Frederick's paternal heritage—the supreme importance of duty. It is at this point, and in this "sad creed," that the diluted Calvinism of the Scottish stone-mason's son and the enlightened stoicism of the Prussian monarch intersect.

The reader may well become exasperated by the constant intrusion of Carlyle's philosophy of history and his personal struggle for "reality" and truth. At the same time, he must be willing to admit that Carlyle successfully manages to set a breeze of destiny blowing through the work, to convey the feeling that above and beyond the substance of the events and personalities he depicts, important forces are at work shaping the fate of Europe in the nineteenth and, for that matter, in the twentieth century. In similar fashion one may, as a reader, resist Carlyle's didactic efforts to involve one in his own battle with the sources. One may well tire of his lengthy and repeated exposition of his working methods, and react by wishing that he had battled alone and in silence, and had merely given us the results of his labors without exposing the bone beneath the skin.

Yet there is something uniquely instructive in being taken into a great historian's workshop, and watching him labor with his raw materials. There is also, as with so much else in Carlyle, something very modern about it. One of the predominant trends of our own time is that, increasingly, spectators, listeners, and readers expect to be more than passive observers of works of art or literature. If they cannot themselves participate in them, they want at the very least to be privy to the effects and the methods that went into the making of these works. Carlyle, in *Frederick,* deliberately lets the reader participate in the making of the work of art. In his important book, *Carlyle and the Idea of the Modern,*[33] Albert La Valley distinguishes four central concerns in Carlyle's work which help to make him part of the modern tradition: concern with the unconscious; exploration of alienation in the individual and in society; awareness of multiplicity; and the urge to unify those three concerns by means of myth-making. Carlyle's pioneering spirit is well exemplified in his historical writing, and in *Frederick* in particular; not merely because he lets us observe his explorations, but because of the manner in which he presents his findings. Here again, it is quite understandable that the reader may be put off by Carlyle's style. The constant oscillation between past, present, and future; the sudden shifts of scene; different voices relating and

commenting upon the same events; all this can be very irritating. It
has put off readers in the past, and will continue to do so.

But one must remember, in the midst of one's irritation, that Carlyle
is still wrestling with the problem he expounded in his essay on "History" many years before: How is the historian able to represent experience, which is multi-dimensional, in a narrative medium which
is linear, that is to say one-dimensional? After reading the first two
volumes of *Frederick*, Emerson wrote to the author that he was "the
true inventor of the stereoscope."[34] The phrase is an apt one for describing Carlyle's narrative technique. In ordinary narrative history,
"A" occurs; then "B" occurs (possibly, but not necessarily, caused
by "A"); then "C" happens, etc. This, of course, is a false rendering
of actuality, since not only do many other events transpire simultaneously, along with "A," "B," and "C"; but it is also true that "A,"
"B," and "C," like all historical events, are anchored in the past and
have repercussions in the future. The historian's usual means of dealing
with this basic problem is to make use of phrases such as "meanwhile,"
"at the same time," "while this was happening here, that was happening there"; and to spell out, in so many words, both the background and the aftermath of the events he is narrating.

The trouble with these stylistic devices is that they completely fail
to capture the historical *process,* in which nothing is stationary, and
everything is constantly in motion and in flux, in which growth and
decay proceed at the same time; in which events do not occur in isolation, but are related each to each in a constantly shifting network
of interconnections. What Carlyle does is not to evade this problem,
but to face it head on, by using linguistic and literary devices to create
the equivalent of living reality.

Thus Carlyle's historical style operates with a liberal use of dramatic
dialogue, and continually attempts to draw the reader into the action
by making him identify himself, in turn, with the principal characters.
He will, for instance, be describing in straightforward narrative how
Frederick William slept for a while in his garden every day after dinner,
regardless of the heat. Then: "We poor Princesses have to wait, pray-
ing all the Saints that they would resuscitate him soon."[35] Note: "We"
poor Princesses, *not* "the" poor Princesses. Carlyle, in the manner of
an epic storyteller or bard, continually intrudes himself into the narrative. Young Frederick chafes under the obligation to engage in close-
order drill. Carlyle imagines the prince asking fretfully: "This, then,
is the sum of one's existence, this?" The historian is ready with immediate comfort: "Patience, young 'man of genius,' as the News-

papers would now call you, it is indispensably beneficial nevertheless!"
And then follows a little lecture on the benefits of discipline and hard
work.[36]

One's first reaction might well be that this activity on his part would
tend to militate against the sense of inevitable fate that suffuses the
history as a whole. For the historian's interventions induce a state of
suspense, a feeling that events were not destined to happen as they
did; that their course could still be changed, as it were in midpassage,
by the historian himself. But since we already know what happened
later, we also know that the suspense is artificial. And Carlyle, who
knows that we know the outcome, is perfectly aware of the artificiality
of his device. What happens, in fact, is that, paradoxically, these dramatic interventions on the part of the historian enhance rather than
diminish the ground bass of the history, which is that destiny holds
sway, and that its course cannot be tampered with.

At times Carlyle comes very close to being a historical novelist
rather than a historian, not only in imagining the thought and speech
of his characters; but, on occasion, in imagining events that he is not
certain ever took place, yet *ought* to have taken place in order to satisfy
his sense of universal interaction, his conviction that the great figures
on the stage of world history must be linked, and, preferably, self-
consciously linked. And so, when Frederick William and the crown
prince undertake their journey into the Reich in 1730, Carlyle must
have them stop at Blenheim to discourse about that battle and about
Marlborough; even though, as he confides to his readers, no evidence
exists for such discourse.[37] A reprehensible thing to do for the historian? Certainly. But it is worth stressing that Carlyle *admits* he is
imagining the scene. He is, in fact, remarkably scrupulous with his
sources, and it is never difficult to distinguish what he is actually
quoting from his own glosses.

In this respect he even feels sufficiently secure to reprimand the great
Ranke himself, "accurate Professor Ranke," for not "comfortably"
supplying provenance and date when he recounts the incident of the
young prince's being publicly beaten by his father. "Why did not the
Professor give us time, occasion, circumstances, and name of some
eye-witness?" Carlyle demands.[38] The question provides a nice footnote to the history of nineteenth-century historiography. Later on in
the work (in a passage not included in this selection) Carlyle will pay
his respects to "ingenious Herr Professor Ranke," whose *History of
Friedrich* consists mainly of matter excellently done; though in referring readers to Ranke's "wondrously distilled" diplomatic history, he

will go on to dub it "a ghost-like fac-simile (elegant grey ghost, with stars dim-twinkling through)," but still ghostlike.[39] As far as Carlyle was concerned, Ranke, like all other conventional historians, failed adequately to represent the multidimensional structure of the past.

Whether or not Carlyle himself succeeded where other historians failed must be left to individual readers. But, in any event, it is well to remind ourselves that the problem remains for the historian today. It confronts him, to be sure, in a somewhat different guise. As the development of sophisticated local histories and detailed investigations in the manner of Sir Lewis Namier—whose work in fact exemplifies Carlyle's dictum about history being the essence of innumerable biographies—makes any sort of generalization ever more difficult for the narrative historian, how is he still to tell a true and intelligible story in such a way that it does not become completely obscured by parenthetical cautions and footnoted reservations? Are not new literary techniques required to try to cope with this problem? And, in any such endeavor, should not Carlyle's work serve, if not as an example, then at least as an instructive and pioneering attempt? The fact that a reading of *Frederick* leaves one with questions such as this shows that in spite of its admitted lacks and weaknesses, it remains a book that, quite apart from the late Adolf Hitler's interest in it, has by no means lost its power.

Carlyle and His Vocation

THOMAS CARLYLE: A BIOGRAPHY

by Fred Kaplan

Once safely past a certain age, iconoclasts and prophets, particularly in England, tend to become national possessions; beloved heirlooms to be cosseted, celebrated, and indulged. What happened to G.B.S. and is now happening to Malcolm Muggeridge—will it, could it possibly, ever happen to E. P. Thompson?—happened earlier to Thomas Carlyle. Fred Kaplan describes how, within the space of a few years after growing a beard—in 1854, aged fifty-nine—he was sought after by commercial photographers, and though in reality still often angry and unhappy, was generally regarded as a "wise, sad, and even gentle man with deep resources of spirit through whose special powers of insight truths that transcended the passing moment had been revealed." It wasn't *all* on account of the beard, either. His *Collected Works* appeared (1857–1858) and duly authenticated his status as a Victorian sage. He had to wait a few more years for the chance of declining a knighthood. That came in 1874 when he was made an offer of one by Disraeli, at the suggestion of Lord Derby, who felt it would be a good political investment; since the putative recipient was "for whatever reason very vehement against Gladstone."

The privileges accorded to the aged usually cease with, or shortly after, their demise. Today, plenty of people are "very vehement"

From the *Times Literary Supplement*, April 20, 1984.

against Carlyle; and some of the reasons for that lie to hand in Mr. Kaplan's biography. His celebration of the virtues embodied by that Teutonic heritage of valor and intellect which he considered to be the crucial element in English history and culture; his antidemocratic outbursts in *Latter-Day Pamphlets*—Trollope remarked, after reading the first of them, that he had long looked on the author "as a man who was always in danger of growing mad in literature and who has now done so"; the attitude of "white supremacy" displayed in his "Occasional Discourse on the Nigger Question" (1849); his stand in favor of Governor Eyre's merciless suppression of black insurrection in Jamaica (1865); his characterization two years later of the Second Reform Bill as "Shooting Niagara"—these attitudes and views are hardly such as to gain him unanimous praise in the late twentieth century. And while Kaplan does his best to put them into perspective, and to correct misinterpretations still widely current, neither he nor anyone else can succeed in making them really palatable to present-day readers.

Not that Kaplan attempts to do that. Indeed, one of the many virtues of his biography is his acceptance throughout of the fact that in the course of a long lifetime Carlyle said and did many foolish, inconsistent, and embarrassing things. Critics both of his ideas and of his personal life in search of more ammunition may find plenty of it in this book. One example must suffice here. Kaplan duly notes that while Carlyle was being lavishly entertained by Bingham and Lady Harriet Baring (they became Lord and Lady Ashburton in 1848) at their small villa at Addiscombe (1844), his "usual criticism of idle aristocracy was suspended." At that very time his wife, Jane, nervous and depressed, as well as intensely jealous of her husband's infatuation with Lady Harriet, was staying with friends of her own, trying to reconcile herself to being Carlyle's "necessary evil." This is what he then wrote to her: "Real good breeding, as the people have it here, is one of the finest things now going in the world. The careful avoidance of all discussion, the swift hopping from topic to topic, does not agree with me; but the graceful style they do it with is beyond that of minuets!" This from the author of *Chartism!*

Carlyle's marriage to Jane, his early life and loss of faith, and his ill health are three subjects familiar to anyone who has ever taken any interest in his life. And Kaplan's biography rightly emphasizes all three. His place and country of birth, Ecclefechan in Scotland, and the hard, relentless Calvinism of his parents, poor farmers making a sparse living from the soil, shaped Carlyle's life beyond all other forces. His childhood and youth were periods of continuous strug-

gle—with school bullies, with sexual impulses that had to be repressed, with doubt and skepticism. His parents intended him for the
ministry. But, with his faith fatally impaired, he renounced that vocation, with their reluctant acquiescence. Hume and Gibbon were the
negative, Goethe and Schiller the positive poles of the intellectual influences acting upon him. But the moral imperatives of Ecclefechan—
work, duty, the need to fight sin and the devil within and without—
remained paramount.

Carlyle tried teaching, and came to hate it. He began to write for
publication, with little success. But the important milestones of his
early life history were spiritual, not professional; internal crises which,
when overcome, gave him strength and hope to go on, in spite of
constant suffering and occasional despair. The first of these caused
him to see his duty to lie not merely in thought and endurance but
in action as well. The second, the conversion experience so memorably
described in *Sartor Resartus,* led him to seek and find a new source
for confidence and inspiration, one to replace orthodox Christian belief. He found divinity within himself; and having done so, felt certain
he could triumph over any obstacles, whether physical or intellectual,
with which the external world might confront him. As Kaplan aptly
puts it: "What religious belief had lost, personal will could provide."
To be sure, one must not imagine that the immediate result of this
experience was a totally changed human being who had now banished
anxiety and depression forevermore. Difficulties remained, even after
he proudly informed his mother, early in 1827, that he was writing
a book; though "only" a novel. The novel, *Wotton Reinfred,* remained
uncompleted.

It was not until almost seven years later that that idiosyncratic work
of genius, *Sartor Resartus,* began to appear in installments in *Fraser's
Magazine.* When Carlyle had first offered it to the proprietor, James
Fraser, in 1831, under the original title of *Teufelsdreck,* Fraser had said
he would publish it, but only on condition that the author pay him
£150. Carlyle had kept his temper and had walked back to his London
lodgings carrying the manuscript openly in his hand, "*not* like a gentleman." Soon thereafter, he almost gave up on the possibility of publication. "Dreck," he wrote to Jane at that time, in words that might
equally well have been used by a contemporary sanitary reformer,
"cannot be disposed of in London at this time."

"Dreck," in any event, was one of the dominant forces in Carlyle's
life. What he referred to as his "thrice cursed stomach" gave him
trouble for years. Stomach pain, constipation, flatulence—he could

never be sure whether they were the cause or the result of depression and despondency—were, a good deal of the time, part of his life. Ill health became as much of an enemy as idleness; and just as only strenuous work could extirpate the latter, strenuous medication had to be deployed against the former. "The harsh laxatives," Kaplan writes, "made matters worse, irritating the intestines and punishing the erring spirit that had allowed itself to become sick." And what an undignified and humiliating sickness it was! "And do but think what a thing it is," Carlyle wrote to his brother Jack, a future doctor, in 1821, "that the etherical [sic] spirit of a man should be overpowered and hagridden by what? by two or three feet of sorry tripe full of—."

His health improved as he grew into middle age. There were periods, for example 1834–1841, when he had little to complain about. That those were also years of literary success for him, in particular with the reception of *The French Revolution* (1837), would not have struck him as mere coincidence. He was all too much aware of the connection between physical and psychological states. Indeed, in his Rectorial address at the University of Edinburgh (1866) he told the students: "If . . . you are going to write a book,—you cannot manage it (at least, I never could) without getting decidedly made ill by it: and really one nevertheless must; if it is your business, you are obliged to follow out what you are at, and to do it, if even at the expense of health. Only remember, at all times, to get back as fast as possible out of it into health." But while he himself got back into health, that of Jane deteriorated. That, too, had roots in the mind as much as in the body.

The Carlyle marriage, between two people of enormous intelligence, talent, and sensibility, one of the most famous and certainly one of the most written-about marriages of the nineteenth century, had come under a good deal of strain from the start. Carlyle's marital credo, which he detailed to Jane just a few months before the wedding—it included the sentence, "It is the nature of a woman . . . (for she is essentially *passive* not *active*) to cling to the man for support and direction, to comply with his humours, and feel pleasure in doing so, simply because they are his; to reverence while she loves him, to conquer him not by her force but by her weakness"—did not bode well. The wedding night, to quote Kaplan, proved "abysmal." There seems no reason to dispute his conclusions, that "sexual intercourse played little or no role in the routine of their relationship during almost forty years of marriage."

Moreover, Jane had to compete with two other women close to

Carlyle: one was his mother, Margaret, to whom he remained deeply devoted during her long lifetime. What he wrote in his last of many letters to her, a few months before her death in 1853, was genuinely felt: "If there has been any good in the things I have uttered in this world's hearing, it was *your* voice essentially that was speaking thro' me: essentially, what you and my brave father meant and taught me to mean, this was the purport of all I wrote and spoke." Not surprisingly, perhaps, Jane did not take quite the same view of her mother-in-law. When, in 1842, there arrived at 5 Cheyne Row, Chelsea, where the couple had settled eight years before, an oil portrait of the elder Mrs. Carlyle—"My good old Mother exactly as she looks" was her son's delighted reaction—she bridled at her husband's urgent proposal that the portrait be framed at once, and then installed directly over the drawing-room mantelpiece. "Not only," writes Kaplan, "were all her favourite mantelpiece ornaments to be scattered around the house but she was to have as a great looming presence in her living room the pervasive features of that dour matriarch." Jane's reaction speaks for itself: "I could never feel alone with that picture over me! I almost *screamed* at the notion." The portrait ended up in Carlyle's study.

Lady Harriet could not be similarly disposed of. Carlyle fell totally under her spell, visited her and her husband constantly at one or the other of their numerous country houses, and wrote her letters of dogged devotion, some of which today's university students, confronted with anonymous texts by their examiners, might well attribute to D. H. Lawrence below top form. *Item:* "Sunday, yes my Beneficent, it shall be then: the dark man shall again see the daughter of the Sun, for a little while, and be illuminated, as if he were not dark! which he very justly reckons among the highest privileges he has at present." *Item:* "Employ me, do, order me this way or that, it is all I am good for at present. . . . See if I will not obey. . . . I must kiss your hand." In fact, Lady Harriet never had the slightest intention of letting the kissing go beyond that region. But one can hardly blame Jane for becoming jealous and upset, or for asking Giuseppe Mazzini, a friend who was far more sensitive to her emotional needs than her husband, whether or not to leave him. He advised her not to do so. She accepted his advice. And though, three years later (in 1849), her state of mind became such that she contemplated suicide, it would be rash to conclude that the Carlyle marriage was altogether unhappy. She rejoiced in the public recognition of the genius she always knew he possessed; while his tribute to her, delivered in a long, rambling, tear-filled monologue to Tyndall after her death (in 1866) was both authentic and well deserved: "He referred to the early days of his wife and himself—to their struggles against poverty and obstruction; to her valiant encouragement in hours of depression; to their life on the moors, in Edinburgh, and in London—how lovingly and loyally she had made of herself a soft cushion to protect him from the rude collisions of the world." That, indeed, had been her sacrifice.

Kaplan has very ably met the challenge, far from easy, of dealing with these crucial aspects of Carlyle's life—his loss of faith, his ill health, and his marriage. But the real contribution of his biography lies elsewhere. Unlike most previous biographers, he has no axe to grind. He is sympathetic to his subject, but at the same time does not let his judgments depend on any particular bias. He knows he is dealing with a complex personality, someone who has in the past been both overpraised and condemned to excess; and that the time is ripe for getting away from those extremes. The result, to my mind, is a Carlyle who makes sense, a Carlyle we can accept.

Let me try to indicate some of the dimensions of this Carlyle. First of all, we must get out of our minds that image of the lonely, craggy, half-crazed prophet of doom, Carlyle *contra mundum*, which still tends to appear on our mental screens when his name is so much as casually mentioned. The book contains a photograph of him taken in July 1854, before he had grown his beard. He looks stern. His hair is grizzled. But, at fifty-nine, in spite of much ill health and many disappointments, his appearance communicates a handsome vigor more reminiscent of the somewhat dandified Maclise engraving of 1832 and the romantic Samuel Laurence drawing (undated) than of the wonderful and justly famous photograph by Julia Margaret Cameron, taken when he was seventy-two, "in a very sensitive lens focused to produce an image of the literary artist as inspired seer."

Nor must we think of Carlyle as perpetually embattled, and therefore antisocial. As Kaplan points out, he had managed by the beginning of the 1840s to create a number of lifelong friendships: "Milnes, Sterling, Thackeray, Browning, Tennyson, Forster, Dickens, soon Edward FitzGerald, and later John Ruskin—together they wove a rich texture of experience, talent, achievement, and mutual affection which created a family connectiveness of the sort that Carlyle thought essential for human relations." The vision of Carlyle in the wilderness might well apply to the years he and Jane spent on the moors, at Craigenputtock (1828–1831), but certainly not to the London Carlyle. Indeed, London is itself a sort of hidden hero of this biography. Time

and again, Carlyle gets fed up with its noise, its crowding, its confusion and longs for the peace and quiet of his native Scotland. Yet,
in the end, he is always drawn back to it, in part because it offers him
the literary friendships he increasingly came to depend on.

It is, of course, undeniable that Carlyle's heightened rhetoric, infused with its peculiar flavor, a mixture of Calvinism, German
idealism, and poetic metaphor, often evoked the understandable reaction, for example from devotees of clearheadedness and common
sense like Macaulay, that his writings could only have emanated from
the pen of a mystical madman. But the truth is that in some ways
Macaulay and Carlyle—each despised the other—were not at all dis-
similar; especially in their respect for the concrete and the particular
which, in the case of Carlyle, went along with his stylistic and philosophical extravagances. Macaulay would certainly have endorsed
Carlyle's stricture on the Utilitarians—"all these people look forever
at some *theory of a thing,* never at any *thing.*" What Thackeray called
Carlyle's "gloomy rough Rembrandt-kind of reality . . . of historic
painting" is something that is as evident in his depiction of his contemporaries as it is in his historical works. Of Daniel Webster he
wrote: "a terrible, beetle-browed, mastiff-mouthed, yellow-skinned,
broad-bottomed, grim-taciturn individual; with a pair of dull-cruel-
looking black eyes, and as much Parliamentary intellect and silent-
rage in him . . . as I have ever seen in any man." Of Adolphe Thiers:
"close-cropped, bullet-headed, of fair weight, almost quite white;
laughing little hazel eyes, jolly hooked nose and most definite mouth;
short, short (five feet three or two at most), swells slightly in the
middle—soft, *sausage-like* on the whole—and ends neatly in fat little
feet and hands." And of Coleridge: "He has no resolution, he shrinks
from pain or labour in any of its shapes. His very attitude bespeaks
this: he never straightens his knee joints, he stoops with his fat ill-
shapen shoulders, and in walking he does not tread but shovel and
slide." Carlyle's "German" metaphysics did not curtail in the slightest
his "British" knack for empirical observation.

His politics show no less of a mixture than his prose. It is possible
to compile an anthology of excerpts from his writings which could
be subsumed under a great diversity of headings; ranging from "revolutionary" to "authoritarian." Kaplan describes him as "an explosive
paradox: the visionary radical, tortured by personal and public misery,
and the visionary conservative, furious at what seemed 'solutions' that
could only make matters worse." His books, Kaplan shrewdly remarks, were bought by "an awkward coalition of readers" many of

whom, while disagreeing with him about his practical policies, were drawn to him above all by "the consonance of the heart." Thus *Sartor* and *Past and Present* appealed to the young who were spiritually adrift and antimaterialistic; *Chartism* to social and political radicals; *Cromwell* to all those, regardless of political affiliation, concerned with English history. As for *The French Revolution,* a great popular success, readers tended to regard it, not in the way Carlyle intended, as a warning that revolutions necessarily break out in order to remove what was false and outdated in institutions, but as a kind of epic poem, like *Paradise Lost.*

The fact that people misread Carlyle was not surprising. Kaplan points out that over the years he created for himself a kind of code language, "in order to obscure a personality and a message for which many were as yet unprepared, while at the same time striking an identifiable theme and chord for the sympathetic and initiated." Gladstone, reading Froude's *Carlyle,* noticed a similar strategy in his letters to his mother in which he still employed Christian phraseology, even though he no longer believed in it. He simply could not bear to give her pain. He was somewhat less averse to giving pain to readers of his published works. On the other hand, since he came to regard himself as a missionary to the English, he wanted to make his message palatable to the widest possible spectrum. Thus the "Aesopian" strategy.

The word "missionary" is of some importance. From the time he had decided on his vocation as a writer, Carlyle was aware of himself not just as an artist, but also as priest and prophet. His aim, from his mid-thirties on, was "a depiction of the state of the human community which would dramatise the decline of spiritual values, communal harmony, and moral sensitivity, while at the same time directing the world toward countervailing modes of mind and behaviour." If that sounds arrogant, one can only reply that modesty has never been a virtue commonly possessed by prophets. It was certainly not one of Carlyle's. In a letter to his mother (September 1831) he even went so far as to compare his own mission to Christ's: "clearly enough also there *is* want of instruction and light . . . as probably for eighteen hundred years there has not been: if *I* have any light to give, then let me give it."

In what way did the light he had to give make him a significant figure, not just in his time, but in ours as well? The answer, according to Kaplan's most eloquent pages, is to be found in the essay entitled "Characteristics," one he began to write just a few weeks after sending the "missionary" letter to his mother. It is encapsulated in Carlyle's insight that the self is contrived in the mind, not the mind in the self:

> He saw what no one in Western culture had seen quite as clearly before: the strongest force within man is Nature, which is unconscious, mysterious, spontaneous, and "the sign of health is Unconsciousness. . . . The true force is an unconscious one." For "boundless as is the domain of man, it is but a small fractional proportion of it that he rules with Consciousness and by Forethought . . . the mechanical, small; the great is ever, in one sense or other, the vital; it is essentially the mysterious, and only the surface of it can be understood.

God was in man, and it was the task of the artist, i.e., Carlyle's own, to create representations of God, the mysteries, the infinite, and the Good from his deepest unconsciousness.

It need hardly be said that there will always be disagreement about the value of this insight for literature, the arts, politics, and human existence in general. One can imagine an eloquent reply to Carlyle on behalf of the tradition of the European Enlightenment which eschews the very "leap in the dark" he favored. Like it or not, however, it is to Kaplan's credit that he singles out this insight as perhaps Carlyle's major contribution to the thought and sensibility of the nineteenth century. Which is not to say that by itself it sums him up. In his works, as in those of other great artists, lie jumbled together profound perceptions, mistaken judgments, repellent rantings, pointless posturings, as well as marvelous flashes of humor and self-knowledge. Jane once said that everyone got him wrong because everyone assumed there was only one Carlyle. Kaplan does not make that mistake. He gives us a figure of genuine complexity; including, as he momentarily assumes Jane's point of view, "the recluse, the friend, the monologuist, the complainer, the mourner, the neurotic, the charitable, the compassionate, the loyal, the loving, the dutiful son, the neglectful husband, the volatile arguer, the self-obsessed artist, the bitter satirist, the brilliant talker." All of those Carlyles are to be found in Kaplan's book, and that is no mean achievement.

Nonetheless, his biography, while undoubtedly "major," lacks the ultimate distinction that might lead readers to rank it with "great" or even "outstanding" examples of the genre. To begin with, it lacks elegance of style. Among the stylistic defects are what G. O. Trevelyan called "jingling lines," such as "Carlyle's unsuitability as a

suitor," and "whatever the threat of steam power, however"; infel-
icities such as "he seemed to hardly get on with his project," and "she
wrote conciliatorily"; and odd uses of words such as a "steamer had
shipwrecked." The standard of proofreading doesn't help. "Crab"
Robinson, "perjorative," and "discretely questioned" are only the
most embarrassing examples of a lack of care which interferes with
one's pleasure in the text. A few weeks after Jane's mother's funeral,
Carlyle traveled by himself to the cemetery at Crawford where she
was buried. He wanted to make a copy of the inscription on the stone.
The stonemason had cut the letters "deep, correct, and very well."
But there were one or two mistakes of punctuation which he could
not bring himself to leave. "So he went to the nearest farm-house . . .
borrowed a chisel and hammer, and succeeded in making it all correct." Kaplan had need of those same implements.

Lack of sufficient context is another weak part of this biography.
Here any critic is on shaky ground. For Kaplan has given us so much
about Carlyle's life, based on what must have been immense labors
in the primary and secondary sources, that to expect him to have dealt
also with, say, the cultural situation of late-eighteenth-century Edinburgh or the key ideas of the German romantics, seems churlish and
ungrateful, to say the least. And yet . . . Carlyle himself is quoted as
writing to Thomas Murray (in 1818) that "I now perceive more clearly
than ever, that any man's opinions depend not on himself so much
as on the age he lives in, or even the persons with whom he associates."
Kaplan is good on the persons, less good on the age. His book is of
such high quality that it deserves to be evaluated by the highest standards. Judged by those, it is deficient; in that while his decision not
to make it a life *and* works seems sensible enough, one would like to
know—indeed, I think it is essential that one know—a little more
about the social and intellectual context, including that of the corpus
of Carlyle's own writings, than he has given us.

One last carping comment: To my mind, Kaplan is overly fond of
talking about Carlyle's "anticipations" of Victorianism. Quite apart
from the fact that there now exists a considerable literature dealing
with the ways in which certain currents of "Victorian" thought and
feeling were to be found in England at least a generation before the
queen ascended the throne, there is an element of question-begging
in the term "anticipation." Shouldn't the real question be, not how
Carlyle "anticipated" one or other aspect of the Victorian age; but,
rather, how it came about that the idiosyncratic amalgam of ideas and
attitudes which he partly inherited, partly constructed for himself,

was taken up and welcomed by readers and auditors whose own form-ative experiences had been very different from his?

The last word about Carlyle, particularly Carlyle within the context of his time, has not yet been spoken. But Kaplan's biography will have to be reckoned with. One of the things he does very well is to communicate the sense of how important family ties, the passage of time, the sense of place, and memories of the past were for Carlyle. In the first section of his essay on Johnson, separately published under the title "Biography," he wrote that "the Past is all holy to us; the Dead are all holy." For him the most touching incident in Johnson's life was the occasion when, fifty years after his father's death, "he stood in the rain—his head bared, tears trickling down his face—on the very spot in the Uttoxeter marketplace where, as a young boy, he had disobeyed his parent." After Jane's death, remembering that incident, Carlyle made it a practice to visit the spot in Hyde Park where Jane had died, baring his head, whatever the weather.

He had long been obsessed by memories of his own early life. One night in 1837 he rode through Ecclefechan: "The old kirkyard tree . . . was nestling itself softly against the great twilight in the north. A star or two looked out, and the old graves were all there, and my father's and my sister's, and God was above us all. I really . . . have no words to speak." As he grew to be a very old man—he lived to the age of eighty-five—and his friends kept dying, one after the other, the acute sense of time passing which suffuses all his works necessarily received greater scope. And Kaplan does full justice to it, as he calls the melancholy roll of the dead and the dying, until, forty-five years after his starlit ride, Carlyle was himself taken on his final journey to the place where he was born.

During the summer of 1849 he had wanted to see for himself the dimensions of the Irish problem, and had gone traveling in Ireland, accompanied by Charles Gavan Duffy. In the coach on the way to Sligo the two men were joined by a young honeymooning couple. Carlyle talked to the bride about sightseeing and the pleasures of travel. When he left the coach for a moment, the bride turned to Duffy and asked: "Who is the twaddling old Scotchman who allows no one to utter a word but himself?" Duffy later repeated her remark to Car-lyle, who was mortified.

There are doubtless more than a few people today who would heart-ily second the bride's cutting comment. Yet the old twaddler refuses to shut up. *Sartor Resartus* can still touch the innermost feelings of those who have lost their way in the spiritual maze of our own time.

The French Revolution has withstood a century and a half of historical criticism; so that when we want to know what storming the Bastille or stopping the King at Varennes or living in Paris during the Terror was really like we turn, not to the statisticians and the retrospective sociologists, but to Carlyle. *Past and Present, Chartism,* and those two marvelously perceptive essays, "Signs of the Times" and "Characteristics," remain essential documents for any student of the nineteenth century in England.

As for Carlyle's political ideas, one may readily agree with Mazzini's critique, that "the forms of government appear to him almost without meaning; such objects as the extensions of suffrage, the guarantee of any kind of political right, are evidently in his eyes pitiful things, materialism more or less disguised." But when Mazzini went on to remark, in a tone of incredulity, that what Carlyle seemed to require was that men should grow better, that the number of just men should increase, who among us, even while at first dismissing such a requirement as beyond reason, or Utopian, does not in some corner of his mind and heart share Carlyle's hope that such a change might indeed come about? And, moreover, that it might be worth working for? Do I sound like a missionary myself? It's all Carlyle's fault. He is alive and well (except for occasional stomach trouble), and living in Mr. Kaplan's biography.

Michelet

MICHELET

by Roland Barthes

translated by Richard Howard

Once upon a time, historians and sociologists defined the advent of modernity in terms of rationality, advances in science and technology, the growth of bureaucracy, the triumph of numbers and facts over magic, myth, and superstition. But nowadays, whether we judge by the work of leading literary critics and historians, or by looking at book titles and the programs of annual meetings of learned societies, all that seems to have changed. The focus of attention of the scholarly avant-garde is not so much on apostles of reason and material progress as it is on practitioners of necromancy and the occult, on mythology and the irrational as the harbingers of modernity. Moreover, it is not the triumph of civilization over nature, but the persistent impingement of the natural world, that tends to take center stage.

A reading of the late Roland Barthes's brilliant book, part anthology, part commentary, about the great French historian Jules Michelet (1798–1874) confirms this new sense of the modern. Michelet was the author of a twenty-volume history of France as well as twice that many volumes on other subjects, ranging from women in the French Revolution to works on birds, insects, mountains, and the sea. Taking Michelet's complete oeuvre into account, Barthes gives us not so much a portrait of an anticlerical, radical democrat as of a magus, imbued with Gnostic notions about the conjunction of opposites and intent on erasing the borders between the world of history and the world of nature.

It is this Michelet who is most relevant to Barthes's own preoccupations as a trenchant critic of tradition and convention in language and society. Barthes published his book on Michelet in 1954, under the title *Michelet par Lui-Même*, a title that underrated the importance of his own commentary as well as the power of the anthologist to pursue his own predilections. Since then, a large and impressive literature about Michelet has appeared in both France and the United States; and the definitive edition of his complete works is well under way. But Barthes's pioneering work is indispensable. It is a great boon to have it available in English at last, most ably translated by Richard Howard.

Barthes tells us at the outset that the chief object of his book is not to depict the influence of Michelet's life on his works, but rather to restore coherence to the historian, to recover the structure of his existence, "a thematics, if you like, or better still: an organized network of obsessions." He attempts to show that Michelet's life and work were dominated and bound together by a series of myths, images, and metaphors that had as their aim the abolition of the distinction between the natural and historical worlds. These devices, since they were crucial to Michelet's view of himself as well as of history, deserve to be called existential rather than historical.

No review can possibly do justice to the subtlety and economy of Barthes's presentation in a volume that barely exceeds two hundred pages. But one can indicate a few of the themes that emerge from the literary archaeology practiced by Barthes with such fruitful results. Take Michelet's assertion that each people has as its prime nourishment a special kind of food, essential for its survival and constant renewal. For the French, from time immemorial, that food has been bread and soup. The strength of the French was ultimately due to their wheat, growing in the flinty soil that gave sustenance to the blossoming plant. Thus France was literally fed on stone, which gave her, at important moments in history, the spark of life and, so Michelet writes, lent her bones a great power of resistance. Now this is not merely a generalization, right or wrong, about food. It is, rather, an integral part of Michelet's Lamarckian doctrine of transformations: forms melt into one another, in this instance from flint to grain to Frenchmen—from stone to living beings.

Another striking example of transformism occurs in Michelet's use of the animal world in his nomenclature for historical personalities. Robespierre is a cat, Marat a toad, Danton a bull, Sade a bird of prey, Choiseul a lapdog. This is not merely a matter of physical resemblances (which, as the illustrations show, did indeed exist). It is a direct attack by the historian on the classical mode of personal portrayal, based on a detailed description of anatomical parts. Instead, Michelet employs natural epithets that get at those "humors" that constitute the essential character of human beings.

Michelet's own awareness of the power of transformation is apparent in his memorable account of mud baths he took in Italy in 1854: "In my splendid coffin of white marble," he recalls, "I received the first application of the black, unctuous slime, which nonetheless never dirties, being nothing more than sand. Another marble tub, beside it, receives you afterwards, and you are made clean in an instant." But far more than that was involved: no less than an exchange of nature. "I was the Earth, and the Earth was man. She had taken for herself my infirmity, my sin. And I, becoming Earth, had taken her life, her warmth, her youth. Years, labors, pains, all remained in the depths of my marble coffin. I was renewed."

Water, as well as earth, wrought that personal renewal. And water, encompassing both smoothness and homogeneity, always meant something desirable as well as beneficent to Michelet, as against the sterility and the discontinuity of dryness. One of his favorite images, or themes, was the Dutch canal boat, which represented for him an ideal site for the family. For Barthes, this image, repeated throughout Michelet's work, reflected his innermost concerns. Barthes describes it thus: "This concave, full object, this egglike, solid space suspended in the smooth element of the water, constantly exchanging the moisture of ablutions and the liquidity of the atmosphere, is the delicious image of the homogeneous. Here the great Micheletist theme is posited: that of a seamless world." Similarly, Michelet's favorite mammal was the whale, creature of milk and blood, product of the primordial sea, itself an epitome of the instability of matter—smooth, viscous, changeable.

Children, too, contained felicitous mixtures of milk and blood, liquids that flowed within them—so Barthes writes—without ever being engorged, diluted, or dried up. That was not necessarily true of the blood of adults, a key substance in Michelet's historical scheme of things. Blood could go sour, as in the case of Louis XIV, in whom it produced tumors (one on his anus that he managed to keep secret for nine months, fearing, rightly, that all Europe would laugh at it).

In blue-blooded aristocracies that had lost their energy and vitality, blood became engorged; and in the two "terrible virgins of modern history," Charles XII and Saint-Just, it turned motionless and inhuman, hard as ice. In kings and queens, whose blood was "sealed" by a closed and static circle of heredity, it became obnoxious and malign.

According to Michelet, benign blood must be in constant motion, must ebb and flow rhythmically. Which is why his principal erotic experience with his second wife, Athénaïs, was to observe and nurse her in the course of her periods: a pleasure, so he believed, far exceeding that of orgasm. For it was only at the moment of her greatest weakness that woman could affirm her magical powers, and was enabled to draw man into that circular, seamless time, superior to the linear time of history, of which he, lacking the natural biological rhythm of the female, could not ordinarily be part.

Woman, for Michelet, was "the gentle mediator between Nature and man." Anticipating a favorite subject of twentieth-century historiography (as he anticipated many of its other current preoccupations), Michelet paid tribute to the beneficial medical functions performed by witches. Woman herself was, in the words of Barthes's gloss, "an ultimate medication, she halts time, and, better still, makes it begin again." And this was crucial. For Michelet historic, that is, male, time came to a stop with the French Revolution. It was up to woman to initiate a new time scheme, mandated by her nature and supported by the nineteenth-century revolution in embryology: natural time.

Does this emphasis on the special role of women imply the permanent separation of the two sexes, with foreseeably tragic results? Not necessarily. Here the powerful Gnostic strain in Michelet's thought comes to the fore. The contradictions and differences between man (idea) and woman (sentiment) can and must be overcome by the ultrasex: the androgynous People, aware that knowledge can discover its object only by means of feeling. The People made the French Revolution—though not the Terror, which was the work of dry and cerebral Jacobins. It is the People that is in possession of the ideal combination of wisdom and instinct, that union of the two sexes of the mind, which Michelet called the source of all that was good and which, so he declared, made him a complete man.

Michelet paid an extraordinary—what to our ears may sound like an extravagant—tribute to the People as the initiator of written history. He believed that nineteenth-century historians, male, cerebral, barren, were unable to find truth. It was the thought of the People, the national legend, that formed the sole true basis for historical credibility. Only the People could dictate true history to the historian. The best historian was the one who had emerged from the People and was thus closest to it. And "people" was not a class-based concept or group. It excluded priests, lawyers, and intellectuals (as opposed to philosophers). On the other hand, it could include wealthy bourgeois.

Like Woman, the People is above history. It "opens Nature." For Michelet, in search of a seamless world, the People is a unique entity that is capable of overcoming contradictions. It includes poets and philosophers, sages and children, the religious and the rational, activists and contemplatives. Yet Michelet's relationship to the People, so greatly loved and admired by him, contained a tragic irony. For he himself, born the son of a printer, ever conscious of his family background, was in the end unable, as he put it, to make the People speak: "The people's language . . . was inaccessible to me." Barthes, himself a pioneer in the analysis of language and its meaning, makes an appropriate comment: "Thus, it is Michelet's entire speech—i.e., his entire work—which bears him, lacerated, far from his paradise: he is perhaps the first author of modernity able to utter only an impossible language."

Barthes succeeds admirably in his declared aim of demonstrating that a "total" reading of Michelet's multifarious writings requires an understanding of the network of themes that both underlies and ties them all together. Still, as a historian, I should like to raise a caution. In a letter to Taine, written around 1855, Michelet squarely rejects the name of "poet" with which his correspondent had saddled him and cites various examples of his own historical positivism, each connected with the history of finance. Michelet's self-assessment needn't be taken as definitive (certainly that goes against the grain of Barthes's approach), but it is a useful reminder that there are other important historical skills to be found in his work—skills that are, perhaps necessarily, slighted in Barthes's treatment, and that do not require, and may indeed be obscured by, the "total" approach.

Consider Michelet's capacity, rivaled only by Marx, to get at the root of the disjunction between power and ideology, the illusion that to call an institution or a party by a new name will somehow change the concrete reality within a particular historical situation; or the related illusion that a political leader's purely tactical declaration that he has changed his mind can, in the long run, seriously affect that reality. To integrate *that* sort of skill, marvelously displayed in Michelet's

French Revolution, into his total thematic system, into the doctrine (I am paraphrasing Barthes) that there are no historical facts, that history is a continuity of identities, that Michelet's belief in vegetal historical growth excludes causality, is to do less than justice to it. And, after all, in the Micheletist scheme, Justice, unlike Grace, is invariably a good thing.

Chosen People

A LIBERAL DESCENT:

VICTORIAN HISTORIANS AND THE

ENGLISH PAST

by J. W. Burrow

Last summer I visited some friends in the house they were then renting in London. It turned out to be the case that their landlord's hobby was collecting pudding molds. Everywhere one looked one could see them—in shapes ranging from bunches of grapes to various birds and animals to a couple of likenesses of famous faces. Some were more beautiful than others; all still seemed redolent with promise of gelatinous bliss.

Reading Mr. Burrow's excellent book on how some Victorian historians interpreted the English past has brought back memories of that visit. For are there not historiographical pudding molds as well as those of a more familiar kind? All historians, whatever their outlook or ideology, must at some point put the results of their researches into a readable form. "Form" means, as battalions of formidable literary critics armed to the teeth with modes and tropes have recently been reminding us, a certain manner of literary construction and presentation. But it also means that, depending on which pudding mold the historian employs, the pattern of events he sets out to describe itself assumes a certain shape; and that, perhaps more often than not, it is the mold, ready to hand, rather than the ingredients of the pudding

From the *New York Review of Books*, June 24, 1982

or even the culinary skills of the chef-historian, that determines the shape.

Mr. Burrow has taken a closer look at one of the pudding molds most frequently used by historians of England over the last three centuries, the so-called Whig interpretation of English history. The term was coined fifty years ago by the late Sir Herbert Butterfield, who used it to characterize those accounts of the English past which celebrated it as revealing a continuous, on the whole uninterrupted, and generally glorious story of constitutional progress, all leading up to the triumph of liberty and representative institutions.

The high points of that interpretation in its original form included an ancient, free, Teutonic constitution under the Anglo-Saxons; the immemorial antiquity of common law and the House of Commons; the continuity of Saxon freedoms, which could not be destroyed either by William the Conqueror or by the feudal system brought to England by the Norman Conquest, but which, indeed, were confirmed and endorsed by Magna Carta; the revitalization after a period of absolutism of the power of the Commons as well as the flowering of constitutional government under the Tudors; and the inevitable as well as providential defeat by the forces of freedom, as they manifested themselves in the English revolutions of the seventeenth century, of the wicked attempts by tyrannical Stuart kings to turn the clock back to despotic, personal rule. It all added up to a story of success that gave grounds for rejoicing over the confident possession of such a marvelous past: "an invitation to national jubilation at which the shades of venerated ancestors are honoured guests."

This particular version of a usable English past went back a long way. In the seventeenth century it was maintained by lawyers intent upon hailing the venerable antiquity of the English common law and by parliamentarians eager to defend what they held to be the ancient rights and liberties of the Commons against royal incursions. It was also heavily attacked. One attacker, Robert Brady, demonstrated, for instance, that writs of summons to the House of Commons could not be traced back beyond the thirteenth century, and argued persuasively that it was indeed feudalism rather than a hypothetical ancient constitution that was crucial for any real understanding of English medieval political history.

Radicals still went on believing in an ideal ancient constitution, somewhere in the distant past. But for those more moderately inclined, more concerned to establish grounds for a "liberal descent," in Edmund Burke's pregnant phrase, than in revolution or nostalgic appeals to democratic rights, what was lacking after Brady and others had gone to work was evidence for continuity between past and present. Continuity, in fact, was and is the essence of any Whig interpretation; and new means had to be found to establish it.

One such means, chiefly developed by the eighteenth-century Scottish school of sociological or "philosophical" historians, was to see the history of civil society as a series of stages, progressing from barbarism to civilization, with liberty a product of the latest or modern stage. Another means will always remain firmly linked to the name of Burke, who yielded to none in his exaltation of the long tradition of English common law, but who regarded that tradition as a flexible one, fruitfully combining continuity and change. A certain amount of innovation and reform could well be absorbed in the course of time by a legal or political tradition, provided that those changes and innovations did not emanate from abstract modes of thought imposed or copied from outside—Burke's *Reflections on the Revolution in France* comes to mind here, of course—but grew naturally from a native stock. One must respect the past without becoming confined by it. Here, then, were two ways in which continuity and progress could still be preserved by those English historians who delighted in the slow but steady growth of freedom, yet at the same time possessed a due regard for historical evidence.

But those same historians had to overcome one more intellectual obstacle—a formidable one—in the shape of the philosopher-historian David Hume. In his *History of Great Britain* (1754–1762) Hume had argued that there had, in fact, been no public liberty under the Tudors, and that because of this there existed no free constitution to be overthrown by the Stuarts. The rights claimed by the Long Parliament from Charles I were new rather than ancient rights. Indeed, as a monarch confronted by attempts at innovation who ended by having his head cut off, he deserved retrospective sympathy rather than censure.

Hume himself belonged to the Scottish school of philosophical historians, and, as such, helped to provide future Whig historians with a model of the advancement of civil society by successive stages. But in stressing the point that this advancement was a European phenomenon of which the development of *English* freedom was a purely local manifestation, the Tory Hume created one further difficulty for his Whig successors.

What eventually happened was that by the early nineteenth century a historiographical consensus had been worked out, something Mr. Burrow calls the "Whig compromise." This assumed that the English constitution was neither Saxon nor merely modern, but arose early in the thirteenth century with Magna Carta and the summoning of burgesses and knights of the shire to Parliament. Under it the monarchy was limited, the sovereign below the law; and kings could neither tax nor legislate without Parliament. The Tudors did make despotic innovations. But those were aberrations which never became an accepted part of the constitution. Thus, in the seventeenth century, there was indeed a free constitution to be defended against the Stuarts; and the Parliamentarians of that time, in defending and improving it, sensed the current of progress that was about to carry Europe as well as England toward the great modern era of wealth and civilization. The "glorious" revolution was both innovative *and* conservative. It resulted in the departure of a monarch, James II; but at the same time it secured English liberty and prosperity.

This Whig compromise, containing elements of both the Scottish school and Burke, as well as taking due account of Hume's historical strictures on the old doctrine of the ancient constitution, was taken over and powerfully displayed, with dazzling literary skill, by Thomas Babington Macaulay, the first of the four Victorian historians to whom Mr. Burrow accords extended treatment in his book. His comments on Macaulay's *History of England* (1849–1861) are original and perceptive to the highest degree.

Take, for example, his observations on the central antithesis of Macaulay's *History:* no longer, as in his early essays, between Whig and Tory as protagonists of party conflict, but between civilization, property, public trust, and liberty under law on the one hand and, on the other, lawless ambition, fanaticism, unbounded passions and appetites.

Macaulay, like many of his contemporaries in the England of the 1840s, feared revolution. He therefore feared the loss of control by governments over those evil passions which it was the office of government to control and to restrain: avarice, licentiousness, revenge, the hatred of sect for sect.

It is this anxiety that lends special force, throughout Macaulay's *History,* to his emphasis on what the proper course of public life ought to be. It makes us understand why it was so important for the historian to use his own book as a potential source for common political memories that would bind together in a common political culture a newly enfranchised electorate. The *History,* then, is much more than a vindication of the Whig Party. It celebrates not merely the worth of public life and the wider progress of society, but also what Mr. Burrow calls "a sense of the privileged possession by Englishmen of their history, as well as of the epic dignity of government by discussion." It is a polemic, not so much on behalf of party as on behalf of that favorite Victorian virtue, respectability.

William Stubbs, author of what became the classic Victorian *Constitutional History of England* (1874–1878), was born in 1825 and belonged to a later generation of historians for whom the key issues were race, nationality, and democracy rather than the power of the House of Commons, and for whom the chief enemies were bureaucracy and centralization rather than revolutionary demagoguery. Those historians, Stubbs among them, were also subject to new intellectual influences, primarily from German legal scholars who laid stress on the *mark*-community as the foundation of Germanic society: this was held to be a free village community, politically democratic, within which a system of communal agriculture was carried on. Brought to England by the Saxons, this "folk-moot," along with other local institutions such as courts of the shire and the hundred, embodied the representative principle and contained dormant seeds of future liberties; seeds that were able to survive the Norman Conquest and the very undemocratic age of feudalism that followed upon it. For Stubbs the continuity of English history rested in the vigor of those humble institutions of local government. Some still existed, so Stubbs believed, in the nineteenth century: for example, the vestry meeting of the English parish incorporated the primitive assembly of the Anglo-Saxon township.

Stubbs himself was a Tory in politics. One would hardly expect a future bishop of Oxford to have been anything else. But so powerful still was the tradition of English historical writing in the mold of progress and continuity that, for the purposes of Mr. Burrow's argument, he can, not unreasonably, be counted as Whiggish in historical outlook. Still, even though the mold may have remained the same, it now contained a new ingredient: the longevity of local institutions. In the old Whig interpretation it was the Parliamentarians of the seventeenth century who fought to conserve a popular ancient institution against innovating monarchs who tried to encroach on it. "But in Stubbs," as Mr. Burrow points out, "the conservative defence was conducted not by parliamentary heroes but by the combination of inarticulate persistence and malleability in the institutions themselves."

Stubbs's successor in the chair of history at Oxford was Edward Augustus Freeman (1823–1892), author of *The History of the Norman Conquest of England* (1867–1879). Unlike Macaulay, he owed his political creed not to the eighteenth century but to Byron and Mazzini. As Mr. Burrow wittily remarks, "the Norman Conquest was his historical consolation for not belonging to an oppressed nation." His historical writings reflect his attempt to assimilate heroic populism to Whig notions of continuity. Though he had begun, when a student at Oxford, as a high church Tory, he ended up as a Gladstonian Liberal. He differed from Stubbs in politics, yet he greatly relied upon him for his constitutional history, thus lending a certain amount of verisimilitude to that well-known Victorian doggerel:

> *Ladling butter from alternate tubs,*
> *Stubbs buttering Freeman,*
> *Freeman buttering Stubbs.*

But while Freeman's assertion that English history had begun in freedom and that the Norman Conquest had made no permanent breach in its essential continuity was very much in accord with Stubbs's stress on the persistence of local institutions, he added something new, an obsession with race.

What that meant as far as Freeman was concerned was recognition of the significance of Teutonic kinship, from the early German forest dwellers to George Washington, along with continuity between village community, tribalism, the nation-state, and the invention of representative government. And to that emphasis on Teutonic exclusiveness Freeman added a corresponding emphasis on "Aryan" inclusiveness. Like some other scholars of his generation, Freeman, taking his cue from the philologists, came to believe in an Aryan race and stock of institutions, in an overarching Aryanism binding together by common ancestry into one noble brotherhood Greeks and Romans as well as Teutons.

In some of his most brilliant pages Mr. Burrow shows how the interplay between Freeman's love of Teutonic homogeneity and his admiration for Aryan inclusiveness—the latter leading him to display in his personal attitudes racial prejudices against "non-Aryans," which have become all too familiar to us in this century—determined the nature and limits of his own special brand of Whig history.

On the one hand, Freeman ran true to type as a Whig historian in regarding England as passing from the village community of the Anglo-Saxons to the modern nation-state in which the principle of representation had successfully taken the place of the ancient liberty of face-to-face democracy. But he was as much attracted by universal as by national history. He wanted to be a Whig on a European scale. And here difficulties arose. For he saw history as a cyclical drama of rebirths and resurrections, with institutions as well as historical actors repeating their roles time and again. Progress occurred only in the guise of restoration.

Cycles and restorations lent themselves to an apocalyptic view of history which posed a major threat to the Whig idea of continuity. Here the concept of a single Aryan race helped to guarantee for Freeman the integrity of European history. But he was never able wholly to resolve either the tensions that were produced by his being equally attached to both English and world history or the intellectual difficulties that were bound to confront one whose love of restoration was almost greater than his love of continuity.

Freeman's views, then, put considerable strain upon those twin pillars of the Whig interpretation of history, continuity and progress. So did the views of James Anthony Froude (1818–1894), whose spiritual odyssey had led him from the Oxford Movement via religious doubt to an aggressive Protestantism; who gained perhaps his greatest fame as the biographer of Carlyle; and who, at the end of his life, like Stubbs and Freeman before him, occupied the Regius chair of history at Oxford. His *History of England from the Fall of Wolsey to the Defeat of the Spanish Armada* (1856–1870) is, on the one hand, a straightforwardly Whiggish paean to the English victory over the Spaniards and the subsequent triumph of the English Reformation. On the other, it contains two elements, both products of his discipleship to Carlyle, the man he called his "master," which were not so easily absorbed into the conventional Whig interpretation.

One is the emphasis on social rather than constitutional history. Froude's ideas, like Carlyle's, were those of a Tory Radical, sympathetic to government paternalism, nostalgically fond of a responsible aristocracy, critical of the inequitable distribution and misuse of wealth, and hostile to the laissez-faire individualism of the classical economists. The other is his adoption, not of the classic Whig pattern of continuity and progress, but of a formula of historical explanation stressing discontinuity, recurrent decay, and renewal.

Mr. Burrow demonstrates how, with Froude, the Whig interpretation once again proved sufficiently resilient to accommodate, more or less comfortably, both radical nostalgia, which yearns for a return to certain aspects of the past, occasionally favors revolution to bring about that return, but militates by definition against a gradual progress from past to present; and messianic views of history that postulate, sometimes in religious, sometimes in secular, guise, a historical pattern consisting of episodes of captivity, deliverance, and release rather than the continuous forward movement that had been the essence of the old Whig view in its pure form.

Froude was an ardent imperialist who hoped to see the virtues of sixteenth-century rural England re-created in the colonies. But while his imperialist tracts caught the mood of the immediate future, his *History* had not dwelt unduly on the expansionist exploits of the Elizabethan age. And neither he nor any other leading nineteenth-century historian grasped what may seem to us now an obvious opportunity to extend the Whig interpretation by propelling it outward to depict in a systematic manner the attachment of American ideas and institutions to ancient constitutionalism. That might have been one way of reinvesting with new vigor a liberal impulse in English historiography, which by the end of the century had reached at least temporary exhaustion.

The combination of a conservative political reaction with a broader and more objective temper in historical writing played its part in diminishing the attraction of a Whig approach for medieval historians. And, in any event, the Whig interpretation, once the property of Parliamentarians and constitutionalists, was getting stretched, broadened, and dispersed to the point where it seemed about to become the national interpretation.

One could say that these are some of the main lines of Mr. Burrow's argument. But no summary can possibly do justice to the richness, subtlety, and originality of this book, to my mind one of the finest volumes on modern English intellectual history to have appeared since his own *Evolution and Society* (1966). Mr. Burrow's deep knowledge of the Victorian age has stood him in good stead in the present book, which he intends not so much as a study of technical historiography as, in the words of Burckhardt, a record of what one age finds of interest in another.

One of the obvious pitfalls of such an approach is, of course, a lapse into excessive relativism. One concentrates to such an extent on the intellectual influences that shaped the historians under discussion that their histories tend to emerge primarily as manifestations of an age, literary documents like novels and poems and tracts, rather than works of history, which, after all, lay claim to dealing with facts and uncovering the truth about the past. Even though one detects a slightly plaintive note in his admission that historians have no duty to make themselves available to intellectual history, Mr. Burrow is well aware of the relativistic danger and manages to avoid it.

He remarks, for instance, that Macaulay's work, with its wider implications, remains within the bounds of responsible history; and that Stubbs's *Constitutional History,* while Whiggish in structure and outlook, is written with a scrupulous respect for the integrity of the historian's materials and for the social arrangements of the past.

At the end of his book, Mr. Burrow confronts a paradoxical situation: having "exposed" the Whig interpretation for more than three hundred pages, how can he himself avoid ending up as a Whig historian? "It would not be hard," he writes, "to idealise the episodes of English historiography described here, aided by the elegiac quality which tends to attach to the conclusions of historical works, often reflecting not so much anything in the history itself as the fact that the story told about it is reaching its end."

Clearly it will not do for Mr. Burrow to end on such a Whiggish note of celebration. So he shocks his readers with a wisecrack. "On the whole," he remarks, "the great Victorian histories now seem like the triumphal arches of a past empire, their vaunting inscriptions increasingly unintelligible to the modern inhabitants: visited occasionally, it may be, as a *pissoir,* a species of visit naturally brief." It is a safe bet that neither Macaulay nor Stubbs nor Freeman nor Froude concluded any of his works in this fashion. Indeed, even Mr. Burrow feels constrained to add one more paragraph in which he duly notes the benefit, offered by a reading of the mid-Victorian historians, of seeing one society and culture reflected through another.

The fact that he does, after all, end on that positive and almost joyful note proves his own thesis that there is an innate Whiggishness in stories as such; and that as long as historians continue to tell stories dealing with entities more enduring than individual lives—crown, Parliament, the constitution, the working class, "or for that matter 'the Whig tradition' "—there must be some depiction of change-in-continuity, just as there is bound to be climax or resolution at the end of the story. In that sense, then, Whiggism is perennial: a pudding mold that will never be melted down or, barring the grim prospect of a total triumph on the part of the cliometricians, retired to the British Museum.

The Victorians from
the Inside

PORTRAIT OF AN AGE:

VICTORIAN ENGLAND

by G. M. Young

The first part of G. M. Young's classic *Portrait of an Age* appeared in 1934, in the form of the last chapter of a two-volume collection of essays by various hands on *Early Victorian England,* edited by himself. His own contribution to these volumes consisted of a panorama of the period from the Reform Act to the death of Palmerston in 1865. Expanded in scope, to take in the rest of the century, *Portrait of an Age* appeared as a separate book in 1936; and, ever since, has held its place as what the late George Kitson Clark justly calls "an historical essay of unique interest and importance." There must be few students of the period, amateur as well as professional, who have not been dazzled by its brilliance, amused and instructed by its mixture of playfulness and profundity, and puzzled as well as shamed by its mandarin allusiveness.

But the actual origin of Young's *Portrait* goes further back and is worth recalling. In the course of World War I, which Young, a former Fellow of All Souls turned career civil servant under Morant at the Board of Education, spent first as Arthur Henderson's private secretary, then in the Ministry of Reconstruction, he set himself "partly from curiosity and partly for comfort" a series of readings about the struggle with Napoleon and the years of peace and distress that had

From the *Times Literary Supplement,* January 20, 1978

followed in the England of a century before. No doubt already true
to his own principle that in order to understand an age one must go
on reading until one can hear the people talking, he was still reading
when the war ended and when there appeared Strachey's *Eminent Victorians,* which he later remembered borrowing from a friend and handing back with the comment: "We're in for a bad time."

The picture of early Victorian England which he had begun to
construct from his own reading was indeed very different from that
conveyed in Strachey's mocking and irreverent essays. Much of the
English reading public, however, proved all too ready to enjoy, if not
to adopt, the outlook and attitude of Strachey and his imitators. Thus,
"in a fit of wrath over what seemed to me a preposterous misreading
of the age," Young wrote an essay entitled "Victorian History" which
first appeared (1931) in *Life and Letters* and, the following year, in
revised form, in a collection of modern English essays issued by the
Oxford University Press as part of its World's Classics series.

It was this essay which was, in fact, the real starting point of *Portrait
of an Age.* In it, having sketched the outline of his own periodization
of the age, Young expressed the view that the authors of most Victorian histories lacked *les grandes entrées:* "they are writing, at the best
from the muniment room, at the worst from the servants' hall. Mr.
Strachey has much to answer for." (Could this help to explain the
epigraph—a "Victorian Precept"—which Young was to put on the
title page of his book: "Servants talk about People: Gentlefolk discuss
Things"?) Thus *Portrait of an Age* came to serve a polemical as well
as a scholarly purpose: to supply sympathetic insight into the historical
significance of the Victorian age as a counterweight to fashionable
raillery and emotional antipathy. The polemical note, though less stridently sounded than in Young's early essay, can still be heard in the
later and more finished work; as in Young's comment to the effect
that "much nonsense about 'the Victorians' is dissipated by the reflection that it was the French Government that prosecuted *Madame
Bovary*"; and, perhaps above all, in the accompanying tone of exasperation: "I read constantly that the Victorians did this and the Victorians believed that; as if they had all lived within the sound of the
town-crier's bell, and at all times behaved, and thought, and worshipped with the disciplined unanimity of a city state on a holy day."

Young's own difficulty was to find anything—besides representative institutions and the family—on which the Victorians agreed;
any assumption that was not at some time or other fiercely challenged.
There was, for Young, something strange about the fact that

Victoria should, by the accident of a youthful accession and a long reign, have been chosen to give her name to an age, to impose an illusory show of continuity and uniformity on a tract of time where men and manners, science and philosophy, the fabric of life and its directing ideas, changed more swiftly perhaps, and more profoundly, than they have ever changed in an age not sundered by a political or a religious upheaval.

And if we ask, as confronted with this annotated edition of an essay now over forty years old we must ask, why it has retained its power and its readability, the answer is largely to be found in the manner in which Young was able both to identify the nature of those changes and to write about them in such a way that the reader seems to become an actual participant in as well as an observer of that shifting flux of ideas and institutions that constitutes the process of history. Like his idol Gibbon, Young was not afflicted with false modesty, and he was quite right when he noted, some years after it had appeared, that "my *Portrait of an Age* differs from most other works on that oceanic theme in that it was written wholly from the inside."

After all, born in 1882 (he died in 1959), Young had still been able to catch a glimpse of Gladstone, his face "half eagle, half lion"; had been taken during the dock strike of 1889 to see the Thames crowded reach after reach with shipping that could not be unloaded; had caught sight of the queen twice; and "my earliest recollection of the Abbey brings back the flowers fresh on Browning's grave." But if personal experience alone produced excellent historians, the world's libraries would be bursting at the seams with masterworks. What Young brought to his task, apart from a few vivid memories of the 1880s and 1890s, was a formidable intelligence buttressed by a classical education, a particularly fruitful interest—fostered by his own career—in administrative and educational history, and, above all, familiarity with many of the sources of nineteenth-century English social, cultural, and political history. His knowledge ranged from the major and minor poets, novelists, and writers of prose to the parliamentary papers, reports of assorted boards and committees, to memoirs and miscellaneous periodical and ephemeral literature. It seemed to cover almost the entire range of life as it was led during the Victorian age by all sorts and conditions of men and women.

Young also brought to his task a command of English style which, for all its allusiveness, enabled him to express matters of the utmost complexity with clarity and to vary the pace of his narrative with

memorable flashes of affectionate irony. As one rereads the *Portrait*—
and it is one of those few works to which one returns time and again
with an anticipation that is never disappointed—one encounters certain sentences as if they were old friends:

> The greater part of what passes for diplomatic history is little
> more than the record of what one clerk said to another.

> On one of its sides, Victorian history is the story of the English
> mind employing the energy imparted by Evangelical conviction
> to rid itself of the restraints which Evangelicalism had laid on
> the senses and the intellect; on amusement, enjoyment, art; on
> curiosity, on criticism, on science.

> Of all decades in our history, a wise man would choose the eight-
> een-fifties to be young in.

(All of the above, by the way, pass one of the supreme tests of historical prose for that rather special group of people who must spend
a certain proportion of their time setting and grading examinations.
What wonderful questions these quotations have often made—and
will presumably continue to make!)

> Born in 1800, in a Lancashire farmhouse where the children were
> washed all over, every day, the mainspring of Chadwick's career
> seems to have been a desire to wash the people of England all
> over, every day, by administrative order.

> When Wellington said on the morrow of the [Birmingham Char-
> tist] riots that no town sacked in war presented such a spectacle
> as Birmingham, he did not mean that he had gone to see it for
> himself, any more than when Lord Shaftesbury said that *Ecce
> Homo* was the foulest book ever vomited from the jaws of hell,
> he meant that he had read all the others.

As one observes and admires the learning that informs Young's (163)
pages, a learning now displayed in all its panoply in Kitson Clark's
footnotes (206 pages), one is quite willing to believe that Young *had*
read all the others, at least all those published in England in the nineteenth century; and had put the information he derived from them at
the service of what he defined as the ultimate task of which the historian is capable, that of presenting as best he can a picture of the past

as it strikes him, the individual observer. Like Burckhardt before him, Young was convinced that events and personalities in history could, indeed must, be seen from different points of view.

His own portrait of Victorian England is really a triptych. Its first panel depicts the 1830s and 1840s, still part of the post-Waterloo generation, a period full of tensions and dislocations due to rapid increase of population and to social and economic crises resulting in part from industrialization. It was a period marked by constant threats of subversion and, possibly, revolution. In the face of this danger from below, Evangelical and Utilitarian attitudes worked hand in hand to supply for both bourgeoisie and clerisy a creed of duty, self-restraint, and respectability. The Reform Act of 1832 was meant to fortify the state by admitting the bulk of the respectable classes to the franchise. Philanthropy, too, was intended to some extent to act as a means of social control. It helped to lessen the shock of bad times. But private endeavor proved to be insufficient. The state had to intervene, and, thanks in large part to the Benthamites, it increasingly did; whether through centralized inspectorates, health and education codes, or factory acts to control hours of labor. Indeed, Young sees the Factory Act of 1847 rather than the repeal of the Corn Laws during the previous year as the crucial turning point: "The cataclysm of 1830 proved to have been the beginning of a slow evolution, by which, while an aristocratic fabric was quietly permeated with Radical ideas, an individualistic society was unobtrusively schooled in the ways of State control."

To the turbulent 1830s and 1840s succeeded the stable 1850s and 1860s. Economic prosperity helped to create a brief period of equipoise which saw the growth of a respectable and nonthreatening working class as well as a relaxation of discipline on the part of those in power. A new middle-class patriciate emerged, a far cry from the austere constraints of the previous age. The universities were doing their part in civilizing the plutocracy. Meanwhile, civil servants, municipal administrators, engineers, and doctors were coming into their own. "Released from fear and insecurity, the English mind was recovering its power to speculate, to wonder and to enjoy. The dissolvent elements in Early Victorian thought, romance and humour and curiosity, the Catholicism of Oxford, the satire of Dickens, the passion of Carlyle; the large historic vision of Grote and Lyell and Arnold, were beginning to work." A knowledgeable middle-class public took an active role in discussing the works and ideas of the great figures of the age—Mill, Macaulay, Newman, Tennyson, Darwin, Ruskin among them—who lent both power and a special lustre to this age of equipoise.

But the third and final act, tragic in outcome as far as Young was concerned, was about to begin: and that he depicted on the third panel of his triptych. Agnosticism, aesthetic revolt, agricultural depression, new military and economic threats from abroad, socialism, imperialism—these are some of the major forces marking the breakup of an equilibrium that turned out to be quite brief. To be sure, there were some hopeful portents. In the professions and the universities women were at last beginning to come into their own. Knowledge about how to limit families was becoming more widespread and, more important, increasingly used. But the Irish problem loomed ever more largely, without a real solution. And the century's end witnessed what Young felt most keenly, the failure within the Victorian public of that disinterested intelligence which during the century's middle decades had begun to operate so well over the whole range of human life and circumstance. Now, "the English mind sank towards that easily excited, easily satisfied, state of barbarism and childhood which press and politics for their own ends fostered, and on which in turn they fed."

It hardly needs saying that this is not the only way to look at nineteenth-century England. Some, keeping in mind W. L. Burn's marvelous *Age of Equipoise,* may feel that there existed more tensions than Young allows for in that period. Others may fault him for not sufficiently concentrating on the working-class view of things or for underrating the more positive aspects of the late Victorian decades. Young explicitly called his portrait a personal one, and would have been the first to recognize the legitimacy of other angles of vision, though he might not have agreed with them.

What does need saying is how difficult it is to do even partial justice to the thickness of Young's texture in a brief and necessarily inadequate summary. So much has been written about the period since his book was first published that we now accept as commonplaces ideas and suggestions that were very far from routine forty years ago. Young's emphasis on the importance of the family and the role of women in the Victorian age; his insistence that the major currents of the time needed to be seen within a European context; his stress on the continuing strength of the aristocracy, the vital role of the private MP, the significance of the contrast between Manchester and Birmingham; above all, perhaps, his awareness of the fact that many of the really heroic figures of the time were unsung civil servants and administrators—men like Leonard Horner, Southwood Smith, Tre- menheere, Simon, and Kay-Shuttleworth—all these things we take for granted today, in great part because a good deal of subsequent work has proceeded along lines first indicated by Young. Not to men- tion some of his incidental insights, usually to be found in his Gib- bonian footnotes: e.g., his suggestion that it was phrenology that helped to keep the idea of personality alive under the steamroller of respectability, or that the first "Old —an," so called, turns out, not unexpectedly, to have attended Rugby.

To identify and to chronicle major elements of change in a period as complex as the Victorian age is hard enough. What is even harder is to accomplish this in such a way that the reader is enabled to observe the changes that are taking place from at least three vantage points: that of the historian writing about them several generations after they took place; that of the generations that came before; and that of a contemporary living at the time those changes actually made them- selves felt. To have carried off this feat successfully is, to my mind, G. M. Young's real triumph. His very first sentence—"A boy born in 1810, in time to have seen the rejoicings after Waterloo and the canal boats carrying the wounded to hospital, to remember the crowds cheering for Queen Caroline, and to have felt that the light had gone out of the world when Byron died, entered manhood with the ground rocking under his feet as it had rocked in 1789"—deftly manages to place the reader into the midst of time passing; and, from then on, he remains caught up in the dilemmas and uncertainties of the Vic- torians, always under the firm guidance of an author who, of course, knows very well how he wants it all to come out, but who, by skillful sleight of hand, creates the illusion of uncertainty about what comes next, one of the real secrets of historical narrative at its best.

I can think of no other piece of historical writing in which the contingent, the possible, the conditional aspects of those changes of mood and atmosphere which, according to Young, underlie all other changes, have been better conveyed. Young's manipulation of tenses and question marks is never less than masterly: "In the sixties even well-disposed men might wonder anxiously whether the Church was still the bulwark it had once been against Popery and Infidelity." "Few could have guessed through what misery the country would have to pass before the clouds lifted again." "Birmingham . . . where old Radicalism might in one decade flower into a lavish Socialism, in another into a pugnacious Imperialism." "If we put to ourselves the question—of all the doings of the mid-seventies which in the long run mattered most?—we might find that our difficulty lay in deciding between the municipal administration of Chamberlain and the industrial legislation of Cross."

Young's preoccupation with the "ifs" of Victorian history and his clever use of certain phrases—"first mutterings," "tidal surge," "chill in the air," "taint in the air," "creeping in," "subtle shift," "temperature is rising," are just a few examples—contribute to the vividness and immediacy with which he is able to depict changes and transformations. So does the way in which he continually switches the angle of vision from himself to old people he knows remembering the past, to contemporaries looking backwards and forwards, and then back to himself again. In his early essay on Victorian history, Young recommended to students that a study of the methods used by the great historians might do more for them than five years in the Public Record Office. Those heeding his advice might well make *Portrait of an Age* a part of their course of reading.

If they do so, they will find it a much easier task than it was before, thanks to Kitson Clark, his two chief assistants, D. R. Fisher and J. M. Collinge (both of whom, along with R. Robson, saw the present edition through the press), and no less than thirty-five other experts on the Victorian period who helped to track down almost all of Young's references and allusions. Young's own footnotes are amusing and informative, but they neither refer to his sources nor identify quotations and allusions. This omission has challenged and exasperated two generations of readers. As far as Kitson Clark himself was concerned, this annotated edition originated as "a game to be pursued by myself and my friends in the intervals of what seemed to be more important work." The desirability of publishing the results was, it appears, first brought home to him when he found that he and other university teachers of nineteenth-century English history had trouble in getting young men and women to read *Portrait of an Age*. This reluctance, Kitson Clark felt, had something to do with the feeling on the part of those students that Young's failure to supply references and full quotations was intended as a mark of superiority on the part of the author: "This was no doubt unfair on Young, but if this was what was thought, it seemed possible that to publish as many references as could be identified might restore the essay's usefulness, as it would also be of use as a starting point for research."

And so Kitson Clark set to work in earnest. He himself was, of course, one of the most knowledgeable students of Victorian history of his time; and it is perhaps the greatest tribute *Portrait of an Age* has received that this distinguished scholar spent what turned out to be the last years of his life (he died in 1975) tracking down Young's references. The phrase *veritatis cupidus,* which forms part of his epitaph in the antechapel of Trinity College, Cambridge, is indeed an appropriate commemoration of such an unselfish activity which, for all the pleasures of the chase, must often have proved laborious and sometimes frustrating.

The edition we now have begins with an evocative biographical memoir of Young by Sir George Clark. That is followed by Kitson Clark's own introduction, which is in turn followed by G. M. Young's preface to the second edition of *Portrait of an Age* (1953). That is reprinted in its entirety, in thirty-one sections, with Arabic numerals in the margins of each page indicating the footnotes by Kitson Clark and his helpers. These are printed, in groups corresponding to Young's sections, at the end of the volume. Apart from two printer's errors (repetitions of words on pages 88 and 153) the text reads clearly and cleanly. There is a minimum of inconvenience in referring to the new notes.

What about these notes? They are of various kinds. Some merely identify persons or supply complete and correct documentary quotations where Young, who often relied on his memory alone, quoted fragments only, and those sometimes incorrectly. Many notes go further and refer to relevant scholarly work which has appeared since the publication of Young's book. In some cases, as, for example, the electoral situation after 1832, Kitson Clark then indicates how such work has changed generally accepted views. Young's mistakes—and he made a good many, perhaps, as Kitson Clark suggests, because he did not check his references—are corrected. Some are more serious than others. Certainly, loyal readers of *Portrait of an Age* will want to know that Mary Russell Mitford was publicly rebuked not for calling a pudding a roly-poly, but for applying that word to the innocent beauty of two coursing bitches, "like that of a roly-poly child."

Occasionally, Kitson Clark takes issue with Young's emphases or expresses his own skepticism about Young's interpretations. Thus he believes that Young overestimated the importance of the Evangelicals in 1830 and in one or two passages treated the High Church party unfairly. He is also doubtful about how much difference it would really have made to the history of Europe, *pace* Young, if Robert Morier had stayed in Berlin as British Ambassador from 1866 to 1870. Once or twice, on matters where he himself has particular knowledge, such as the role of the civil servant in the early nineteenth century,

Kitson Clark supplies his own essay in miniature, in the form of a lengthy note serving to elucidate Young's statements or put them into historical context.

At least once he permits himself the well-earned luxury of contributing to that stock of irrelevant trivia of which most students of the Victorian age can never quite get enough. We now know that the undertaker William Banting, who was *not* the undertaker William Banting who took it upon himself to apply a fresh coat of paint to the Coronation Chair at the Jubilee celebrations of 1887, was so corpulent that he was unable to tie his shoes before he reached the age of sixty; tried exercise, Turkish baths, and medicines without success; but, as a result of a special diet, finally lost so much weight and enjoyed such improved health that he described his experiences in *A Letter on Corpulence* (1863) which introduced the word "to bant" into the language and thus into the *OED*.

Each note bears under it the initials of that person who helped to track it down, the great majority of them the three letters GKC. They testify to his enormous labors and to his devotion to getting things right. One could object to one (the Headmaster of Eton's reply to a question put to him by the Clarendon Commission) that it creates more rather than less work for the reader; to another (on Chamberlain and the Jameson Raid) that it fails to take account of much recent writing on the subject; to yet another (on Bishop Colenso) that it supplies additional information not strictly relevant to what Young wrote. But that would be quibbling in a situation where admiration and gratitude are due above all; in the first instance to Kitson Clark, but, in the end, just as much to G. M. Young, whose work triumphantly survives even the most rigorous procedures of forensic medicine. That work is now intellectually accessible to all, and one can only hope that the Oxford University Press will put it into paperback promptly so that it may become physically accessible as well. For who, apart from libraries, can pay the price now charged?

An occasion for rejoicing, then. And I hope it will not be considered churlish if, echoing the sentiment of Peel's translation of *suave mari magno—suave:* "it is a source of melancholy satisfaction" (or, in the alternative version of Peel's translation supplied by Kitson Clark: "it is a source of gratification")—I conclude with the news that some of Young's allusions have thus far resisted the combined efforts of two-score Victorian scholars, with Kitson Clark at their head. Those who have always found the mysteriously allusive quality of Young's essay one of its greatest attractions can still wonder where Byron expressed his disapproval of mixed bathing, "even when the parties are married"; on what occasion Gladstone called the English habit of deference "a sneaking kindness for a lord"; and who that Liberal adherent was who ambiguously described the Newcastle Programme of 1891 as "a Blooming Plant." That, come to think of it, is perhaps not such a bad description (and one meant quite unambiguously) of what G. M. Young's *Portrait of an Age,* newly fertilized by Kitson Clark and his assistants, continues to be. Long may it flourish!

IV

CONTEXT
AND
COMPARISON

The Social Background of the Scottish Renaissance

The question of the origin of the "Scottish Renaissance"—that remarkable efflorescence of the mid-eighteenth century, with its roll call of great names: Hume, Smith, Robertson, Kames, and Ferguson—is one of those historical problems that have hitherto stubbornly resisted a definite solution. This is not to imply that attempted explanations have failed to be forthcoming. On the contrary, ever since a learned Italian named Carlo Deanina applied himself to the problem in *An Essay on the Progress of Learning among the Scots* (1763), historians have suggested different reasons for that striking and apparently sudden outburst of creative energy. Macaulay saw the principal cause for what he considered to have been "this wonderful change" from the barren wastes of seventeenth-century theology in the act passed by the Estates of Scotland in 1696 which was designed to enforce previous legislation setting up a school in every parish. Buckle, sounding a suitably Darwinian note, observed the energies displayed in the Scottish political and religious struggles of the seventeenth century surviving those struggles and finding another field in which they could exert themselves.

There is something to be said for both these points of view. The

From *Scotland in the Age of Improvement,* edited by N. T. Phillipson and Rosalind Mitchison (Edinburgh, 1970)

national system of education, though in practice never quite as ideal as in conception, enabled many a poor father's boy to go on to one of the universities as well prepared as his socially superior classmates. Nor can it be denied that in spite of the Fifteen and the Forty-five the general atmosphere of eighteenth-century Scotland was more conducive to peaceful pursuits than that of the strife-torn decades of the seventeenth century. But it requires no more than a little reflection on cultural history to perceive that neither peace nor public education, nor their conjunction, guarantees the intellectual achievements suggested by the word "renaissance."

Similar objections can be advanced concerning some of the other so-called "causes" of Scotland's golden age. Thus it is certainly true that the eighteenth century, in contrast to the seventeenth, was for Scotland a period of increasing economic prosperity. However, the disastrous Darien scheme of the 1690s ate up that capital fuel without which even the most rigorous Protestant ethic could not become economically efficacious. The immediate effect of the Union of 1707 was not the expected sudden prosperity, but, rather, increased taxation and loss of French trade. Nor, until much later, was there a compensatory expansion of commerce with England and the colonies. Real economic advancement did not come until later in the century, too late to serve as a satisfactory reason for the first stages of Scotland's great creative period.[1]

The Union, of course, had effects more immediate than those in the economic field. It was not only the sixteen Peers and forty-five Members of Parliament making the annual pilgrimage to London who acquired English tastes and aped English fashions. Scottish society did not want to lag behind its southern counterpart, and the tremendous popularity of London literary periodicals among its members exemplifies only one of the countless means by which English cultural influence reached the North. What a mere listing of English influences leaves unexplained, however, is the high degree of receptiveness to those influences, which might, after all, have fallen on barren ground. That school of thought which sees Scotland "forced back upon herself" by the Union avoids this problem by laying prime stress on the vernacular revival and the strength of native Scottish literary tradition. There is no gainsaying the importance of a tradition that helped to inspire Ramsay, Macpherson, Burns, and Scott. But it must be remembered that their achievements were part of a literary production bifurcated throughout in terms of "pure" English and Scottish vernacular.[2]

As for the influence of "New Light" Hutcheson, his Glasgow lectures—effusions on the marvelous powers of the "moral sense" by an enthusiastic disciple of Shaftesbury—no doubt "contributed very powerfully to diffuse, in Scotland, that taste for analytical discussion and that spirit of liberal enquiry, to which the world is indebted for some of the most valuable productions of the eighteenth century."[3] But holding them solely responsible for the Scottish enlightenment is surely expecting a little too much, even from the most lucid philosopher. Furthermore, it is worth noting that after Hutcheson's first year at Glasgow, at least one contemporary observer singled him out for praise because he was maintaining the cause of orthodox Christianity in a university shot through with free thought. The fact is that by the time Hutcheson began his lectures, considerable breaches had already been made in the dam of orthodox austerity so laboriously constructed during the embattled decades of the previous century.

Adequate explanations of the origins of the Scottish Renaissance, therefore, must take account not only of a variety of social factors at the moment of fullest flowering, but also of the conditions of growth in the previous period. It is always dangerous to confuse origins and causes, but a knowledge of the former often helps to elucidate the latter. To what extent had enlightened ideas broken through Presbyterian orthodoxy by 1729, the year of Hutcheson's appointment? Did this process date from the Union, or had it begun before? What kind of people were interested in secular intellectual activities? What was the role of the Scottish Kirk and the Universities in these developments? The city of Edinburgh is bound to be the principal focus for seeking answers to such questions. For one thing, it is well to keep in mind Lecky's caution that intellectual currents such as Moderatism in the Church were almost wholly confined to the big cities; so that, for instance, over the greater part of Scotland, the empire of the old Kirk was little shaken in the course of the eighteenth century.[4] For another, Edinburgh remained, even after 1707, the administrative, legal, ecclesiastical, and intellectual center of Scotland, a position which could be disputed only by the growing commercial wealth and the influential university teaching of Glasgow. Studying the genesis of eighteenth-century Edinburgh culture is thus really tantamount to studying the origins of the Scottish enlightenment.

Any such study—and here no more is intended than to suggest possible lines of investigation—would have to begin with the consideration that apart from David Hume there were no professional men of letters in eighteenth-century Scotland. We find Dugald Stew-

art, in his *Life of Robertson,* commenting on the fact that in the 1730s
the trade of authorship was unknown in Scotland, and that her high
rank among the learned nations of Europe had, for many years, been
sustained entirely "by a small number of eminent men, who distinguished themselves by an honourable and disinterested zeal in the
ungainful walks of abstract science."[5] Boswell, writing in 1763, noted
after a supper with Johnson and Goldsmith that "I had curious ideas
when I considered that I was sitting with London authors by profession."[6] The main reason for the difference between Scotland and England in this regard is not far to seek. The Scottish reading public was
not sufficiently large for the support of professional authors; and,
whereas in London patrons and booksellers had in turn assumed a
tutelary function—with authors bound to them in varying degrees
and often in unsavory fashion, but free to devote their entire time to
writing—in Edinburgh literature remained, for the most part, the by-
product of men engaged in other professions. Lawyers, professors,
and clergymen produced most of the outstanding literary works of
the Scottish Enlightenment.

Of the three, the lawyers undoubtedly played the most important
role. Not only do individual names, such as Mackenzie, Kames, Monboddo, Scott, Jeffrey, and Brougham, indicate the significance of the
legal profession for Scottish literary history. But lawyers and judges
of lesser renown contributed as much through their active interest in
literature and philosophy which formed part of their continuous concern for intellectual and cultural pursuits, a concern that befitted their
aristocratic class standing in Edinburgh society. Peter Williamson's
first *Edinburgh Directory* (1773–1774), which listed citizens in an order
of rank originally sanctioned in 1532, was headed by Lords of Session,
Advocates, Writers to the Signet, and Lords' and Advocates' Clerks,
in that sequence. The category of "noblemen and gentlemen" followed after.[7] It must, of course, be remembered that both the Faculty
of Advocates and the Writers to the Signet were closed corporations
of gentlemen, with high entrance fees and exclusive regulations. Dr.
Phillipson has shown that between 1707 and 1751, 96 percent of en-
trants to the Faculty of Advocates came either from landed families
or from families with close landed connections. The corresponding
percentage for the period 1752–1811 was almost as high, i.e., 88 percent.[8] In any event, because Scotland kept her own legal system after
the Union, and the principal Law Courts were located in Edinburgh,

judges and lawyers there possessed an importance that transcended their rank by birth.

Such a desirable profession naturally attracted a great many unsuccessful aspirants. An English visitor to Edinburgh, writing shortly after the publication of Williamson's *Directory,* commented on the "almost innumerable" number of gentlemen styled advocates, few of whom had much business. He added, more acerbly than accurately, that "every man who has nothing to do, and no better name to give himself, is called advocate."[9] One wonders whether this same observer, who declared himself vastly impressed with the literary attainments of Edinburgh society, was aware of the intimate, though hardly illicit, connection between the Law and the Muses that had long characterized the city.

A good example of this connection is provided by an analysis of the membership of the Select Society, founded in 1754 for the dual purpose of philosophical inquiry and improvement in public speaking. By 1759 this society had come to include all the Edinburgh literati, in addition to many of the nobility and gentry. A membership list of that year totaled 135, of whom 119 can readily be identified by profession. Of these at least forty were associated with the law in one way or the other.[10] A generation earlier, the membership list of the Rankenian Club, a philosophical society of "learned and respectable men" founded in 1716, had included five lawyers as against only four university professors.[11] Is there any explanation for this affinity between Scottish law and Scottish culture? Why did the lawyers indeed constitute "a body of men who in Scotland had all along taken a decided lead in matters of taste and literature"?[12]

In dedicating his *Institutions of the Laws of Scotland* to Charles II (in 1681) Viscount Stair, perhaps the greatest legal mind produced in Scotland during the seventeenth century, made the proud boast that Scottish law could be compared to any in the world, noting that "those that applied themselves to that profession amongst us, have given great evidence of sharp and piercing Spirits, with much Readiness of Conception and Dexterity of Expression."[13] He might have added that it was not just the professional lawyers who concerned themselves with the study of Scottish law. An edict by James I (of Scotland) and an Act of Parliament under James IV had decreed that all barons and freeholders must have their oldest sons instructed in the law.[14] The tradition, thus dating back to the fifteenth and sixteenth centuries, which linked the Scottish gentry with the attainment of legal knowledge and which, in this way, helped to give the law such an influential place in society, was steadily carried on; so that Blackstone, in 1758, could single out Scotland as a place where "it is difficult to meet with a person of liberal education, who is destitute of competent knowledge in that science which is to be the guardian of the natural rights and the rule of his civil conduct."[15] He made a contrast between Scotland and England in this respect and connected the more pervasive role played by the law in the national life of "the northern parts of our own island" with the fact that municipal laws were there frequently related to the civil (i.e., Roman) laws. And there is no doubt about the crucial significance of this relationship for the theme of this essay.

Roman Law came to Scotland mainly at second hand from French practitioners and the French courts, through Scottish students who studied in France in the course of the sixteenth century.[16] On the one hand, it is well to guard against overestimating its influence: though Scottish municipal law was in many respects founded upon it, the instances in which customs and statutes differed from it were in fact so numerous that it could be said that to understand Justinian was far less difficult than to perceive his application to Scottish practice.[17] On the other hand, the undoubted emphasis placed upon Roman Law in the training and qualification of Scottish lawyers meant that many law students pursued their studies on the Continent, first mainly in France, later in Holland, and were thus exposed to the intellectual influences current there. A reliable estimate reveals that between 1600 and 1800 approximately sixteen hundred Scottish students (many of them future lawyers) studied at the University of Leyden alone, the greater number during the latter part of the seventeenth century.[18]

The continental course in "natural jurisprudence" made for a close association of legal studies with moral philosophy and political science, and brought a philosophical and scientific tinge into the realm of Scottish law.[19] The influence of Grotius and Thomasius is particularly important in this context, since it tended towards a humanistic rationalism alien to the prevailing intellectual temper of seventeenth-century Scotland, and since it helped to cement a fruitful union between law and philosophy at the Scottish universities. It is of some significance that Hutcheson's predecessor at Glasgow, Gershon Carmichael, edited Grotius (1724), and that Hutcheson's own lectures on moral philosophy can be said "to form perhaps the most complete view of legal philosophy of the time."[20]

Grotius had carried his secularism so far as to assert that the laws of reason would remain valid, even if no God existed.[21] Stair, whose

Institutions long remained the most influential commentary on Scottish law, was a militant Presbyterian, in spirit far removed from the Dutch jurist; though, significantly enough, he had begun his career as a regent in philosophy at the University of Glasgow. Stair denied the validity of the Decalogue for all nations and all times not because Roman Law had taken its place, but because man's "pravity" had so much increased vice and deceit since then that what had been sufficient in the simplicity of the time of the Old Testament now fell short of what was needed. Stair specifically cited Grotius in support of the doctrine of law as a rational discipline, having principles from which its conclusions could be deduced; and, exalting law as the dictate of reason, he adduced the argument that even God chose to determine Himself by His goodness, righteousness, and truth.[22] But Peter Stein has acutely observed that Stair differs from continental natural lawyers such as Grotius and Pufendorf in maintaining that a rational theory of law cannot be independent of theological assumptions. Law is founded primarily in the will of God. Reason remains a subsidiary instrument. Logic has its limits. No legal system can dispense with authority. Law is neither entirely logic nor entirely experience, but a mysterious mixture of the two. Professor Stein points out that Stair was only the first of a succession of Scottish legists who challenged natural law theory and thus paved the way for a sociohistorical conception of the law.[23]

The study of Roman Law and the study of history were in any event in close alliance. In 1689, when Sir George Mackenzie delivered his inaugural address at the opening of the Advocates' Library in Edinburgh—while the town was swarming with his Whig enemies—he declared that this library was to be purely legal, differing in this way from all other libraries. Nevertheless, historical works had to be included, as essential adjuncts of legal studies.[24] It was thus entirely appropriate that in 1719 the Faculty of Advocates sponsored the appointment of Charles Macky, a lawyer, as the first Professor of Civil History in the University of Edinburgh. The names of Hume, Robertson, and Ferguson bear witness to the important place of history in eighteenth-century Scottish letters. The Scottish Bar can rightly claim a share in planting the seed from which these fruits were to spring.

The share Edinburgh lawyers had in the appointment of a history professor in 1719 did not mark the first such contact between the university and the legal profession. In 1590, only a few years after the founding of the College of Edinburgh, Lords of Session, Advocates, and Writers to the Signet joined the Town Council in making provision for a professor of law.[25] But the appointees under this grant never taught law, perhaps because the ministers of Edinburgh followed the example of the Venerable Pastors of Geneva who had remonstrated strongly against the law faculty there, and had singled out the dissolute habits of the young men of quality who wanted to study under that faculty.[26] Whatever the reason, the failure of this project is indicative of the failures that were to mar Scottish university education during the seventeenth century. In the *First Book of Discipline* the early Scottish reformers had made radical proposals for the improvement of higher education, but these were never carried into effect. The Scottish nobility and gentry generally went abroad to study; the majority of the student body at the College of Edinburgh consisted of theological students "from the middling ranks of society"; and the quality of learning in the School for Theological Studies is reliably described as "very slight."[27]

To what extent can the Kirk of Scotland be held responsible for the low state of higher education during the seventeenth century? Can that revisionist history which has exonerated the New England Puritans from obscurantism be made to yield the same results for the Scottish Presbyterians? It must certainly be granted that there is no ineluctable antithesis between Calvinism and secular culture; though Max Weber's reference to its fundamental antagonism to sensuous culture of all kinds does have particular validity for Scotland. What must be kept in mind, however, is the fact that the spiritual distance between Geneva and the Scottish Kirk remained far smaller than that, say, between Geneva and English Puritanism. The fundamental and irreconcilable conflict between the English Independents and the Scottish Presbyterians illustrates one aspect of a difference which, as Tawney suggested, may have "depended, above all, on the question whether Calvinists were, as at Geneva and in Scotland, a majority, who could stamp their ideals on the social order, or, as in England, a minority, living on the defensive beneath the suspicious eyes of a hostile government."[28]

It may be argued that even an authoritarian theocracy can buttress itself with learning; and that the classics can be persuaded to declare the glory of the Lord even as the Heavens. But perhaps on account of its embattled state, perhaps because its original alliance with the nobility was only briefly resumed during the seventeenth century, the Scottish Kirk, for most of that century, constituted an inhibiting force in matters of culture and learning. The universities naturally tried to free themselves from this inhibition. Thus a joint Universities Commission, in 1647, advocated freedom from church control in all except ecclesiastical matters, and drew up a uniform course of studies. But the last sentence of one of the reform proposals submitted reveals the fate of all of them: "This is to be understood ordinarily, and in peaceable tymes."[29]

If the Church of Scotland is to be held solely responsible for the low state of university education, it is only proper to ask whether the period of the Restoration produced any remarkable changes for the better. To raise this question is to open up a complicated field of inquiry that will yield no simple answers. If one is to believe Dr. Alexander Monro, Episcopalian Principal of the University of Edinburgh from 1685 to 1690, those years in particular were a golden time, "when the government of the city of Edinburgh was lodged in the hands of the first and best order of citizens and gentlemen"—note this social emphasis!—and the Masters of the College "had all the encouragement they themselves could wish," guarded by the magistrates against "the little efforts of censorious and talkative Fanaticks."[30] Monro is no unprejudiced witness; since, in 1690, he, along with four other professors, was dismissed from the University as a nonjuror. It is, nonetheless, undeniable that a certain upswing took place during the seventies and eighties, especially in the sciences. By 1690 David Gregory had begun to lecture on Newton, thus making the University of Edinburgh the first in all Europe where the *Principia* were publicly taught; and Sir Robert Sibbald had established the Medical School, soon to become justly famed far beyond Scotland. Before their day the Scottish universities had hardly concerned themselves with science.[31] The fact that neither Gregory nor Sibbald was a Presbyterian may serve as a warning to those who would apply too readily to Scotland Robert Merton's thesis in regard to the elective affinities between Puritanism and science in seventeenth-century England.[32]

Yet to conclude from this that the new winds of doctrine that were blowing so hard all over Europe during the last four decades of the seventeenth century left the Scottish Presbyterians unaffected would be inaccurate. The Kirk itself was changing in character, especially in the course of the second half of the century; approximating less and less to the ideal type postulated by Buckle. Hume Brown writes about the "mighty force of Presbyterianism," broken by repression and concession, the latter in the form of three Indulgences (1669; 1672; 1679) issued by Charles II that were accepted by the majority of the Presbyterian clergy. In so doing these ministers compromised the essential principles of their creed—by accepting the king's supremacy—but supplied a potent stimulant for the idea of toleration.[33] Meanwhile, the more liberal currents of Dutch theology had begun to exert increased influence, specifically the *De Veritate Religionis Christianae* of Grotius, whose steadily growing popularity foreshadowed the intellectual orientation of the eighteenth-century Moderates in the Church of Scotland.[34]

The main argument against crediting Episcopalians alone with the new spirit of the universities, which found one means of expression in the falling off in attendance at "dictation" sessions by students dissatisfied with the antiquated teaching methods, is the continuance of this spirit after the reestablishment of Presbyterianism. This is not to say that the difference between the two confessions had by then disappeared. On the contrary: while during the period of the Restoration their liturgical disagreements had been remarkably small, these were greatly intensified after the Revolution Settlement, when the Episcopalians "drifted in a definitely English direction."[35] And there was no lack of occasion for conflict in the political and social realms. But Covenanting days and ways were over. A man such as William Carstares, elected Principal of Edinburgh University in 1703, exemplifies this change. Though twice tortured with "thumbikins" for his knowledge of the Rye House Plot, he continued to count several Jacobites among his close friends. His great dream was of a revival of learning through the importation of professors from abroad; and although he was unable to accomplish this, under his administration the university curriculum was increasingly modelled on that of Utrecht and Leyden, the old "regenting" system being replaced by formal lectures.[36]

Glasgow University, meanwhile, had begun to send its theology students to Holland on an increasingly large scale, usually for postgraduate studies.[37] One of the results was a greater spirit of tolerance, which made itself felt in frank theological discussion. To observe the extent to which this tendency developed in a relatively brief time it is instructive to examine the comments of the Rev. Robert Wodrow, a Presbyterian of the old school, on the activities and attitudes of Edinburgh and Glasgow University students in the mid-1720s; remembering that this was some years before Hutcheson "officially" inaugurated the Scottish enlightenment.

In December 1724, Wodrow (not one to take these matters lightly) noted that the divinity students at Glasgow were openly opposing the Confession of Faith; that there was much reading of Deists and anti-Confessionists; and that thirty to forty students, finding these conditions unbearable, were reputed to have left for Edinburgh. He added that the professor (of theology) allowed the students "lightness and liberty of speaking."[38] A few months later (February 1725) Wodrow once again voiced concern over Glasgow where student clubs were debating such questions as "the role of moral goodness" and "whether God could make the sun better than it is"; where other clubs ventured to "declare against reading, and cry up thinking"; and where, *horribile dictu,* a farce about the ministers of the town had been composed. Little more than a year after this, accounts reached Wodrow of atheistical clubs in Edinburgh, meeting very secretly, and taking their origin from a Hell-fire club in London. Wodrow's comment about all this was succinct and to the point: "Wickedness is come to a new height!"[39]

It was not the first time that club life in Edinburgh had supplied material for Wodrow's Jeremiads. In December 1724, in the course of the very month in which the band of pious Glasgow students was reported to have sought the reputedly more orthodox atmosphere of the capital, word had reached him that for some years Edinburgh had been harboring a club whose members, including several ministers, were convinced that "we're in a way of too narrov [*sic*] thinking in this country; and that some of the younger students inclined to have some great freedom of thoughts."[40] This club, as is clear from the names of the members supplied by Wodrow, was none other than the Rankenian Club, the philosophical society whose membership list of nineteen we found to have included five lawyers.[41] The number of clergymen amounted to no less than seven. The old Kirk still had its adherents. But a Presbyterianism mollified to the point where it produced (in Ramsay of Ochtertyre's phrase) "cluster[s] of clerical *literati*" was in the ascendant. An Edinburgh philosophical club consisting mainly of lawyers, ministers, and professors, its membership in sympathy with the desire for greater freedom of thought on the part of university students—there could be no better illustration of the thesis of this essay up to this point. What must be primarily emphasized is the fact that while by the 1720s the cultural results of the Union had certainly begun to take effect, autonomous developments in the realms of the law, the church, and university education, dating back at least as far as the end of the seventeenth century, had done much to prepare the ground for the reception of English influences.[42]

The diffusion of those influences owed a great deal to the Scottish nobility and gentry, especially to those among them not prosperous enough to look on London rather than Edinburgh as their proper metropolis. In the course of the seventeenth century, the old alliance between the Scottish Presbyterians and the nobility had been only

briefly revived. That revival was impelled by Charles I, whose Act
of Revocation (1625) threatened to annex to the Crown all church and
crown lands alienated since the accession of Mary Stuart. The nobles
saw, at this point, that their interests were tied to the anti-Royalist
cause, and a majority of them signed the Covenant of 1678. The General Assembly of the Kirk, in its sittings that year, might have established a moderate Episcopacy, embracing all ranks of the people. But
its intransigence on all issues involving theology and church organization prevented this compromise whose political and cultural results would have been considerable.[43] By mid-century the nobility
found itself still in the possession of its estates; while the Bishops, of
whose new powers it had been jealous, had ceased to exist. From this
time on it drifted away from Presbyterianism; working very hard for
the restoration of Charles II, and, after this had been accomplished,
loyally supporting Episcopacy and the Stuarts. Hume Brown goes so
far as to state that after the Revolution and William's accession, only
one solitary Scottish noble, Crawford, displayed pronounced Presbyterian sympathies.[44] Most of the nobility and a large part of the
gentry certainly remained Episcopalian and—what almost invariably
followed—Jacobite.[45]

In matters of taste, manners, and culture they were thus unencum-
bered by those ascetic proclivities against which even the growing
body of moderate Presbyterians still had to struggle; and this made
it easier for them to supply the essential froth for the potent mixtures
starting to brew around the turn of the century.[46] Their study and
travel abroad had given them at least a modicum of cosmopolitan
propensities, from which Edinburgh derived much benefit. For the
Darien failure left many of them too poor to travel abroad, and
brought them to the capital each winter.[47] They had already played
the principal role in the amusements and—as some said—the excesses
that shocked and delighted the citizens of Edinburgh after the Restoration.[48] And their strong hold on Edinburgh society continued in
spite of the return of Presbyterianism. For their religion was not pro-
scribed; and they were not persecuted for their politics. They kept
alive the spirit of sports, concerts, dancing, gaiety, and general *bon-
homie;* and thus set a tantalizing example for the more liberal-minded
of the Presbyterians.[49]

There is little doubt about the fact that in the years immediately
following the Union, Episcopalianism became increasingly fashionable—perhaps because it was considered an emollient for the painful
wound left by a growing awareness of provincialism. "Such was epis-

copal influence among the professional classes and gentry in the early years of the century," Douglas Duncan writes about the Jacobite Thomas Ruddiman, "that his beliefs seem to have helped rather than hindered his career."[50] As usual, Wodrow found the *mot juste*. There was, he noted, "a disrelishing of Presbyterian Government."[51] Some Presbyterian ministers, seeing which way the wind was blowing, changed their tack: "The peculiar doctrines of Christianity would, they hoped, be more acceptable to the nobility and gentry for being set forth in a language worthy of a Tillotson and an Atterbury whose works were universally admired in those days" (i.e., after 1714).[52] And while a large proportion thus appealed to remained equally loyal to Episcopalianism and Jacobitism, there is a good deal of significance in the strangely sweet modulations with which they were now being enticed. Episcopalianism had already acquired something of the aura which, many years later, impelled Boswell to end a catalogue of the things he wanted most to do during his lifetime with the desire to attend the "Church of England Chapel" in Edinburgh.[53]

The cultural stirrings of the early eighteenth century owed much to the Jacobites, and not just to those of noble birth. Nearly all the Edinburgh printers and booksellers at this time, among them the anthologist James Watson, were Jacobites and Episcopalians.[54] So were two of the most influential figures in the city's intellectual life: Dr. Archibald Pitcairne—physician, wit, and, by repute, close to a freethinker; and Thomas Ruddiman, Librarian of the Advocates' Library, publisher and scholar. One must not forget, furthermore, the debt of the vernacular revival to "disaffection." Opposition to the Union meant an intensified patriotism that found cultural outlets. The works of Ramsay, Burns, and Scott serve as the best illustration of Jacobite influence on Scottish literature.[55]

One reason for the important part played by Jacobites in the cultural life of Edinburgh derives from the fact that this cultural life was largely fostered by gentlemen's clubs and societies, many of whose members were politically "disaffected." The significance of the legal profession for Scottish culture has already been emphasized. In 1707 the great majority of the Faculty of Advocates was strongly attached to the Stuarts, as were most of the Writers to the Signet.[56] Ramsay of Ochtertyre reported that "near a majority" of the Lords and Earls of Session were similarly inclined, and raises the question of how they could reconcile this inclination with their oaths of allegiance. His answer is the cynical one that oaths of allegiance will not make men refuse lucrative and honorable offices.[57] However that may be, the fact that these judges and lawyers, whose political sympathies were, of course, well known, could keep their positions shows that the seventeenth-century atmosphere of struggle and persecution had been largely dissipated. When the Jacobite scholar Thomas Ruddiman founded Edinburgh's first purely literary society, for the purpose of mutual improvement in the classics, the original members declared in their charter that there was to be no meddling with the affairs of Church and State. That this injunction was indeed followed is proved by the membership of the society, which came to include Presbyterian ministers as well as Jacobite lawyers.[58] It may well be taken as symbolic of a new era.

The attempt has been made to show that the cultural revival in Scotland can best be understood in the light of the social and intellectual background of the late seventeenth and early eighteenth centuries; and that this approach yields a clearer view of the causes of that revival than those hitherto set forth, which have generally concentrated on the educational system, the Union of 1707, and assorted mysterious forces. English influence resulting from the Union fell on fertile soil: the Scottish bar constituted a force congenial to new philosophical currents, historical studies, and other intellectual activities. The Kirk had changed greatly since Covenanting days and had begun to develop within itself the roots of that Moderatism that was to come to flower in the course of the eighteenth century. This process went hand in hand with a more liberal spirit among faculty and students at the universities, where curricula and teaching methods had also begun to undergo some improvement. In all these fields Dutch influence, transmitted through the large number of Scottish students at Dutch universities, had a significant and fruitful part to play. A portion of the Scottish nobility and gentry stood ready to foster cultural activities, with Edinburgh as their focus. And these activities owed something to the Episcopalianism and Jacobitism that many of these leading families professed.

One further question should be asked. When the flowering came, did Edinburgh's provincial cultural situation vis-à-vis London serve to inhibit or to enhance it? Throughout the century, certainly, life in Edinburgh was affected by the mere fact of physical removal from the cosmopolitan center. For though the Scottish border lay less than three hundred miles from London, as late as 1763 only one regular stagecoach traveled between Edinburgh and the British capital. The trip took about two weeks, and those few who could afford to make it considered it so serious an expedition that they frequently made their wills before setting out. As far as the English were concerned, Smollett's Mrs. Tabitha, who thought one could get to Scotland only by sea, represented no great advance over those of her countrymen earlier in the century to whom "many parts of Africa and the Indies . . . are better known than a Region which is contiguous to our own, and which we have always had so great a concern for."[59] Even toward the middle of the century, there were occasions when the London mailbag for Edinburgh was found to contain only a single letter.

But isolation, as the late Perry Miller pointed out, "is not a matter of distance or the slowness of communication: it is a question of what a dispatch from distant quarters means to the recipient."[60] News, literature, and personal messages from London did not merely convey information. They carried with them standards by which men and events were judged. In them was involved a definition of sophistication. *Tatlers* and *Spectators* were eagerly devoured in Edinburgh. Scottish ladies ordered all sorts of finery, from dresses to wallpaper, from England. And Wodrow complained that "all the villainous, profane, and obscene books and plays, as printed in London, are got down by Allan Ramsay, and lent out, for an easy price, to young boys, servant weemen of the better sort, and gentlemen."[61]

Communications from England exerted such authority because they fell upon minds conscious of limited awareness. A sense of inferiority pervaded eighteenth-century Scottish culture, affecting the great no less than the common. It lay behind David Hume's lament, in 1756, that "we people in the country (for such you Londoners esteem our city) are apt to be troublesome to you people in town; we are vastly glad to receive letters which convey intelligence to us of things we should otherwise have been ignorant of, and can pay them back with nothing but provincial stories which are in no way interesting." And it led Adam Smith to admit that "this country is so barren of all sorts of transactions that can interest anybody that lives at a distance from it that little intertainment is to be expected from any correspondent on this side of the Tweed." A young Scot returning to Edinburgh after a journey to the continent and London felt he had to "labour to tone myself down like an overstrained instrument to the low pitch of the rest about me."[62]

The manners and idioms that labeled the provincial in England were stigmas that Scotsmen tried strenuously to avoid. There was no subject about which they were more sensitive than their speech. Lieutenant Lismahago may have proved to his own satisfaction that "what we generally called the Scottish dialect was, in fact, true, genuine

English." But Dr. Johnson laughed at Hamilton of Bangour's rhyming "wishes" and "bushes." And when in 1761 Thomas Sheridan, the playwright's father, lectured in Edinburgh (and in Irish brogue) on the art of rhetoric, he had an attentive audience of three hundred nobles, judges, divines, advocates, and men of fashion. Hume kept constantly by his side a list of Scots idioms to be avoided, and was said by Monboddo to have confessed on his deathbed not his sins but his Scotticisms.

The sense of inferiority that expressed itself in imitation of English ways and a sense of guilt regarding local mannerisms were, however, only one aspect of the complex meaning of provincialism. Ramsay of Ochtertyre, for example, inveighed against the slavish imitation of English models as such a confession of inferiority "as one would hardly have expected from a proud manly people, long famous for common-sense and veneration for the ancient classics."[63] Awareness of regional limitations frequently led to a compensatory local pride. It was the conviction that in spite of its "familiarity," life in Edinburgh possessed a congeniality and vigor all its own that made Robertson refuse all invitations to settle in London. Hume, too, in the midst of his Parisian triumphs, longed for the "plain roughness" of the Poker Club and the sharpness of Dr. Jardine, to correct and qualify the "lusciousness" of French society.[64] Hume's complex attitude toward his homeland is significant. It is typical of a psychology which rarely failed to combat prejudice with pride.

For Scotsmen this pride was reinforced by the treatment they received in England, where their very considerable successes remained in inverse proportion to their popularity. One day Ossian, Burns, and Highland tours would help to wipe out even memories of Bute. Meanwhile, in spite of their own "Breetish" Coffee House, life in London was not always easy for visitors from north of the Tweed. "Get home to your crowdie, and be d—d to you! Ha'ye got your parritch yet? When will you get a sheepshead or a haggis, you ill-far'd lown? Did you ever see meat in Scotland, saving oatmeal hasty pudding? Keep out of his way, Thomas, or you'll get the itch!"[65] The young Scotsman thus recounting his London reception added that little real malice lay behind such common jibes. But Boswell's blood boiled with indignation when he heard shouts of "No Scots, No Scots! Out with them!" at Covent Garden. Yet only a few months later, he can be found addressing a memorandum to himself to "be *retenu* to avoid Scotch sarcasting jocularity," and describing a fellow countryman as "a hearty, honest fellow, knowing and active, but Scotch to the very backbone."[66]

The deepest result of this complicated involvement in British society was that the provincial's view of the world was discontinuous. Two forces, two magnets, affected his efforts to find adequate standards and styles: the values associated with the simplicity and purity (real or imagined) of nativism, and those to be found in cosmopolitan sophistication. Those who could take entire satisfaction in either could maintain a consistent position. But for provincials, exposed to both, an exclusive conception of either kind was too narrow. It meant a rootlessness, an alienation either from the higher sources of culture or from the familiar local environment that had formed the personality. Few whose perceptions surpassed local boundaries rested content with a simple, consistent image of themselves or of the world. Provincial culture in eighteenth-century Scotland was formed in a mingling of these visions.

Undoubtedly, provincialism often served to inhibit creative effort. But there existed important factors which more than balanced its deleterious effects. The complexity of the provincial Scotsman's image of the world and of himself made demands upon him unlike those felt by the equivalent Englishman. It tended to shake the mind from the roots of habit and tradition. It led men to the interstices of common thought where they found new views and new approaches to the old. It cannot account for the existence of men of genius, but to take it into consideration may help us to understand the conditions which fostered in such men the originality and the creative imagination that we associate with the highest achievement of the Scottish Renaissance in the eighteenth century.[67]

Looking over a Four-Leaf Clover: A Quartet of Nineteenth-Century Historians

I want to treat four major historians—Macaulay (1800–1859), Tocqueville (1805–1859), Burckhardt (1818–1897), and Henry Adams (1838–1918)—as a group, on the assumption that such comparative treatment might elicit fruitful questions and reflections about the nature of their achievement. They were all great historians. They all lived in the nineteenth century, though they actually overlapped in time for only twenty-one years (1838–1859). But the resemblance seems to end there. A middle-class Whig essayist and politician, a Norman aristocrat, a Swiss professor, and a Boston brahmin: what, besides a consuming interest in history and the ability to write it supremely well, did they have in common?

Their historical subjects were certainly very different. Macaulay's *History of England* (1848–1861) celebrates the beneficial consequences of the Glorious Revolution of 1688: Protestantism and economic progress secure, English freedom and national power soundly established under just laws. Tocqueville's *Old Régime and the French Revolution* (1856) also deals with a revolutionary theme, but far less encomiastically. For Tocqueville, the men of 1789, far from furthering the triumph of liberty, carried on and made worse pernicious tendencies already at work under the Bourbon kings: centralization, the

From *Critical Review*, 1985, no. 27

isolation of social classes one from another, the erosion of public spirit. Burckhardt's *Civilization of the Renaissance in Italy* (1860) depicts on the one hand the creative ferment of individualism in all spheres of human activity, manifesting itself in fifteenth-century Italy with almost explosive force; on the other, the violence and immorality that appeared to be inevitable concomitants of high cultural and artistic achievements. Adams's *History of the United States under the Administrations of Jefferson and Madison* (1889–1891) shows how, in the course of the opening years of the nineteenth century, Thomas Jefferson's agrarian democratic ideal was forced to give way to the necessities of power politics, the pressures of war, and the demands of an increasingly industrialized and economically competitive society.

Why, then, consider these particular historians together? Though their subjects were different, there were in fact some obvious similarities among the authors. All of them were multitalented, and at some stage of their lives exercised those talents, whether as statesmen, poets, novelists, journalists, editors, or travel writers. All of them, even when not themselves actively engaged in politics, showed great interest in the political trends and tendencies of their time; and, like all great historians, each of them had developed a certain view of the world in general, certain attitudes about the ultimate meaning and aims of life, which helped to shape his historical endeavors. They were not professional historians in the sense in which that phrase is now used; but one calls them "amateurs" at one's peril. Macaulay never tired of ransacking appropriate archives and visiting the sites of his *History*. Tocqueville was a pioneer in the use of French provincial archives. Burckhardt, a professor of history himself, despised the *viri eruditissimi*, the "capricorn-beetles"; but he had served his apprenticeship in Berlin under Ranke, and knew all about the new critical method of writing history. So did Adams, who, while teaching medieval history at Harvard, introduced the German seminar method there. By considering these four historians as a group, we come a little closer not only to an understanding of the role of the historian in the nineteenth century, but also to a view of him within the context of the more general framework of ideas and attitudes that characterized the period.

It is worth notice at the start that, though their origins and nationalities were different, each of these four historians was from birth part of a "nest" or family group that had its own powerful traditions and possessed its own strong civic consciousness. Tocqueville's paternal ancestors, Norman aristocrats, could trace their origins back to the

Middle Ages. The château de Tocqueville, which the historian and his wife were to occupy, provided concrete testimony of that tradition. His father, Hervé de Tocqueville, something of a historian himself, was imprisoned during the French Revolution, and escaped execution only by great good fortune. His mother was the granddaughter of Malesherbes, a lawyer of legendary courage and principle, who, having defended the people's rights before Louis XVI, subsequently defended the King before a revolutionary tribunal. Jacob Burckhardt's ancestors had for centuries supplied clergymen, mayors, and professors for his native city of Basel. His own father was minister of the Protestant cathedral there; and the Burckhardt family name, then as now, was synonymous with civic pride and achievement. Macaulay called himself a "parvenu"; and far from being to the manner born, penetrated to the outer sanctum of the great English Whig connection by sheer cleverness and ability. But he, too, came by his family pride and civic consciousness in legitimate fashion. His father, Zachary, was a leading member of the Clapham sect, that public-spirited group of leading Evangelicals residing in prosperity and neighborly amity in what was then still an outer suburb of London. The members of this group, in and out of Parliament, fought unrelentingly for the abolition of the slave trade and slavery, for the reformation of manners and morals, and for the spiritual welfare of English society. Henry Adams, born a member in supreme standing of the Boston patriciate, was able to recall in his *Education* sitting in childhood "in Quincy church, behind a president grandfather and . . . [reading] over his head the tablet in memory of a president greatgrandfather." Henry's father became a member of Congress and minister to the Court of St James's. His mother was the daughter of Boston's richest merchant, a brahmin in her own right.

I suspect it is more than a matter of coincidence that each of our four historians emerged from a "nest" that fostered awareness of family tradition, civic consciousness, and an interest in public affairs. To argue that all great historians must necessarily emerge from such a family background would be absurd. But what seems incontrovertible is that here is one link between these historians that may help to account for the kind of history they ended up writing. When public service and family pride run in the blood, and when one grows up in an atmosphere where such values are accepted as the norm, then it is really not surprising that historical awareness and practitionership will reflect those values. Indeed, the responsibilities of civic life, the public role of the citizen, the moral obligations and dilemmas of statesmanship—these are themes that resound throughout the works of our four historians. Thus, as John Burrow has pointed out, in spite of its justly famous third chapter on social history, a description of England in 1685, Macaulay's *History* remains "obstinately political," a veritable epic of discussion under law, public accountability, and public trust. Burckhardt's *Renaissance* epitomizes cultural history. Still, it starts with a long section on "The State as a Work of Art," and the problem of what happens to civic virtue in a period of violence and disorder constitutes one of its major emphases. A similar thread runs through Tocqueville's *Old Régime,* a devastating commentary on the failing health of the French body politic in the eighteenth century, through loss of vigor and public spirit. And Adams's *History* is, in large part, both study and evaluation of the means and ends of American statesmanship during a critical period in the history of the young republic.

Late in life, Burckhardt remembered that in 1839 Berlin, where he attended Ranke's lectures, was not only the best place to learn history, but also the best place to master the arts. It was, for him, the place where "I received an indelible impression of Gluck's operas and of old church music, at least to the extent of recalling the beginning of an understanding." Twenty years later, in 1859, Henry Adams, too, found himself a student in Berlin. He had gone there to learn German, which he tried to do by joining a class at a local *Gymnasium.* That experiment was not successful, but he learned other things in Berlin, one of them to love classical music. He supposed, so he recalled in the third person in which his *Education* is couched, that except musicians, everyone thought Beethoven a bore, as everyone except mathematicians thought mathematics a bore. "Sitting thus at his beer-table, mentally impassive, he was one day surprised to notice that his mind followed the movement of a Sinfonie. . . . Among the marvels of education, this was the most marvellous."

One could dismiss those two reminiscences as merely coincidental, and thus of no particular import or consequence. On the other hand, they may serve to remind us that Burckhardt and Adams could afford to be youthful travelers whose *Lehrjahre* took them to Berlin in early life; that both had strong aesthetic propensities which made memorable their first experience of listening to certain music. And that, in turn, helps to recall the fact that both historians went on to write guidebooks on art and architecture: Burckhardt his *Cicerone,* at the beginning of his career, and Adams his *Mont-Saint-Michel and Chartres,* towards the end of his. Burckhardt painted and drew throughout his life. Adams tried his hand at watercolors, with notable success, during his Far Eastern travels.

Other links and resemblances form part of the mosaic. Adams, who, so far as we know, never read Burckhardt's *Renaissance,* called himself "a quintessence of Boston, devoured by curiosity to think like Benvenuto," of whom Burckhardt had written, "whether we like him or not, [he is] a significant type of the modern spirit." A chance similarity? Of course. But it reflects the fact that both historians were obsessed with the meaning of modernity for their own lives and thought: the Swiss, who went searching for the origins of the modern spirit of rationality and calculation in fifteenth-century Florence and Venice, and who wanted to portray the Renaissance "in so far as she was the mother and native source of modern man, in thought and sensibility as well as in the shaping of form"; and the American, who concluded that his own education had inadequately prepared him to live with full awareness and commitment in an age of science and technology that continued to baffle him to the end of his days.

In the course of his Indian sojourn as Legal Member of Council, Macaulay recorded, in 1836, that "my mornings, from five to nine, are quite my own. I still give them to ancient literature. I have read Aristophanes twice through since Christmas; and have also read Herodotus, and Thucydides, again. I got into a way last year of reading a Greek play every Sunday." Thirty-five years later, Burckhardt noted that "I read the Greek tragedians, etc. lying on my sofa, so as to devote every moment possible to the daily routine practice of Greek." Of course, they reread the classics for very different purposes: Burckhardt because he was in the process of preparing his lectures on the history of Greek civilization, Macaulay to remind himself, even in the midst of what he considered to be an alien and backward culture, worthy neither of respect nor of study, of those peaks of Western literary culture to which he had become attached for life, while an undergraduate at Trinity College, Cambridge. It is well to recall, however, that that attachment did not alter the fact that the chief literary product of Macaulay's Indian stay was his enormous essay on Lord Bacon, in which he argued that while the ancient philosophers had filled the world with long words and long beards, they had left it as wicked and ignorant as they had found it. Bacon's practical philosophy of "fruit" had been triumphantly vindicated by the increase of bodily comforts and the results of technological and scientific progress in the course of the nineteenth century. Comparative vignettes can help us to make distinctions as well as to find similarities.

In any event, one does not need vignettes to make connections among our quartet of historians. There are direct links. It is all too easy to forget—more especially if one discusses the great historians one by one, devoting a chapter or essay to each as one proceeds along the giants' causeway—that historians write in the context of two traditions, always assumed though not always made explicit. One is the "long" tradition, reaching back to Herodotus and Thucydides, and proceeding majestically from St. Augustine, Sarpi, and Machiavelli, to Montesquieu and Voltaire, Robertson, Hume, and Gibbon; the other, the "short" tradition established by their immediate predecessors. Treating any group of more or less contemporary historians together serves to remind us of that fact.

Macaulay and Tocqueville met when the French historian visited London in 1857. We are told that Macaulay made the—for him—supreme sacrifice, and honored the distinguished visitor with a sample of his French. Alas, we do not know what was said. Perhaps there was talk of Burke, for whom both men had boundless admiration. We do know that through his writings on American democracy, Tocqueville had become a life-long model for Adams. As the latter wrote from London in 1863, "I study his life and work as the Gospel of my private religion." Indeed, Tocqueville's observation that scientific history was more appropriate than heroic history when it came to writing about democracies—it comes from *Democracy in America*—was to find both echo and fruit in Adams's *History*. In that work, as Adams pointed out,

> War counted for little, the hero for less; on the people alone the eye could permanently rest. The steady growth of a vast population without the social distinctions that confused other histories—without kings, nobles, or armies; without church, traditions, and prejudices—seemed a subject fit for the man of science rather than for dramatists or poets.

Various links exist between Macaulay and Adams as historians. Perhaps it was almost inevitable that Adams's chapter on "The Anglo-Saxon Courts of Law," which served as the introduction to those *Essays in Anglo-Saxon Law* (1876) that emerged from his Harvard seminar on medieval English history, was cast in the mold of "the ancient constitution," shaped by the search for continuities between medieval and modern English political institutions. It had become the conventional mold, including Macaulay's own, for describing the growth of English institutions, and had duly crossed the Atlantic. There were, however, more explicit links.

When Adams came to write his *History,* he wondered whether he should have his general introduction, a sort of historical conspectus of the United States in 1800 (similar in many ways to Macaulay's depiction of England in 1685 in his third chapter), stand by itself, or run it into the narrative: "Macaulay actually broke off his narrative to insert his introductory chapter. On the other hand, I admit that my first seven or eight chapters are wholly introductory. . . . They ought to stand by themselves." And so they did. But in those very chapters are to be found deliberate echoes of Macaulay. Where the latter had written that "the noblest of Protestant temples . . . [was] steadily rising on the ruins of the old Cathedral of St. Paul's," Adams, in describing the building of Washington, D.C., in 1800, adverts to the place where, across a swamp, a mile and a half away, the shapeless, unfinished Capitol was seen, two wings without a body, "ambitious enough in design to make more grotesque the nature of its surroundings." Whereas Macaulay had inveighed in his third chapter against "fools in that age who opposed the new light as strenuously as fools in our age have opposed the introduction of vaccination and railroads," Adams pointed out that Robert Fulton's new invention, the steamboat, was viewed by the public "either with indifference or with contempt as a visionary scheme." These small touches—and there are others—may be said to constitute mere pleasantries, fraternal tributes across the years from one historian to the ghost of another who had once cast a long shadow, and whose pioneering effort to survey the society of his country at a certain period within a small compass of pages had influenced the younger historian to attempt something similar. But they are also tokens of Adams's conviction, which he shared with Macaulay, that in some respects human nature does not change, that the average human mind, when confronted with something radically new, will always tend towards inertia and resistance.

All four historians faced existential crises in the course of their lives. For Macaulay and Adams these were largely personal, though there can be little doubt that they exerted considerable influence on the particular direction their work and achievement were to take. For Burckhardt and Tocqueville, they were closely connected with contemporary public affairs, and the political context within which their careers unfolded. From his early twenties on, Macaulay was strongly attached to his youngest sisters, Hannah and Margaret. In a family dominated by the stern presence of their father, Zachary, these two young girls responded with admiration and affection to both the brilliant public successes and the private drollery and fantastic imagination of their gifted brother, who, himself possessed of a more uninhibitedly emotional temperament than his father, found only in their presence the warmth and love he craved. When Margaret got married, her brother suffered agonies of loss and deprivation. He persuaded Hannah to accompany him to India; and when she, in turn, found her husband there in 1834—it was Charles Trevelyan—Macaulay's private world of happiness collapsed. When he heard the news of her engagement, so Hannah recalled, Macaulay became so mentally disturbed that the then governor general became frightened about his condition.

As it turned out, Margaret died of scarlet fever a few weeks later. Macaulay found some immediate comfort in the classics, more lasting comfort later on as a devoted and beloved uncle, adored by his nieces and nephew. But Margaret's marriage and subsequent death, as well as Hannah's marriage, had not a little to do with his decision, taken in India, to relinquish the thought of any major career in politics in favor of writing history. Though the Trevelyans and their children remained close to him for the rest of his life, he had lost the only audience he really cared about. The *ménage* of which he had dreamed, life with his favorite sisters, who would applaud his parliamentary triumphs as he returned from the House of Commons, had turned out to be a castle in the air, and had collapsed.

Adams never mentions the suicide of his wife, Marian Hooper (1885) in his *Education;* though it has always been assumed that the description he gives of his sister Louisa's agonizing death from lockjaw thirteen years earlier was also meant to serve as a paradigm for his wife's death. After his wife's suicide, he wrote to a friend that fate had at last smashed the life out of him. To another, he confided that "if you compare the tone of my first volume [of the *History*]—even toned down, as it is, from the original, with that of the ninth when it appears, you will feel that the light has gone out. I am not to blame. As long as I could make life work, I stood by it as though it was my God, as indeed it was." It was Marian's suicide that drove him to his world travels and to a search for spiritual meaning, not merely in the Mariolatry of Roman Catholicism, and the architectural masterworks it had inspired in the Middle Ages, but also in the worship and religion of the East. The mysterious sculptured female figure that he commissioned from Saint-Gaudens for his wife's tomb in Washington's Rock Creek Park cemetery attests to his spiritual travail, as do his travels and the books he wrote late in life—*Mont-Saint-Michel and Chartres,* and his autobiography, *The Education.*

Both Tocqueville and Burckhardt underwent personal crises closely related to the political situation in which they found themselves. Tocqueville, that proud aristocrat who valued liberty and individuality above all else, had to endure the regime of Napoleon III, who valued neither. His own brand of liberal conservatism put him out of favor with reactionaries; on the other hand, radicalism was repugnant to him. He felt surrounded by a sea of mediocrity. To his friend and confidante, Madame Swetchine, he wrote late in life:

> The most essential of the conditions of happiness fails me, the power of quietly enjoying the present. . . . I have a wife who for the last twenty years has kept my mind from giving way, but has not rendered it perfectly and habitually steady. . . . I have relations, neighbours, people who are close to me; but my mind has neither family nor motherhood. I assure you, my dear Madame, that such spiritual and moral isolation often gives me a sense of loneliness more intense than any I ever experienced in the primeval forests of America.

For his part, Burckhardt lost virtually all the friends of his German student days after he broke with the young Liberals who were preparing for the revolution of 1848 but who, increasingly, seemed to him to be aiding and abetting the worst aspects of nationalism and the new power state. After he had returned to his native Basel, leaving behind the heady days of university life in Berlin and companionable travel in the Rhineland, these former friends saw him only as a social conservative and as someone with an aesthetic distaste for the realities of life. As one critic has remarked, "he who was 'nothing without the stimulation of friends' sat in the frigid, intellectually alien city of a crumbling world, alone with his thoughts" (James Hastings Nichols, "Introduction to Burckhardt," in *Force and Freedom: Reflections on History,* New York, 1943, p. 9). For Burckhardt, this turned out to be a temporary crisis: not because European politics became any more to his liking—quite the contrary—but because he found a personal *modus vivendi* revolving around Basel and his teaching there. Tocqueville, on the other hand, was unable to adjust himself to the France of the Second Empire. He died lonely and embittered.

The crises I have just described were essentially personal, even when politics and public life had some part in their making. Other crises, common to the four historians, may more readily be linked to general trends of the century which, in one way or the other, affected a great many thoughtful men and women. One such trend was that toward secularization, a widespread fading of orthodox Christianity under the impact of science, Biblical criticism, and, often, the mere exhaustion of the formally theological impulse in an increasingly rationalistic environment. Individuals coped with these matters in very different ways. Still, the example of our quartet of historians should serve to illustrate the power and pervasiveness of the trend.

Greatly to the disappointment of his father, Macaulay neither became a clergyman nor, though reared in the most thoroughly Evangelical of households, was touched by the descent of divine grace in the prescribed and expected manner. Perhaps to avoid giving pain to his family, he rarely adverted to his own religious beliefs; though when, in the course of electioneering at Leeds in 1832, he was asked at a public meeting about the nature of those beliefs, he told the assembled throng: "My answer is short, and in one word. Gentlemen, I am a Christian." The most revealing clue to his real feelings on the subject is to be found in one of his marginal notes to an essay by the eighteenth-century freethinker and deist Conyers Middleton, who had himself written: "But if to live strictly and think freely, to practise what is moral and to believe what is rational, be consistent with the sincere profession of Christianity, then I shall acquit myself like one of its truest professors." Macaulay's marginal note reads: "Haec est absoluta et perfecta philosophi vita." His Evangelical father would certainly not have agreed with that statement. But, like so many other former Evangelicals in Victorian England, his son retained the moralistic impulses of the persuasion. To quote Peter Gay:

> As his religious beliefs faded . . . he retained the energy of the Claphamites, their detestation of evil and their solemn desire to aid good causes. In fact, his dramatic perception of his history as a combat between two clearly delineated forces translated the Evangelicals' faith of things into secular terms (*Style in History*, New York, 1974, p. 128).

The young Burckhardt, too, was destined for the ministry, but came to find himself unable to believe in the tenets of Christian theology, though he continued to believe in an eternal Providence. "As God," he wrote in 1844, "Christ is a matter of indifference to me—what can one make of him in the Trinity? As man he is the light of my soul, because he is the most *beautiful* figure in history." Readers of the *Renaissance* need not be told that Burckhardt continued to value the moral beauty and power of Christian currents of thought and feeling, particularly in a period when they tended to flow together with currents of paganism. In his *Reflections,* he predicted the evaporation of the shallow, optimistic, latitudinarian Christianity of his own time, which, he said, would give way to a return to pessimism about man's nature and earthly fate. At the outbreak of the Franco-Prussian war, he hoped for a religious revival in Germany, "for without a transcendent urge which outweighs all the clamour for power and money, nothing will be any use."

Tocqueville, born a Roman Catholic, lost his faith early in life under the impact of reading the writers of the Enlightenment. He, too, remained convinced, however, about the value of religion for society, whether American or French. And it has been pointed out that the Jansenism with which he was inculcated in childhood made itself felt in that powerful sense of doubt about everything—including himself—which remained all his life perhaps the most pronounced ingredient of his personality. As for Adams, growing up in Boston, the chief citadel of American Unitarianism, "the boy went to church [he himself recalls] twice every Sunday; he was taught to read his Bible, and he learned religious poetry by heart; he believed in a mild deism; he prayed; he went through all the forms; but neither to him nor his brothers or sisters was religion real. . . . The religious instinct had vanished, and could not be revived, although one made in later life many efforts to recover it." Those efforts at recovery, whether in the cult of the Virgin or the Dynamo, or in his travels to the East, led to Adams's most personal books, *Mont-Saint-Michel and Chartres,* and *The Education.*

Secularization, then, meant more than merely loss of faith; but it was a trend that affected all four historians. Another was love of country and locality. In 1860 Adams, as proud of his ancestry as he was of American democracy, wrote his mother from Dresden that Europeans were "not great enough to understand and appreciate the state of society in which the equals of their princes are only private persons, and they cannot conceive how a person whose ancestors have held in succession every position of dignity and power which their nation could give, can consider himself as their equal." The "equal of their princes" was, of course, himself. In the same vein, he tells his mother that "we Americans here are rather proud. We don't lick boots like the English nor court notice." That pride in the United States and its democratic ideal surfaces time and again in the course of Adams's works. Even when he is critical, as he often is, of one or the other aspect of American politics and culture, that criticism comes from one who loves and, even as he censures, wishes the object of his affections to become even better than it is.

In Tocqueville and Macaulay, love of country and locality was no less pronounced. At the age of twenty-two, Tocqueville, while traveling in Sicily, saw a fishing boat at sea, and on it a three-year-old child being lovingly caressed by its family. This was his comment:

> Never in my life as at that moment did I understand the horror of exile and the reality of those patriotic instincts which return us to our country from so far and in spite of all obstacles and dangers. I felt myself moved by such a strong desire to see France again that I've never been moved in the same way for anything else.

Twenty-seven years later, in 1854, Macaulay encountered a group of Surrey hop pickers while taking a country walk:

> As I walked back from Esher, a shower came on. Afraid for my chest, which at best is in no very good state, I turned into a small ale-house, and called for a glass of ginger-beer. I found there a party of hop-pickers, come back from the neighbourhood at Farnham. I liked their looks, and thought their English remarkably good for their rank of life. It was in truth the Surrey English, the English of the suburbs of London, which is to Somersetshire and Yorkshire what Castilian is to Andalusian, or Tuscan to Neapolitan.

He bought them a pot of foaming ale, and rejoiced in the encounter. What is perhaps most remarkable about this passage is that it shows the historian, usually and rightly depicted as a John Bull impatient with foreign habits and ways, revealing a fondness here for region as well as nation. It reminds us that he was a product of the Romantic movement, and an avid reader of Scott.

For Burckhardt, as a student in Berlin and during his period of close friendship with the student Liberals, Germany became his all in all. To his sister he wrote at the time: "I am like Saul, the son of Kish, who went out to look for lost asses and found a king's crown. I often want to kneel down before the sacred soil of Germany and thank God that my mother tongue is German. I have Germany to thank for every-thing! What a people. What a wonderful youth. What a land—a par-adise." And he told a German friend: "Now, I recognise the embrace of our common great fatherland which I, like most of my fellow Swiss, used to mock and repel. . . . I will make it my life's purpose to show the Swiss that they are Germans." This enthusiasm, a product of the discovery of German art and architecture, music and history, and above all of friendship with like-minded young Germans, did not last. Burckhardt came to fear the nation-state and the harmful effects it could produce, in terms of both power politics and the homoge-nization of all that was individual and particular. And so he made himself the defender of diversity, the keeper of Basel tradition who refused all calls to go elsewhere and to accept more exalted posts. His patriotism became entirely local, and its object was his native city to whose academic and civic welfare he devoted himself for the rest of his days.

It is possible to claim that the social and political history of the nineteenth century in the West is, in fact, a series of footnotes to the French Revolution. If such a claim be made, our four historians might certainly form part of the evidence for it. Tocqueville wrote one of his two great books about the Revolution, and was literally obsessed with its meaning for his time and the future. In Adams's *History,* concerned in large measure with the battle between conservative Fed-eralists and democratic Republicans, it becomes apparent that in early-nineteenth-century America, Jefferson and his supporters were said by their opponents to stand for the principles of the French Revo-lution. In New England, for example, conservatives answered every democratic suggestion with "Look at France!" France, it has been pointed out, remained "red revolution" to the Federalists, democracy to the Republicans, "long after she had ceased to be either" (Herbert Agar, "Introduction to Henry Adams," in *The Formative Years,* 2 vols., London, 1948, vol. I, p. xv).

Within the space of less than two decades, both Macaulay and Tocqueville appealed to their respective legislatures to grant reforms lest revolutionary violence, on the model of France in 1793, ensue. This is what Macaulay told the House of Commons in 1831, during the Reform Bill debates:

A portion of the community which had been of no account ex-pands and becomes strong. It demands a place in the system, suited, not to its former weakness, but to its present power. If this is granted, all is well. If this is refused, then comes the struggle between the young energy of one class and the ancient privilege of another.

The Reform Act did in the event grant a modicum of political power to the middle classes by enfranchising a good many of their members and taking at least some borough-mongering power from the aristocracy. And Macaulay himself expressed the feeling that perhaps the time had arrived to come to terms with the French Revolution. It had, after all, begun as a struggle of the people against princes and nobles, for political liberty. The spirit of democracy, which it brought in its train, had indeed produced crimes and excesses that one could not palliate. But then the Reformation—a self-evidently happy event for Macaulay—had been full of violence as well. Thus

> experience surely entitles us to believe that this explosion [the French Revolution] like that which preceded it, will fertilise the soil which it has devastated. Already, in those parts which have suffered most severely, rich cultivation and secure dwellings have begun to appear amidst the waste. The more we read of the history of the past ages, the more we observe the signs of our own times, the more do we feel our hearts filled and swelled up by a good hope for the future destinies of the human race.

In January 1848, Tocqueville couched his famous warning to the French deputies in similar terms, though, unlike Macaulay, he was less concerned with the demands of new social and economic forces than with what was going on in men's minds. The mere absence of riot and disorder was not necessarily a sign that there would be no revolution:

> Do you not see that men's passions have changed from political to social? Do you not see that opinions and ideas are gradually spreading among them that tend not simply to the overthrow of such-and-such laws, such-and-such a minister, or even such-and-such a government, but rather to the overthrow of society, breaking down the bases on which it now rests?

It was the *spirit* of the government that needed to be changed.

A generation later, Burckhardt (in 1867), though recognizing that "we are all children of the revolution" because it had engendered democratic feelings which became dominant in the nineteenth century, passed a more pessimistic judgment. Undoubtedly, the Revolution had brought complete equality before the law, disposability of real property, freedom of industry, equality of religions, and the beginnings of absolute political equality. "However, it is doubtful whether the world has on the average become happier for all this. . . . The chief phenomenon of our days is the sense of the provisional. In addition to the uncertainty of each individual's fate we are confronted with a colossal problem of existence." Burckhardt saw events like the Paris Commune of 1871, and rumored events like that of the destruction of the Louvre, as ultimately deriving from Rousseau's notion of the native goodness of man. There was a definite link, he wrote in the *Renaissance,* between Rabelais's "fay ce que vouldras" and that misguided faith in the goodness of human nature that had inspired the men of the second half of the eighteenth century, and had helped prepare the way for the French Revolution.

Burckhardt's pessimism about his own time and the future extended beyond his sense that the nature of things in general had become provisional. He was appalled by the all-pervasive materialism he detected in the Western world, symbolized by one of President Ulysses S. Grant's speeches (1873) in which he enunciated "the necessary goal of a purely money-making world." That was, of course, the same Grant about whom Adams was to write sardonically that it was indeed matter for wonder that "two thousand years after Alexander the Great and Julius Caesar, a man like Grant should be called—and should actually and truly be—the highest product of the most advanced evolution. . . . The progress of evolution from President Washington to President Grant was alone evidence enough to upset Darwin."

Both Adams and Burckhardt, the former with self-deprecating irony, the latter with real anger, expressed reservations about the value of at least one convenience produced by modern technology. Just two years after Adams, in 1868, had "accepted the hospitality of the sleeper, with deep gratitude, the more because his first struggle with a sleeping-car made him doubt the value—to him—of a Pullman civilization," Burckhardt inveighed against those men of his time who really hated every form of diversity: "They would readily give up all their individual literatures and cultures, if it had to be so, for the sake of through sleeping cars." When he visited London, in 1879, he noted that "a disgusting, high, straight, cast-iron bridge has been built slap across the main vista of the town, a main-line railway laid across it, and a hideous great round-topped lady's suitcase [Charing Cross] built above it." A similar monstrosity was being erected in the vicinity of London Bridge: "O, Lord, what is not going to be sacrificed to the *practical* sense of the nineteenth century?" The Swiss historian despised the "mere trance" of urban money-making, the close quarters, the haste, the crowding, the constant excitement of modern living. It would all lead to the end of creativity, diversity, and cultivation.

Macaulay's view of material and practical progress was very different. He frankly rejoiced in the comforts and conveniences it brought, not least because they enabled a much larger public to be quickly and efficiently informed about what had gone on in Parliament the day before. Like not a few of his fellow Victorians, he glimpsed beauty where others saw only ugliness. "Can there be a stronger contrast," he asked the House of Commons in 1831, during the Reform Bill debates, "than that which exists between the beauty, the completeness, the speed, the precision with which every process is performed in our factories, and the awkwardness, the rudeness, the slowness, the uncertainty of the apparatus by which offenses are punished and rights vindicated?" In *The History*, he compared Torbay at the time Dutch William landed there in 1688 with its nineteenth-century successor:

The newly built churches and chapels, the baths and libraries, the hotels and public gardens, the infirmary and the museum, the white streets, rising terrace above terrace, the gay villas peeping from the midst of shrubberies and flower beds, present a spectacle widely different from any that in the seventeenth century England could show.

Lytton Strachey's comment on that passage was to consist of three words: "They do indeed!" That was part of Bloomsbury's revenge against Clapham—though even Strachey reluctantly granted Macaulay his place on Parnassus.

But Macaulay did not merely celebrate material progress. "It is pleasing to reflect," so he wrote in his *History*, "that the public mind of England has softened while it has ripened, and that we have in the course of ages become not only a wiser, but also a kinder people." Burckhardt disagreed. "As for moral progress," he in turn reflected some years later, "if even in bygone times men gave their lives for each other, we have not progressed since." The Swiss historian, perhaps not surprisingly for someone who like his friend Nietzsche valued

Schopenhauer as "the philosopher," had no use at all for the exaltation of progress. In 1875 he bleakly remarked that "as the illusions of the 'progress' which has dominated since 1830 come to disappear, it is essential to have someone to tell us all *that* belongs to the kingdom of illusions, and how to give up our own hopes in time." Adams, on the other hand, while certainly far from an optimist about progress— on Papeete he noted that the natives had "the look of sadness that always goes with civilization"—required an evolutionary theory of history in the name of science and objectivity. To his student, Henry Cabot Lodge, he wrote in 1878:

> Unless you can find some basis of faith in general principles, some theory of the progress of civilization which is outside and above all temporary questions of policy, you must infallibly think and act under the control of the man or men whose thought, in the times you deal with, coincides most nearly with your prejudices.

For Adams, then, progress was not so much a concomitant of a sanguine temperament as a metaphysical necessity.

"Necessity" is a word that might well be applied to Tocqueville's view of democracy—though here the qualifying adjective should probably be "providential" rather than "metaphysical." "Why [God] is drawing us toward democracy," he wrote, "I don't know. But embarked on a vessel that I did not build, I am at least trying to use it to gain the nearest port." For Tocqueville, the great task of his time was to construct countervailing barriers against those leveling tendencies that, if left to exert themselves unhindered, would inevitably lead to a despotism of the masses more oppressive than that of any single tyrant. Tocqueville was himself certainly no democrat. But, persuaded of the ineluctable advent of democracy, providentially decreed, he decided that one had to cope with it as best one could.

Macaulay, too, knew that franchise reform could not really end with the Reform Act of 1832, on whose behalf he had labored with such eloquence and passion. His own hope was that the next instalment of franchise reform, which he knew had to come at some point, might be put off for as long as possible. After the crucial second reading of the bill was carried in the House of Commons in late March 1831, he wrote to his friend Thomas Flower Ellis: "I called a cabriolet and the first thing the driver asked me was 'Is the bill carried?' 'Yes, by one.' 'Thank God for it, Sir.' And away I rode to Gray's Inn—so ended a scene which will probably never be equalled till the reformed parliament wants reforming; and that I hope will not be till the days of our grand-children." That was, of course, the essence of the Whig approach: put off reforms as long as possible, but make concessions, when necessary, in order to prevent violence and revolution.

Given this outlook on the part of Macaulay, it should occasion no surprise that he was the last person to have been enamored of American democracy. "All sheet and no anchor" was to be his mature judgment of the United States Constitution. "When I left college," he once recalled, "it was the fashion of young liberals—I cannot say that it was ever exactly mine—to consider the American institutions as the very model of good government." He would certainly not have sympathized with Adams's intention to write his *History* in the light of "the infinite possibilities of American democracy," though he might well have endorsed the American historian's formulation that one of the great problems for American statesmen in the early nineteenth century—Jefferson in the lead among them—was whether being at the same time a democracy and a great power might not constitute a contradiction in terms. Burckhardt himself never doubted that democracies were power states like any others. "The sense of power and democratic feeling are for the most part indistinguishable," he wrote. "Statesmen no longer seek to combat democracy, but in some way or other to reckon with it, to eliminate risks as far as possible from the transition to what is now regarded as inevitable."

Our four historians agreed in fearing some of the deleterious effects of democracy upon the kind of society they wished to preserve. Adams, with all his democratic idealism, put his own version of that fear succinctly: "Democracies in history always suffered from the necessity of uniting with much of the purest and best in human nature a mass of ignorance and brutality lying at the bottom of all society." It was this fear—the possible threat from the poor and uneducated masses—which haunted nineteenth-century Liberals as well as Conservatives, including even some of those who were themselves in favor of a considerable measure of political reform. Macaulay, for instance, wrote of "the human vermin which, neglected by ministers of state and ministers of religion, barbarous in the midst of civilization, heathen in the midst of Christianity, burrows among all physical and moral pollution, in the cellars and garrets of great cities, [and] will at once rise into terrible importance." Burckhardt, while editing the *Basler Zeitung,* felt that he was getting a sense of what the masses could really be like when in the hands of demagogues—"a beast," a "roaring pack." When, in Tocqueville's *Recollections* of the Revolution of 1848, one reaches his description of Blanqui, the socialist leader—"he had sunken withered cheeks, white lips, and a sickly malign dirty look like a pallid mouldy corpse. . . . He looked as if he had lived in a sewer and only just come out"—or notes the praise he bestows on his servant for not being a socialist, one is made aware of the fact that Tocqueville himself had the same limited sympathy with "the lower orders" that he was to condemn with such eloquence in his *Old Régime*. All four historians were certainly very conscious of the underside of democracy, the threat from below—a consciousness frequently reflected in their attitudes as well as in their writings.

For both Burckhardt and Macaulay, the road to history had led by way of poetry. For both, daydreaming and reveries continued to play a significant role in the process of literary creativity. Thus Burckhardt wrote to a friend from Berlin, in 1840: "My poetry, for which you prophesied fair weather, is in great danger of being sent packing now that I have found the height of poetry in history itself." Two years later, to a different correspondent: "My entire historical work, like my passion for travel, my mania for natural scenery and my interest in art, springs from an enormous thirst for contemplation [*Anschauung*]." For his part, Macaulay once told his sister Margaret that his factual accuracy was due to his love of castle-building. From childhood on, she related, he had retained the habit of constructing the past into a romance. As soon as he found himself in the streets he imagined himself in Greece, in Rome, in the midst of the French Revolution. And in these daydreams, in the course of which he composed conversations between the great people of the time in the style of Sir Walter Scott, precision in dates, the day or hour in which a man was born, was of crucial importance. More than a quarter of a century after that conversation, in 1857, while engaged in what turned out to be the final chapters of *The History of England*, he confided to his journal that if he lived long enough, he would one day write a disquisition on "the strange habit of day-dreaming," to which he imputed a great part of his literary success.

Adams, as we know, admired Macaulay, but found him inimitable: "One might as well imitate Shakespeare." For Adams, inability on the part of others to imitate a great historian seemed somehow wrong: "For the poet and the historian ought to have different methods, and Macaulay's method ought to be imitable, if it were sound." The reason was, of course, that Adams wished historical writing to become a science, like any other science. In his *Education*, he referred to his own

History as an experiment in scientific history: "He had even published a dozen volumes of American history for no other purpose than to satisfy himself whether by the severest process of stating with the least possible comment such facts as seemed rigorously consequent, he could fix for a familiar moment a necessary sequence of human movement." That was certainly a long way from Macaulay's unashamedly literary approach, his advocacy of the art of narration, of "interesting the affections and presenting pictures to the imagination." It was an even longer way from Burckhardt's belief that each observer of an historical event must bring to it his own, subjective way of looking at it. It was closer to Tocqueville, who said of himself that he was employing the method of the anatomist, "who dissects each defunct organ with a view to eliciting the laws of life and [whose aim] was to supply a picture that while scientifically accurate, may also be instructive."

But Adams was not satisfied with the results of his experiment: in part—and this he was willing to admit—because there was as yet no general agreement about the units of measure by which one could test and evaluate the validity of a historical sequence; in part—and this he did not admit—because he was himself too much the intuitive artist and stylist ever to write the sort of history that would qualify as "scientific." It was certainly true that Adams dealt by preference with types rather than with individuals—to the extent that in the *History* Jefferson is depicted as someone representing rather than forming the American character, as the anti-hero rather than the hero (J. C. Levenson, *The Mind and Art of Henry Adams,* Stanford, 1968, p. 124). In choosing this approach, Adams was simply carrying further a tendency one can already find in Macaulay's depiction of the typical English country gentleman at the end of the seventeenth century, in Tocqueville's memorable comments on his French equivalent in *The Old Régime,* and in Burckhardt's brilliant attempt to distill the salient characteristics of the Renaissance personality by looking at representative figures, whether despotic princes or court humanists. The motives of our four historians were, to be sure, different. Macaulay's was to put his knowledge of Restoration drama at the service of his history; Tocqueville was convinced that the historian's proper business was to deal with classes; Burckhardt wrote in that increasingly powerful historicist tradition, according to which each historical period could be said to possess its own unique "spirit," expressed by means of politics, literature, art, or representative personalities.

Here, then, is one methodological approach shared in varying de-

grees and for different reasons by our quartet of historians. It makes
for one bond between them. But there is another bond, which reaches
beyond the realm of method and technique into that of underlying
pattern, of basic action. In each of the four works written by our
quartet of historians, that pattern is essentially moral; and in all but
Macaulay, where it is clear and unequivocal, some mystery remains.
When Jeffrey wrote to a correspondent in 1849 that "the doubts dis-
pelled—the chaos reduced to order" were crucial elements in the success of the first two volumes of Macaulay's *History,* he put his finger
on the basic duality that underlies that work. It consists, as John Burrow has pointed out, not merely of a battle between Whig and Tory,
but rather of the perennial struggle between civilization, property,
public trust, and liberty under law on the one hand; lawless ambition,
fanaticism, unrestrained passions and appetites on the other. Law and
order, and above all, respectability, triumph over the forces threatening them (*A Liberal Descent: Victorian Historians and the English Past,*
Cambridge, 1981, pp. 80–93). Rationality prevails.

In Tocqueville's *Old Régime,* the pattern is less hopeful. It is not
just that tendencies towards administrative centralization under the
French monarchy laid the real groundwork for that despotism that,
beginning with the later stages of the Revolution, comes even more
to the fore under the first and third Napoleons; but that there exist
mysterious forces—feelings and beliefs, habits of mind and heart—
which at critical moments in history may lead, as they did in the case
of the French nobility, to a loss of nerve, and to the sort of moral
isolation of classes that carries with it nefarious effects even more
powerful than the worst results of misguided administrative arrangements. Some nations, Tocqueville writes, have freedom in the blood.
Others do not. Genuine love of freedom "defies analysis. For it is
something one must *feel* and logic has no part in it." The anatomical
approach does not necessarily lead to clear and definite answers,
whether used by physicians or by sociologists. Indeed, in reading
Tocqueville, one is tempted to conclude that, in the final analysis, it
accentuates mystery. "In all human institutions," Tocqueville writes,
"as in the human body, there is a hidden source of energy, the life
principle itself, independent of the organs which perform the various
functions needed for survival; once this vital flame burns low, the
whole organism languishes and wastes away, and though the organs
seem to function as before, they serve no useful purpose." The moral
costs of aloofness and isolation are clear, and central to Tocqueville's
grim commentary on the crumbling of community feeling under the

old regime in France. But why do such things happen? What is the nature of the "curious internal malady" that attacks the French nobles, and, without external pressure, makes them crumple up? As in real life, there is a great gulf fixed between diagnosis and cure.

If that reminds us of Burckhardt, it is for good reason. For here too, at the heart of his great work on the Renaissance, lies a mystery: on the one hand, the growth of self-conscious individualism leading to towering artistic achievement, the presence on a large scale of the beauty and dignity of exceptional human beings; on the other, the crimes, the violence, the bloodshed, the moral abyss, the abuse of power that accompany triumphs and attainments. Is it possible to have one without the other? That question finds no resolution. For "the ultimate truth with respect to the character, the conscience and the guilt of a people remains for ever a secret; if only for the reason that its defects have another side, where they reappear as peculiarities or even as virtues." The puzzle remains.

Adams's *History* deals with the survival in the United States of the early nineteenth century of the democratic ideal, against all the odds and obstacles of faction, power politics, and skepticism. The democratic ideal did indeed survive, though Adams ends his work with a series of questions about the future of the American people: "What interests were to vivify a society so vast and uniform? What ideals were to ennoble it? What object, besides physical content, must a democratic continent aspire to attain?" Those were moral questions, having to do with men's minds and ideals. But even the most scientifically inclined of our quartet of historians leaves us with a mystery. The growth of social and national character, he writes, more interesting than any territorial or industrial growth, "defied the tests of censuses and surveys." Just as his mentor, Tocqueville, had glimpsed even in the midst of the very prosaic life of the American people the poetry of democracy, the hidden nerve, "which gave vigour to the whole frame," Adams found the essence of the democratic impulse in "an emotion which caused the poorest peasant in Europe to see what was invisible to poet and philosopher,—the dim outline of a mountain-summit across the ocean, rising high above the mist and mud of American democracy." The instinct for democracy was ultimately mysterious. So deep an instinct was it for the Pennsylvanians, the people living in the most genuinely democratic state in America, "that they knew not what to do with political power when they gained it; as though political power were aristocratic in its nature, and democratic power a contradiction in terms." One critic has remarked that the baffling simplicity of these essential democrats presents the riddle on which Adams's entire *History* is based (Levenson, p. 145).

Adams, then, celebrates the survival of the democratic idea, just as Macaulay had celebrated the triumph of order over chaos. What for the one could be ascribed to the happy exercise of reason and good judgment remained ultimately baffling and mysterious for the other; just as ultimately baffling and mysterious as the causes of class isolation in eighteenth-century France for Tocqueville, and the moral character of the Italian people in the fifteenth century for Burckhardt. Perhaps that is the chief lesson our quartet of historians can teach us: as the nineteenth century advanced, even as historical writing became more critical and scientific, the moral conflicts and dilemmas that lie at the heart of all great literary and historical works remained central. But the mystery deepened.

> *We dance round in a ring and suppose,*
> *But the Secret sits in the middle and knows.*

V

ENGLISH CLIOGRAPHERS

English Cliographers

The number of outstanding biographies—whether in the form of books or of essays—of modern English historians may not be large enough to merit "official" consideration as a separate genre of the art. But it is certainly varied, ranging as it does from monumental classics like Trevelyan's *Macaulay* and Froude's *Carlyle* to the delicate filigree of Lytton Strachey's *Portraits in Miniature*. Varied enough, perhaps, to serve as a sounding board for the question: What can one expect to find in the biography of a historian that will best illuminate the relation of his life to his work as well as instruct current practitioners of the art of history?

One obvious component of any answer to that question comes readily to mind: formative influences. We want to know why the great historians chose to write history in the first place, and what it was that led them to write the kind of history they eventually produced. Native talents and childhood influences (nowhere better depicted than in Sir George Otto Trevelyan's *Life and Letters* of his uncle, Thomas Babington Macaulay) can be highly revealing. The extraordinary little boy who, at the age of four, replied to Lady Waldegrave's question as to whether he was still feeling pain from some hot coffee a servant had accidentally spilled over his legs, "Thank you, madam, the agony

From *Harvard English Studies*, 1978, no. 8

is abated," and who, before he had reached the age of ten, was already working on a compendium of universal history, composing hymns and epics, and displaying awesome powers of memory, emerges graphically from Trevelyan's early chapters. And so does the atmosphere of political activism and moral endeavor that characterized the Clapham Sect and helped to shape young Macaulay's mind and character. Just as the stern presence of that leading Evangelical reformer Zachary Macaulay, the historian's father, dominates the son's early life, so does the far more jovial presence of Thomas Babington Macaulay dominate the entire life of his nephew and future biographer, G. O. Trevelyan.

Indeed, in reading G. M. Trevelyan's memoir of his father, George Otto, one cannot help but be struck by the extent to which the Trevelyan family had fallen under the magic spell of the author of *The History of England*. Macaulay, who must surely rank at or near the top in any enumeration of devoted Victorian uncles, lived long enough to take intense interest and pride in his nephew's attainments at Harrow and Cambridge. And the younger man amply repaid his debt, not only with the masterly *Life and Letters* of his uncle but also with his *Early Life of Charles James Fox* and his *American Revolution,* both of which bear unmistakable traces of consanguinity with Lord Macaulay's work. When, in addition, we remember that George Otto's own son (and memorialist), George Macaulay Trevelyan, not only bore his great-uncle's name but himself wrote a series of books that carried on the family tradition of combining Liberal sentiments with a special interest in social history, we cannot help but reflect that there exist historiographical as well as royal dynasties, and that, at least in the case of the House of Macaulay, they seem to supply their own best biographers.[1]

Lord Acton was distantly related to Edward Gibbon. But that particular family tie was hardly decisive in molding the younger historian's spiritual outlook or approach to history. As Gertrude Himmelfarb demonstrates in her study of Acton, the drama of his life was the drama of his ideas; and the forces that shaped those ideas derived as much from teachers and guides, living and dead, as they did from the historian's Catholic family background.[2] Among the living guides, the chief was Ignaz von Döllinger, who purged his pupil of those Whiggish and Macaulayite sympathies he had brought with him to Munich in 1850. Another was Ranke, whose lectures and writings instilled both Döllinger and Acton with the necessity of writing history, whenever possible, from original manuscripts and documents.

Among the dead, perhaps the principal influence was Edmund Burke. As Professor Himmelfarb points out, it was partly to reinstate Burke and to expel Macaulay as the sage of politics that Acton undertook his first major task, the editorship of the *Rambler*.

If Acton's life, then, illustrates the influence that powerful minds, past and present, may exert over a historian's intellectual development, so does the biography of John Richard Green, author of *A Short History of England,* as set forth in his *Letters* (edited by Leslie Stephen). There we learn not only that the sixteen-year-old Green was, like Gibbon at the same age, tempted to become a Roman Catholic—a temptation to which, unlike the historian of the Roman Empire, he did not yield—but also that his reading of Gibbon at about the same time had an enormous effect on him: "What a new world that was!" he later recalled. Along with Addison and Steele, Gibbon remained one of his favorites at Oxford. Another was Macaulay, whose *History* apparently suggested to Green his own first historical work, a description of eighteenth-century Oxford (1859). Three years later it was a reading of Sismondi that finally persuaded Green to abandon the more limited theme of a history of the English Church and to write his own history of England. Stephen's edition of Green's *Letters* shows that a historian does not merely benefit from actual discourse with his contemporaries (in Green's case, Stubbs and Freeman) but also that the influence of the great historians through their writings may do much to determine the direction his own work takes.

Much, but not everything. We need only recall how Gibbon acknowledged the usefulness of his service in the Hampshire militia in writing the history of the Roman Empire to remind us that practical experience as well as books helps to shape both the work and the life of the historian. Green himself is a good example. For some years he was the incumbent of an Anglican parish in the East End of London. This experience strengthened his sympathies with different types of human beings. Indeed, as Leslie Stephen remarks, "The history might have been written in a very different tone had the writer passed his days in academical seclusion."[3] Green himself, by the way, carried the environmental interpretation of English historiography to the point where he saw something in the English atmosphere of freedom that made it impossible for any historian living there to sink into a "paper-chaser" on the German model. Even those historians of his own day who consciously strove to be merely external and pragmatic failed in their aim: witness, Green pointed out, the contrast between Freeman and Pauli, and between Gardiner and Ranke.[4]

Macaulay, of whom it cannot be said that he ever attempted to be a "paper-chaser," gained practical experience in public life. Trevelyan's *Life and Letters* shows how, first as a Member of Parliament during the Reform Bill debates and subsequently as Legal Member of the Indian Council, Macaulay acquired the knowledge that enabled him to deal more effectively with the public transactions of the past in *The History of England*. And from Lady Namier's biography of her late husband, Sir Lewis, the reader learns that that great prober into the practical affairs of politicians and statesmen in eighteenth-century England had himself garnered ample practical experience in both business and diplomacy. That experience must be kept in mind in any appraisal of the empirical and anti-ideological nature of Namier's method. One should also be aware, from Namier's own account, of his rejection in turn of what he came to consider two delusive ideologies: his parents' belief that the principal difference between Jews and Gentiles was religious, and the formularies of socialist doctrine. Finally, one should recognize the intellectual context of what Sir Isaiah Berlin has called Namier's "deflationary" approach to history in a Viennese milieu that included Mach, Freud, Loos, and the members of the Vienna Circle.[5]

Childhood and family influences, intellectual and social environment, teachers and guides (living and dead), practical experience in the affairs of the world—all these are shaping forces that we expect to see delineated in any worthwhile biography of a major historian. But those of us who try to write history ourselves want something more: at least a glimpse, preferably a long look, into the master's workshop, which will go some way toward satisfying our curiosity about how the great historians went about the workaday business of actually writing their histories. Macaulay told his young nephew in 1843 that he was going to spend five more years collecting materials to write a history of England. "The little boy thought he meant to spend five years buying the very best pens and plenty of blue and white foolscap paper."[6] But readers of Trevelyan's *Life and Letters* know better! They know that the historian tirelessly visited archives and battlefields in search of documents and local color; that he sometimes read twenty books to write a single sentence; that Macaulay the historian, unlike Macaulay the essayist, did not rely on his famous memory, but filled scores of notebooks before putting pen to paper; and that he wrote only when he felt at his best, first a rapid rough draft, with gaps filled in and revisions and corrections made later. The manuscript of the last volume of the *History* (now at the Morgan

Library in New York), with its innumerable crossings out in the search for the perfect word or phrase, amply confirms what Trevelyan tells us.

One thing Macaulay did not have to do, however, was to rewrite a whole volume of his history after it had been inadvertently destroyed. That, as we know, was the heroic task facing Thomas Carlyle after volume 1 of *The French Revolution* was thrown into the fire by John Stuart Mill's careless maid. Even after he decided to rewrite what had been lost, Carlyle, who had by this time destroyed his notes and could remember nothing of the volume, failed for some time to make any progress. As his biographer, James Anthony Froude, remarks: "A man can rewrite what he has known; but he cannot rewrite what he has felt."[7] Finally, he decided to read nothing but novels for two weeks; thereafter he was able to rewrite the volume in a version he judged to be worse, but not much worse, than the original.

In his early days, Froude tells us, Carlyle made no "foul" copy. "The sentences completed themselves in his head before he threw them upon paper."[8] He was no longer able to do this when he wrote *Cromwell* and *Frederick*. At the start of any literary work, he was distracted by every trifle. Noise in particular was anathema to him while he was trying to write, and he complained bitterly about being disturbed by a young lady who practiced the piano at the time he was attempting to begin his *Cromwell*. Froude's comment here (unlike that piano) will strike a sympathetic chord with anyone who has ever been engaged in writing history: "And after all it was not the piano, or very little the piano. It is in ourselves that we are this and that, and the young lady might have played her fingers off, and he would never have heard her, had his work once been set going, and he absorbed in it."[9]

Like many other historians since, Carlyle knew that the British Museum contained the best collection of the materials he needed for *Cromwell*. But he was reluctant to work there since, Froude explains, "he required to have his authorities at hand where his own writing-tackle lay round him, where he could refer to them at any moment."[10] Unlike those other, later historians, he did something about the situation: he founded the London Library, still (because its books circulate) a blessing to those who, like Carlyle, prefer to work at home. It was there, in any event, that J. R. Green had to work after the museum closed and he had finished his daily parish duties—sometimes staying up from midnight until two a.m., at other times from two to five a.m. In 1866 Green got into a fight with the British Museum staff.

He had lost his ticket, and they, rather than issuing him a new one, told him to "search" for the old one. He was furious about the delay this caused in his work. But at least he finished his magnum opus, *A Short History of England,* or, as he liked to call it in his letters, "Shorts."

Acton never did finish his "Madonna of the Future," the *History of Liberty,* that "greatest book that was never written." And if Froude, Trevelyan, and Stephen, in their biographies of great historians, supply some positive hints for aspirants to that class, Professor Himmelfarb's biography contains some implicit warnings about what *not* to do if one intends to complete a major historical work. She shows how Acton was unable to stop himself from prolonging research at the expense of writing. Every week, he complained to Mary Gladstone, brought new publications to throw fresh light on or add fresh difficulties to his subject. He could not make the necessary decision to ignore these new materials and go forward without them. Instead, he threw himself into the *Cambridge Modern History,* which in the end prevented him from doing any major work of his own. What really defeated him, as Professor Himmelfarb perceptively concludes, was his own restless, dissatisfied, ambitious mind.

Thus it is possible to learn from existing biographies of modern English historians not only how to finish but also how not to finish work in hand. Of course, we do not read those biographies primarily as "how to" manuals, or even as "how not to" manuals. Nor should we. What concerns us most is, I suppose, to find an answer to the question: Is there such a thing as a special historical imagination or temperament and, if so, how does it work? Richard Ellmann, in his essay "Literary Biography," has admitted that "we cannot know completely the intricacies with which any mind negotiates with its surroundings to produce literature. The controlled seething out of which great works come is not likely to yield all its secrets."[11] That applies equally well to the creative process out of which comes great historical writing. But at least we can keep trying to come close to that process, to gain a greater understanding of it. Namier, singling out a "historical sense" as the crowning achievement of historical study, defines it as "an intuitive understanding of how things do not happen (how they did happen is a matter of specific knowledge)." Alan Bullock has drawn an analogy between the historian's preference for the concrete and particular, his distrust of the abstract and the general, and the approach of the painter and novelist. "Probably," he writes, "it is a question of temperament, of the way your mind works."[12] It is worthy of note that these two twentieth-century historians, neither of them noted for lack of realism, stress suprarational elements in their definition of the ideal historian's cast of mind. Namier, as his widow's biography reveals, always wanted to write a novel—to be entitled *The Torn Out Pages*—whose highlights and turning points he sketched out over the years. Another eighteenth-century historian of note, J. H. Plumb, actually wrote a novel in his twenties that, we are told, came very close to publication.[13]

Few biographers of English historians have dealt in an adequate manner with this difficult subject of the historian's imagination. Some skirt its edges, usually in the process of pointing out some defect in their subject. Thus William Ewart Gladstone, whose brilliant essay about Macaulay still remains one of the best things ever written about the historian, quotes him to the effect that "some books which I would never dream of opening at dinner, please me at breakfast, and vice versa." Gladstone's comment on this remark (largely, but perhaps not wholly, unjust) is: "There is more subtlety in this distinction, than could easily be found in any passage of his writings."[14] Lytton Strachey, equating the virtues of the metaphysician with the vices of the historian, criticizes Hume's historical style in these terms: "A generalized, colorless, unimaginative view of things is admirable when one is considering the law of causality, but one needs something else if one has to describe Queen Elizabeth."[15]

Neither Gladstone nor Strachey gets us very far. Nor, for that matter, does Lady Namier, even though she makes us privy to the result of her late husband's Rorschach test: "Intelligence superior and concrete. Approach often intuitive. There is also evidence of imagination."[16] The most interesting attempt to analyze the historical temperament of a famous English historian was made a hundred and twenty years ago by Walter Bagehot in his essay on Macaulay. He spoke there of "the temperament which inclines men to take an interest in actions as contrasted with objects."[17] Some people, Bagehot remarks, are (and, truth to tell, he precedes the next two words with the adverb "unfortunately") "born scientific." They are curious about shells, snails, horses, and butterflies. As the result of the absence of an intense and vivid nature, their minds are directed to scenery rather than to man's actions. In their intellectual makeup, "the abstract reason, and the inductive scrutiny which can be applied equally to trees and to men, to stones and to women, predominates over the more special qualities solely applicable to our own race,—the keen love, the eager admiration, the lasting hatred, the lust of rule which fastens men's interests on people and to people."[18]

Scientific men, Bagehot continues, are calm men. Euclid may be compared to fine ice, Newton to a peak of Teneriffe. The historian's mind differs from that of the naturalist, because he has more interest in human affairs. But it is also characterized by a certain quality of passivity. "It can bear not to take part." That is why Gibbon, as a Member of Parliament, could watch Fox and Burke debate without ever intervening himself. That is why Macaulay, who *did* speak memorably in Parliament, was not a debater, but rather a man for great occasions: "Somebody had to fetch him."[19] Why, Bagehot asks (tongue partially in cheek, as usual), is history dull? "The answer is, that it is written by men too dull to take the common interest in life, in whom languor predominates over zeal, and sluggishness over passion."[20] It was Macaulay's "inexperiencing nature" that made his greatest speeches so abstract; that prevented him from absorbing and learning more than he did from his sojourn in India; that explained his ultimate lack of real sympathy with either Cavaliers or Puritans.

But, granted the truth of all of this—and a twentieth-century reader would have to say that that is granting a good deal—why, Bagehot asks, is Macaulay's *History* as readable as it undoubtedly is? The answer is that he was able to unite two apparently discordant qualities: a flowing fancy and a concern for the coarse business of life. He could "throw over matters which are in their nature dry and dull,—transactions—budgets—bills,—the charm of fancy which a poetical mind employs to enhance and set forth the charm of what is beautiful."[21] And he was able to do this because he combined a vivid imagination with an impassive temperament.

Curiously enough, the appearance of Trevelyan's *Life and Letters* twenty years after that of Bagehot's essay confirmed much of what Bagehot had written about Macaulay's cast of mind. It contained a letter from him, written in 1830, in which the historian described individual items of furniture in the Duc de Broglie's salon in such detail that he himself felt obliged to add: "You will think that I have some intention of turning upholsterer."[22] At the same time, it revealed that what Macaulay loved more than anything else was to build castles in the air, to daydream; so that walking the streets of London, he would fancy himself in Greece, in Rome, in the midst of the French Revolution. He himself, so he told his sister Margaret, felt that those two ways of looking at the world—she for her part referred to them as a combination of a romantic disposition and a common-sense way of looking at things—stood in a fruitful relationship to one another. For, he told her, it was precisely when he built his castles in the air, when he daydreamed about the past, that factual accuracy became absolutely imperative: "Precision in dates, the day or hour in which a man was born or died, becomes absolutely necessary. A slight fact, a sentence, a word, are of importance in my romance."[23]

Is it possible that this seemingly paradoxical union of daydreaming and factual accuracy characterizes more than one historian, past and present? It is difficult to answer that question, since—Bagehot aside— few biographers of historians have hitherto occupied themselves with the nature of the connection between the historian's personality and his imagination. What, if anything, differentiates historians in this regard from other creative artists—or from scientists? One can make a quick list of desirable qualities for historians: love of puzzles and gossip; interest in power and personalities; a vigorous fantasy life; above all, perhaps, the negative capacity for not taking anything for granted, an ingrained skepticism about human motives and human testimony of any sort, as well as a fierce determination to get to the roots of matters. But is it axiomatic that all Western historians, from Herodotus to Toynbee, have needed to possess those qualities in similar proportions? After all, even in the course of just the last two centuries there have been fundamental changes in the sort of history generally praised and accepted as "great" by the society in which it is written. Gibbon's distantly ironical approach to the past went out of fashion after Herder and the historicists made *Einfühlung* the key to historical insight. Subsequently, Ranke and the "scientific" school that derived from him have given way to an awareness that a treatment of the past that is to some degree subjective is at once inevitable and desirable. As these changes in historiographical modes occurred—and England was not immune from them—has the result been to set up new kinds of elective affinity between certain personality traits and the ability to write history?

One might confidently assert, in answering that question, that Clio's many-mansioned house has always contained rooms to accommodate the whole range of human personality. Certainly, today, one need do no more than look around the table at the meeting of any history department (or to compare the *Journal of Economic History* with the *Journal of the History of Ideas*) to conclude that it takes all kinds. . . . Nevertheless, this should not deter biographers of historians, whose task it is, after all, to study character and psyche in relation to achievement, from at least raising the question as to whether there exists a "historical" personality type, and whether that has always been the same.

Other questions suggest themselves: Why do historians write?
J. H. Plumb has given one answer: "to try and understand the forces
which impel mankind along its strange course; to justify a religion,
a nation or a class; to make money; to fulfil ambition; to assuage
obsession; and a few, the true creators, to ease the ache within."[24] It
would be of special interest to hear more about the last category, those
"true creators." How do they achieve those breakthroughs in historical interpretation that revolutionize the field when they occur? According to one recent writer on this subject, the crucial element in the
breakthroughs made by four twentieth-century historians is their capacity to conceive of not just a single problem or issue or theme, but,
like the great novelists, of an entire self-contained world.[25] The late
Helen Maud Cam called Maitland's brilliant conclusion—a real break-
through—that in the thirteenth century the English parliament was
not primarily a national assembly or legislature but rather a session
of the king's council whose function was chiefly judicial and administrative "a magnificent attack on after-mindedness."[26] Is the essence
of such a revolutionary insight, then, as one historian has suggested,
the ability to see the past not through the distorting medium of what
followed after, but in its own terms?[27] Yet by no means all historians
who are able to look at the past in that manner achieve greatness or
even distinction. What else is required from the historians who really
made a difference? The biographers have not as yet supplied us with
more than approximations to an answer.

Yet another question they might well pose concerns the language
and style of historians, in particular their use of imagery and metaphor.
Lady Namier tells us, for example, that in the course of his early visit
to the United States, Sir Lewis was particularly struck by the New
York skyscraper. Thenceforth, he used it as an ideograph for man's
creative adaptability, since to him it represented a felicitous example
of interplay between independence and interdependence. He even
wrote an essay entitled "Skyscrapers."[28] Was Namier's fascination
purely accidental, or is it of some significance for his work as a historian? Do historians, especially those dealing with abstract entities
like groups and classes and movements, have to possess a special met-
aphorical capacity, a plastic or tactile imagination that can detect
shapes and configurations where others less gifted see only jumble
and confusion? In what ways is the sort of imagery any great historian
chooses integrally related to his personality and his general outlook
on the world? Did these historians, consciously or otherwise, derive
inspiration and verve for writing particular passages of their histories

not merely from contemplation of their sources but, to some extent, from extraneous experiences? One thinks of Macaulay's noting in his journal after a visit to the Great Exhibition (1851) that the sight had produced in him a "glow of eloquence" that supplied him with just the right touches for his description in *The History of England* of the battle of Steinkirk.[29] Was this experience unique to Macaulay? Surely not. But how often does it occur? And what are its psychological dimensions?

What the ultimate answers to those questions will turn out to be is uncertain. What is certain is that there remains a good deal to be done by that group of writers, present and future, whom (at the risk of perpetual obloquy and derision) I shall here refer to as Cliographers.

Peter and the Wallah:
from Kinsfolk to Competition

There are at least two fortuitous links between John Gibson Lockhart and George Otto Trevelyan. Both produced justly admired and still eminently readable biographies of close and famous relations—Lockhart that of his father-in-law, Sir Walter Scott, Trevelyan that of his uncle, Thomas Babington Macaulay. And both while still in their mid-twenties wrote series of pseudonymous letters about aspects of British society, in Scotland and India respectively, which caused shock and amusement at the time, and are now largely, and undeservedly, forgotten. It is to their common role as epistolary authors that this essay addresses itself. Beneath their leisurely and often playful use of the epistolary genre lay serious concerns and polemical intentions.

Lockhart and Trevelyan were both twenty-five years old, bright young men, gently born, on the way up, when they published their fictitious letters—Lockhart his *Peter's Letters to his Kinsfolk* (1819) and Trevelyan (in 1863) his *Competition Wallah*. Lockhart, a son of the manse on both sides of his parentage, had by then received his education at Glasgow University and at Balliol College, Oxford, where, like Adam Smith before him, he was awarded the Snell Exhibition.

From *History and Imagination: Essays in Honour of H. R. Trevor-Roper*, edited by Hugh Lloyd Jones, Valerie Pearl, and Blair Worden (London, 1981)

At Balliol he had immersed himself in German and Spanish literature as well as in the classics. He thought of joining the Spanish patriots who had risen against Napoleon, and offered to take Anglican orders if his father would allow him to serve as a chaplain in Wellington's army. His father would have none of it. Those who knew Lockhart at Oxford were struck by his satirical bent and by his ability to draw vivid and telling caricatures of his contemporaries. That was a habit he carried with him to Edinburgh, where he arrived in 1815 with the intention of pursuing a legal career. "A mischievous Oxford puppy" is how his close friend James Hogg, the Ettrick Shepherd, described him, "dancing after the young ladies, and drawing caricatures of everyone who came into contact with him."

His real bent was literary, not legal. When he returned to Scotland after getting a first at Oxford, he thought of writing a novel in the style of Galt. Later he was to write several novels; one of them, *Adam Blair,* is still in print. For the moment, however, he was a willing recruit for the magazine founded in 1817 by William Blackwood, whose aim it was to counteract from the Tory side the triumphant reign of the *Edinburgh Review.* In the so-called Chaldee Manuscript, a satirical commentary in biblical idiom on some of the leading Edinburgh literati, which appeared in an early number of *Blackwood's,* one verse read: "There came also from a far country the Scorpion which delighteth to sting the faces of men." The scorpion was Lockhart, who was then doing his best to live up (or down) to that sobriquet. Writing as "Baron von Lauerwinkel," he reprimanded two prominent Scottish figures, the theologian Dr. Chalmers and the mathematician Professor Playfair, for their association with the *Edinburgh Review,* and lambasted the "Cockney School of Poetry" and its guiding spirit, Leigh Hunt. Perhaps most notoriously, it was Lockhart who wrote that scabrous and wrong-headed review of Keats's *Endymion*—"back to the shop Mr John, back to 'plasters, pills, and ointment boxes' "— which impelled the mortally ill poet to exclaim to a friend: "If I die you must ruin Lockhart." Meanwhile, his interest in German literature and philosophy remained unabated. He translated Friedrich von Schlegel's *Lectures on the History of Literature Ancient and Modern* into English, and used the publisher's advance to finance a visit to Germany, where he had a (for him) ever memorable meeting with Goethe—"the finest specimen of humanity I ever beheld."

George Otto Trevelyan was born in 1838. His father, Charles Edward, was a prominent civil servant descended from an old and distinguished

Cornish family; his mother was Macaulay's beloved sister Hannah. They had met, fallen in love, and married in Calcutta, where she had accompanied her brother when he took up his post as Legal Member of Council in 1834, and where Trevelyan was then secretary to the Bengal political department. George attended Harrow under Vaughan, won all the prizes, and went on to his uncle's Cambridge college, Trinity. There he gained a certain local fame by his satirical verses; he shone at the Union; he became an "apostle," as well as a friend of the Prince of Wales; and he emerged from the Tripos as second classic. But, much to his chagrin, he failed to get a Trinity fellowship. So he tendered a "non-fellowship dinner" to his friends and, at the end of 1862, took ship for India with his father, who was returning there in the role of financial member of the Council. His son was to be his private secretary.

The India to which they sailed was still under the impact of the mutiny of 1857. The cruelty and violence of the mutineers had been matched by the cruelty and violence with which the mutiny had been put down. That had left deep scars on both sides. In 1862, the year of G. O. Trevelyan's arrival in India, panic was caused by a report that the assassination of all Europeans was being planned: "Even British officials became savage. The life of an Indian, according to the Viceroy [Elgin], was estimated by most Europeans no higher than that of a dog."[1] The phrase "even British officials" implies, correctly, that it was not usually they who showed the greatest antagonism to Indians. It was, rather, the large body of traders and planters who, even before the mutiny, had felt that the East India Company did not sufficiently favor British commercial interests. Parliament had wanted to reassure them, by taking over direct control of the Company from 1858, that they were not forgotten. Now, less concerned with responsible government than with maximum profits, they had become the principal opponents of a "soft" attitude towards the Indians. The result was tension between settlers and civil servants, or, as they were called, civilians. That tension was memorably recorded in the "improving exercise of writing about what he has seen" which, according to his father, G. O. Trevelyan "imposed upon himself" during his Indian sojourn, and which resulted in *The Competition Wallah*.[2]

"Competition wallahs," in Anglo-Indian usage, were those among the higher ranks of the Indian Civil Service who had received their posts since 1853, when Parliament had abolished patronage and had opened all appointments to competition. Macaulay, helped and advised by his brother-in-law, chaired the committee to implement the legislation. Until the mid-nineteenth century, directors of the East India Company could nominate candidates to "writerships." Those candidates then sat an examination and, if successful, spent two years at the company's college at Haileybury, before proceeding to India. All that was now changed. Any student at Oxford or Cambridge could compete for an Indian Civil Service appointment. Haileybury was closed in 1857.

The impulse was reformist; but it was scarcely democratic. The new system was intended to produce civilians who conformed to the ideal of the gentleman. In the event, however, it failed to appeal to the higher social echelons. Those competitioners who got to India— where they had to take two more examinations, in Indian law and languages—were attacked as too bookish, as lacking in manners, and as weak in field sports.

"Henry Broughton," the ostensible author of *The Competition Wallah,* was one of those civilians selected under the system that resulted from the act of 1853. The letters he addressed to his Trinity (Cambridge) friend, "Charles Simkins," were first published in England in successive numbers of *Macmillan's Magazine* between January 24, 1863, and July 20, 1864. They appeared in book form in the following year, with certain omissions. By that time all pretense of anonymity had been dropped, and Trevelyan's name was on the title page. *The Competition Wallah* describes life in British India as seen through the eyes of a young civilian, a former Trinity man, who has just arrived there after receiving his degree. It depicts the competitioners' way of life in India, their contacts with Anglo-Indian society, a railway journey, visits to a government school and an opium factory, conditions in Calcutta, a tiger hunt, a Hindu religious festival, and a sojourn in the interior. We are given vignettes of Anglo-Indian life which, in their descriptive power, are reminiscent of Kipling. At the same time, the letters discuss some of the major issues of contemporary controversy: the effects of the mutiny; the desirability of the law of contracts which, on pain of criminal penalties, prevented workers from leaving their jobs; the position of Christianity; and, above all, relations between English settlers and native Indians in the postmutiny period.

The narrative framework of the book is cleverly established at the beginning, when "Charles Simkins, B.A." writes to *Macmillan's Magazine* in order to introduce the letters addressed to him by "Henry Broughton," his closest friend at Radley and then at Cambridge. When they were at Trinity, Broughton was the man of action who rowed for the college and spoke at the Union, while Simkins "con-

versed with a few kindred souls"—presumably the apostles—about
the problems of existence. Both take the competitive examination
for the Indian Civil Service. Broughton triumphs, coming third.
Simkins—the very name seems to whisper failure—fails. The two
friends had agreed in advance that the "survivor" of the examination
should write a full account of his Indian experience to the less fortunate
competitor. That is the ostensible origin of *The Competition Wallah,*
where Broughton, in his letters to Simkins, assumes an affectionate
indulgence befitting a correspondence between a proconsul and a
bookworm.

Peter's Letters to his Kinsfolk were published forty-four years before
The Competition Wallah. As well as the distances of time and of geography between the two works, there is the distance of subject-mat-
ter. The chief concern of Dr. Peter Morris, the ostensible author of
Lockhart's three volumes, is with the prominent literati, lawyers, professors, and judges of Edinburgh, whose activities are held as a mirror
to the intellectual and, so to speak, the spiritual state of the city. As
a reviewer for *Blackwood's,* Lockhart had taken the Tory side in the
war against the reigning Whig literary-legal establishment. The *Letters*
must be read in that context; although they also contain much nonpolitical, primarily descriptive material, and although, as we shall see,
their intellectual scope far transcends the battle between the reviews.
On one level, *Peter's Letters* may certainly be read as a cultural gaz-
etteer, with emphasis on the direct observation—and overhearing—
of leading civic and literary personages. Lockhart's descriptive powers, like Trevelyan's, are considerable. He has a highly developed sense
of the ludicrous, and an exact and delightful ear for the local argot.
By courtesy of the ostensible author, we attend dinner parties and
university lectures in both Edinburgh and Glasgow. We visit Jeffrey's
house at Craigcrook and Walter Scott's Abbotsford. We inspect book-
shops, critically examine books and paintings, meet bluestockings and
dandies. We are present at the law courts, at a Burns dinner, and at
a General Assembly of the Scotch Kirk.

Lockhart, whose characterizations are more subtle than Trevelyan's,
employs the more complex narrative device. Many observations in
Peter's Letters are filtered through the eyes of two persons rather than
one. The two are Morris, a convivial and bibulous Welsh physician
whose mother was Scottish but who, himself educated at Oxford, is
imbued with English rather than Welsh or Scottish national feeling;
and one Wastle, an Episcopalian Scottish laird who alternately resides

in his Berwickshire castle and in lodgings in the old town of Edinburgh. A former contemporary of Peter Morris in Oxford, Wastle acts as a guide during the doctor's Edinburgh visit. He is said to be the keenest Tory in Scotland; his Toryism, approaching that of the old Cavalier school, was, Morris noted, "far more keen and intolerant than that of any man of superior attainments I ever met with on either side of the Tweed." Unlike Morris, who is impressed by the absence of party spirit in the social intercourse of the Edinburgh literati, Wastle is wholly intolerant of Whigs and Calvinists; being too great a bigot, Morris writes, to feel much happiness in the presence of men who differed from him on important points. Whereas Morris (who has a particular interest in phrenology) is keenly observant and prides himself in taking nothing on trust, Wastle lives almost wholly in the past, his head full of Gothic antiquities and of the history, the poetry, and the romance of the Middle Ages.

Professor Francis Hart may well be right in viewing Morris and Wastle as the projections of a conflict in Lockhart's own mind and experience, between the unbending Toryism of *Blackwood's* and the less rigidly conservative outlook of Scott, whom Lockhart had first met during the summer of 1818, who had lost no time in inviting him to Abbotsford, and whom he already greatly admired.[3] The question of the relationship between Lockhart and his two fictitious protagonists is complicated by the appearance in *Peter's Letters* of the author *in propria persona;* described by Morris as a very young man who might soon find that there were better things in literature than satire. Morris-Wastle-Lockhart—perhaps we should not be surprised to find so solipsistic a preoccupation with the different facets of an author's own psyche and personality in a Calvinist country, and in a city that within half-a-dozen years was to witness the publication of *The Confessions of a Justified Sinner* by Lockhart's friend James Hogg.

The general target of *Peter's Letters* is Scottish Whiggery. Its particular targets are the *Edinburgh Review* and its editor, Francis Jeffrey. In the Edinburgh of 1819, Dr. Morris observes, the Tories had all the political power, but the Whigs were still lords of public opinion. One reason for this, Morris argues, is that whereas in England important literary figures like Wordsworth, Coleridge, and Southey could be counted on the Tory side, in Scotland the leading literary lights— Scott, of course, was the exception—tended to be Whigs. And the leader of the pack, by virtue of his immense power as editor of the *Edinburgh Review,* was Jeffrey. Listening to "the sharp, shrill, but deep-toned trumpet of [Jeffrey's] voice in court," Morris finds it impossible to conceive of a more fertile, towering intellect; but he adds: "There cannot be a finer display of ingenuity than his mode of addressing a set of plain conscientious men [the jury], whom it is his business to bamboozle." Jeffrey seemed to exert the same power over the jury that his journal exerted over Edinburgh opinion. And, in Morris's view, to much the same effect. He recognizes the *Review*'s "wonderful authority . . . although it never did anything to entitle it to much respect from English scholars, English patriots, and English Christians."

As we learn in the course of *Peter's Letters,* English Christians were repelled by the *Edinburgh*'s infidelity, English patriots by its defeatist posture during the Napoleonic wars, and English scholars by its lack of critical judgment. For the last, Morris holds Jeffrey altogether responsible. How, for example, could he have launched such a long, deliberate, and elaborate attack on the character of Robert Burns? It was all too easy to rail against the dissipation of those who were poor, and in drudgery. An attack of that kind was a defeat both of nationality and of humanity of feeling. For Lockhart, who may have derived the idea from Schlegel, literary and national genius were, or ought to be, inextricably linked. A great national author, he proclaims through Morris (the author in question was William Robertson), "connects himself for ever with all the better part of the nation, by the ties of an intellectual kinsmanship—ties which in his own age are scarcely less powerful than those of the kinsmanship of blood, and which, instead of evaporating and being forgotten in the course of a few generations, as the bonds of blood must inevitably be, are only riveted the faster by every year that passes over them."

Morris thoroughly approved of the great Burns dinner which, with all the leading Edinburgh literati, he was privileged to attend, and at which the requisite national enthusiasm was displayed in honor of a lowborn peasant genius. But his hope that the dinner would be nonpolitical was to be disappointed. The toasts had been prearranged by the Whig reviewers. Not one of them had the common candor or manliness, at a dinner that honored poetical genius, to propose the health of Wordsworth, Southey, or Coleridge; while Crabbe, Rogers, and even Montgomery were duly toasted. The lack of respect shown by the *Edinburgh* for the Lake school, and for Wordsworth in particular, seemed to Lockhart unforgivable. In his eyes, Wordsworth was as much a great moral guide as he was a great poet. The finest introduction to any book of psychology or ethics in the world was the opening of *The Excursion,* that poem of which Jeffrey had written in a famous review that it would "never do." Lockhart himself was embarrassed by the fact that *Blackwood's* had only recently savaged Coleridge's *Biographia Literaria,* in an article filled with personal venom. So Peter Morris expresses shock at this "sad offence," adding that "if there be any man of grand and original genius alive at this moment in Europe, such a man is Mr Coleridge."

Students of the conservative school of European romanticism in the early nineteenth century can have a field day with *Peter's Letters.* All the expected indicators are present, beginning with love of history, "the only study which presents to all our endeavours and aspirations after higher intellectual cultivation, a fast middle-point and grappling place." But history ought not to be a mere chronicle of names, years, and external events. It ought to be a study that "seizes and expands before us the spirit of great men, great times, and great actions." Morris is stirred by his visits to cathedrals in South Germany and Spain, and laments the discontinuance of Gregorian chant by the Church of England. Lockhart's nostalgia is evident too in Morris's reaction to the roll call of the venerable Henry Mackenzie's heroes and heroines of days gone by, which "sounded in my ears like the echoes of some old romantic melody, too simple, and too beautiful, to have been framed in these degenerate over-scientific days." Morris most sympathetically describes Mackenzie's loving evocation of Edinburgh life as it used to be, when all the genteel population lived in the tall citadels of the town, and when the general style of entertaining was less formal and at the same time heartier and friendlier. Lockhart's antimechanism emerges in the doctor's strictures against contemporary Scottish philosophers like Thomas Brown and Dugald Stewart, who favored the investigation of human thoughts and feelings by mechanical modes of observation. That approach, Morris thought, was bound to fail: for human affections could never become an object of successful scientific inquiry. Antimechanism is associated with a revulsion against urban industrialism. During his visit to a Glasgow cotton factory, Morris's spirits are "not a little depressed" by the eternal rack and buzz of wheels and spindles. He finds relief by quickly escaping for a walk in the fields.

Morris's values are starkly opposed to those held dear by Jeffrey and his colleagues on the *Edinburgh Review.* They aimed to bring Whiggery into touch with the forward-looking outlook of the middle classes and with the lessons and the values of political economy. Lockhart's romantic Toryism was repelled by most manifestations of modernity. But *Peter's Letters* give evidence of a philosophical conflict more fundamental than the contrast between past and present, one that cut more deeply than Lockhart's quarrel with Jeffrey over the appropriate responses to Burns and Wordsworth. From Lockhart's point of view, the *Edinburgh* reviewers were chiefly dangerous because they were the spiritual heirs of Hume who, with his pervasive skepticism, had spared no pains in "convulsing the whole soil, wherein feelings both religious and national had taken root."

Hume's writings on religion, Lockhart thought, had increased the prevalence of infidelity. Commenting in 1851 on a review of Cockburn's *Life* of Jeffrey, Lockhart remarked that "I fancy the whole set [of *Edinburgh* reviewers] were really most thorough infidels and S[ydney Smith] at the top of them in this respect as in all others." But Hume's pernicious influence had done more than foster infidelity. The doctrine of trying everything by the standard of mere utility, set on foot by Hume, Adam Smith, and the other philosophers of their sect, had undoubtedly been "the most dangerous present ever conferred by men of high and powerful intellects upon the herd of the species." Hume's Toryism was another matter, of course. But the Whigs contrived to dismiss that as "David's one little foible." At the same time, they fortified the influence of his deleterious philosophy by giving them prominence in the *Edinburgh*. Wastle, while recognizing Jeffrey's intellect and his general rectitude of feeling and principle, "regards the Scotch philosophers of the present day, and among them or above the rest, Mr Jeffrey and the Edinburgh Reviewers, as the legitimate progeny of the sceptical philosophers of the last age." Morris agrees. It is particularly unfortunate, he thinks, that at the present time a thoroughgoing skepticism has no object on which the disinterested affections might exercise themselves. Self-gratification, therefore, had become the principal aim of common minds; and when there were no longer any earnest notions about what it meant to be loved and respected, the reading public easily fell in with the skeptical critic's tendency to despise everything and to admire nothing. Moreover, by not sufficiently emphasizing the study of the classics, the Scottish universities provided no barrier against the spirit of mockery. Only acquaintance with the great models of antiquity moves men to love and reverence the great authors of their own time, who are the intellectual kinsmen of the ancients and who "seem to revive the greatness of the departed, and vindicate once more the innate greatness of our nature."

There are connections between those concerns and Lockhart's political beliefs. On the one hand, there was the self-love of those conceited blockheads who, egged on by Jeffrey's sarcasm, were convinced that they themselves were superior to anything the age could produce. On the other hand, there was the self-love that had characterized the worst periods of the French Revolution, one "gratified with the downfall of so many kinds of distinction, that at last it grew to be a blind, infuriate, ungovernable impulse, which could not remain quiet, while any individual yet retained qualities which raised him above the multitude." Here were two kinds of self-love that were closely linked. For both were inevitable results of religious skepticism, of substituting the self-sufficing, self-satisfied reason of the speculative human intellect for divine wisdom.

Thus Lockhart's critique of the *Edinburgh Review* and its editor derives not merely from his stance as a romantic partisan, but also, and more significantly, from a congeries of ideas in which theology and politics are blended with literature and philosophy. The real enemy was not so much Jeffrey as the destructive influence of Hume, which, seen from this point of view, resembled the "Geist der stets verneint" of Lockhart's beloved Goethe. It was no accident that Jeffrey, when he pleaded before the Scottish bar, showed little sympathy for the simple and unadorned workings of the affections. Equally, as Professor Hart has argued, it was no accident that Dr. Morris was so enamored of phrenology, a branch of study that because it threw light on the primitive or elementary faculties and feelings, was, like Lockhart's Germanism, a critical vantage point against Scottish metaphysics.[5] Far more than the reputation of the Lake poets was at stake for Lockhart when, through Morris and Wastle, he took aim at Jeffrey and the *Edinburgh Review* in *Peter's Letters*.

G. O. Trevelyan's declared purpose in writing his *Competition Wallah* was to make Englishmen at home aware of the harshness and contempt with which so many European settlers in India, most of them English, treated the native population. Their slogan was "a Criminal Contract Law, and damn the Niggers!" Whereas, on the whole, people in England had soon repented of their enthusiasm for a severe and retributive policy, many of the settlers had, if anything, become even more firmly attached to the great principle of the debasement of the native, the domination of the "Anglo-Saxons," and the development of the resources of British India for the benefit of English pockets.

The political creed of at least one of the English characters in Trevelyan's play *The Dawk Bungalow: or Is his Appointment Pucka?*, performed at the residence of the Lieutenant-Governor of Bengal on

December 21, 1863, included the sentiment that "when you hit a nigger, he dies on purpose to spite you." At the Sanapore race meeting, Henry Broughton watches an incident which he reports to Simkins with a passion clearly derived from Trevelyan's own: "I saw—with my own eyes I saw—a tall, raw-boned brute of a planter" rush at a number of well-dressed, well-to-do natives (respectable shopkeepers, men of business, gentlemen of rank) who had as good a right to be there as the governor general himself, "and flay them with a double-thonged hunting-whip, until he had driven them in humiliating confusion and terror for the distance of many yards." One or two civilians remarked to each other that it was a shame. But no one seemed astounded or horrified. No one interposed. No one prosecuted. "No one objected to meet the blackguard at dinner, or to take the odds from him at the ordinary."

Trevelyan was enough of a realist to understand that any hope of the complete amalgamation of rulers and ruled in India was utopian. But he saw no reason why the two races should not live side by side in amity. For that to happen, however, there would have to be a marked improvement in the "tone" of the settlers. "The intense Anglo-Saxon spirit of self-approbation, which, though dominant at home, is unpleasantly perceptible among vulgar Englishmen on the Continent, becomes rampant in India." Enlightened opinion in England must keep a close watch on the nonofficial English in India. That was one theme, and by Trevelyan's own account the most important, of *The Competition Wallah*.

Another clearly enunciated theme is the sympathetic portrait of the life of the young civil servants who had come out to India under the new competitive system. There was no better company in the world, Broughton declared, than a rising civilian; for he altogether lacked "that carping spirit of discontent" which was so painfully apparent in able men in England who found themselves kept in the background for want of interest or money. The competitioner and his colleagues were kept busy enough with practical problems in a dangerous setting where men had to help each other to survive and where tolerance was essential. "In spite of Dr Pusey," Broughton writes, "I cannot help greeting as a brother Protestant the little Danish missionary who has changed those blackguard murderous villagers of Kurnam into Christians and payers of rent. Flanagan rides twenty miles every fortnight to Dinagegur to hear mass; but I can remember when he rode as many leagues, through the September sun, with my baby in the saddle before him, a musket-ball in his shoulder, and his cheek laid open by a sabre cut." Was not that sort of life better than the heartsickness of briefs deferred, dreary chambers, or drumming Latin verses into dull English schoolboys?

It is not, I believe, merely coincidental that a work dealing with life in India contains references to briefs and chambers, Latin verses and Dr. Pusey. *The Competition Wallah* may have been written partly in condemnation of the racist attitudes of English settlers, partly in praise of the new civilian's mode of life. But it is as much a revelation of the general outlook of a young Whiggish Radical as it is an account of a sojourn in India. As such, it provides a fascinating counterpoint to the Tory views expressed in a very different context by the young Lockhart four and a half decades before. Broughton-Trevelyan welcomes the triumphs of technology. He rejoices that the entire Indian subcontinent is now covered with a network of telephone wires and that railways connect all the chief cities, with light tramways branching out from the trunk lines. Never has he been so impressed by "the triumph of progress, the march of mind," as during his first railway journey in Bengal: "those two thin strips of iron, representing as they do the mightiest and most fruitful conquest of science. . . ." On and near the railway line there are signs of England's handiwork everywhere to be seen—viaducts, iron sheds, the refreshment room, even the true British station master. But a hundred yards from the embankment, one found oneself amidst "scenes that Arrian might have witnessed": bullock litters, trains of pilgrims, filthy beggars—"these are sights which have very little in common with Didcot or Crewe Junction."

Trevelyan does more than point the obvious contrast between ancient and modern civilization. When he takes us inside an Indian train and imagines Simkins asking how "our countrymen manage to appropriate to themselves the first-class carriages without a special regulation to that effect," he uses a purely English class analogy to underline his outrage at one of those Anglo-Indian customs that impeded good race relations. How is it, Simkins is asked in return, "that there are no tradesmen's sons at Eton or Harrow? There is no law, written or unwritten, which excludes them from those schools, and yet the boys take good care that if one comes he shall not stay there very long."

Trevelyan does not idealize the Indians. He notes their lack of stamina, their indolence, their want of truthfulness, their litigiousness. But mendacious habits, however deeply engrained in the mysterious Hindu nature, could be corrected and modified in time, if only the

English settlers would stop using their "damned Nigger style" and try, by an act of imagination, to put themselves into the position of the Hindus, and to see themselves as they were seen. After all, Hindu civilization went back to an ancient social order, "with titles which were borne by his forefathers, when the ancestors of English dukes still paddled about in wicker canoes, when 'wild in woods the noble marquis ran.' "

The Indian mind, Broughton points out, is bound to be outraged by much English behavior. Imagine, for example, the horror with which a punctilious Brahmin must regard people who eat cow or pig flesh, and consume liquor. English energy and earnestness must strike the languid and voluptuous aristocracy of the East as oppressive and importunate. English honesty must appear contemptible to the tortuous Hindu mind. English disregard of *les convenances,* in matters of hygiene for example, must seem inexplicable and hateful. Add to that the mysterious awe in which Englishmen were shrouded in native eyes, "and you will have some conception of the picture presented to the Hindu mind by an indefatigable, plain-spoken, beer-drinking, cigar-smoking, tiger-shooting collector." To the Indians, the English probably seemed a species of quaint and somewhat objectionable demon, with a rare aptitude for fighting and for administration, but foul and degraded in their habits.

While Trevelyan is anxious that the English in India should learn to recognize the profound differences between the two races, he does not advocate a policy of cultural laissez-faire. That would be expecting too much of Macaulay's nephew who, like his uncle, believed firmly that the rulers had a civilizing role to fulfill. It is our duty, he writes, to educate and to enlighten, to strike off the fetters of custom and superstition. Schools and railroads had already done much to set "the fresh air of European civilisation" circulating freely through every pore of the vast Indian community. But after sixty years of European missionary activity, the proportion of heathens to Christians was still a thousand to one; indeed, in northern India, ten thousand to one. Why, "under the very shadow of the Christian churches and colleges, do men cry aloud to Seeva, and cut themselves after their manner with knives and lancets, till the blood gushes out of them"?

The answer to that question elicited, once again, Trevelyan's awareness of cultural relativism, in this case his recognition that an elevated and philosophical religion, adapted to the needs of an enlightened and progressive society, could not achieve success as a proselytizing creed in India; and that Protestant simplicity could not appeal to a people accustomed to elaborate ritual. If an English clergyman "chose to stand for twenty years at a stretch on the top of the Ochterlony monument, or take up his abode under a cocoa-nut tree in the Sunderbunds, he would have thousands of worshippers and admirers; but the Bishop of Oxford or Dr Guthrie might preach through all the cities in the north of India without making two dozen proselytes." To be effective in India, Christian missionaries would be well advised to abandon their European way of life; not to hesitate to sacrifice comfort, society, and respectability for the cause of Christ. Certain groups of German Lutherans, Broughton notes, had succeeded in this. They lived simply and austerely. They spoke Indian languages with fluency and precision. Their children ate rice and curried lentils. The Lutherans had retained their remarkable influence over the people in their territory.

Both of our authors came to regret the manner, if not the substance, of what they had written. Yet it may be worth pondering certain other similarities between these two epistolary works, published almost half a century apart, by men whose outlooks differed in so many ways. To begin with, both series of letters were, in a very real sense, footnotes to great political events; and both were violently attacked in certain quarters. In the case of *The Competition Wallah,* that is hardly surprising. The mutiny, so W. L. Burn has written, was like "a red-hot poker thrust into the face of the Englishman."[6] The desire for revenge, accompanied by undisguised hostility to Indians, was slow to evaporate. Trevelyan himself tells us that after the publication of his ninth letter, which condemned the bloodthirstiness of some of the "Anglo-Saxons," the leading Calcutta journals that had hitherto spoken of the *Wallah* "in terms of extravagant and unmerited eulogy" discovered that he was an ignorant, conceited coxcomb, fresh from college, "whose effusions could only be received with silent contempt."

But why did *Peter's Letters* give offense? Sir Walter Scott, who was in on the secret of the authorship from the start, had a ready answer. It was, he wrote, because "few men, and least of all Scotchmen, can hear the actual truth in conversation, or in that which approaches nearest to conversation—a work like the Doctor's, published within the circle to which it refers." In fact, Scott believed, Lockhart had been too gentle and had refrained from depicting Edinburgh's embattled and vindictive literary society in its true colors. After first reading the letters, in July 1819, he had told him that "the general tone is perhaps too favourable to the state of public society and of individual character." But Lockhart had been right to "throw a Claude Lorraine tint over our Northern landscape," since Scots could not tolerate the bare truth, either in conversation or in a work like *Peter's Letters*.

Coleridge informed Lockhart that the spleen and criticism provoked by the book had been exceptional. If that was so, Lockhart replied in a postscript to the third edition, the true reason for the anger of the Scottish Whigs went much deeper than annoyance at their sharp delineation by Dr. Morris. Peter's real crime was to have declared himself "an enemy to the pestilent genius of Scottish republicanism and Scottish infidelity." It was not merely that Morris had exposed the Scottish Whigs' lack of patriotism, a deficiency exemplified, he observed, by the failure of the *Edinburgh Review* to have rendered steady support for the Spanish patriots who rose against Napoleon. Something more was at stake now. Eighteen nineteen, the year of the book's publication, was, after all, a year of domestic crisis for England. Afflictions beyond the reach of human aid were being fancifully interpreted by a suffering populace as symbols and consequences of oppression. And what had the Scottish Whigs been doing? Pouring oil on the kindling embers of disaffection, and, according to Morris-Lockhart, hailing England's internal enemies with the same fervor with which, for so many years, they had hailed Bonaparte. No wonder they were furious with Dr. Morris, whose Tory loyalty to church and state matched his still evident joy at the triumph of English arms and honor over Napoleon.

Peter's Letters, then, are as much a by-product of Waterloo, and of the postwar social and economic dislocations that led to Peterloo, as *The Competition Wallah* is a belated by-product of the Indian Mutiny. Both works can be read, on one level, as polemical tracts, and they were certainly assailed as such. But there are deeper similarities between the two books than those to be found in their common membership of the epistolary genre and in the hostility that their publication aroused. In the first place, both Lockhart and Trevelyan were fervent English patriots. Lockhart's revenge for the attacks made on him by the Scottish Whigs consists, so he tells Coleridge, of taking special pleasure in every present and future assertion of English honor, and in every spectacle of English glory. Trevelyan, for his part, celebrates the heroic defense of "the little house at Arrah" by the outnumbered English against the rebels with an eloquence that reminds us of his uncle's account of the siege of Londonderry. He rejoices that, in the mutiny, "the blaze of Oriental fanaticism . . . at length yielded to the courageous perseverance, and the unconquerable energy of our race." Trevelyan praises not only English heroism but the sacredness of the English marriage tie, the purity of English literature, and his compatriots' capacity for charity and humanity. As for the English reputation for snobbery, "what is the champagne from the public-house round the corner, and the greengrocer in white cotton gloves making off with a cold chicken in his umbrella, to the gigantic, ruinous pretension and display of a highborn Zemindar? I hate this ignorant abuse of everything English."

Both Lockhart and Trevelyan valued classical learning—both had performed brilliantly in that subject at university—and their pages are studded with classical allusions and quotations. For Lockhart, a classical education, by making men acquainted with human nature displaying itself under the guise of manners very different from their own, makes it possible for them to understand their own manners and nature better than they could do otherwise. If there is an awareness of cultural relativism in Trevelyan, it is present in the romantic Tory Lockhart too. Trevelyan, for his part, turns to the classics to increase his understanding not so much of English as of Indian institutions, manners, and customs; particularly when he discusses Indian religion. He observes that the introduction of Western learning has produced the same effect on that religion, that is to say a clandestine turning to deism, which the progress of civilization had produced on the ancient classical creeds. What Trevelyan and Lockhart both valued in religion was authenticity. The Indians found it, Trevelyan believed, in elaborate oriental ritual: Lockhart found it in a simple rustic gathering that took the sacrament in a Scottish country kirk.

For all his praise of material progress, rationalism, and tolerance, Trevelyan finds that there are times when an oppressive sense of the nineteenth century weighs heavily upon the soul—

> when we shudder to hear Mr Cobden pronounce that one number of the *Times* newspaper is worth the eight books of Thucydides. There are moments when we feel that locomotives and power-looms are not everything; that black care sits behind the stoker; that death knocks with equal foot at the door of the Turkey Red Yarn Establishment. Then it is good to turn from the perusal of the share-list; from pensive reflections on the steadiness of piece-goods, the languor of gunnycloths, and the want of animation evinced by muletwist, to the contemplation of qual-

ities which are recognised and valued by all ages alike. It is good
to know that trade, and luxury, and the march of science, have
not unnerved our wrists, and dulled our eyes, and turned our
blood to water. There is much in common with Leonidas dressing his hair before he went forth to his last fight, and Colvin
[one of the defenders of the little house at Arrah] laughing over
the rice and salt, while the bullets pattered on the wall like hail.

Those sentiments are not so far removed from Lockhart's suspicion
of the test of mere utility, from his dread of uniformity in an age when
"so much oil is poured upon the whole surface of the ocean," or from
his celebration of national heroes, whether of the past or in the shape
of contemporaries like Wellington, Scott, and Wordsworth.

Trevelyan, indeed, was no more a pure Utilitarian than his uncle,
or, for that matter, the later John Stuart Mill. His literary tastes—
though, to be sure, not his literary knowledge—ranged far more
widely than Macaulay's. He liked not only Browning and Carlyle,
but also Wordsworth and Ruskin. He was to call Goethe, in hyperbolic
language that echoes Lockhart's, "the greatest master who ever consciously made art out of literature." That is not the only reminder of
Lockhart to be found in *The Competition Wallah*. We notice, for example, Trevelyan's comment, during his comparison of the civilians
of his own day with those of the eighteen-thirties, that while his contemporaries could certainly be said to be doing their duty on behalf
of the Hindus, that task was no longer a labor of love. *The Competition
Wallah* is, in large part, an appeal by an English patriot for a revival
of that spirit as well as for an end to race hatred on the part of the
English settlers; just as *Peter's Letters,* in their turn, are largely an appeal
by an earlier English patriot—Lockhart's patriotism was as much English as Scottish—for the replacement of self-love, mechanism, and
artifice by genuine love of country and authentic depth of feeling.
Hunting lions in Edinburgh was, perhaps, not all that different from
hunting tigers in India.

Peter's Letters to his Kinsfolk and *The Competition Wallah* are youthful
and idiosyncratic productions, *jeux d'esprit,* and it would no doubt be
unwise to search too hard in them for broad conclusions about the
intellectual history of the period. "From Kinsfolk to Competition" is
merely a conflation of the two titles, and thus less portentous than it
may sound. Its evocation of echoes of "from status to contract,"
"from *Gemeinschaft* to *Gesellschaft,*" is, however, not entirely acci-

dental. Lockhart's "kinsfolk" connotes community, history, and hierarchy. Trevelyan's "competition" is linked to science, reason, and progress. Yet his *cri de coeur* against the "oppressive sense of the nineteenth century" recalls Albert Hirschman's recent observation that

> as soon as capitalism was triumphant and "passions" seemed indeed to be restrained and perhaps even extinguished in the comparatively peaceful, tranquil, and business-minded Europe of the period after the Congress of Vienna, the world suddenly appeared empty, petty, and boring and the stage was set for the Romantic critique of the bourgeois order as incredibly impoverished in relation to earlier ages—the new world seemed to lack nobility, grandeur, mystery, and, above all, passion.[7]

Are we not mistaken if we think in terms of a rigid intellectual barrier between the old regime and the new world of capitalism and democracy?

Marx had an answer. "The bourgeois viewpoint," he declared in the *Grundrisse,* "has never advanced beyond the antithesis between itself and the romantic viewpoint, and the latter will accompany it as its legitimate antithesis up to its blessed end." But that answer, though brilliantly suggestive, is not wholly satisfactory. Neither Lockhart nor Trevelyan fits snugly into the "bourgeois" pigeonhole. And the romantic viewpoint, to accommodate both, needs more stretching than Marx allows. Yet, in a very real sense, it does accommodate them. That is some measure of its triumph. One ends by hoping that there will soon appear more books like Raymond Williams's *Culture and Society,* broadly conceived studies of nineteenth-century ideas in their relation to politics and class. But one ends too with the conviction that such studies must concern themselves, not with England alone, but with Britain as a whole, including Scotland and Anglo-India. After all, those Utilitarian ideas that had their origins north of the border, and which Wastle and Dr. Morris found so sinister, were to hold partial sway, in one form or another, over British India in the nineteenth century. And Macaulay, who had not a little to do with that, knew and loved his Scott almost as well as did Peter Morris. Reading provocative pseudonymous letters can be instructive as well as amusing. As for writing them—ah, but who, in (to recall Lockhart's phrase) "these degenerate over-scientific days," would hazard that rash undertaking?

Macaulay, History, and the Historians

December the twenty-eighth, 1959, marked the centenary of Lord Macaulay's death. On one occasion, worn out by long hours of re-writing and polishing, all part of his endless effort to make the meaning of his *History* crystal clear to all its readers, he spurred himself on with the reminder: "*Corraggio!* And think of 2850." And he would, no doubt, be pleased to know that his fame easily survived the first hundred-year stage on the road to this distant date.

It has not, however, survived unimpaired. Ours is an age of doubt, of cautious pessimism, of minor keys—not one to take kindly to the brash, metallic clangor of symphonies in C-major. And Macaulay, self-acknowledged composer of such symphonies, has become the symbol of a misinterpretation of history that sees the past not in its own terms but merely as preparation for the present.

Unfortunately, the debate on the extent to which Macaulay was in fact a "Whig historian," in the narrow as well as the broad sense, is nowadays apt to form the only point of scholarly interest in him. Let us admit that he was blind to the seamy side of material progress in the early Victorian age, that he carried a certain amount of political and personal bias—without disguise—into his historical writing. What remains important is his mastery of the art of narrative history

From *History Today*, December 1959

and his personality and character that—thanks to Sir G. O. Trevelyan's *Life and Letters* of his uncle—we know better than those of any other modern historian and that, marked at once by charm and prejudice, wit and affection, continue to exert a lively fascination.

Perhaps it is appropriate to recall some of the features of Macaulay's personality, since he is at present so often condemned and dismissed as cocksure, arrogant, and insensitive, a sort of human counterpart to the Great Exhibition. This kind of description does not begin to do him justice. One might certainly expect, for example, to find in someone like Macaulay—who rose by sheer talent from an Evangelical middle-class background to an eminence that made him in the eyes of the Whig aristocracy both a welcome guest and, eventually, a popular host—at once a great consciousness of his advancement and a great pride in it. It is, indeed, a long way from his writing to his sister in 1831, no doubt jocosely, about a dinner party including various members of the nobility—"Listen and be proud of your connection with one who is admitted to eat and drink in the same room with beings so exalted"—to the story recorded in his journal twenty-eight years later that tells of the proprietor of the *Illustrated London News* edging close to him "and saying with an insinuating grin and in a most tender tone: 'And 'ow [sic] do you find it being a Lord?'"

Yet this considerable change of status seems to have left few marks, beyond a possibly excessive awareness of the fact that it *had* left few marks. As early as 1833, Macaulay called himself "the only *parvenu* I ever heard of, who, after being courted into splendid circles, and after having succeeded beyond expectation in political life, acquired in a few months profound contempt for rank, fashion, popularity, and money—for all pleasures in short but those which arise from the exercise of the intellect and the affections." Even then, fresh from his oratorical triumphs in the Reform Bill debates, this was on the whole an accurate self-appraisal. Many years later, he recalled that: "there was a time when I was half ashamed of being related to vulgar people. That was when I was fighting my way against all sorts of difficulties. Now it is quite different." Macaulay never did learn to show patience in the face of what he considered to be folly and dullness; but to one who could call Buckingham Palace "the dullest house in London," impatience knew no social discrimination. Neither money nor social position, his own or other people's, ever became fundamentally important to him.

Thus, one must not put too much stress upon the effects on his personality of his youthful struggles for financial solvency and his change of social *milieu*. Yet it is important to remember that there were other strains and difficulties, and to modify somewhat the view, still widely current, of Macaulay as a paradigm of continuous happiness and self-confidence. At school he suffered not only from homesickness—"*la maladie du Clapham*," he called it; he was regularly beaten and taunted by bullies, "a child among young men, a little boy unaccustomed to being away from home and crying for my papa and mama and sisters, among hardened, thoroughbred schoolboys." His school years, as well as his years at Cambridge, were darkened by clashes with his father, that most devout and dedicated of Evangelicals, who had once had hopes of seeing his brilliant son take Orders; who thought that if he could only add his own qualities of concentration, energy, industry, and patience to Tom's rather disorderly genius, a being might be formed who could regenerate the world. That is why he reprimanded his son at school for writing the lines: "And if at Eastertide thou makst us work, Thou mightst as well have been a Jew or Turk," citing the example of "Young Wollaston" who, when he wished for a reward, never asked for a holiday, but for a quadratic equation. That is why he forced Tom to apply himself to mathematics at Cambridge and discouraged him—with notable lack of success—from novel reading, which he considered a sign of idleness. And that is why, as Tom's sister later revealed in a memoir of her brother, "with all the love and reverence with which [Macaulay] regarded his father's memory, there mingled a shade of bitterness, that he had not met quite the encouragement and appreciation from him he received from others."

From Cambridge Macaulay assures his worried father that: "I never had a higher ambition than that we might, if it please God, triumph together over the enemies of humanity." But there is a bitter undercurrent in what he himself calls an "undutiful reflection," addressed to his sister some years later: "My father . . . holds swearing, eating, underdone meat, liking high fame, lying late in a morning, and all things which give pleasure to others and none to himself to be absolute sins." That this strain between father and son helps to account for Macaulay's reaction against his Evangelical heritage is certain—in middle age he, who won his first oratorical spurs addressing the annual meeting of the Anti-Slavery Society in 1824, will be found referring to the "nonsense" of an Exeter Hall antislavery gathering. But it may perhaps be credited with a more positive contribution. The numerous lengthy letters that Tom addressed to his father during adolescence and youth—the majority argumentative, forcefully disputing with him upon such subjects as the advantages of reading for pleasure, the uselessness of mathematics, the unjustifiable neglect of modern in favor of ancient literature, the pedagogical function of history as a school of freedom—these polemical missives supply at least a partial answer to the conundrum Jeffrey posed upon receipt of Macaulay's first *Edinburgh Review* contribution, the essay on Milton: "The more I think, the less I can conceive where you picked up that style." The vigor of the historian's style was forged on the anvil of filial revolt, just as its clarity—so his sister Margaret was to point out—came out of his constant contact with the family circle, "from the habit of conversing with very young people to whom he has a great deal to explain and impart."

Behind Macaulay's astounding precocity and his brilliant achievements at Cambridge, then, lay some shadows: unhappiness at school and conflict with his father. And it was at Cambridge that he was first assailed by those morbid bouts of incapacity for work, to which he remained subject all his life. Time and again, in his journal, one comes across references to "this peculiar impotence," this "old malady of mine," this "shell of indolence." Sometimes he struggles against it, sometimes he gives in to it, knowing from past experience that it would pass away. Always he notes it down as a failing; though, by the end of his Cambridge days, no longer—after the manner of his father and his fellow Claphamites—as a sin. These periods of depression and inactivity evince a delicate and sensitive temperament behind the flamboyantly omniscient aggressiveness, so characteristic of much of his writing and conversation. The "hardness" of Macaulay, on which so many critics and commentators have harped, is confined to his official style and manner; and its outward manifestations there may, indeed, have helped to mask an almost feminine inward sensibility, an intense craving for giving and receiving affection. In his journal, Macaulay recalls that, when he was seventeen or eighteen, he was half in love with a girl named Mary Parker. "But," he adds, "her conversation soon healed the wound made by her eyes." One thinks of Gibbon, almost a hundred years before, confiding to *his* journal, about "a pretty, meek but I am afraid insipid girl," who had been "talked of" for him: "Tho' she will have a noble fortune, I must have a wife I can speak to." It was on his family, first his sisters, then his nephew and nieces, that Macaulay "poured out," as his sister Hannah wrote after his death, "a world of love."

Hannah accompanied Macaulay to India in 1834, thus softening the blow of that "complete revolution in all the habits of life—an estrangement from almost every old friend and acquaintance—fifteen thousand miles of ocean between the exile and everything that he cares for," which he imposed upon himself in order to accumulate enough money for the support of his family, and of which he later said that no temptation of wealth or power could make him go through it again. In India, Hannah met and married Charles Trevelyan. Macaulay liked and admired his brother-in-law; but the separation from his favorite sister, who had helped to make his exile bearable, was a severe blow to him, intensified by the news of the death in England of his sister Margaret, which reached him shortly afterwards. The dimension of a grief-stricken Macaulay, reconciling himself to a life of lonely bachelorhood, must be kept in mind, alongside the much better known dimension of hard-headedness and glibness that made it so easy for Matthew Arnold, and many others since Arnold, to castigate him as an apostle of the philistines. In Macaulay, one is confronted by a complex personality, that of a man occasionally capable—in his *Essays* and in conversation—of roughness of manner and crudity of thought; at the same time, that of a man who lavished affection on his family, shed copious tears over Homer and Herodotus, as well as over his own poems, and who endured without complaint the pain of self-inflicted exile and personal tragedy.

It is of some interest to observe the interaction between Macaulay's personality and his historical imagination. This interaction exists at several different levels. There is, first of all, the level of observation of men and manners. By nature, the historian responsible for that pioneering achievement in the field of social history, the great third chapter of the *History* on the state of England in 1685, possessed the gift of casting a shrewdly appraising eye on the society, events, and personalities of his own day. The results of this appraisal are apparent in his journal and correspondence, which reveal him, not unexpectedly, as a model traveler who never left a foreign country or city without noting the state of roads, inns, buildings, and sanitation; or without reflecting upon the nature of social class distinctions, the appearance of the women, and the general spirit and character of particular places. In a characteristically pithy comment, he compares the difference between Rome and Naples with the difference between Sunday and Monday.

Secondly, there is the level of what might be called an irresistible disposition to glee and empathy—sheer joy in the drama and pageantry of history in the making, and the ability to identify himself with actors past and present on the historical stage. It is this disposition, at the age of thirteen, that makes him wish to have seen the King of France enter London—"what a scene for future historians and poets"; and some months later to comment as follows on Napoleon's escape from Elba: "All my detestation of his crimes, all my horror at his conduct, is completely swallowed up in astonishment, awe and admiration at the more than human boldness of his present attempt." It also makes him record verbatim for his sister's delectation a conversation he overhears in the Library of the House of Commons, with the remark: "To the historian three centuries hence this letter will be invaluable"; and, on the aesthetic level, finds expression in his desire to see the walls of St. Paul's "incrusted with porphyry and verde antique, and the ceiling and dome covered with mosaic and gold."

This same disposition—in a striking revelation of how his imagination could transform a momentary personal experience into fuel to be used in the actual process of writing history—evokes this comment from him after a visit to the Great Exhibition: "I felt a glow of eloquence or something like it come on me from the mere effect of the place, and I thought of some touches which will greatly improve my Steinkirk." And, on the eve of his departure for India, he is impelled to compare his state of mind with that of those suffering death on great occasions—and to conclude that on the scaffold he would probably have been as tranquil as Russell or Sidney. He is also moved to send to the friend and benefactress of his childhood, Hannah More, the text of a "wicked" Radical war-song, the purpose of which was to turn the Radicals into ridicule, but whose lilt had a wonderfully authentic ring:

> *We'll stretch that tort'ring Castlereagh*
> *On his old Dublin rack, Sir.—*
> *We'll drown the King in eau de vie,*
> *The Laureate in his sack, Sir.*
> *Old Eldon and his scolding hag*
> *In molten gold we'll smother;*
> *And stifle in his own green bag*
> *The Doctor and his brother.*

No wonder the mature Macaulay defined his historical method in these terms: "I try to get as fast as I can over what is dull, and I dwell as long as I can on what can be made picturesque and dramatic. I believe this to be the most instructive, as well as the most popular way of writing history."

The third and, at the same time, the most intangible level of interaction between personality and historical imagination we might
call, taking our cue from Macaulay himself, "Kenneth Macaulay."
On a trip to Weybridge in 1858 with the Trevelyans—his sister, her
husband, and their children—there is talk of daydreaming, "a habit
in which Lady Trevelyan and I indulge beyond any people that I ever
knew. I mentioned to George [his future biographer, Sir George Tre-
velyan] what, as far as I know, no critic has observed, that the Greeks
called this happiness κενὴ μακαρία [empty happiness]. Alice, who
was some way off and did not hear distinctly, said 'Kenneth Macaulay!
What did the Greeks say about Kenneth Macaulay?' I shall always call
the unreal world in which I pass a large part of my life Kenneth Macaulay." The historian attributed much of his success in historical writing to his unlimited capacity for castle building or daydreaming; and
planned, shortly before his death, to write a disquisition on what he
called "that strange habit." In what may at first sight appear a paradoxical fashion, he saw in this habit a spur to factual accuracy; for,
in the romance of the past that he constructed in his mind, the slightest
and most minute touches assumed as great an interest as, or perhaps
an even greater interest than, important events.

An inclination to fantasy, then, linked to a marvelous histrionic
talent, should be recognized as a part of Macaulay's personality that
bears a significant relation to his work. When, as a boy, he addressed
a letter to "one of the high and mighty triumvirate of girls, member
of the most Honourable Committee for Circulating the Bride of Abydos"—in short, his sister; when, many years later, he delighted the
Trevelyans by acting out an old clothesman and romancing about a
secret embassy to America on which he pretended to have been sent
twenty years before: "I told G[eorge] . . . how we visited an encampment of Red Indians,—how they gave me the name of the Great
White Beaver"; and when, sometime later still, he sent an April Fool's
Day letter to his sister Hannah, informing her that Mrs. Beecher
Stowe had invited herself to dinner, bringing along a Negro parson
named Caesar Ugbark—these were *jeux d'esprit* that not merely betokened a powerful imagination but were also essential to its working
when it turned to history and historical writing.

Not that the writing of history ever became for Macaulay as painless
and easy a process as daydreaming. A few brief extracts from his letters
and journal, all concerned with the composition of *The History of
England,* eloquently demonstrate what we sometimes tend to forget,
that even the greatest historians have to grapple with the practical

problems that continue to confront their lesser successors: "The words drop slowly from my pen; and the corrections and polishing will be endless."—"The plague is that my work cannot be spun out of my own brain. I must have my materials around me."—"Arrangement and transition are arts which I value much, but which I do not flatter myself that I have attained."—"I must positively get over that business [the Grandval conspiracy] tomorrow. It has long hung in hand. I do not know why I dislike it."—"I can truly say that I never read again the most popular passages of my own works without painfully feeling how far my execution has fallen short of the standard which is in my mind."—"I could review myself better, whichever side I took, than any of my reviewers."—And, finally—this from the "cocksure" Macaulay when, as an historian, he had scaled the pinnacles of worldly success in terms of honors, money, and admiration: "Alas! How short life and how long art! I feel as if I had but just begun to understand how to write. And the probability is that I have very nearly done writing."

He was right. He had less than two years to live, and did not have the time to carry his great *History* beyond the death of its hero, William the Third. Shortly before his death, he noted in his journal that "it is pleasant to think that though we pass away, the world goes on improving," a perfect foil to the prophetic letter written to his mother from school as a French language exercise more than forty years before: "Peut-être on peut se promettre le retour d'un âge d'or quand les jeunes demoiselles entreront dans nos universités et deviendront 'Senior Wranglers.'" He was rightly convinced that his *History* would live; though not always as confident as on the one occasion when— after becoming fatigued with reading Thiers—he confided to his journal that he did not acknowledge himself inferior to any historian except Herodotus and Thucydides. Even then, he added with characteristic candor: "Thiers would probably rate me very differently." It was to the great Greeks, as well as to his other favorites—Livy, Tacitus, and Sarpi—that he returned time and again, reading and admiring anew, knowing that the great historians of the past must always supply both measure and inspiration to those who follow in their footsteps. He would be happy to know that he, in his turn, is now fulfilling this function for his successors.

More or Less
Eminent Victorians

Nineteen fifty-eight marked the fortieth anniversary of Lytton Strachey's *Eminent Victorians;* which almost persuades one to believe that life may indeed begin at forty. For not only are these four short biographical essays—about Florence Nightingale, General Gordon, Cardinal Manning, and Dr. Arnold—still widely read and reprinted; they and their author continue to constitute a bone of contention on which scholars and others are willing, even eager, to gnaw: an infallible sign of at least a certain kind of vitality.

In the Preface to *Eminent Victorians,* which is for some the sort of landmark in the history of biography that the *Communist Manifesto* is in the history of the working classes, Strachey invited biographers to throw off the chains with which they had dragged those twin-boxed Victorian coffins, otherwise known as Standard Biographies, their slow length along. The first duty of the biographer, he proclaimed, was to preserve a becoming brevity; the second, to maintain his own freedom of spirit. "It is not his business to be complimentary; it is his business to lay bare the facts of the case, as he understands them." Furthermore, the end of biography, as Strachey practiced it in his essays, was not merely to depict the lives of some famous personages. His subjects were selected to serve as samples of the visions of an age,

From *Victorian Studies,* September 1958

characteristic specimens brought up for examination from an ocean of material now so immense that it could hardly be studied in any other fashion.

Any readers to whom this image—it was Strachey's—gave promise of a strictly scientific procedure were doomed to quick disappointment. What they found were four elegantly written essays based on printed sources; crackling with wit, verve, and irony, and indicating in no uncertain manner that some of the great Victorian idols had possessed feet and, on occasion, heads of clay. The lives of the ecclesiastic, the educational authority, the woman of action, and the man of adventure—Victorian heroes all—gave evidence of crass stupidity alongside heroic endeavor, of selfish ambition alongside high idealism, of confusion and muddling alongside purposeful determination. Those "certain fragments of the truth which took my fancy and lay to my hand" revealed hidden depths and shadows where all had seemed plain and sunny before. The angelic Florence Nightingale turned out also to have been a demon who drove her associates and helpers as mercilessly as she drove herself. Dr. Arnold, the stern preceptor of English youth before whom even the Sixth Form quaked, was seen to be a man whose intellectual perspicacity by no means matched his moral certainty. Behind Cardinal Manning's ascetic countenance lay ruthless ambitions as well as spiritual struggles. The martyred General Gordon, gentle soldier of God, proved to have been no less a mystical fanatic than his opponent, the dreadful Mahdi.

Nor were Victorian institutions sacrosanct to Strachey. Army, church, public schools, political leaders—all supplied ready targets for the ironical and irreverent shafts loosed at them by the author. *C'est le ton qui fait la musique.* The essays were written in a tone of amused detachment expressing the reasonable man's disbelief in the extent to which folly and self-deception had actually come to take possession of such distinguished personages, living in such a respectable age. One by one, bubbles of sham and hypocrisy were pricked, sometimes with evident delight by the author, more often by the eminent persons themselves made to utter their most inane thoughts in their own words by means of Strachey's diabolically clever use of quotation and indirect discourse. Yet, though Strachey seemed to have cast himself in the double role of Mr. Sneer and the King of Brobdingnag, his portraits communicated more than mere contempt and amusement. In them he raised problems of character and circumstance, reason and unreason, the individual in relation to the spirit of his age, and ideas in relation to action. Behind the ironical title and the strictures lay a certain recognition of achievement, and, above all, a curiosity in the motives and impulses that moved human beings, which went beyond the obvious debunking aspect of the book.

Whether or not its immediate success may be ascribed in part to the postwar disillusionment with formerly accepted values and institutions, *Eminent Victorians* rapidly and solidly established itself as a biographical classic. Rarely, if ever, had psychological penetration, a talent for dramatic depiction of character, and a brilliant style been employed together to better effect. In the space of two hundred pages, by what Asquith called his "subtle and suggestive art," Strachey succeeded in reabsorbing English biography into the realm of literature. Not that the chorus of acclaim was unanimous or wholehearted. Almost everyone, then and now, was and is willing to grant Strachey stylistic excellence. But in the forty years since the first appearance of *Eminent Victorians,* the book has been under more or less continuous and vehement attack; and has, in turn, been no less vigorously defended.[1]

The case for the prosecution can be summed up as follows: Strachey misused and occasionally distorted historical evidence. He may have been a member of the Bloomsbury Group, but he did not carry its passion for absolute truth and honesty in the expression of thought and feeling about personal relations into the pages of *Eminent Victorians*. Dr. Arnold did not have short legs; Gordon was not a drunkard; Manning did not go over to Roman Catholicism because Pio Nono offered to make it worth his while. These are examples of inventions and insinuations which Strachey deliberately inserted into his essays. And even where he did not deliberately distort, he gravely misinterpreted. Since he set out to discredit the age, he ended up by drawing caricatures rather than portraits. Men and women of high seriousness and goodwill became in his hands mere puppets going through ridiculous motions in order to raise sniggers from readers. Contradiction and complexity, to be found in all human beings, supplied Strachey with ammunition to score off hypocrisy and stupidity against the subjects of his essays. And, worst of all, the innuendoes, the irreverence, the witticisms were but the outward and visible signs of a basically flippant view of the world. Strachey, in short, was a wicked and clever alchemist who had mastered the secret of turning gold into dross.

The defense might reply as follows: True, Strachey's dishonesty disqualifies him from consideration as a serious historian. But he never pretended to write chapters of history; his essays were artistic inter-

pretations, written from a definite point of view. Occasional distortion
does not alter the essential verisimilitude of his portraits. What remains
remarkable about these is the frequency with which, by a brilliant use
of imagination and intuition, he was able to hit the nail on the head.
Moreover, though Strachey's particular view of the world may at
present be unfashionable, it is not for that reason to be dismissed. It
is detached and amused rather than flippant. It exalts moderation,
modesty, affection, and intelligence; and eschews stupidity, humbug,
and misdirected zeal, officially sanctioned though these may be. It was
held by an author who belongs in the great tradition of those comic
writers for whom the world is full of paradox and folly, and who
hope to effect at least the first stage of a cure by making people laugh
at themselves.

As, forty years after *Eminent Victorians,* we look at current trends
in Victorian biography, Strachey's contribution appears at first glance
to have been both absorbed and superseded: absorbed in the sense that
most biographers now assume that in order to succeed they must be
as much artists as chroniclers; superseded in the sense that debunking
has been followed in due course by understanding, laughter by sympathy; scorn by insight. We have discovered new dimensions in the
great Victorians. Figures once irritatingly ebullient, confident, and
self-satisfied we now find more and more frequently staring at us in
anguish out of some strange and awful chiaroscuro. And our hearts
go out to them.

And yet—is the pendulum perhaps beginning to swing too far the
other way? Admitting Strachey's sins of both omission and commission, is it conceivable that a reading of some recent Victorian biographies might show that present students of the age could benefit
by looking to him for more than diversion or target practice?

A brief look at post–World War II biographies of Strachey's four
eminent Victorians is in itself sufficient to discourage a categorical
dismissal of Strachey the biographer. With one exception, these biographies can be called defensive in tone. They are out to show that
their subjects, far from having been amalgams of strength and weakness, intelligence and stupidity, singlemindedness and contradiction,
religiosity and practical self-seeking, were great and good and altogether worthy. Sir Shane Leslie's *Manning* (London, 1953), though
useful in presenting a full survey of the cardinal's activities, is chiefly
remarkable for a sort of breathless awe before the institutions and
grandeur of the Roman Catholic Church, not unfairly represented by
sentiments such as the following: "The Holy See waiteth at one time,

and at another time waiteth not. Inscrutable are her judgments."[2]
Manning's character, motives, and actions are examined at length and
found to be admirable. However that may be, the last thing Manning
was was dull; and that is what this pedestrian treatment makes him.
Lord Elton's *General Gordon* (London, 1954) is a much better book,
noteworthy for a detailed and illuminating discussion of Gordon's
highly individualistic theology and its practical expression in his apos-
tolate to the poor. Yet one cannot help feeling that the author, justly
eager to clear Gordon's personal character from Strachey's imputations and, somewhat less justly, to establish his role in the final tragedy
as blameless, too often has let his indignation control his focus. The
reader is never moved to exclaim: "With all his faults and virtues,
what a man!"

Those seeking such a reaction will not find it induced, either, by a
reading of Norman Wymer's *Arnold of Rugby* (London, 1953). Lionel
Trilling and Basil Willey had already established, in contradiction to
the poorest of the essays in *Eminent Victorians,* that the doctor's intellect
was not so absurdly out of kilter with his moral stature as Strachey
had tried to make us believe.[3] But Mr. Wymer, while using some un-
published materials and supplying the first full biographical treatment
of his subject, does little more than relate in a pleasant though overly
lyrical manner the success story of a reforming headmaster who
triumphs when his students begin to gain academic honors. He may
have felt that analysis and critique of Arnold's writings and ideas did
not come within his purview. Yet his rather inadequate coverage of
Arnold's intellectual background, as reflected, say, in the Oriel Common Room when he was one of its members, raises the question of
the extent to which the life of an intellectually significant figure can
be fully and fairly estimated without placing him in his setting. Like
Lord Elton and Sir Shane Leslie, Mr. Wymer has performed a service
in correcting the distortions of *Eminent Victorians.* But will their biographies be read forty years hence, even (to use the antonym of Lord
Rosebery's characterization of Strachey's *Queen Victoria*) as nonfiction?

That is perhaps too high a standard by which to judge. But it is by
that standard that one can safely render judgment in favor of Cecil
Woodham-Smith's *Florence Nightingale, 1820–1910* (London, 1950).
Confirmed Stracheyans—a contradiction in terms?—may say with
some justice that the main outlines of Miss Nightingale's character as
they emerge in this lengthy and amply documented study do not differ
materially from those already familiar through *Eminent Victorians.* But
if Strachey's intuitions are thus vindicated, it must be added that

Woodham-Smith has laid bare for the first time in awesome and moving detail the inner life of a woman of genius who could write as well as minister like an angel. Her youthful spiritual struggles and agonies emerge especially clearly, revealing how that hardness of spirit, the demonic force that could lead to both triumph and grief, came to be forged. The author, concerned neither with defense nor with attack, but with the re-creation of a personality, lets the sources speak for themselves as much as possible, often directly and without commentary. There is no doubt that she has brilliantly succeeded in thus letting her subject reveal herself fully as a human being. Yet this method of writing biography brings with it the risk that the biographer's presentation of his own point of view may exist only in his power of selecting from his sources. Strachey doubtless favored exposure at the cost of exposition. Woodham-Smith's approach tends to favor exposition at the cost of analysis. But what she set out to do, she did superbly.

These particular biographies raise certain questions of general importance: to what extent, and with what consequences, Strachey's strategy of attack has given way to a strategy of defense; in what ways recent biographers have handled the problem of providing background and setting; and in what proportion they have given the reader on the one hand selection from the sources, on the other analysis and judgment. These questions can only be answered by examining other examples of recent biographical writing, especially since we are today interested in aspects of the Victorian age that would not have attracted the attention of Strachey's generation.

The increasing emphasis on economic and administrative history has produced a number of biographies dealing with prominent figures in those areas. L. T. C. Rolt, in the preface to his fine biography of *Isambard Kingdom Brunel* (London, 1957), notes the curiously impersonal character of the few books written about the great figures of the Industrial Revolution. "We do not know what sort of men they were, or what impulses drove them on their momentous course" (p. vii). No good biographies of engineers exist, he writes, because these would have to deal with technicalities hitherto considered fit subjects only for juvenilia and arid treatises; and yet a man like Brunel must be regarded as a key character of the century, the archetype of the heroic age of engineering. Rolt attempts to probe the sources of Brunel's fabulous and fruitful energy, and, with the help of extracts from a diary unfortunately covering all too short a period, he succeeds in presenting us with a good likeness of the man. But when all is said and done, the book tells us more about railroad engineering in the nineteenth century than about Brunel. This may be inevitable. The monuments of scientists, engineers, and administrators are to be found in their works far more than in their lives.

That is by no means to imply that artistry is irrelevant in writing about such men. For an example of biography as an art one need only turn to S. E. Finer's *The Life and Times of Sir Edwin Chadwick* (London, 1952).[4] The author tells us at the start that what follows is to have only the slightest reference to Chadwick's private life—since that was all of a piece with his public life. But he has injected such suspense into the record of Chadwick's administrative activities that before one has finished reading the book, defective drainpipes and leaking sewers have assumed greater consequence than even the most elaborately painful Victorian neuroses.

How has Professor Finer achieved this? Scholarship, mastery in the use of primary materials, clear organization—all these factors help. But the real secret lies in the author's assumption that just as Chadwick's private and public life were in effect one and the same, so also must the biographer describe his public life *as if* he were describing his private life. Instead of setting up a mental reservation positing a division between personal history (interesting and lively) and institutional history (instructive and dull), he has proceeded with the aid of style, art, and gusto to invest something like the squabble over the exact nature of Chadwick's appointment to the Poor Law Commission with the same sort of drama ordinarily reserved for spiritual crises and military engagements:

> As Nicholls, fresh from hearing Melbourne confirm his appointment, rushed out of the Prime Minister's study, he ran up to Chadwick, pressed him warmly by the hand, and said how delighted he was to serve with him. T. F. Lewis followed him, with cold hauteur and with Melbourne's last words ringing in his ears—"Beware of theory and speculation; in you I have confidence, you are a man of business—but there are others, others who were connected with the Commission of Enquiry, in whom I have not the same confidence." Disdainfully, Lewis remarked his Secretary; and then, drawing himself up to his full height, turned away Pecksniff-like to order mahogany tables and plush chairs for the Commissioners' offices, and for the Secretary's cane-bottom chairs and tables of plain deal (p. 111).

No novel could communicate more tension and sense of immediacy. In his book Mr. Finer has raised the curtain on the inner workings of the Poor Law Commission and the Boards of Health; has revealed the role played by newspapers like the *Times* in shaping public opinion on the subject of health, the tangled relations and jurisdictions of central and local authorities, the importance of vested interests such as the powerful railroad engineers; and has thrown light on the internal politics of boards and commissions. But, above all, he has managed to keep Chadwick in the center of the scene. Chadwick's ideas as shaped by Benthamite philosophy, his passionate devotion to the cause of reform, the sharp edges of his personality, these, "the life," are at no point swamped by "the times."

The few biographies that have been written about men of science, industry, and administration whet the appetite for more knowledge about the psychology of the Victorian engineer, the Victorian civil servant, the Victorian banker and businessman. That is not to say that the biographer's sole concern must be with those who have achieved or successfully exerted power. In some ways Richard Monckton Milnes, for instance, can be regarded as a failure. Yet, in Mr. Pope-Hennessy's masterful biography of the Bird of Paradox, *The Years of Promise, 1809–1851* (London, 1949) and *The Flight of Youth, 1851–1885* (London, 1951), not only does he come to life in all his paradoxical plumage, but, because he was important in Victorian literature and society, a lovingly detailed account of his life in effect becomes a social history of the age. One of the dangers of this sort of kaleidoscopic biography, in which a man's life and times are reconstructed, so to speak, day by day, lies in the inevitable intrusion of trivia. We are told that when Monckton Milnes called on Varnhagen, he was out; and that when Varnhagen subsequently called on Monckton Milnes, *he* was out. We hear about the carriage horses slipping one day, with no ill effect to anyone. But the author may well feel that the bright colors of a mosaic are best set off by darker stones; that in order to communicate the texture of life, he must chronicle huggermugger and humdrum along with the rest. And a passage like this—one example of many such—amply justifies his approach: "At Derby they [Carlyle and Milnes traveling together to the West Riding] sat up late in the travelers' room at the Royal Hotel, Milnes reading a tragedy of Landor's at one side of the table while Carlyle wrote to Jane at the other. Across the room two bagmen dined and talked. Overhead the gas jets blazed relentlessly" (*Years of Promise*, pp. 139–140). Here the past lives again.

The ramifications of Monckton Milnes's friendships and interests were such that any biography must naturally and inevitably depict him within the context of his society. This is of course far from necessarily so when a less sociable man of letters attracts the biographer's attention. Wilfred Stone's manifold aims in his *Religion and Art of William Hale White ("Mark Rutherford")* (Stanford, 1954) illustrate the range of problems faced by an author writing about the sort of major-minor literary figure who must be brought into the framework of his time so that each may shed light on the other. Mr. Stone wants to introduce an author of merit, to study the transitions and tensions of the nineteenth-century milieu in which White found himself, and to elucidate his writings—fictional, scholarly, and confessional—by his life. These writings and the spiritual agonies they reflect he treats at one and the same time as the product of a peculiar personal neurosis, the sufferings of the highly nervous son of a highly nervous mother, forced, because he could not love her, to seek affection outside the home, and finding the religious springs from which he is aching to drink dried up and turned to dust and ashes before his eyes; and as a case history in the psychological experience of an age. A striking final chapter devoted to an analysis of the revised version (1912) of an article White first wrote in 1879 shows how he turned processes of particular experience, feeling, and thought into generalized principle, not merely on stylistic or aesthetic grounds, but as part of his attempt to make himself at home in the world.

The distinction between "dynamic" background, as it is to be found in the last chapter of Mr. Stone's book, and background of another kind is illustrated in Sir Geoffrey Faber's *Jowett: A Portrait with Background* (London, 1957). An example of the former, in this instance the relation of individual psychology to the general atmosphere of the age, is Sir Geoffrey's perceptive comment on Arthur Stanley, who, like so many other Victorians, found "in the rarefied moral code of his age so perfectly devised a protection for his own fastidious repugnances that he never dreamed of questioning it, or of seeking to find rational support for his extreme assumptions" (p. 121). Examples of a more static kind of background are the long set pieces on *Essays and Reviews,* on the affair of Bishop Colenso, and on the dispute concerning the Regius Professor's salary. Not all of this scaffolding is essential. Some of it might have been better constructed. But behind it the personality of the Master of Balliol may be clearly observed.

The popular image of the stern and remote Victorian taskmaster gives way to that of the undersized human being with the highly pitched voice who triumphantly overcomes poverty and a heritage of weakness and failure. In this book, as in his *Oxford Apostles: A Character Study of the Oxford Movement* (London, 1933), Sir Geoffrey considers comment on the sexual proclivities and problems of his subjects an important part of his task as a biographer. Jowett's sexlessness is obviously an important factor to be weighed in any estimate of his personality. If, in his hypothesis of a traumatic experience the Master of Balliol may or may not have undergone at St. Paul's, just as in his interpretation of Newman's nightmare after overindulgence in cheese at Brighton in the previous book, the author is skating on rather thin ice as far as the evidence is concerned, at least he is willing to go skating. We can applaud his efforts to probe the relation of emotional disposition to character and ideas. It is less easy to accept his passionate and at times almost petulant defense of Jowett's opinions and ideas on practically all subjects, because this defense tends to become part and parcel of Faber's treatment of Jowett throughout as a man of his time who had to make the best of it and deserves recognition for so doing. Someone of Jowett's influence and position, after all, helps to shape the moral and intellectual climate of his age at the same time that his actions may to some extent be its product. There is a delicate problem here. To weigh men and their thoughts out of the context of their time is patently dangerous and unfair. On the other hand, when motives, actions, and ideas are regarded primarily within their setting, judgment and critical evaluation are at a discount.

This problem is but another aspect of the difficulty of merging life and times, foreground and background, with no loss of either perspective or understanding; perhaps the greatest challenge facing the biographer today, when he is aware as never before of the extent to which circumstances help to shape personality and thought. It is a challenge that becomes particularly demanding when the biographer tackles a man of ideas. He need not be either a Marxist or a Freudian, he must be a bit of both, to be properly conscious of the relation of life to thought. He need not be a professional philosopher, but he must have a certain proficiency in the anatomy of ideas. Should the ideal result be textual analysis tempered by anecdote? Or should he forgo all claims to completeness, substantive critique, and originality in dealing with the thought of his subject, confining himself to the analysis of personality? And, if he adopts the latter course, is there not a perpetual danger of *Hamlet* without the prince?

In his *Life of John Stuart Mill* (London, 1954) Mr. Michael St. John Packe has not solved all these problems. The summaries of Mill's major writings give the reader an impression of the range of his thought. But more could perhaps have been done in the way of analyzing the interconnection between its political and philosophical aspects as well as the relation of both to Mill's active involvement in public affairs. Nonetheless, this is a notable book. For as the first to make full use of the Mill Papers, the author sets forth in detail as readable as it is scholarly the complete story of the friendship of Mill and Harriet Taylor, an account triply significant: as a human document of pathos, dignity, and passion; as a commentary on the totems and taboos of Victorian society; and as the record of an intellectual collaboration of unique and supreme importance. Here is compulsory supplementary reading for all readers of Mill's *Autobiography;* and an oasis for those who have tended to regard that work as a classic of desiccation as well as one of dedication.

In some ways Mr. Packe may be said to have deliberately sacrificed background to foreground. Noel Annan, in *Leslie Stephen, His Thought and Character in Relation to His Time* (London, 1951), proceeds in a precisely contrary manner, deliberately stressing background rather than personality in accordance with his view of the time that biography then suffered from an overemphasis on personal relations to the detriment of their social and intellectual context.[5] Having sketched out Stephen's life and achievements in the first two chapters, he devotes the remaining two-thirds of the book to placing him in his Victorian setting. The technique works, primarily because the background, far from being a mere "fill-in," constitutes in effect a highly original series of essays on the relation of Stephen's writings to Victorian modes of thought.

One might complain that the author has used Stephen the man primarily as a peg on which to hang these essays; but the complaint would be captious. For more light on Stephen's personality we can always turn to Maitland's *Life,* a masterpiece of its kind. But there is nowhere else to turn for such penetrating pages on topics like the continuing (and paradoxical) search for ultimate sanctions in Stephen's evolutionary ethics, the psychological basis of Victorian athleticism, and the exact route of the intellectual omnibus from Clapham to Bloomsbury. At the same time, the ideal blend of background and foreground—the Renaissance portrait in which the open window behind the seated figure leads the eye as if by an inevitable progress to distant mountains, castles, and rivers—that ideal has eluded Mr. Annan as it has eluded Sir Geoffrey and Mr. Packe. Perhaps it cannot be attained today. For the biographer, even when he possesses the two skills necessary for its attainment—ability to delve into the mysteries of the individual human personality and mastery of a large body of intellectual, social, or political history—must also be able in the writing to blend them in such a way that for the reader the transitions from one aspect to the other occur, as it were, with an ineluctable logic of their own. Two outstanding recent examples of political biography, Sir Philip Magnus's *Gladstone, A Biography* (London, 1954) and Lord David Cecil's *Lord M., or the Later Life of Lord Melbourne* (London, 1954), illustrate this problem of emphasis. Sir Philip paints Gladstone in frock coat and wing collar, addressing the House of Commons. Lord David gives us Melbourne in his dressing gown.

Any biographer of Gladstone, shadowed by Morley's Ghost and faced with the manuscript mountains of Hawarden and the British Museum, achieves heroic stature by definition. Sir Philip not only manages, in a reasonable amount of space, to depict the principal stages of Gladstone's political career clearly and dramatically. He is also that rare and refreshing phenomenon today, a biographer not afraid to make judgments, occasionally even adverse judgments, about his subject. He makes no bones about the high esteem in which he holds Gladstone's moral stature as well as his facility for never shutting the door on his mind. Nevertheless, he does not let this respect deter him from pointing out his blunders—his deportment in the American Civil War and in the Gordon episode are two instances—nor does he refrain from suggesting that Gladstone might have acted with more acumen in his relations with Palmerston and with the queen. Such knowledgeable hindsight is neither easy nor reprehensible.

Inevitably the continuous chronicle of public affairs can begin to weigh rather heavily on the reader. A. C. Kennedy, in his fine *Salisbury, 1830–1903, Portrait of a Statesman* (London, 1953), tried to avoid this effect by occasional variations; supplying, for example, a connected and complete discussion of Salisbury's religion early in the book, and later on imagining him in soliloquy after his Turkish mission. Sir Philip shuns such diversionary tactics and takes us over the course from start to finish, including, it is true, occasional rest periods for holidays and lighter moments as they occur. But his subject took appallingly few holidays, and the number of his lighter moments barely exceeds that of his ministries. In his analysis of Gladstone's political behavior as a revelation of the way in which his mind worked, the author's seismic simile may be deemed causally true without being causally sufficient. Can the analogy of a series of earthquakes really catch the full complexity of this process? Involuntarily one's gaze wanders from Sir Philip's full-length portrait in oils to the pen-and-ink sketch Strachey drew in his Gordon essay, too unkind, perhaps, but still revealing by a line here, a bit of shading there, certain elements of the true likeness which have eluded the portrait painter.

The massive pomp of Sir Philip is apt to induce occasional longings for Strachey's subtlety. But lest we jump to the conclusion that long and solid biographies of prime ministers do not invite the essayist's flexible manner, born of more freedom and less responsibility, we need only turn to Lord David Cecil's volumes on Melbourne. His style, polished, urbane, slightly ironical throughout—in short, reminiscent of Strachey's, serves him supremely well as an instrument of character analysis and as a lens through which human passions and follies may be observed with Gibbonian detachment. *The Young Melbourne* (London, 1939) presented the subtly drawn picture of a young man whose own temperament, half animal vigor and hard common sense, half dreamy speculation and delicate sensibility, mirrored the transition from eighteenth- to nineteenth-century habits of thought and feeling. The second volume, in which politics begins to compete for attention with character, does not quite reach the superlative standard set by the first. Even the combination of Queen Victoria and Mrs. Norton cannot make up for the tempestuous Caroline Lamb. And Melbourne the prime minister does not hold the same psychological interest as Melbourne the young man between two worlds. Lord David's artistry has fullest play wherever the human element rules supreme, as in his masterly treatment of the relationship between the young queen and her first prime minister. And since this relationship happens to have been perhaps the most significant aspect of Melbourne's premiership, the book qualifies as an outstanding political biography as well as a moving human portrait.

Literary biography, in the form of new full-length studies of major figures, continues to flourish alongside political biography. It is a special field, with problems of its own, and deserves separate treatment.[6] But no essay concerned with recent Victorian biographies can omit mention of Edgar Johnson's *Charles Dickens: His Tragedy and Triumph* (New York, 1953), a magisterial treatment of the man and his work that might have restored even Strachey's faith in two-volume biographies. And to this must be added two other outstanding biographies of major literary figures, Charles Carrington's *Rudyard Kipling, His Life and Work* (London, 1955) and Sir Charles Tennyson's biography of his grandfather, *Alfred Tennyson* (London, 1950). What is perhaps most significant for the present purpose about all these books is that they deal sympathetically and respectfully with writers who have been underrated in the past, in part because one of the consequences of the reaction against Victorian values and standards was that the popular authors of the period were automatically assumed to have been in harmony with those values and standards, and therefore lacking in depth and complexity. Both these assumptions are now being widely questioned.

All the biographies hitherto mentioned have dealt with individuals, some great, others not so great; some primarily interesting in terms of character and personality, others more in reflecting the age. What of the genre of collective biography to which, after all, *Eminent Victorians* belonged? For though he called the choice of his four subjects "in one sense haphazard," it is quite clear that Strachey's four Victorians were in fact carefully (some might say maliciously) selected as outstanding examples of respectable achievement, moral earnestness, probity, and religious conviction. Some of the most striking biographical works of recent years also concern themselves with groups brought together by the biographer to point a moral or adorn a tale. Woodham-Smith's *The Reason Why* (London, 1953) is one of these. A study in part of those institutional and administrative weaknesses of the British Army in the nineteenth century that contributed to the disaster of "The Charge of the Light Brigade," it is built around the lives and characters of three men, Lord Lucan, Lord Cardigan, and, to a lesser extent, Lord Raglan. But instead of writing biographies of these men—there would have been little point in doing so in the case of the former two—the author has crossed the threads of their lives with those of institutional history and has attempted to demonstrate how personal character, chance, and institutional pressures interact in the shaping of historical events.

Frances J. Woodward's *The Doctor's Disciples: A Study of Four Pupils of Arnold of Rugby* (London, 1954) is another kind of collective biography. Here the unifying factor is not, as in *The Reason Why,* a series of events, but the influence of a teacher on four of his students— Stanley, Gell, Clough, and his own son William Arnold—all of whom played significant parts in the drama of the age. The book is part of a tendency to turn from preceptors to disciples, to pursue Victorian ideas from closet and classroom to the world of action—or, indeed, as in the instance of Clough, to the world of inaction. Arnold did not always see where his ideas might lead others when carried to their logical conclusion. Woodward shows that the quest for truth inculcated at Rugby could have unexpected results and makes good use of the biographical method in her demonstration.

Easily the most important of the collective biographies of recent years is Asa Briggs's *Victorian People: Some Reassessments of People, Institutions, Ideas, and Events, 1851–1867* (London, 1954) in which the author sets out to examine the unity of that period by studying selected people active in affairs at the time. These people, "specimens," as Strachey's characters were, include Roebuck, Bright, Lowe, Disraeli, Hughes, Trollope, Bagehot, Applegarth, and Smiles. The book is important for several reasons. First, in its supposition that it is possible to penetrate to the "mood" of a period by isolating certain expressed and unexpressed assumptions that underlie that mood. Secondly, because it does not merely list the components of that mood—the gospel of work, the idea of the gentleman, the concept of self-help—but also traces its crosscurrents. Thirdly, because Professor Briggs leaves the beaten path to such advantage. Where countless others have studied the diplomacy of the Crimean War he probes its influence on domestic affairs; where much has been said about economic class distinctions in the nineteenth century, he stresses the continuing strength of habits of deference and proaristocratic feelings in English society. Lastly, the book is important because it makes biography the vehicle for general ideas about the age. Here it is not entirely successful. The biographer tends to be submerged by the historian. And in spite of the title, Victorian people emerge far less vividly than Victorian institutions and habits of thought. The author has resisted the temptation to treat picturesque personalities like Smiles and Hughes as "characters." But the resultant gain in sympathetic understanding also brings with it a certain loss of liveliness. Moreover, the thought is never allowed to occur to the reader that some Victorian people, however socially significant, may have possessed amusing eccentricities and may even have made fools of themselves on occasion. The book could have done with a dash of Stracheyan bitters.

Strachey himself figures in yet another species of collective biography, that concerned with families rather than heterogeneous groups of individuals. C. R. Sanders's *The Strachey Family: History of a Family, 1588–1932* (Durham, N.C., 1953) attempts to find continuities and inherited characteristics in tracing the story of a distinguished English family that made great contributions to public and cultural life through the centuries. But neither this book nor Paul Bloomfield's *Uncommon People: A Study of England's Elite* (London, 1955)—concerned with the Wedgwood-Darwin, Barclay, and Villiers connections—really sustains the sociological note. For the most part, both these books supply what turns out in the main to be a mixture of genealogy and anecdote. Perhaps it is difficult to do much more than that in following a family through several centuries. External factors making for variety and differences tend, then, to outweigh common traits.

But that far more can be done within the limits of a shorter period has been proved by Noel Annan, who followed up his stimulating remarks on the English intellectual aristocracy of the nineteenth century in the Stephen biography by an article setting forth its ramifications in detail.[7] Here, in what might be called an essay in intellectual prosopography, he shows how in the course of the century an aristocracy of intellect gradually spread over English intellectual life, criticizing the assumptions of the ruling class above it, and forming the opinions of the upper middle class. The families composing this new aristocracy were united by their emphasis on intellectual freedom, on a public service open to talent, on the improvement of society by an analysis of its needs and the calculation of the possible course of its development, and (on the negative side) by their limited aesthetic responses.

When E. M. Forster, at the end of the "domestic biography" of his great-aunt, *Marianne Thornton, 1797–1887* (London, 1956), remarks that the impressions he received at the Hertfordshire house where he spent his early years had given him a middle-class, atavistic slant upon society and history, he is really putting himself forward as a living example of family continuity. The book, based on the Thornton family papers, and written with grace, subtlety, and occasional playful irony, shows how in the course of almost a century, and in spite of vast changes in thought and activity in the outside world, a closely knit family may retain traits of thought and feeling as significant to the social historian as charts of prices and wages or files of long dead periodicals. One could hardly expect authors of similar books to have Mr. Forster's talents—when he writes about Henry Thornton that "he never pens a sentence that is clumsy or feeble, and he knows exactly what he wants to say," that applies equally to himself—but it is clear that the path of intellectual or domestic family biography is one that can lead to rewarding discoveries.

What does all this add up to? Certain glimpses come to mind first of all, glimpses reminding one once again of the diversity and color the period holds: Salisbury testing the telephones at Hatfield by shouting nursery rhymes through them; Jowett and Tennyson tossing the two little Tennyson boys in a blanket; William Arnold's first reaction to the Himalayas—he was "reminded of Papa"; Lord Tankerville saying he liked a rainy Sunday because the people could not come out and enjoy themselves; Gladstone and his wife in front of the fire singing "A ragamuffin husband and a rantipoling wife, we'll fiddle it and scrape it through the ups and downs of life"; Swinburne reading *Les Noyades* at Fryston in the presence of the Archbishop of York; Monckton Milnes spraining his ankle at Bagnières dancing the cachuka down a mountainside; Macaulay running through the Athenaeum, shouting "It's out, it's out!" in reference to the coin lodged in Brunel's windpipe. An easy answer to the three questions raised earlier—regarding the proportions of background and foreground, analysis and exposition, praise and blame—would simply be to match the variety of the Victorian scene with a similar variety in biographical writing about its inhabitants. And it would not be an incorrect answer. Yet beyond this undoubted variety certain tendencies, both in the art of biography and in the general view of the age, may perhaps be discerned.

First, it is probably fair to say that the approach to the period taken by most Victorian biographers writing today is sympathetic; and that this has as its corollary some abdication of critical judgment on their part. Things have indeed come round since Strachey wrote. No longer do we dare mock the Victorians or condescend to them. On the contrary, their struggles, their predicaments, their agonies have become paradigmatic of our own. And the fact that they were often able to surmount them without benefit of psychoanalysis has further enhanced their standing. Some writers relate Victorian problems directly to the twentieth century, either in intellectual terms, as when Basil Willey links *Essays and Reviews* with Bultmann's *Kerygma and Myth* to show the relevance of the former for contemporary liberalism and "demythologization";[8] or, more frequently, in terms of the mutual perplexities that bind us together. Others prefer to see the age "as it saw itself," that is to say sociologically, and are thus bound by method rather than inclination to practice *Einfühlung*. As Sir Geoffrey Faber has put it: "Sympathy and respect are necessary conditions for the understanding of any ideas whatsoever" (*Oxford Apostles,* p. 13). And this dictum must certainly be applied in some degree to motive and action as well as thought. But the sociological approach has its perils. "*Tout comprendre*" can all too easily become not only "*tout pardonner,*" but "*tout applaudir*." It is well to remember the injunction that "ideas must be viewed, not only as early or late, but also as sound or unsound."[9]

One danger signal is the readiness with which some recent writers seem to assume that the Victorian age in all its manifestations was preordained; and that the people living it in could do no other than adjust themselves to the inevitable. This is a variant of the historicist fallacy, perhaps found in its most harmless and unavoidable form in statements such as Lord David Cecil's, to the effect that "the spirit of reform was out to make itself felt in every established department" (*Lord M.*, p. 144)—where a literary and space-saving device takes the place of historical analysis. A slightly different result ensues when Asa Briggs writes (about *Tom Brown's Schooldays*): "It needed a jolly book to popularize the public school with the middle class, and later on with the working-class reading public, just as it needed a serious biography [of Arnold] to provide a convincing assessment for Christian intellectuals" (*Victorian People*, p. 158). No doubt. But seeing these books as sociological phenomena tends to preclude any value judgments about them. Sir Geoffrey Faber defends Jowett's subscription to the Articles as a sign of strength rather than weakness: "A strength which kept itself for a real occasion, and refused to be dispersed in useless friction with an imperfect, but not alterable environment."[10] One need not quarrel so much with this view of Jowett as with the implication (1) that to accept one's environment is the path of virtue as well as wisdom, and (2) that Jowett's "strength" could somehow foresee the occasions upon which it must exert itself more fully.

Professor Willey performs yet another variation based on this theme of whatever must be, must be. In discussing the kinship between the Oxford Movement and Methodism, he writes about the latter: "But occurring in the eighteenth century it had had other tasks to perform, and could melt the spiritual ice-pack by reaffirming the old Protestant certainties" (*Nineteenth Century Studies*, p. 74). The question of who decides what tasks are to be performed suggests itself. The implication that they *must* be performed at certain times makes critical evaluation difficult, since value judgments have already been weighed in advance, so to speak, by the taskmaster. In this particular instance, because Protestantism *needed* a deepened understanding of the grounds of faith and the nature of religious experience, the author claims for Newman "a place, not amongst the reactionaries or obscurantists, but amongst the light-bearers of the nineteenth century." Again, the question here is not so much whether he should or should not occupy such a place as whether a necessitarian interpretation such as this can allot him any other.

In short, on the one hand, sympathy growing out of our own inability to solve our problems any better than the Victorians did theirs, on the other the sociological approach that regards a society in its own terms without judging it, have combined to produce a phase of Victorian biography characterized by great good will and understanding. And if, to those still critical of some Victorian values, there is perhaps too much of a tendency to conduct the study of the age like a religious service, the silence in church is not being broken by Freudian firecrackers. Fears that the increasing emphasis on the psychological approach in many fields would have a deleterious effect on the writing of biography because it would lead to too much scientific or pseudo-scientific categorization have on the whole proved groundless. The best biographies of recent vintage show that their authors can and do use subtlety, tact, and at times almost excessive caution in their psychological analyses. They are, of course, preoccupied with childhood and adolescence. But none of them pretends to be writing case histories. Readers must not expect diagnosis, but the biographer ought to be able to raise the right questions when the facts warrant his doing so.

As for the view of the age as a whole that emerges from a reading of some recent biographies, granted that an arbitrary selection of books about diverse people makes it difficult to see the wood for the trees—and that there is always another part of the forest—one major point at least can be made. The old and simple categories which seemed to visualize Victorian England as an enormous playing field, with a series of teams in distinctively colored jerseys engaged in fierce yet expertly refereed combats—Christians vs. Doubters, Liberals vs. Conservatives, Extroverts vs. Introverts, Optimists vs. Pessimists—these, it is clear, no longer apply. For one thing, they do not account for the fact, increasingly apparent, that so many of the players wore jerseys of clashing colors (which sometimes concealed hair shirts, underneath). Scratch a Victorian, and find a split personality? Reading some recent books on the period almost persuades one to answer in the affirmative.

Here are Monckton Milnes, at once philanthropist and Master of Aphrodisiopolis; "Mark Rutherford," the conscientious civil servant undergoing spiritual martyrdom; Florence Nightingale, outwardly the devoted daughter and young society lady, inwardly in secret turmoil through her mysterious "calls"; Melbourne, the gay and cynical man of the world, worried about ultimate problems, poring over his Greek Testament, his bland exterior concealing a troubled spirit; Leslie Stephen, at the same time James Russell Lowell's "lovable man" and egocentric family tyrant; Browning and Tennyson, torn between creative impulse and social conformity; Jowett and Brunel, incarnations of hardheadedness and self-confidence to the outside world, confiding their weaknesses and faults to private journals. The conflict of action and belief depicted in Clough's "Dipsychus"; that "clash between conventional poise and secret catastrophe" observed by the late Michael Sadleir (quoted by Briggs, p. 105); the extent to which, as we have recently learned from Walter E. Houghton's *Victorian Frame of Mind, 1830–1870* (New Haven, 1957), the Victorian subconsciousness was haunted by fear and worry, by guilt, frustration, and loneliness—all these symptoms of the syndrome of the age duly make their appearance in the lives of its notable men and women. Perhaps this should occasion no surprise. A period which saw such immense changes as the growth of an industrial civilization, the development of a democratic society, and the decline of faith naturally left its marks on sensitive people living through it. And if it is foolish to expect to find no contradiction, no struggle, no complexity in the individual psyche, it is even more foolish to expect to be able to categorize the age as a whole in clearly distinct social and political terms, to choose obvious "teams."

A few examples, picked at random from books mentioned in this essay, should suffice to illustrate this point: Monckton Milnes wrote tracts in defense of the Oxford Movement as well as of the Revolution of 1848. The Christian Socialists requested permission to reprint the chapter on the future of the working classes from Mill's *Political Economy*. Leslie Stephen, the real founder of muscular Christianity, was not a Christian. Smiles's gospel of self-improvement was admired by the socialist Robert Blatchford; it was an outgrowth of Radicalism, not an antidote to it. Dr. Arnold was liberal in politics and theology, yet at the same time in favor of the old classical education. Lowe, on the other hand, supported progressive education while opposing the extension of the franchise. Carlyle and Sterling wrote for the *Westminster Review*. Conventional political nomenclature breaks down when one recalls that Bagehot and Trollope were Liberal Conservatives, Bright essentially conservative, and Disraeli something of a radical. And just as any simple generalization about Toryism vs. Democracy is put to flight by a mere glance at the life and career of Disraeli, so is any hasty ranging of laissez-faire vs. state intervention placed in doubt by figures such as Chadwick and Shaftesbury, both in their different ways unwilling precursors of the Welfare State.

Tension is often not present where we might most expect to find it: the Balliol Common Room remained friendly throughout the Ward controversy; Carlyle was a regular visitor at Whig parties; Swinburne read Plato under Jowett as well as reading Sade under Monckton Milnes. "Influence" does not always flow in textbook channels, nor is the *Zeitgeist* evenly distributed: Chadwick took no direct impress from his Nonconformist background; apart from the Bristol Riots of 1831, no single historical event occurred that had any bearing on Brunel's life and work; there were even more than the usual worlds of difference between the intellectual atmospheres of Oxford and Cambridge during the years of theological strife.

All this does not add up to chaos, nor is it insusceptible of analysis. It constitutes, rather, the sort of complexity that demands new categories, emphasis on crosscurrents, on unexpressed underlying assumptions, on hitherto unsuspected groupings and combinations. And we are beginning to get that new structuring of the age. Dr. Kitson Clark has shown, in the economic sphere, that all landlords did not necessarily oppose the repeal of the Corn Laws, that an explanation of English society purely in terms of industrial against agricultural interests breaks down on closer examination.[11] In the intellectual sphere Mr. Annan has stressed the parallel point that political alignments cut across religious as well as economic differences, and (following in the footsteps of A. V. Dicey and G. M. Young) has further pursued the variations and transpositions of the Evangelical theme in the Victorian symphony. Professors Houghton, Willey, and Briggs have begun the work of discarding the old labels and of devising a set of fresh ones capable of describing the complicated texture that recent biographers have helped to reveal.

It is apparent that the old periodization, roughly a sort of prolonged *accelerando* from eighteenth-century libertinism to progressively increasing respectability and reform, no longer holds water. On the one hand Regency Respectables, whether hailing from Edinburgh or Clapham, bid fair to outweigh Regency Bucks in number and significance. Some scholars even go so far as to see the high point of what used to be called "Victorianism" reached in the age of Bowdler and

Mrs. Sherwood. On the other hand, the high moral tone of the Victorians themselves, their emphasis on family life and on proper deportment, has come to be understood more and more as a line of defense against the chasm perpetually threatening under the respectable crust.[12] Then, too, we are learning to beware of the linear fallacy, and beginning to regard political, social, and intellectual controversy in terms of the ebb and flow of generations rather than in those of ineluctable progress. Certain families or groups may build nests of views and assumptions that maintain an existence over a long period of time, little or not at all affected by a supposedly dominant "climate." We still have too much of a tendency at times to think of nineteenth-century English opinion as an entirely passive substance, reacting to successive assaults made upon it by certain books—*On Liberty, Essays and Reviews, Robert Elsmere*—and to forget that the people who wrote these books were, after all, themselves shaped to some extent by the very atmosphere they are said to be "assaulting."

What is the biographer's future role to be in these new approaches to the Victorian age? The last few years have made it clear that excellent biographies of major figures, based on new materials, will continue to be written. It is to be hoped that Finer's *Chadwick* and Rolt's *Brunel* have set examples for equally instructive biographies of Victorian administrators, engineers, and businessmen. Much scope is offered by the genre of collective biography. There have been studies of groups of doubters and of groups of believers. Parliamentary history is increasingly being written in terms of the biographies of members. And there will undoubtedly be more biographies of Victorian families and influential groups. Other themes suggest themselves: Victorians abroad and in the colonies; their deathbeds; their illnesses; their successes and failures in academic examinations; their love of landscape; their conversions and mystical "moments of truth"; changes in their epistolary style and modes of humor; their school experiences; different kinds of provincialism; family rifts and emancipation from family influence; the effect of literary fashions on domestic life. A single remark of E. M. Forster's, to the effect that the gradual reduction in the intensity of mourning and deathbed emotionalism also implied a reduction in love and loyalty of soul (*Marianne Thornton,* p. 71), opens up a fertile field for psychological study through family biography. Is there any reason why the method and scope of contemporary sociological investigations like Riesman's *Lonely Crowd* should not be projected backwards? The Victorian age certainly offers a great deal of source material, in its literature, its diaries, its correspondence, its journals and autobiographies. It is up to the biographers to meet this challenge.

We seem to have traveled a long distance from Strachey's *Eminent Victorians*. And yet, have we really come as far as all that? It has been the fashion to damn Strachey with faint praise by expressing admiration for his style, his humor, his wit, his artistry—for everything except the substance of what he said. He was capable of willful distortion; he mocked too much; he pitied too little. These are sins inexcusable in serious students of the past, and it is all to the good that they are not being committed today. But in rereading *Eminent Victorians*, after reading some of the better biographies of Victorian figures that have appeared since the Second World War, one is struck by more than mockery and stylistic brilliance. In his four Victorian specimens Strachey saw contradiction and complexity—conflicts between religiosity and worldliness, belief and action, idealism and practice, self-love and self-sacrifice. We may not like his attitude towards what he found; we can certainly condemn him for too readily finding what he wanted to find. Yet the more we learn about the period, the more it becomes apparent that it was an age of strains and stresses—social and psychological—which often resulted in individual neurosis and confusion of purpose. Strachey put his finger on some of these strains and stresses. He also saw, though from the vantage point of the scoffer, that religion can probably serve as the best key to the period as a whole. Furthermore, he passed the judgment that stupidity and vulgarity were part and parcel of the age. Our present sympathy for the Victorians, combined with our tendency to "sociologize" them, threatens to rob us of a similar power of judgment.

No less a scholar than the late Humphry House warned that it would be disastrous if Victorian stupidity, failure, vulgarity, and unhappiness were all to be explained away, or minimized, or accepted as something else. "For many Victorians were in many respects stupid, vulgar, unhappy, and unsuccessful, and these aspects of the age remain visible in the objects, the buildings, the pictures, and the literature that have been left to us."[13] I am not suggesting that we should again make a laughingstock of the Victorians, or denigrate their achievements. But, at a time when there is little danger of either contingency, it may not be totally inappropriate in this fortieth-anniversary year of Strachey's book to remind ourselves that to think critically, to judge, and, once in a while, to be amused will not necessarily spell disaster for Victorian studies.

VI

LIFE
IN LETTERS
AND
MEMORIES

The Education of
Alexis de Tocqueville

OF ALEXIS DE TOCQUEVILLE

edited by J. P. Mayer

In the late summer of 1850 the English economist Nassau Senior visited his friend Alexis de Tocqueville at the latter's ancestral mansion in Normandy. In the journal he kept of this visit he noted the presence of Tocqueville's father, a "fine old man" of seventy-eight, whose hair had turned gray during the Terror of the first French Revolution, when he was barely saved from trial and certain execution by the fall of Robespierre. The old count recalled that "the disagreeable time in every day was about half-past three," when those selected for trial were summoned from prison. For this reason he accustomed himself to sleep each afternoon between three and four. The anecdote is doubly significant: it evokes a psychological atmosphere heavily charged with *noblesse oblige,* and it reminds us that by the middle of the nineteenth century there were still eyewitnesses to lend additional vitality to a powerful revolutionary tradition.

The revolutionary heritage of modern French history and the aristocratic heritage of Alexis de Tocqueville provide the counterpoint for his *Recollections,* the complete text of which has now appeared for the first time in an English translation. At the time of Senior's visit Tocqueville had just finished setting down the first part of what he resolved would be "... a mirror in which I will amuse myself in

From the *Partisan Review*, September–October 1950

contemplating my contemporaries and myself, not a picture painted for the public." It was a mirror that came to reflect nine months of the French revolutionary period of 1848–1849: the four months beginning in February 1848, which saw the proclamation of the Second Republic, the establishment of a provisional government, the election and deliberations of the Constituent Assembly, and the bloody "June days" when the *bourgeois* Republicans who had begun the revolution defeated the insurgent Paris workers who had wanted to make it social as well as political; and the five months beginning in June 1849, during which Tocqueville served as foreign minister in a cabinet dismissed by the president in October of that year because it refused to make itself subservient to his wishes. The president was Louis Bonaparte, Victor Hugo's *Napoléon le Petit,* who had been overwhelmingly elected in December 1848, by that universal suffrage that seemed to so many the infallible guarantee of democracy.

Tocqueville, who had not actively helped to bring about the revolution but did his best to support the Republic once it was proclaimed, had no illusions about universal suffrage. He predicted the coup d'état of Louis Napoleon and the eventual ruin of the Second Republic just as he had predicted the outbreak of the revolution itself. Like Marx in his *Eighteenth Brumaire,* he recognized the social elements in the revolutionary process he described. The middle class had achieved its triumphs in 1789 and 1830 and had monotonously consolidated them during the July Monarchy. In 1848 the turn of the working classes seemed to have arrived. "Socialism will always remain the essential characteristic and the most redoubtable remembrance of the Revolution of February. The Republic will only appear to the onlooker to have come upon the scene as a means, not as an end."

Tocqueville wrote this late in 1850. A little more than two years earlier, in September of 1848, the Constituent Assembly, made up for the most part of moderate Republicans, had debated the critical issue of incorporating the "Right to Work" demanded by the Left into the new constitution. In his speech opposing this demand Tocqueville had explicitly denied what he was to assert in the *Recollections,* maintaining—on that occasion—that the character of the February Revolution was neither socialist nor social, but political, and that one must have the courage to say so. He himself, whose honesty in self-analysis verges on the painful, would have been the first to admit the discrepancy. As an active participant in the political events of the revolution, he saw his duty in saving the Republic from socialism. If this could be done by denying the social character of the revolution, he was willing to try. But when, in the *Recollections,* he came to probe into the deeper meaning of the events through which he had lived he felt free not only to emphasize the importance of socialist currents in the revolution, but to envisage the possibility of their eventual success. Like his spiritual kinsmen, Jacob Burckhardt and Henry Adams, Tocqueville devoted a great deal of effort to predicting what he could not but detest.

His political career during the revolution exemplifies that tragic irony that keynotes the *Recollections.* Fear of socialism with its "tyranny of equality" drove him who was perhaps the most "enlightened" conservative of the century into the Party of Order. There were few, if any, in that camp who shared either his selfless passion for liberty and justice or his clearsighted awareness of the dangers that lay ahead. None knew better than he that the successful quelling of the workers' risings was all too likely to prove a Pyrrhic victory. None was less convinced than he that 1848 constituted the end of the revolutionary process that had begun in 1789. And not even Marx was more contemptuous than Tocqueville of the claptrap employed by Republicans of all shades to re-create the atmosphere of that first great revolution. His wit is never more mordant than when he is describing the procession of secretly armed deputies to the "Feast of Concord," there to be bombarded with bouquets by three hundred young girls dressed in white "who wore their virginal costume in so virile a fashion that they might have been taken for boys dressed up as girls"; or when he notices the single deputy who obeyed the decree of the provisional government which suggested that the representatives wear the costume of the members of the National Convention of 1792–1795, "especially the white waistcoat with turn-down collar in which Robespierre was always represented on the stage."

Tocqueville's contempt for these antics is part of a theme sounded more than once in the *Recollections:* that history does not repeat itself, and that those who act as if it did do so at their peril. But the problem of Tocqueville's views on this matter is not so easily solved. One may discover three Tocquevilles in the *Recollections,* and three *Weltanschauungen* corresponding to them. Their constant interweaving produces a tension that permeates the book and lends it its classic stature.

There is first Tocqueville the sociologist, the author of *Democracy in America,* who has long foreseen that the inevitable transition to the age of the masses would be attended by such disturbances as the Revolution of 1848. For him there are no surprises and no mysteries. To each event he wearily reacts with an "I told you so," for the processes of history proceed according to plan. The second Tocqueville is the politician: as a deputy in both the old and the new legislative assemblies and in the Constituent Assembly that intervenes, later as foreign minister, he refuses to be overwhelmed by any ineluctable laws or movements and fights with tireless tenacity for his "middle way." The third Tocqueville is the curious human animal who looks into his brain and heart to seek there the secret springs of his thoughts and actions: for him the destinies of the world proceed as the contrary result of the intentions that produce them; for him neither events nor persons (including himself) are ever what they appear to be; and for him the unpredictable passions and sentiments of men are the only reality.

It is this last Tocqueville who gives the *Recollections* an astringent melancholy and a bitter humor. A supremely able observer, aristocrat by birth and temperament, impatient of mediocrity and sham, records a period of revolution marked by nothing more than platitudes and histrionics. Like a lepidopterist, he is forever out to catch new specimens for his collection: his victims are human, his net is the fine network of his intelligence, and the labels under the mounted specimens all read alike—*genus vanitas*.

He may, at times, be hypercritical; that, after all, is the privilege of the moralist. But he is always incisive and never dull: whether he comments on the rhetorical style of Louis-Philippe—"Jean-Jacques with a touch of nineteenth century kitchenmaid"—on the peculiar gait of Lamennais, who "glided through the crowd with an awkward, modest air, as though he were leaving the sacristy," on George Sand's affair with Mérimée, conducted, he hears, "in accordance with Aristotle's rules of time and place," or on his own psychological insecurity, whose source he finds not in modesty but in "a great pride . . . as restless and disquieted as the mind itself."

A Nephew's Tribute

THE LIFE AND LETTERS OF
LORD MACAULAY
by Sir George Otto Trevelyan

This special edition (three hundred numbered copies) commemorates the hundredth anniversary of Lord Macaulay's death, and provides an opportunity to pay tribute once again to one of the classic Victorian biographies, first published in 1876, seventeen years after the death of the historian. It now appears with a brief preface, written especially for this edition by Dr. G. M. Trevelyan, the author's son and the subject's great-nephew, and with an enlarged and comprehensive index.

As Dr. Trevelyan points out in his preface, the two great qualities that have made contemporary and later critics hail this biography as one of the masterpieces of the art are its readableness and its clear, truthful picture of Macaulay's character and personality. It is readable because with uncanny skill Sir G. O. Trevelyan built the thread of his narrative into a mosaic of vivid and amusing extracts from the great historian's letters and journals. And it is truthful because, unlike that multitude of Victorian biographers who regarded their function as primarily eulogistic, Trevelyan was not afraid to give his readers the whole man, inclusive of rough edges and minor blemishes. As a result, we can still read the book today in the certainty of encountering

From *History & Theory* 1, No. 11 (1961)

a person of flesh and blood—argumentative, affectionate, opinionated, playful by turns; but always human and alive.

Macaulay, as we know, was much more than a "mere" historian. Member of Parliament and for a time of the Cabinet, Indian administrator, poet, man of letters—it is possible to argue that in these capacities alone he deserves biographical consideration. However, those professionally concerned with the history of historical writing have particular reasons for being interested in his biography, for it raises a question about the degree of relevance that knowledge of a historian's life bears to an understanding of his written history. Therefore, it is in the light of this question that we shall consider the book here.

It may well be argued, of course, that what finally counts is the work a historian leaves behind, that it is his contribution to the stock of historical knowledge or his artistry in the writing of history that ensures his survival; and that details about his personality are pleasant to have, but largely irrelevant. Others may feel that, since there is no such thing as "pure" or "objective" history, since, therefore, the prejudices and value judgments, the crotchets and predilections of the historian are always bound to emerge from between the lines of any historical work, it is sufficient to look for them there.

It is certainly true that a good deal of historical writing readily lends itself to this particular game of hide-and-seek. "Was" William the Third Macaulay? "Was" Julian Gibbon? In order to answer these questions, we must know something about the authors' lives. But, coming to *The Decline and Fall* with no knowledge whatever of Gibbon's life and personality, one would not have to read more than a few pages to conclude that the author of that work was not, in all likelihood, a humorless clergyman of the Church of England, with Evangelical views. One or two chapters of von Ranke should suffice to persuade the general reader that here was no jolly fat uncle chuckling over wondrous tales of a golden past for the delectation of his nieces and nephews.

The game becomes slightly more risky when we begin to play it with figures such as Thucydides and Herodotus. The one stern and austere, the other garrulous and hail-fellow-well-met? It would appear so. But Professor Toynbee, for one, has called the real Herodotus subtle and ruthless. And we must be careful. For our quarry in this game of hide-and-seek often proves more elusive than we at first suspect.

Macaulay, for instance, seems to emerge from his essays as a cantankerous, ill-tempered, occasionally even brutal Philistine laying about him with fierce and near-sadistic vigor, delighting to catch out his literary victims in error and chastising them to his own smug satisfaction. Yet, as his letters and journals show, behind this blustering façade there lurked a delicate, an almost feminine sensibility— the sensibility of someone fanatically devoted to his family, easily prone to tears, and reconciled not without pain to the lonely life of a bachelor.

It may be objected that there is no contradiction here. After all, Macaulay himself, in the essay on "Milton" that brought him fame and fortune overnight, had this to say about that line of defense for Charles the First which held that he was a good father and a pious churchgoer:

> We charge him with having broken his coronation-oath—and we are told that he kept his marriage-vow! We accuse him of having given up his people to the merciless inflictions of the most hot-headed and hard-hearted of prelates—and the defense is, that he took his little son on his knee and kissed him! We censure him for having violated the articles of the Petition of Right, after having, for good and valuable consideration, promised to observe them—and we are informed that he was accustomed to hear prayers at six o'clock in the morning!

But the point is that we could never have guessed the complexity of Macaulay's personality, the extra dimension of affection and sensitivity, without seeing him in the circle of his family and friends, accompanying him on his travels, and sharing his hours of leisure—in other words, without reading Trevelyan's *Life and Letters*. Knowing that the complexity exists at least makes it possible to speculate that there may have been some connection between the rough manner, the occasional crudities, the bluster, and the painfully shy interior of the man—that one may have served as a mask to hide the other.

This, admittedly, is speculation. But the *Life and Letters* of Lord Macaulay bring into sharp relief various other, far less speculative connections between the man and the historian which dramatically underline the importance of knowing as much as possible about a historian's life in order fully to understand his historical writings. Take the question of "The Whig Interpretation of History." This is certainly writ large in the pages of the *Essays* and of *The History of England*.

The Whig bias is perhaps not as strong as it has sometimes said to have been; but it is undoubtedly present. Are we not helped in accounting for it when we are reminded that Macaulay himself was a member in good standing of the Holland House set, that last and most glorious preserve of eighteenth-century aristocratic Whiggery? That he played a most prominent role in the House of Commons in the passage of the Great Reform Bill? That, as he wrote his father from Trinity at the time of Peterloo: "I am not one of those advocates of anarchy and confusion with whom you class me. My opinions, good or bad, were learned not from Hunt and Waithman, but from Cicero, from Tacitus, and from Milton"?

Or take the question of Macaulay's moral judgments, which ring so unhesitatingly through the pages of everything he ever wrote. We may not approve of them; indeed, we may deplore them. But if we are to understand them and their source, the *Life and Letters* will take us back into the atmosphere of the Clapham Sect, of Zachary Macaulay's superhuman devotion to duty, of the Evangelical discipline that forced upon its adherents the severest criticism not alone of themselves and their consciences, but (perhaps even to a greater degree) of others who failed to meet the high standards which betokened the converted. It was in this atmosphere that young Tom wrote one of his earliest poetical productions, a hymn composed at the age of seven:

> *Almighty God of all below,*
> *Thou canst protect from every foe;*
> *The Heavens are made by Thy great hands,*
> *One word of Thee the earth commands.*
> *Some men make Gods of red and blue,*
> *And rob their Sovereign of His due*
> *The good shall go to Heaven. The fell*
> *Blasts of Thy wrath can bear to Hell.*

And, though he was to shake off the religious aspects of this strict Evangelical heritage (in middle age he, who won his first oratorical spurs addressing an annual meeting of the Anti-Slavery Society, will be found referring to the "nonsense" of an Exeter Hall antislavery gathering), he continued to think in the well-defined, black-and-white moral categories impressed upon him during his childhood and early youth.

As for the belief in progress so fervently held by Macaulay and nowadays often so fervently held against him, we come a little closer to its nature and origins when we watch him visit and revisit the Great Exhibition and see him astounded by it, even inspired to write part of a chapter of his *History* by the sight; or when we listen to him, in his speech on the Anatomy Bill of 1832, celebrate the great achievements of the medical profession of his time, which enabled any bricklayer falling off a ladder in England to obtain better surgical assistance than that which the sovereign of Austria could command in the twelfth century.

But the linkage of life and work, of personality and written history, may be far more subtle than merely environmental. Two of the principal components of Macaulay's greatness as a historian are to be found in his style and his historical imagination. Ever since Jeffrey, upon receipt of Macaulay's first brilliant contribution to the *Edinburgh Review*, wrote to the young contributor, "The more I think, the less I can conceive where you picked up that style," there has been some mystery in regard to the origin of the historian's vividly polemical manner of writing. A careful reading of the *Life and Letters* does not entirely solve the mystery. But in the letters which young Tom Macaulay, writing from Cambridge, addressed to his father—the majority argumentative, forcefully disputing with him such subjects as the advantages of reading for pleasure, the uselessness of mathematics, the unjustifiable neglect of modern in favor of ancient literature—may be found a valuable series of clues. The vigor of Macaulay's style owes much to the impetus of filial revolt, just as its clarity very likely came out of his constant contact with his family circle, out of his habit, as his sister Margaret put it, of conversing with very young people to whom he had a great deal to explain and impart.

From a reading of Trevelyan's biography we discover that when it comes to the realm of the historical imagination the interaction between personality and written work takes place at several different levels. One is not surprised to find in the author of the great third chapter of the *History* an acute and shrewd observer of the social scene. Furthermore, from boyhood on, Macaulay loved the picturesque and the dramatic. An avid reader of novels (much to his father's indignation), he was fascinated by the colorful and the dramatic both in history and in his own times. Finally, we find what is perhaps the most complex level of interaction—the relationship between the historian's personal fantasy life and the particular quality of his imagination as displayed in his historical writing. And here a careful reading of the *Life and Letters* can pay unexpected dividends. For there is undoubtedly some connection between the man who, as he said of himself, passed a large part of his life in the unreal world of fantasy and the historian who could let his imagination play on the past to such vivid effect.

Reading large extracts from the journals and letters of a historian brings home to us the fact, often forgotten, that even the great masters of the craft had to struggle, that writing history is hard work at any level. We watch Macaulay rewriting and polishing and revising again and again; we see him all too often depressed and dissatisfied, even when the applause of the multitude is still ringing in his ears; we see him as his own severest critic, always holding up for himself the highest standards, always engaged in the endeavor of emulating the very greatest historians who preceded him, yet never completely convinced of his success.

In sum, it is good to be reminded by this reissue of Macaulay's *Life and Letters* of the general proposition that it is important to know the human being behind the work. Gibbon in the Hampshire Militia, Parkman using his writing machine in the agony of his suffering, Carlyle undismayed by the destruction of his manuscript of *The French Revolution,* Burckhardt running to commiserate with Nietzsche at the false report of the destruction of the Louvre, Macaulay acting out a Red Indian chief for his family—these glimpses remind us that behind the history stands the historian and that in order fully to understand the one it is well to become familiar with the other.

An Odd Couple

LOVE IN A COOL CLIMATE:

THE LETTERS OF MARK PATTISON AND

META BRADLEY, 1879-1884

edited by Vivian Green

The letters on which this remarkable book is based provide a moving and fascinating record of the romantic friendship that flourished just over a century ago between the elderly Mark Pattison, formidable Oxford scholar and academic reformer, and a young woman forty years his junior who, lonely, awkward, and unattractive, craved intellectual guidance and human affection and received both from the notoriously rebarbative Rector of Lincoln College. The two had met briefly in 1878, but the crucial meeting took place in the autumn of the following year, when, having encountered Meta Bradley at an Oxford party—her uncle was Master of University College, and one of his daughters, Meta's cousin, was married to a Fellow and future President of Trinity—Pattison asked her to tea in his lodgings at Lincoln. That was the real beginning of what turned out to be a close relationship between two difficult people, one in his mid-sixties, the other in her mid-twenties, each thirsting for sympathy and love. (One is initially put off by Vivian Green's use of "Mark" and "Meta" in referring to the two principal characters in his story. The conjunction of names inevitably conjures up prospects of television romance. But, after considering possible alternatives that might have been used, such as "The Rector" and "Miss Bradley"—shades of Brighton Pier—or

From the *Times Literary Supplement,* April 18, 1986

the repeated use of both Christian and last names, one tends to respect Dr. Green's decision and, with some trepidation, to emulate it.)

That they were difficult people was doubtless due, in part, to their family backgrounds, which in both cases could have been included in a medical textbook on Victorian neuroses induced by Evangelical clergymen. Meta's father, Charles Bradley, living in retirement in London with his second wife, had previously owned and taught at the school near Southgate that figures in Augustus Hare's *Story of My Life*. Hare recalls that among the punishments Bradley tried to impose on him for committing trivial grammatical faults—he was then almost nineteen years old—was "wearing his coat inside out running with a tin kettle tied to his coat-tail through the village." Meta adored her mother, long-suffering and kindhearted, who died when she herself was thirteen. (By an odd error, Green lists her in his dramatis personae as the daughter of her father's second wife.) She never got over that loss; in particular since to her father, so Green writes, "she seemed an ugly duckling whose wayward opinions had to be countered." Understandably, she came to loathe her father. But, as an unmarried daughter financially dependent on him, she had no choice but to live at home in Paddington. Lacking the independence her father repeatedly refused to grant her, she increasingly occupied herself with good works. Her views were indeed unconventional for her household: she once declared that, were she a politician, she would propose to pull down and rebuild workmen's houses, alter the marriage laws, and open public places on Sunday.

That streak of unconventionality was no doubt part of her attraction for Mark, who, having early in life fallen for some years under the spell of Cardinal Newman and Tractarianism, even to the point of considering going over to Rome, had subsequently taken distinctly liberal views on religious matters—he had been a contributor to *Essays and Reviews*—and had broken many a lance in his efforts to change Oxford from its preoccupation with undergraduate and college life to a place centered on scholarship and learning.

Mark's father, like Meta's, was an Evangelical clergyman. After a nervous breakdown and some time in a mental home, he became so infuriated and obsessed with the Tractarian influences under which his daughters, having taken their cue from their brother, had fallen, that he would greet visitors to his North Riding rectory at Hauxwell with, "Will you join the Papists in the dining-room or be content to partake the fare of the poor solitary persecuted Protestant here?" He was as appalled by his son's liberal as by his Romanizing views. The grim goings-on at Hauxwell cast a shadow over Mark's life; though, unlike his sisters, he did not have to endure the perpetual presence of a demented father. He pursued his own course at Oxford, first as an undergraduate at Oriel, then as Fellow and, from 1861, Rector of Lincoln College, a position that required him to remain in Orders, but allowed him to marry.

Thus in 1861, at the age of forty-eight, he married Francis Strong, an exceptionally beautiful and highly intelligent woman twenty-seven years younger than he was. She had romanticized her future husband's personality as well as the attractions of Oxford academic society. After some years she became disillusioned with both; and, beginning in 1875, spent increasingly long periods in France, first on the Riviera, then in Provence. There she devoted herself to the study of art history, a field in which she eventually became an international authority, and began the friendship with the radical Liberal politician Charles Dilke that would, a decade later, lead to their marriage. Mark was outraged by his wife's frequent and prolonged absences; and, even more, by a letter she wrote him from Nice in 1876 in which she informed him that sexual relations could no longer take place between them: "It is a physical aversion which always existed, though I strove hard to overcome it, and which is now wholly beyond control."

It is therefore not wholly surprising that when Mark, who, in any event, liked the company of young women—Walter Pater once observed that his favorite pastime was "romping with great girls among the gooseberry bushes"—encountered immediate trust and adoration in the person of Meta, he responded with enthusiasm. For three years they met, either for walks and meals in London, or in Oxford, where Meta would come to stay at the Rector's Lodgings. When they were apart, which was most of the time, they wrote frequently to one another. It is their correspondence, 450 letters in all, ingeniously excerpted, summarized, and glossed by Green, that forms the substance of *Love in a Cool Climate*—which can truly be said to rival many a novel in depicting a relationship that, with all its bizarre aspects, brought genuine happiness to two lonely and emotionally starved people. After meeting her (in 1880) at Grasmere, where Meta was staying with her sister Jessie, Mark wrote to her that "There is now no one from whom I get the special form of attachment which you have found it in your heart to bestow upon me." Meta's reply was that "I felt so happy merely in being with you that I didn't care very much about anything else. I don't think I've ever been so happy since I was a child." Before long the letters became more passionate in tone, with

Meta writing to Mark—he was absent from the lodgings for a night while she was staying there—"I don't suppose you will ever understand the sort of feeling which I have for you, a unique mixture of what people feel for their God, their husband, and their child." A few weeks later, Mark addresses her as follows: "Dear love, I must have you back again! Seeing does not satisfy me. I must have my arms tightly around that waist, with infinite possibilities of kissing."

There is no way of knowing whether actual intimacy ever took place. Green, for cogent reasons, doubts that it did. But whether it did or not, there can be no possible doubt about the passionate affection that bound the two together. There were intellectual as well as emotional bonds. Meta wanted Mark to "Improve" her. They read aloud to one another: Dante, Ruskin, Ouida—and, needless to say, *The Prelude* at Grasmere. Beyond that they were linked by their inability to believe in orthodox Christianity—in his case the product of his troubled journey from Newman to *Essays and Reviews,* his extensive studies of theology and history; in hers the result of feeling and thinking for herself at a time conducive to such intellectual independence on the part of those temperamentally inclined to exercise it. Meta linked her inability to believe in a personal God with the intensity of her love for Mark: "It is so awfully hard to feel absolutely alone in the world, to have no God to breathe a prayer to," she tells him in 1881. "If I could only know that there was some Power whom I could love, say as much as I do you."

It is one thing to read in books about the late Victorian decades that they were a period of fading beliefs, of groping for new certainties; and quite another to find confirmation in this intimate correspondence between an old and famous scholar, biographer of one Casaubon and probable model for another, and a young, self-educated woman looking to him for comfort and sympathy. The ethical problems raised by the Incarnation, troublesome for not a few sensitive spirits since the start of the century, worried both of them. Meta, granting "the Christian account of Christ," could not see what was so wonderfully self-sacrificing about His spending thirty-three years "down here, very trying years no doubt, but then I look at the result, which he knew all the time. Why, it seems to me that if one could even cure one human being's anguish one would sacrifice oneself gladly to help them, and as Christ was supposed to see into everybody's heart I don't see how he could have done a lot less than he did." The thought is hardly new, the tone almost jarringly informal; but the feeling genuine and powerful. Mark agreed with her. "Yes, that is a very staggering thought, the infinitesimally small effect produced by the intervention of the Almighty 1,800 years ago."

A good deal of middle-class opinion, in Oxford and elsewhere, remained censorious about the sort of relationship that seemed to be developing between the married head of an Oxford college and a young woman less than half his age. Tongues wagged; letters were purloined—Francis Pattison saw some of them; and, at the end of 1882 Meta's father forbade his wayward daughter either to meet or to write to her friend. Mark himself increasingly feared a major scandal, and became more cautious. In the event, Charles Bradley died soon after issuing his edict. So, in 1883, Mark and Meta resumed their correspondence, though they now met less frequently than before. And Mark (who in a rare moment of self-knowledge referred to "a certain chilliness of manner" in his own nature) sometimes felt impelled to adopt a tone of irritated frankness in his letters. About her voluntary social work he remarked: "I should have thought all this sanitary occupation could have been sufficient to have diverted your thoughts in a healthier channel." And, shortly thereafter, about her appearance: "I was so sadly grieved to see you look so thin, wan, and haggard on Thursday." There were reasons for this. Her father had practically disinherited her, and she was mourning the recent death of her friend Grace Toynbee's brother Arnold. So she replied, a little sharply: "You must know that I would do anything on earth to please you, but I can't make my face look young and fat! I may have been 'bright and vivacious' when you first knew me, but I never was 'hearty.' " Mark, for his part, did not become more tactful. Only a few weeks later, responding to Meta's report that someone had suggested she might try her hand at teaching: "I don't think you would like teaching, and have great doubts if you could teach with effect."

Meta's devotion could weather such wounding words. It could even weather Mrs. Pattison's visits to Oxford, in the course of which meetings with Mark were necessarily rare. But ill health was another matter. In the autumn of 1881 Mark had written of his awareness of death, "galloping towards me all the while"; and the following January, complaining of a feverish cold, he added: "This in addition to gout, rheumatism, no teeth and inactive liver! Is life worth preserving?" But really serious illness did not strike until the end of 1883. Expecting imminent death, he told Meta that he did not wish to see her: "I have told you over and over again what I think of those dying interviews and leave takings. They are odious ceremonial." He did receive a visit from the octogenarian Cardinal Newman, who nobly insisted on coming from Birmingham to call on his mortally ill onetime disciple. The Rector suspected that Newman was possibly cherishing "the hope, however slight, that I might still be got over in my last moments." The cardinal made no such attempt, perhaps because during their talk of old times he saw that "he had not realised the enormous distance at which I had left behindhand the standpoint of 1845." What a scene! The letters to Meta describing it should be read with his reminiscences of the Oxford Movement in his *Memoirs*—whose existence, by the way, we owe to her.

If the Newman visit brought back the very distant past in dramatic form, there was a different kind of drama in Francis Pattison's return to England, to nurse her husband in his final illness. The closing pages of Green's book abound with memorable vignettes: Mark's last encounter with Meta in London, where he and Francis had taken a house during a temporary improvement in his health. Mrs. Pattison insisted on accompanying her husband to Paddington, only to espy "her" copy of Carlyle's Dante on the drawing-room table. The Rector's progress in a Bath chair round the Oxford Parks, as described by Stephen Gwynn, "drawn . . . by a shambling menial, lying more like a corpse than any living thing I have ever seen. And yet there was a singular vitality behind that parchment covered face, something powerful and repellent. Beside him walked his wife, small, erect, and ultra Parisian, all in black with a black parasol." And then the end, in Mark's beloved Yorkshire, at Harrogate, where Francis nursed her dying husband with untiring devotion. She even offered to ask Meta to pay a visit. But he refused, saying, "You are *all*-sufficing. You do not know how good you are to me. You are my comfort and consolation, the only one I want."

He died in excruciating pain, of cancer of the stomach. On the day before his death, so Francis Pattison reported, "the morphine passed off and then till the doctor came nurse and I stood for 4 hours witnessing the terrible fits of terror with shrieks which went through the house and trying to ease and calm. Let not my last days be like his! The moral misery is awful."

That evening, his last, two sides of his complex personality showed themselves. After his wife read him Gray's "Ode on a Distant Prospect of Eton College," with its grim lines about "the painful family of Death," he commented on the poem "with all his old aptness, pregnancy and refinement." After which he dictated a cruel farewell letter to his sister Eleanor.

So ends a moving story, told in masterly fashion by Green who, as the present Rector of Lincoln College, and its historian, is of all possible authors the most qualified to tell it. "Our letters," so Meta once wrote to Mark, "would be invaluable in 1983 as showing the life of this age." Indeed, there is much to be garnered from these pages by those in search of light on Victorian Oxford, the intellectual currents of the time, and the habits and constraints of certain segments of English middle-class society in the early 1880s. But, in the end, what chiefly remains in the reader's memory is the human drama, the story of an incongruous friendship between a young woman radiating gush, goodwill, and common sense in just about equal proportions, and a selfish, sardonic, cantankerous scholar not immune to the warmth of human affection. It was a friendship that brought some measure of love and happiness to both. As Dr. Green aptly puts it: "Normally the passion of love seems romantic when it concerns only the handsome and beautiful of both sexes, young in mind, body and spirit. But love's frontiers are never closed nor exclusive, in terms of either gender or appearance, or age or looks. Meta and Mark came tentatively within its territory." This is one more valuable stone to be added to that ever more strangely glowing mosaic called the Victorian age.

Laura, A Stonemason's Daughter

LARK RISE TO CANDLEFORD

by Flora Thompson

In any future history of historiography, the present time may well turn out to be known as "the age of *mentalités*." More than ever, historians of all periods interest themselves not only in how ordinary people lived in the past, but also in how they felt and thought about the world and themselves. The latest research techniques, ranging from statistics to oral history, are used, with varying degrees of success, in the service of this curiosity. Meetings and conventions abound with learned debates about past ways of thought and feeling. And many young historians, following in the footsteps of a few pioneering elders, are hoping to make at least their academic fortune in this new and exciting field. What is often forgotten in all the excitement is that there are already certain books that, thanks to that most reliably effective of all historical methods, the intelligence and sensitivity of their authors, have gradually attained the stature of classics and that are still unrivaled in supplying insight into the mental habits of former generations. One of these, now happily available again, is Flora Thompson's *Lark Rise to Candleford,* her reminiscences of Oxfordshire country life, published in three separate volumes between 1939 and 1943 and first issued as a trilogy in one volume bearing the present title in 1945.

From *University Publishing,* Spring 1981

In her book, the author herself appears as Laura, a stonemason's daughter, who at the age of fourteen leaves the hamlet of Lark Rise in order to become assistant to the postmistress at the nearby village of Candleford Green. The end of the volume sees her as a letter-carrier, an occupation that enables her to exercise to the fullest her shrewd and sympathetic powers of observation. The circumscribed world of rural Oxfordshire in the 1880s and '90s is seen through Laura's eyes. But Laura herself—sensitive, intelligent, and above all endlessly curious—is always referred to in the third person. This literary device enabled Flora Thompson to keep her distance and to produce a work that is much more than an autobiography, one that may be said to constitute the reconstruction of an entire locality and its way of life during the last two decades of the nineteenth century.

Three places form part of that locality: the hamlet of Lark Rise, the village of Candleford Green, and the small country town of Candleford. Those names, like Laura's, are imaginary; but there can be no doubt about the reality on which the description is based. In the 1880s Lark Rise consisted of about thirty cottages, inhabited in the main by farm laborers earning no more than ten shillings a week. Some of the cottages had two bedrooms, others only one that had to be divided by a screen or curtain to accommodate parents and children. Families were large in those days; and beds were often so closely packed together that sleepers had to climb over one bed to get into another. The one hot meal of the day, called tea, was taken in the evening and usually consisted of a bit of bacon, vegetables and potatoes from the garden, and a "roly-poly," containing fruit, currents, or jam, which appeared as the first course in order to take the edge off the appetite. Everything was cooked in one utensil. Only three of the thirty cottages had their own water supply. There was no public well or pump; people had to get their water where and how they could. Deep pits with seats set over them served as privies whose emptying twice a year caused every door and window in the vicinity to be sealed. Coal and paraffin, like house rent, had to be squeezed out of the weekly wage. For clothes, shoes, books, illness, holidays, and amusements there was no provision whatever. By the standards of today, then, a grinding poverty prevailed.

Yet, on the whole, people were not unhappy. Lark Rise was not a slum set down in the country. The inhabitants lived an open-air life. They kept their cottages clean. Their health was good. "Though food was rough and teeth were neglected, indigestion was unknown, while nervous troubles, there as elsewhere, had yet to be invented." Good manners prevailed. Special occasions, like May Day or Harvest Home, or the killing of the family pig once or twice a year, were celebrated with great feasts and helped to break up the monotony, as did relics of old country customs and the last echoes of country songs, ballads, and rhymes. In the eighties the children of Lark Rise still had a large repertory of traditional games. For the adults, there were dances, storytelling, singing, and the occasional visit of a German band. Most of the men sang or whistled as they dug or hoed. People knew the secret of being happy on little. Their favorite virtue was endurance. "In spite of their poverty and the worry and anxiety attending it, they were not unhappy, and, though poor, there was nothing sordid about their lives."

What Flora Thompson communicates so well is how the old country civilization lingered on into a period bringing new circumstances and new values. "All times are times of transition," she writes.

But the eighteen-eighties were so in a special sense, for the world was at the beginning of a new era, the era of machinery and scientific discovery. Values and conditions of life were changing everywhere. Even to simple country people the change was apparent. The railways had brought distant parts of the country nearer; newspapers were coming into every home; machinery was superseding hand labor, even on the farms to some extent; food bought at shops, much of it from distant countries, was replacing the home-made and home-grown. Horizons were widening; a stranger from a village five miles away was no longer looked upon as "a furriner."

But traditions and customs that had lasted for centuries did not die out in a moment. State-educated children still played the old rhyme games. Women still went gleaning, or "leazing," although fields were now cut by mechanical reapers. And men and boys still sang the old country ballads and songs, along with the latest music-hall successes.

Meanwhile, machine-made lace had killed cottage lacemaking. Good, solid, handmade furniture had given place to "the cheap and ugly products of the early machine age." Babies did not pour as quickly into the cottages occupied by new families as they had into the others. Wages went up early in the nineties. Prices soon followed suit. "Penny-farthing" bicycles could be spotted on the roads. The innkeeper's wife got in cases of tinned salmon and Australian rabbit. "The Sanitary Inspector appeared for the first time at the hamlet and shook his head over the pigsties and privies." In the big towns suburban villas as well as new churches and chapels, railway stations, schools, and public houses were being built. Of those changes the hamlet people of Lark Rise saw nothing. They might have taken place in a different world. But in Candleford Green, the neighboring village, the wives of villagers who had had a stroke of good luck in the way of a better job or higher wages would soon be exclaiming: "Now we can go to live in one of the villas!" And on the newly opened building estate, a few village families would join their fellow readers of *Answers* and *Tit-Bits,* the clerks and shopkeepers from Candleford town who fancied country life or wanted to reduce their rent. We tend to know all of this social history in general terms, from textbooks, and articles, and statistics. But in Flora Thompson's book it comes to life in the memorable concretion of individual instances and distinct personalities.

The same is true of politics. If Flora Thompson had confined herself to telling us that at Lark Rise, in the eighties, "a mild Liberalism prevailed, a Liberalism that would be regarded as hide-bound Toryism now, but was daring enough in those days," we should simply regard that as confirmation of our preconceived notions. But she does not so confine herself. She tells us of Sam at the pub, relating his meeting with Joseph Arch, the farm workers' champion. " 'Joseph Arch!,' he would cry. 'Joseph Arch is the man for the farm laborer!' and knock on the table and wave aloft his pewter mug, very carefully, for every drop was precious." And of the landlord's replying: " 'It's no good you chaps think'n you're goin' against the gentry. They've got the land and they've got the money, *an*' they'll keep it.' " And of all voices then carrying away the resultant chill with

> God bless the people's William,
> Long may he lead the van
> Of Liberty and Freedom,
> God bless the Grand Old Man.

Some were secret Liberals. One old man, taken by elegant Tory carriage to the polling station, whispered to Laura a few days afterwards: " 'Tell y're dad I voted Liberal. He! He! They took th' poor old hoss to th' water, but he didn't drink out o' their trough. Not he!' " But at Candleford Green, the laboring class was the most conservative of all: " 'I know my place and I keep it,' some man or woman would say with a touch of pride in the voice, and if one of the younger and more spirited among them had ambition, those of their own family would often be the first to ridicule and discourage them."

Thus Flora Thompson, in her quiet and understated way, sheds light on both history and politics. But, in the end, what lingers most persistently in one's memory after reading her book is her preoccupation with popular language and culture, what some historians nowadays might well call her anthropological approach, a label that most likely would not have pleased someone who remained above all a literary artist. We learn about nicknames—"not used among the women, and only the aged were spoken of by their Christian names, Old Sally or Old Queenie or sometimes Dame—Dame Mercer or Dame Morris." We relish the vividness and economy of " 'Ain't he a regular dog?,' a fond parent would ask, when a boy, just starting work, would set his cap at an angle, cut himself an ash stick, and try to walk like a man." We listen to the lingo of the early cycling clubs: quite common things were "scrumptious," or "awfully good," or "awfully rotten," or "bally awful." And we take note of the new style of preaching sermons on familiar topics that was coming in, with the clergyman out to capture immediate attention by starting with "The other day I heard a man in this parish say—," or "You may have read in your newspapers last week—."

Linguistic usage, however, only forms part of something larger, the mental outlook of a generation in transition between old and new values and attitudes. This was a time when in the fields "men's tales" were still told, "a kind of rustic *Decameron* which seemed to have been in existence for centuries and increased like a snowball as it rolled down the generations." At the "Wagon and Horses," ghost stories and tales of dread vied with politics and old ballads like "Lord Lovell" and "Outlandish Knight." Neighborly talk still included capping proverbs; so that one who had helped another solve some knotty problem would remark "Two heads be better n'r one," with the other replying either "That's why we fools get married," or "Aye, specially if 'um be sheep's heads." Some of the older mothers and grandfathers still threatened naughty children with the name of Cromwell: "If you ain't a good gal, old Oliver Crummell'll have 'ee!," they would say. But new fashions were coming in: "novelettes," romantic love stories in which the poor governess always married the duke, or the lady of title the gamekeeper; and London "slum books" like *Christie's Old Organ* and *Froggy's Little Brother*. Throughout, it is apparent, and much to our benefit, that when Flora Thompson grew up, her sharp ears and eyes missed nothing. She was as fine a writer as she was an ob-

server. Even after many rereadings it is hard to resist a catch in the
throat when one comes once again to the last paragraph of *Lark Rise:*

> And all the time boys were being born or growing up in the
> parish, expecting to follow the plough all their lives, or, at most,
> to do a little mild soldiering or go to work in a town. Gallipoli?
> Kut? Vimy Ridge? Ypres? What did they know of such places?
> But they were to know them, and when the time came they did
> not flinch. Eleven out of that tiny community never came back
> again. A brass plate on the wall of the church immediately over
> the old end house seat is engraved with their names. A double
> column, five names long, then, last and alone, the name of
> [Laura's brother] Edmund.

VII

WHERE ARE WE HEADING?

Trevelyan: The Muse or the Museum?

In July of 1962 George Macaulay Trevelyan, the distinguished British historian, died in Cambridge at the age of eighty-six. As his middle name indicates, history was in his blood: Thomas Babington Macaulay was his great-uncle. His father, George Otto Trevelyan, was the author of a history of the American Revolution and of that brilliant and sparkling masterpiece of the art of biography, *The Early Life of Charles James Fox*. His grandfather, Sir Charles Trevelyan, who had married Macaulay's sister in India, had himself helped to *make* history. He had been the guiding spirit behind the introduction of the competitive examination principle into the English civil service.

Thus it was no wonder that when G. M. Trevelyan's first book, *England in the Age of Wycliffe*, was reviewed by the *Times Literary Supplement*, the anonymous reviewer was impelled to quote the French saying: *Bon chien chasse de race*. Nor was it any wonder that the object of his praise thenceforward adopted that proverb as his secret motto. For, as far back as he could remember, he had always wanted to become a historian, to keep up the family tradition. Trinity College, Cambridge, where he received his university education, had been his father's college as well as Macaulay's. Bertrand Russell and G. E. Moore were his contemporaries there, and the Cambridge his-

From *The Nation*, February 16, 1963

torians of his day included such luminaries as Maitland and Acton. Both recognized the bent of Trevelyan's talents, and encouraged him in his determination to write literary history, history intended for the delectation and instruction of a large audience. But in this they were out of tune with the principal academic tendency of the period, which was "scientific" and therefore antiliterary.

The great and growing prestige of the physical sciences, the pervasive influence of the German seminar method practiced with such signal success by Ranke and his pupils, the need to make history respectable as an academic subject by making it as rigorous as possible—all of this put a premium upon history that was "true" because it was based on laws of evidence. Constitutional history was in the ascendant, since legal documents lent themselves particularly well to such scientific analysis. The result was history written for scholars by scholars. During Trevelyan's first year at Cambridge (1893) Sir John Seeley, then Regius Professor of History, enraged the young historian by telling him that Carlyle and Macaulay had been charlatans. Ten years later, J. B. Bury, Acton's successor in the Regius Chair, resoundingly proclaimed that history was "simply a science, no less and no more."

It was in response to this challenge that Trevelyan, who had by then left Cambridge in order to devote himself entirely to historical writing, stated his own lifelong credo in an essay entitled "Clio: A Muse." Here he maintained that history was more than the accumulation and interpretation of facts. It was not worthy of the name until those facts and interpretations had been presented to a wide reading public by the historian in his essential role of literary artist. History was not a science. Unlike the physical sciences, it was of no practical utility. Nor could causal laws of general application be deduced from it. The true function of history was educational: to cause the minds of men to reflect on the past. To be sure, it was the historian's responsibility to attempt to establish, as conscientiously and as painstakingly as possible, the accuracy of the events and transactions he was describing. Furthermore, while he could never hope to formulate historical laws, he should certainly regard it as part of his task to make what Trevelyan called imaginative guesses at the most likely generalizations. But his main business was to tell the story, to bring home to the present generation the deeds, thoughts, feelings, and achievements of men and women who had lived in the past. Not just of kings and queens and lawmakers, but of men and women of all sorts and conditions. The principal task of the historian must inevitably be narration:

> Round the story, as flesh and blood round the bone, should be gathered many different things—character drawing, study of social and intellectual movements, speculations as to probable causes and effects, and whatever else the historian can bring to illuminate the past. But the art of history remains always the art of narrative. That is the bed rock.

Trevelyan remained true to his own principles. Over the years he produced many books on a variety of subjects: three volumes on Garibaldi's part in the unification of Italy, volumes he was inspired to write when his father, standing with him on the Janiculum in 1897, told him the story of Garibaldi's defense of Rome half a century before; general political and social histories of England as well as more detailed treatments of England under the Stuarts and during the nineteenth century; biographies of his father, of John Bright, and of Lord Grey of the Reform Bill of 1832, as well as of Sir Edward Grey, British Foreign Secretary in the years before the First World War; and, his *chef d'oeuvre,* a masterly account of *England Under Queen Anne,* in which he brought to completion the story that death had prevented his great-uncle from carrying to a close.

These books are not immune from criticism. Trevelyan had been taken to task more than once for his historical optimism, his liberal prejudices, his simplistic moral judgments, his failure at times to do full justice to the complexity of human motives and events. It is both refreshing and amusing to hear him dwell, late in life, on some of the qualities for which he was often reprimanded:

On optimism:

> I have always had a liking for those bits of history that have clear-cut happy endings . . . partly because such sections have more artistic unity than history as a whole, which is a shapeless affair; and partly no doubt because they are more cheerful to contemplate.

On bias:

> I once wrote three volumes on Garibaldi. They are reeking with bias. Without bias I should never have written them at all. For

I was moved to write them by poetical sympathy with the passions of the Italian patriots of that period, which I retrospectively shared. Such merit as the work has, largely derives from that.

On moral judgments:

If all historians . . . had condemned aggressive wars, including those begun by their own kings and countrymen, we should not be where we are today.

Here is the voice—frank, civilized, not without a touch of dry humor—of the liberal and humane tradition from which he sprang and which he never ceased to represent.

One accusation against which Trevelyan never had to defend himself was lack of readability. Some of his books sold in the hundreds of thousands. The *Social History* has become a popular classic. Everything he wrote shows the touch of the poet upon which he, who had been in his youth the friend of Meredith, prided himself all his life. His last book was a series of lectures entitled *A Layman's Love of Letters*. He had returned to Cambridge as Regius Professor of History in 1928 and had become Master of Trinity College early during the Second World War. His comment on this great honor was characteristic: "My appointment would probably have pleased Macaulay and my father as much as the destruction of Holland House [by German bombs] would have pained them." To the end, he rightly thought of himself as the continuator of a family tradition. And this, in fact, remains his primary achievement as a historian. He was neither a daring innovator, striking out along new paths, nor a royal intellect, probing into fresh depths of meaning. He will be remembered as one who carried on with distinction two great traditions of British historiography: the tradition of history as a literary art, dating back to Hume and Robertson and Gibbon in the eighteenth century; and the tradition of social history, history not merely as the story of battles and politics and institutions, but above all as the story of the ways of life and thought of people in the past. This second tradition dated back to Carlyle and to Macaulay. For it was Trevelyan's own great-uncle who in the famous third chapter of his *History of England* had pioneered this great extension of the subject matter of history.

How have these traditions recently fared in British historiography? As one looks at the scene today, the battle that Trevelyan waged on behalf of the muse Clio seems to have been won on all fronts. Popular interest in history has rarely been higher. The most prominent members of the younger generation of British historians are, almost without exception, gifted writers who, far from confining themselves to the production of esoteric tomes for a limited audience, regularly enter the lists in the weekly magazines, on the radio, occasionally even on television. As far as the substance of their serious historical writings is concerned, social history, the sort of history that Trevelyan stood for, has gained the day. True, academic curricula, and more especially those at Oxford and Cambridge, habitually lag behind the main currents of the times. Thus R. W. Southern, the new Chichele Professor of Modern History at Oxford, still felt it necessary to devote part of his inaugural lecture in 1961 to a plea for a revised history syllabus that would permit more venturing away from the well-trodden paths of politics and institutions, into the realm of the thoughts and visions, moods, emotions, and devotions of articulate people in the past. Yet, a look at the table of contents of the *Festschrift*, presented to Trevelyan on his eightieth birthday seven years ago by a group of outstanding younger historians, reveals the extent to which their preoccupations have departed from those of their predecessors taken to task in "Clio: A Muse." The subject matter of the various chapters ranges from "An Elizabethan Provincial Town: Leicester," through "The English Woman, 1580–1650" and "Comedy in the Reign of Charles the First," to "The Romantic Element, 1830–1850" and "The Intellectual Aristocracy in the Nineteenth Century."

Even those historians engaged in what that perpetual *enfant terrible* of the British historical profession, A. J. P. Taylor, writing about the late Sir Lewis Namier, has called "Tory History"—that is to say, those more interested in what made institutions actually work than in movements of ideas—can hardly be regarded as the residuary legatees of the narrow constitutionalists against whom Trevelyan took up the cudgels sixty years ago. For at the center of their concern lie neither legal texts nor official documents, but flesh-and-blood individuals. Why did men go into Parliament in the eighteenth century? What were their party affiliations there? The answer, as Namier showed it, is not to be found in speeches and manifestoes, but in their letters and diaries and journals, studied not haphazardly but systematically; so that in the end we know the thoughts and feelings and special interests of each one. The Namierites have been upbraided, with some justice, for routinizing a method which in their formidable master's hands never lost the excitement of a pioneering venture. But there is no doubt about the fact that in the truest sense of the word they, too, are social historians.

Yet, paradoxically, the very triumph of social history all along the line may constitute a new and unexpected threat to the art of narrative history. For the more we broaden our approach to the past, leaving behind the conventional categories of politics and institutions in favor of the study of society as a whole, the more we are apt to find interconnectedness rather than sequence. This presents serious problems for the historian who wants above all to tell a clear and coherent story. Take, for example, the question of why family limitation became widespread among the middle classes in late Victorian England, a question of paramount interest to the social historian, and one recently discussed by Joseph A. Banks of Liverpool University in a brilliant book entitled *Prosperity and Parenthood: A Study of Family Planning among the Victorian Middle Classes* (London, 1954). It is plain that one very important component of the answer to this question must lie in the sphere of economics. When mid-Victorian prosperity came to an end, those who had managed to attain a high standard of living were naturally reluctant to give it up. They had to cut down on something. Housing? Holidays? Quality and quantity of food and clothing? Good schools? The answer, if all of this was not to be given up, was to produce fewer children. The means had been at hand for some years. And so we see the gradual decline of the huge Victorian family and the coming into existence and fashion of the "two-child" family.

So far, so good. If this were indeed the whole answer, the historian of nineteenth-century England would have an easy time of it. All he would have to do would be to write at the appropriate point in his narrative that in order to maintain an accustomed standard of life, the middle classes reduced the size of their families. But Mr. Banks shows in convincing fashion that this is by no means the whole answer. He tells us with disarming candor that he doesn't yet know *what* that is. But we *do* know that in order to find it, we must take into account factors such as the following: the ebbing away of religious faith, and thus of the view that it was Providence alone which ought to decree the number of children in a given family; the growing strength of the feminist movement, the new and much less sheltered role that women were beginning to play in society; and the ever more pervasive scientific attitude which made for an increased acceptance of the whole *idea* of artificial family limitation. The conscientious historian must also take account of the threat to pride and status posed by working-men who, thanks to the coming of cheaper and more efficient means of transport, were beginning to move out into those suburbs which the middle class had considered as its own secure preserve; and of the beginning of a process that has reached its culmination in our own day—the reluctance of people to become domestic servants when less demeaning occupations offer equal or better wages.

Here, then, is interconnectedness: intellectual currents, class movements, economic and technological trends, moral and religious attitudes, all involved one with the other in creating a situation in which reduction of family size gradually becomes the norm. The historian of demographic change cannot say with any confidence: A caused B. Nor even, more modestly: First came A, then came B. He can only describe a whole congeries of factors deriving from different realms of human endeavor—A, B, C, D, E, etc.—and wait for further studies like that of Mr. Banks to enable him to assign relative weights of importance to each. This may satisfy the specialist.

But what of the historian who is trying to tell the story, not merely of demographic change, but of modern English history as a whole? What is he to do when he comes to this as well as to many other, similar problems? Is he to turn to what Crane Brinton has called retrospective sociology, contenting himself with a description of the structure of English society in the late nineteenth century?

That is certainly one possibility. Yet structural analysis is static. History, being process and not structure, is essentially dynamic. People lived and thought in this way. Now they live and think in another way. The narrative historian's principal preoccupation must remain change. What he *can* do, of course, is to adduce all the relevant factors that touch upon a particular problem at one point in time, and then look at them again, say, one generation later; remembering that his job is to take moving and not still pictures. But whatever he decides to do, one thing is certain. It has become increasingly difficult for him to succeed, within the brief compass that artistry (if not his reader) demands, in taking due account of the widening ramifications of his subject while at the same time telling his story with grace and economy. Can the historian of today do justice to Clio the Muse without turning her into Clio the Museum? Let us hope that among the many able historians who are following in Trevelyan's footsteps there are those who will enable us to answer in the affirmative.

The Prying Yorkshireman:
Herbert Butterfield and
the Historian's Task

Herbert Butterfield, one of the outstanding English historians of his generation, died in 1979, full of years and honors. To those unfamiliar with his work and personality, even an abbreviated list of his distinctions—professor of modern history and subsequently Regius Professor of History at Cambridge, Master of Peterhouse and Vice-Chancellor at the same university, holder of a knighthood—may convey the image of an Establishment figure. That would be far from the truth. A Yorkshireman who never lost his native manner of speech and who, out of earshot, was frequently referred to, at times affectionately, at times sneeringly, as "Bootterfield," a Methodist lay preacher in the bargain, he could hardly be said to have fit either into the ranks of the elegant Cambridge grandees or into those of the fashionable rebels represented by the Apostles with their glittering Bloomsbury connection. Like the man himself, his books, of which the best known are probably *The Whig Interpretation of History* and *Christianity and History,* do not easily fit an expected category. Most of them, like the two just mentioned, could be called contributions to historiography, the history of historical writing. But that classification, while broadly accurate, does not get to the essence of Butterfield's en-

From the *New Republic,* June 23, 1982

deavor—which was to raise searching questions not just about the technical ways in which historians were going and had gone about the exercise of their craft, but also about the fundamental assumptions, conscious and implicit, underlying their treatment of both past and present.

When Butterfield died at the age of seventy-nine, after a long illness, he had only half finished what he once called "the most impracticable adventure of my life," no less than the attempt to answer the double question as to how and why men first became aware of the past beyond living human memory; and how and why it then came about in the West that history gradually developed into a self-explanatory system of cause and effect, excluding chance and divine intervention. Enough of the manuscript was left in finished form and in draft to enable Adam Watson to piece together *The Origins of History* (New York, 1981) in accordance with the author's intentions, though there are inevitable gaps and omissions in the argument and presentation, and though, for obvious reasons, this posthumous volume lacks the clarity and economy of style that characterized the rest of Butterfield's work. The book is by no means easy reading. But we must be grateful to Mr. Watson for having given it to us, not only because it shows that to the very end of his days Butterfield wrestled with the sort of basic and often recalcitrant questions that would have taxed the scope and ambition of even the most energetic and erudite younger historian, but also because it serves to remind us of the interconnectedness of both the subject matter and the problems to which he had devoted his entire scholarly life.

It is, of course, hardly surprising that someone like Butterfield, who had for so long concerned himself with the ways in which men wrote about, and both used and abused, the past, should have come to ask himself how what we take for granted—society looking behind itself, organizing its memory, reflecting on long-term tendencies and the directions they might take—actually started. Why did some men, but not others, begin to keep records, to meditate on possible connections between events, and to see continuities between past, present, and future? From the beginnings of civilization there has been official history, celebrating the powers that be. The chief reason the Egyptians, Hittites, Assyrians, and Babylonians produced lists and records, annals and commemorative tablets, was concern on the part of rulers and monarchs over their future fame. Epics, too, the earliest forms of history as literature, were essentially commemorative. It was religion that played a major role in providing a genuine sense of the past.

From early on, the history of history involved priests as well as official scribes. For great empires required powerful gods as well as powerful rulers. Thus the rise of Babylon to imperial status provoked attempts to exalt Marduk, hitherto a merely local and minor god, into a major deity. But it was with the Hebrews that history and religion came together to greatest effect, that there emerged a people more obsessed with history than any other nation that had ever existed. For it was the message recorded in the Old Testament, but already existing in much older documents, that Yahweh had promised to bring the children of Israel out of Egypt, out of the house of bondage, that provided the unique historical memory which helped to make the Hebrews into a nation. Yahweh was not only the god of nature who had created the world, but even more so the god of history who had made a covenant with Abraham, whose promise had kept alive hope in the wilderness, and who would renew that promise, so that in spite of all its vicissitudes and sufferings Israel would be able to fulfill its mission as the chosen people. For the ancient Hebrews, as Butterfield puts it, history was really going somewhere; it was not cyclical, as it was for the Greeks, but linear, irreversible, and unrepeatable. Furthermore, in the book of Genesis, the history of the Hebrew nation became part of the history of mankind, starting from the Creation. Thus the Old Testament provided an enormous stimulus for both national and universal history.

As it turned out, Christianity tied itself to ancient Judaism by its acceptance of the Old Testament as holy Scripture, its recognition of the identity of Christ and the Messiah. That was of tremendous importance for the history of historical awareness; for it made people see that antecedents could be both significant and fruitful. It is when Butterfield continues his discussion of the Christian impact on historiography, and in turn follows that with some considerations on the subsequent effects of secularization, that we begin to realize the extent to which this last work of his marks a final return to themes which had preoccupied him all his life. One of those themes appears in his comments on St. Augustine who, though writing as a believing Christian, recognized the existence of profane history and almost conceded to it a certain autonomy. A second theme is closely tied to Butterfield's conviction that the doctrinal struggles of the Reformation, with all the passionate partiality they produced on both sides, nonetheless promoted a more judicious approach to history: "The conflict kept each side on its toes, making both more scientifically critical." Yet a third theme finds an echo in his warning, in the last and most fragmentary chapter of *The Origins of History*, entitled "The Great Secularisation," that historical writing treating mundane history in a wholly mundane manner does not necessarily denote a secular spirit on the part of its author. Indeed, he raises the question whether Christianity does not provide a clearer version of the facts and the factual setting than the pagan beliefs of the past or the present, and whether there might not be something in the view that links modern science and modern historiography with Christianity, seeing both those features of Western civilization developing out of Christian soil.

The theme of how the Christian historian ought to view the secular realm had always been particularly close to Butterfield's mind and heart, since it was a very personal one, reflecting his own life and experience. The theme of the origins of modern science provided the title for a pioneering set of lectures he delivered in Cambridge in 1948, published to great acclaim during the following year. And the theme of the historiography of the Reformation constituted a crucial part of his *Whig Interpretation of History* (1931), that subtle and ingenious essay of his youth, which, though now over half a century old, shows no signs of having lost its power to stop in their tracks, even if only momentarily, historians of all ages and persuasions. For it treats— and condemns—the psychological tendency of many historians to look in the past for "roots" and "anticipations" of their own time, and to single out and praise only those personalities and parties who turned out to have been successful in fighting for causes and values dear to the hearts of the twentieth century—in the case of English liberal historians, freedom, progress, toleration, humanitarian reform, democracy.

At its crudest, this interpretation saw the past as a Manichaean struggle between the forces of light and those of darkness, with Protestants and Whigs on the "good" side, Catholics and Tories on the "bad." Not surprisingly, the Reformation often proved to be the crux of the matter, with Protestants fighting for the future, Catholics for the past, and Martin Luther cast as the champion and father of libertarianism to whom all gratitude was due. Two years after the appearance of *The Whig Interpretation,* the Nazis came to power in Germany, and some Anglo-American historians found a different role for Luther—as a precursor of Hitler. That, too, was looking at the past through the eyes of the present, though from a very different vantage point, and the history it produced was no better. Looking for anticipations of villains can prove just as "Whiggish" as looking for anticipations of heroes.

It was easy to take up arms against such a crude view of things. It was much harder to emphasize, as Butterfield did, the more subtle and insidious ways in which historians—and not just English historians—could be led into a "Whig" interpretation of the past, not so much by actual religious or political party bias, but by the "pathetic fallacy" of abstracting events and ideas from their historical context, and judging them apart from it; stressing the achievements of congenial great individuals and the triumphs of forces that later proved to be agents of enlightenment, rather than the complex process of clash and collision that had marked all great historical movements. In the depiction of that process the losers deserved as much attention and sympathy as the winners. But they rarely got it.

Thus, while (as we learn from *The Origins of History*) the actual struggles of the Reformation had contributed positively to the rise of critical history, looking at those same struggles in retrospect often produced an opposite effect, resulting in history that catered to present preoccupations rather than illuminating the past in its own terms. In order to avoid such misreadings, historians would have done much better if, instead of looking for likenesses to the twentieth century in the sixteenth century, they had regarded Protestants and Catholics of the earlier period as distant and strange, as men whose quarrels were "as unrelated to ourselves as the factions of Blues and Greens in ancient Constantinople."

It is quite clear that Butterfield believed that a Christian historian like himself was particularly qualified to adopt such a distanced approach to history. What he wrote in his last work about Augustine's allowance of a certain autonomy to the realm of mundane events and about the fallacy of assuming that a purely secular approach to the past did not necessarily reflect a secular spirit on the part of the author was, as far as he was concerned, nothing new. In his *History and Human Relations* (1951) he had reminded his readers that "there is in the Christian tradition a healthy regard for the material world, compared with which some of our modern liberals have seemed to savor of Manichaeism." Two years earlier, in his *Christianity and History*, Butterfield had pointed out that the assured Christian could easily undertake empirical research into history, "for, having in his religion the key to his conception of the whole human drama, he can safely embark on a detailed study of mundane events, if only to learn through their inter-connection the ways of Providence." The concluding sentence of that book makes the point even more strongly by enunciating the principle: "Hold to Christ, and for the rest be totally uncommitted."

A scientific view of history (so Butterfield wrote in *History and Human Relations*), arising out of man's habit of reflecting on observable connections between events, was by no means inconsistent with Christianity, which regards the historian as "a person under a certain kind of discipline for the purpose of examining the ways of Providence and the structure of the providential order." Western science itself, after all, had developed in the heart of Christian civilization; and many of the people who developed it thought they were glorifying God while doing so. Butterfield went on to recall the seventeenth-century argument that a divine miracle could never be justified unless it could be shown that the world in its normal processes was regular. Certainly, so he wrote in *Man on His Past* (1955), natural scientists must not be presumed to be atheists, merely because they observed the rules of the game and left God out of the argument.

Butterfield delivered his own lectures, entitled *The Origins of Modern Science,* at a time when the subject was far from fashionable and had by no means yet become the major branch of historical study it is today. He had written the lectures, he said, in order to interest the historian in a little science and the scientist in a little history. He himself maintained that the scientific revolution of the sixteenth and seventeenth centuries, overturning as it did the scientific authority both of the ancient world and the Middle Ages, outshone in importance everything since the rise of Christianity, and reduced both the Renaissance and the Reformation "to the rank of mere episodes, mere internal displacements, within the system of medieval Christendom." For his own part, he was to write in *Man on His Past,* he would like to cry from the house tops that "the publication of Newton's *Principia* in 1687 is a turning point in history for peoples to whom the Renaissance and Reformation can hardly mean anything at all—peoples among whom the battle of Waterloo would hardly be calculated to produce an echo." But, apart from the intrinsic importance of the subject, it had other, methodological aspects which clearly interested him because they were analogous to those encountered in the writing of general history.

Thus when we hear him say that it had proved especially useful to learn about the misfires and the mistaken hypotheses of early scientists, and to pursue courses of scientific development which ended in blind alleys, but still had their effect on the progress of science in general, we are reminded of the "losers" in the great ideological and party struggles whom the Whig historians were ignoring at their peril. When he speculates that the most remarkable turns in the current of intellectual fashions, the most fundamental changes in outlook, might in the last resort be referred to an alteration in men's feelings for things, he himself draws the analogy between the possible changes in men's feeling for matter itself in the seventeenth century, and the change in feeling men had had in England a century earlier for the territorial state. Habits of mind were as important for political history as they were for the history of science.

In *Christianity and History,* which appeared in the same year as the lectures on the history of science, Butterfield proceeds quite naturally to draw a parallel between Galileo's doctrine of inertia, which opened the gateway to modern science, but which he could never have seen in its purity, and the Hegelian-Marxist triad of thesis-antithesis-synthesis, which could still be of interest to historians, "even though it were to be shown that no such case ever existed in a state of absolute purity." Certainly, here is yet another echo of *The Whig Interpretation.* Might it not sometimes be preferable to try to understand history by means of the triad, rather than to see it invariably in terms of lineal development, of simple, unequivocal progress?

Butterfield was not averse to the use of occasional autobiographical reminiscence to illustrate some of the points he was making; and those anecdotes not only conjure up the man, but also serve to show that the links between his personal experience and his historical themes were as strong as the links between the themes themselves. When he argues that it was not so extraordinary that in the sixteenth century students watching dissections would believe the orthodox verities of Galen rather than the evidence of their own eyes, he remembers his own physics master at school, a certain Mr. Jones, who was giving a demonstration and who called on a boy named Booth to watch the actual experiment while he, Jones, was doing the mathematics on the blackboard. Booth reported that nothing was happening, to which the master replied, "The liquid is rising in the tube." But the boy persisted in maintaining that nothing at all was going on. "Whereupon Mr. Jones grew red in the face, dashed across the little platform, and boxed his ears." In fact, the liquid was *not* rising in the tube. But the boys were not greatly worried. Great men had performed that experiment in the past, and if their successors couldn't make the answer

come out correctly, they were no doubt themselves in the wrong.
When, in *History and Human Relations,* Butterfield makes the point
that there is a great difference between a good diplomatic historian
and a good diplomat, he recalls that he once had to induce the governing body of Peterhouse to try to agree on the color of a new carpet
for the college library: "A person who has had to undertake such a
task and who has discovered all the maneuverings, all the delicate
tactics, the persuasions, the whole science of give-and-take, that are
necessary to get twelve men to agree on the color of a carpet—such
a person may be said to have had his first lesson in diplomacy." In
the same volume there is to be found an autobiographical dimension
to account for Butterfield's life-long obsession with the dangers of
letting the present shape one's view of the past. Before 1919, he remembers, he had been taught the kind of history that saw in the
sovereignty of nation-states the culmination of centuries of progress,
the very end toward which history was moving. After 1919 history
and the textbooks were reshaped, now proving that everything had
all the time been advancing toward the League of Nations. Neither
use was good history. Both simply served to ratify existing prejudices.

One must take care, nonetheless, not to categorize Butterfield as
an enemy, *tout court,* of present-mindedness in any form. There was
no doubt that he wished to guard himself and others against the optical
illusion that could so easily result from regarding the past through
the eyes of the present. On the other hand, he was by no means
opposed to making use of those lessons of history that could be derived
from an unprejudiced study of it. He was convinced that "technical
history" permitted such an unprejudiced approach and could help to
build an agreed and cumulative body of facts that could be used to
bring greater understanding to the problems and dilemmas of the
present.

For example, as he wrote in *Christianity and History,* the delusions of
messianism were just as strong in the twentieth century as they had
been in the sixteenth or, indeed, in biblical times. Messianic slogans
like "the dictator as savior," "making the world safe for democracy,"
or "the four freedoms" had done great harm, and showed reversion
to "a primitive messianism not only over two thousand years old, but
representing a somewhat inferior version of the ideas of that ancient
period." The implication here is that a knowledge of history might
have done something to save us from such delusions. History, then,

could teach lessons. Not all of them were as uncontroversial as the one that could be learned from the British having helped to install a strong Prussia in the Rhineland after the defeat of Napoleon in 1815, wrongly convinced that it was the French who would always be the aggressors and enemies of mankind. Butterfield's generally neutralist approach to ideological warfare, past and present, not only put him into the camp of those who, since they believed that all men were sinners, could not decide whether Napoleon or Hitler was better or worse in the eyes of eternity; it also led him to argue, in 1951, that the West would have faced the same problems with Russia, even if the czars had still been the rulers of that country.

But not all of those who might have agreed with him on that or who might have shared his conviction, expressed two years before, that the key fact of recent European history was the struggle for a dominating position between Germany and Russia, would necessarily have gone along with his appeal to the Christian to be diffident about believing that the fate of God and all His angels in all the future was going to depend on Russia rather than Germany dominating the Continent in another age of history. *Life* magazine, for one, did not go along. It devoted a special, denunciatory editorial to those lectures on *Christianity, Diplomacy, and War* (1953) in which Butterfield had expressed the opinion just cited. In *Life*'s view, the historian's major premise—that a truly Christian diplomacy must be based on belief in original sin and the universality of guilt, and must therefore play down ideological differences—resulted in myopia toward communism, a dubious faith in Britain's traditional balancing act, and an ill-timed appeal not to be beastly to the Russians.

Butterfield's approach to international politics is probably even more controversial today than it was a generation ago. But he would not have minded that in the least. He did not so much crave agreement on the part of his students or readers as he wanted to make them think. The more difficult and uncomfortable the problems, the better. He felt that the tough questions had to be asked, both about the past and about the present; and he had both the courage and the wit to ask them, never pretending that his were the only possible answers. He also had a dislike for orthodoxy and unqualified generalizations which he was as ready to turn upon himself as upon others. In *Man on His Past,* for example, he wrote that while he personally did not believe that "the conflict with the world behind the Iron Curtain should be regarded as the all-important issue for the men of the West at the present time," he was not prepared to write off the map as either villains or fools those who thought that the issue of external relations should be viewed as supreme and decisive.

Two years later, in *George III and the Historians,* he took to task those students of the eighteenth century in England who, following their mentor, Sir Lewis Namier, concentrated in their histories on underlying political structures rather than the expressed aims of politicians. Butterfield himself, of course, had brilliantly exposed some of the weaknesses of that Whig interpretation that Namier could be said to have laid to rest. But what disturbed him now was not merely the growth of a new, Namierite orthodoxy, but also the tendency, particularly on the part of Namier's disciples, to see eighteenth-century English politics primarily as the play of faction and self-interest. Selfishness, love of place, corruption—these were not sufficient, in Butterfield's view, to explain human behavior. Ideas, ideals, conscious purposes always played a role as well, which had to be taken into account. Furthermore, the Namierites were not always so original as they claimed. Those of us, he wrote, who had spent our lives in combat against the Whig interpretation of history were still perturbed by the way in which the new school treated its predecessors. He called the members of that school "Whigs in reverse."

That line of attack was characteristic of the man who had himself celebrated the value of the Whig interpretation for the English political tradition in lectures he had delivered during World War II and published, in 1944, under the title *The Englishman and His History.* There may have been a good deal wrong with an interpretation of English history that saw a direct and inevitable progression running from the Teutonic idea of freedom to the Magna Carta, the independence of the House of Commons, the constitutional struggles of the seventeenth century, the Reform Act of 1832, and those English liberties the country was fighting for in World War II—and Butterfield knew better than anyone what was wrong with it. But that vision had helped, along with the common law, to tighten the bonds that held Englishmen to their past, and had produced that consensus on love of precedents, affection for tradition, desire for gradualness of change, and adherence to ancient liberties which had stood England in such good stead in 1940.

When he wrote a new preface to *The Englishman and His History* (1970 edition), Butterfield, who could be as hard on himself as he was on others, called it "comic" and "a museum piece." At the same time, he repeated what he had said a quarter of a century before, that the story of English historical awareness could not be studied merely as the history of a branch of historical scholarship. The story of historical interpretation was connected with the way in which men in general had experienced the past, felt about it, and found themselves committed to it. That conviction informs *The Origins of History* as well. It is hard to believe that it is Butterfield's last book. Whether we always agree with him or not, we shall miss his searching intelligence, his knack for asking the hard questions, his quiet tone of voice, and his forceful pen.

The Great Historians in the Age of Cliometrics

Not all history is amusing. In 1832 Macaulay reviewed a three-volume life of Lord Burleigh by the then Regius Professor of Modern History at Oxford. This is what he wrote:

> Compared with the labour of reading through these volumes, all other labour, the labour of thieves on the treadmill, of children in factories, of negroes in sugar plantations, is an agreeable recreation. There was, it is said, a criminal in Italy, who was suffered to make his choice between Guicciardini and the galleys. He chose the history. But the war of Pisa was too much for him. He changed his mind, and went to the oar.

All of us can no doubt think of works by our contemporaries that might exert similar effects even now. But, ever since ancient rhetoricians talked of the *voluptas* as well as the *utilitas* of history, its practitioners—at least those who wished to have readers—have tried to be entertaining; though few have emulated Herodotus, who is reputed to have sung his history. In one of his early essays Gibbon noted that the contemplation of human life "should be the favourite amusement of man. It is his easiest and yet least mortifying method of studying

From the *Times Literary Supplement*, March 7, 1975

himself." And it is, of course, for that very reason that his own great work will never cease to be read.

There is surely no need to stress the readability of the great historians: all one has to do is to open their books. But instruction? That word has a forbidding sound, smacking of schoolrooms, sermons, and Samuel Smiles—indeed, smacking of smacking. No doubt the lessons of Thucydides will remain, as he hoped, a possession for all time. No doubt, to quote Gibbon once again, Tacitus will endure as "the philosophical historian whose writings will instruct the last generations of mankind." And it may be that some would argue that never have so many stood in so great a need of moral lessons. But I shall not argue thus; preferring to leave the high road of moral inculcation to others while myself turning on to the byways of rhetoric.

Here, too, there exists a great tradition of instruction. One need only recall those Renaissance humanists who held up great classical authors such as Caesar, Sallust, and Livy as rhetorical models for the historians of their own day. Not only were the latter to learn from their great predecessors what aspects of history were most worthy of description. They were also to look to them for specific guidance on matters of literary style and structure. Thus, in Pontano's dialogue, *Actius,* Altilius demonstrates in detail to his interlocutor Pudericus, with examples drawn from Livy and Sallust, how "the same thing holds true . . . in composing history as in building houses and ships, that one has to make many junctures of things, and, so to speak, connections of the parts among themselves." Excellent advice, which—in a manner of speaking—brings me to the question of what today's historians can learn about the rhetoric of history from the classical historians of *modern* times.

When I refer to "today's historians" (unlike the department of history of a major university which recently advertised a "full professorship in the New History") I draw no distinction between new and old history. Which is not to say that there is perpetual amity between the two. Those who, deep down, feel a possibly perverse sense of satisfaction about the ultimate recalcitrance of the local, the particular, the individual to general laws and scientific formulae will continue to remain suspicious of the computer; and their suspicions will no doubt be reciprocated by the cliometricians. But, if some of the great historians were suddenly to come to life today, they would be among the first to welcome the many ways in which the new historians, with the help of machines, have managed to breathe life into dusty parish and census records and into mildewed business ledgers. There are, to be sure, cliomeretricians as well as cliometricians. But they live in both camps and may be left to their own devices.

But, it might well be asked, need the new historians learn anything at all about the rhetoric of history? It has been said that some subjects do not lend themselves to dramatic or elegant presentation. True enough, though one should not be too categorical about this. Take, for example, the findings of a recent New Historian who devoted himself for many years to the problem of whether there is to be found any relationship between number of siblings and extent of baldness among the clockmakers of southeastern Ohio between 1823 and 1859. Employing the latest sampling, data-collecting, and computer techniques, he established beyond controversy that 47 percent of those clockmakers with three or more siblings were totally or partially bald; whereas of those with two or fewer siblings 49 percent were totally or partially bald. Those, baldly stated, were his conclusions. But, had he had his Gibbon at his side, he might have phrased them somewhat differently:

A melancholy duty devolves upon the historian who wishes to delineate the progress of luxury and error among those sullen and rebellious subjects whose occidental peregrinations led them to enjoy and abuse the hospitality proffered by the verdant declivities of the Ohio valley. He must, though, with becoming submission, inquire whether the divine clockmaker, had he foreseen that the descendants of those fierce and foolish sectaries would one day attempt to emulate his handiwork, could have brought himself in the first place to countenance the creation of the universe. Moreover, were it not an act of singular impiety to do so, an analogy might be drawn between the Calvinist economy, which arbitrarily consigns a chosen few to eternal felicity, and untold multitudes to tortures so exquisitely refined that only the most devout annalists have been able to bring themselves to depict them, and the respective destinies of those capable of preserving intact their hirsute integument and those irremediably doomed to a state of calvity.

It would, in any event, be salutary for those engaged in the effort to retain their hair to reflect upon what the Emperor Augustus discovered about the prosecution of remote wars: the undertaking becomes every day more difficult, the event more doubtful, and the possession more precarious. The dignity of history should not entitle the historian to judge between the pop-

ulous beard of Julian and the luminous dome of the first of the
Caesars. Yet the diligent and accurate Suetonius records that
when the Roman soldiers celebrated their triumphs in the Gallic
wars, they chanted with minatory fervor:

> *Men of Rome, keep close your*
> *consorts,*
> *Here's a bald adulterer.*

If, as the naturalists are pleased to tell us, the condition of hair-
lessness be not entirely unconnected with an excess of virility,
then the report that of a hundred bald horologers who plied their
tintinnabulatory trade by the banks of the Muskingum in the
course of the early decades of the last century, those whose fraternal and sororal bonds extended beyond the number of three
numbered forty-seven, while those similarly bound to two or
less numbered forty-nine, must occasion not a little surprise, and
compel even the most candid observer to draw a veil of decency
over the entire subject.

Had our new historian been imbued with Carlyle, he might have
written:

Behold, then, matter for wonder—and tears, too. Two score
and seven timemakers, barepated as cannonballs, ticktocking
away, every man Jack of them, in Nelsonville, Hanging Rock,
and Athens—far from marble Acropolis and Mediterranean sun,
this Athens—but with demos a plenty, as well as brisk Ohio
air—. In Marietta, too, named for sad Queen Toinette, of bread
and cakes and tumbril fame. All of them with three or more
strapping and rosy-cheeked brothers and sisters, fit as fiddles
scraping yankee doodle doo. Destiny dim-brooding over shiny
crowns, making us mindful of brother of German Louis, grand-
son of Charlemagne, Kaiser Karl der Kahle—of Mersen and Lorraine renown. Of Stratford William also, in Avon vale, he who
wrote that time himself was bald, and that therefore the world's
end would have bald followers. But look, Reader, look as well
to Hockingport and Zanesville and Gallipolis, where cradles rock
idle and no more than braces of brotherly-sisterly helpmeets
cheer the labor of thatchless *horlogers* to the number of forty-
nine. Time, ever flowing, ever rolling, shall wash them all

away—yes, baldpated Elmer Schlossberg, addle-pated, too, Elmer of the chocolate *Grossvater-Uhr,* and Charity his spouse, and Henry Jones of Pomeroy, who smashed every last cuckoo clock he ever built because, poor vain mortal, he thought that time must have a stop. And did he not learn better? Go easy with them all, for hairy or bald, they were God's creatures, every one.

And if our new historian had been an assiduous student of Macaulay, this is how he might have addressed his readers:

As every schoolboy knows, the population of Marietta, Ohio, in 1826 amounted to 1,051 souls. Since that time, what was then a mere hamlet has become a town and grown to a greatness which this generation can only contemplate with pride and wonder. What not so long ago was a peaceful and tranquil village set amidst green fields has become a busy and opulent center of lively manufactures and commerce, justly famed for its iron and dross castings, its paints and varnishes, its gas engines and ranges, and its household and office furniture. In the year of the Great Exhibition, elderly inhabitants barely living could recall the building of the first frame house, and the start of the first mail route, when the post left Marietta every Tuesday at noon and arrived at Zanesville every Thursday before dawn. It was in 1851 that the Belpre and Cincinnati railroad became the Marietta and Cincinnati. There were fools in that day as in ours who said that the line from Cincinnati could never extend to Baltimore and Philadelphia. But they were confounded when, on April 9, 1857, the citizens of Marietta heard the cheerful and manly sound of whistle and bell as the first train rumbled in from Chillicothe. Among those who watched its arrival were a few honest farmers who expressed their delight by remarking, in the fashion of rustics everywhere, that the engine gleamed like the head of a bald clockmaker.

As baldness becomes more and more common, brothers and sisters become less and less necessary. Why this should be so we shall state as concisely as possible. As civilization advances, the wearing of hats increases. As a greater number of hats comes into the possession of a greater number of families, more hats will be worn. The more often hats are worn in youth, the greater the loss of hair in middle age. It follows, therefore, as night does day that in the Southeastern portion of Ohio, one of the United

States of America, 47 percent of those clockmakers with three
or more brothers and sisters were wholly or partly bald, whereas
of those with two or fewer brothers and sisters as great a number
as 49 percent found themselves in a similar predicament.

Perhaps, then, even the most unexpected subjects may lend themselves, on occasion, to elegant and dramatic presentation. But even if
he is willing to dispense with drama and elegance, the most statistically
minded historian must still employ the medium of language to communicate his findings to those of his readers who are not expert at
scanning graphs and tables. Like his more old-fashioned colleagues,
therefore, he must try to master the art of historical narration. For,
whether he is aware of it or not, he will find himself using the rhetoric
of history.

This is a subject that has more or less lain dormant since the Renaissance, but has recently once again come into prominence. Thus
Hayden White, in his learned and monumental *Metahistory: The Historical Imagination in 19th Century Europe,* has shown the role of linguistic strategy and literary form in the works of some great historians
as well as philosophers of history. And in the suggestive conclusion
of his *Style in History,* Peter Gay has put forward a persuasive argument to the effect that the literary devices employed by the great
historians are not separate from their search for historical truth, but,
rather, precise means of conveying it.

Their books raise profound problems in the domains of linguistic
structure and philosophy. I am neither able nor willing to follow them
into those recondite realms. What I want to do instead is to make a
case for the great historians of modern times as possible models for
what one might call the operational rhetoric of history today, by
which I mean to refer to those workaday problems of the craft of
narrative and arrangement that confront every one of us when we try
to write a book or an article. Jack Hexter, one of the few contemporary
historians who have taken a special interest in this field, has pointed
out that the rhetoric of historical storytelling has received little attention from historians and others, and that the rhetoric of historical
analysis has received none at all. What I have to say here is intended
as a small contribution to the rhetoric of historical storytelling, to
what might be called the historian's tricks of the trade.

I think, for instance, that most historians would agree that it is
desirable to engage and keep the reader's attention, and that there is
always a danger of losing it all too quickly if one gives away too much

of one's hypothesis or conclusion at the start. When a historian has completed his research and has thought about his materials, and before he begins to write, he has presumably made up his mind about how he wants to explain or interpret what he has found. But how is he to avoid letting the cat out of the bag? The great teacher here is Elie Halévy, who in his historical writings managed to make a virtue of what Charles Dickens, writing to Lady Holland about *Chuzzlewit* in 1844, called "the great misery" of serial publication, namely that "conclusions are necessarily arrived at, in reference to the design of the story before the design becomes apparent or complete."

Halévy's *England in 1815,* for example, is built around the question of why in the course of the nineteenth century English society and institutions proved to possess a greater stability than any other in Europe. There can be little doubt that Halévy had reached his own answer to this question before he ever put pen to paper. But he knew better than to give the game away at the beginning by telling his readers that the answer was to be found in the moral and religious sphere, that the foundation of English social order derived from the free organization of the sects and the partial junction and combination of the theoretically hostile forces of Evangelicalism and Utilitarianism. Instead, he first examines England's political and economic institutions in succession, in order to determine whether they would supply the master clue for stability. It is only after he has found that they would not do this that he turns to the realm of religion. He, of course, knew the answer all the time. But by not revealing it until the end, he succeeds in building sufficient tension and mystery to encourage readers through the thickets of complex political and economic history.

If one wants to see Halévy's mastery of this difficult art demonstrated even more strikingly, one should turn to his essays on *The Birth of Methodism.* By the time he finally reveals his hypothesis (whether it be right or wrong is irrelevant in this context) that there existed a direct connection between the revival of 1739 and the economic crisis of the previous year, he has his readers sitting on the edge of their chairs; and, in the case of this particular reader, when he first encountered those brilliant articles, sorely tempted to cheat by looking ahead to the conclusion.

Halévy's works confirm Macaulay's dictum that in writing history arrangement is all important, that it alone makes the welter intelligible and retainable. Macaulay himself had his own models; and devised what he called the declamatory disquisition as a substitute for the speeches used by the ancient historians to present arguments on both sides of an issue. One can look for his use of it in chapter 14 of *The History* where, employing indirect discourse, he states the arguments put forward by the clergy for and against taking the oath of allegiance to William III, or in chapter 23 where he discusses the controversy about whether or not a standing army is desirable. But, if Macaulay looked for help to the ancients, we in turn can look for help to him in regard to that most difficult and, at the same time, most essential aspect of the craft of writing history, the process of getting from one subject to another. He himself was modest about his technical prowess in this sphere; noting in his journal that "arrangement and transition are arts which I value much, but which I do not flatter myself that I have attained." But one need only look at chapter 3 of *The History* to find conclusive evidence to the contrary.

In that chapter—a description of England in 1685—we are led with what appears to be a kind of natural propulsion from Macaulay's account of population, revenue, government, and agriculture to his depiction of social classes, towns, travel, communication, and the state of the arts and sciences. At times the links between paragraphs are purely verbal, deftly managed by the strategic repetition of a key word used in one at the start of the one following. At times they are topical, as when Macaulay's discussion of the post office is immediately followed by a description of the newsletters carried by the mails. At times the links are conceptual, as when, following his portrayal of the large number of wild animals still to be found roaming the English countryside in 1685, the historian turns to the subject of the greatly increased number of enclosure acts to be met with in the statute book.

Then again these links may grow out of antithesis, as when, after recounting the merely ceremonial receptions held by the first Hanoverians for the nobility and gentry, Macaulay begins his next paragraph with the words: "Not such was the court of Charles the Second." More often than not, his transitions succeed by virtue of their apparent inevitability. What could be more natural, for instance, than that a description of Whitehall as the chief staple of news and rumors should be followed by some comments about the coffeehouses where the news and rumors were soon gossiped about? But that "natural" quality was, in fact, the product of long labor and consummate craftsmanship.

We can still learn from Macaulay, then. We can even learn from so crabbed and idiosyncratic a stylist as Carlyle—hailed by Emerson as "the true inventor of the stereoscope"—how literary devices can enable the historian to come closer to capturing actual experience, which is multidimensional, in a narrative medium that has traditionally been linear, that is to say one-dimensional. And we can learn from Maitland and Tocqueville how to manage that delicate and essential enterprise, the striking of a proper balance between generalization and illustration. Maitland's writings demonstrate the truth of his remark that "a large stock of examples, given with details, may serve to produce a body of flesh and blood for the ancient rules which . . . are apt to seem abstract, unreal, impracticable." But, if Maitland can teach us how best to deploy a large number of illustrations, it is to Tocqueville that we may look for guidance on how, when exigencies of space and method permit only a single anecdote in the midst of generalization and analysis, one can really be made to count. After describing the feelings of contempt harbored by the French upper classes for the lower orders during the old regime, Tocqueville writes:

> We are reminded of the conduct of Mme. Duchâtelet, as reported by Voltaire's secretary; this good lady, it seems, had no scruples about undressing in the presence of her manservants, being unable to convince herself that mere lackeys were real flesh-and-blood men.

Who, having once read this, can forget it? Or, should he happen to be a historian, fail to be instructed by it?

Certain problems of style and structure—how to create suspense, how to balance background and foreground, how to produce artful transitions—are built into the craft of historical writing, and will presumably remain to confront our successors as well as ourselves. Are there others which are peculiarly a product of the new history? And are fresh literary devices required to cope with them? Certainly, the development of sophisticated local histories and detailed investigations in the manner of Sir Lewis Namier makes it ever more difficult for the narrative historian to tell an accurate and coherent story in such a way that it does not become completely obscured by parenthetical cautions and footnoted reservations.

Then there are the rhetorical problems raised by the proliferation of statistics, by no means confined to the manner in which to put lists of numbers into sentences without succumbing to tedium. Take one of the classic historical works of our own time, W. L. Burn's *Age of Equipoise*. One finds there that on numerous occasions the author's style is shaped not so much by the figures he cites as by the reservations and exceptions he feels compelled to advance after citing them. Complexity and multiplicity require their own techniques of expression. The sort of social and institutional history written in our time demands a kind of structural tension very different from the dramatic contrasts and antitheses inherent in the older narrative history, preoccupied with the exploits and conflicts of individual personalities, and populated with good and bad men and women rather than with ideal types.

To read Marc Bloch's *Feudal Society,* for instance, is to observe how a great historian of our own generation employs appropriate rhetorical devices to bring suspense and dramatic tension to the art of qualification: "It would be easy to conclude. . . . But it would be wrong"; "It would be a mistake to assume. . . . Rather"; "Let us not picture. . . . Instead." This sort of history requires its own tricks of the trade, and in order to master them we ought to turn to the modern as well as to the older classics of historical writing.

But, if some problems change, others remain the same. One must still begin and end. A distinguished historian once told me that his best guide to ways in which to make his own historical themes grow organically out of background and context had been the opening movements of Mozart's piano concertos. But, for the unmusical, much is to be learned merely by attentively perusing the first and last sentences of some of the great histories. Note, for example, the worlds of difference between Gibbon's opening words—"In the second century of the Christian era, the Empire of Rome comprehended the fairest part of the earth, and the most civilized portion of mankind"— and those of Henry Adams, who not only knew his Gibbon, but had also sat on the steps of Ara Coeli to find inspiration: "According to the census of 1800, the United States of America contained 5,308,483 persons." Or ponder the beginning of Namier's *England in the Age of the American Revolution:* "The social history of England could be written in terms of membership of the House of Commons, that peculiar club, election to which has at all times required some expression of consent on the part of the public." Karl Marx is a master here. One need only recall the start of the *Eighteenth Brumaire:* "Hegel remarks somewhere that all facts and personages of great importance in world history occur, as it were, twice. He forgot to add: the first time as tragedy, the second as farce." And its end: ". . . when the imperial mantle finally falls on the shoulders of Louis Bonaparte, the bronze statue of Napoleon will crash from the top of the Vendôme Column."

These are memorable ways in which to open and close great works of history. It goes without saying that I do not advise that such examples be lifted bodily from their authors for the benefit of aspiring

Gibbons, Adamses, Namiers, or Marxes; though sometimes even that is permissible. Take, for instance, the dilemma of a historian of our own day who has trouble finding a conclusion for a paper on the rhetoric of history that he has prepared for delivery to a historical convention. All he needs to do is turn to the final words of Carlyle's *French Revolution:* "Ill stand it with me, if I have spoken falsely: thine also it was to hear truly. Farewell."

Notes

GIBBON'S HUMOR

1. *Gibbon's Decline and Fall of the Roman Empire (DF)*, Everyman's Library Edition, 6 vols. (London, 1910; reprinted, 1966), chap. 58, p. 48. All subsequent references are to chapter and page of this edition.

2. *DF*, chap. 19, p. 204.

3. *DF*, chap. 23, p. 395.

4. *DF*, chap. 69, p. 471.

5. *DF*, chap. 51, p. 313.

6. *DF*, chap. 1, p. 27.

7. *DF*, chap. 26, p. 1; chap. 51, p. 357; chap. 28, p. 143; chap. 46, p. 503.

8. *DF*, chap. 40, p. 155.

9. *DF*, chap. 27, p. 112. ["drinking a draught of which results in the removal of the signs of virginity"]

10. *DF*, chap. 3, p. 76; chap. 21, p. 273.

11. *DF*, chap. 7, p. 171.

12. *DF*, chap. 68, pp. 448–49.

13. *DF*, chap. 37, p. 14.

14. *DF*, chap. 21, p. 285.

15. *DF*, chap. 15, pp. 430, 499.

16. Ibid., pp. 434, 441.

17. *DF*, chap. 16, p. 68.

18. *DF*, chap. 37, p. 19.

19. *DF*, chap. 32, p. 317.

20. *DF*, chap. 12, p. 339.

21. *DF*, chap. 55, p. 517.

22. *DF*, chap. 50, p. 272.

23. *DF*, chap. 58, p. 56.

24. *DF*, chap. 62, p. 239.

25. *DF*, chap. 70, p. 546.

26. *DF*, chap. 39, pp. 120–21.

27. *DF*, chap. 15, p. 457.

28. *DF*, chap. 41, p. 273.

29. *DF*, chap. 66, p. 374.

30. *DF*, chap. 22, p. 340.

31. *DF*, chap. 35, p. 407; chap. 38, pp. 52, 93, 100.

32. *DF*, chap. 21, p. 310; chap. 22, p. 349; chap. 27, p. 75; chap. 36, p. 437; chap. 37, p. 18.

33. *DF*, chap. 47, p. 27.

34. Ibid., p. 41.

35. *DF*, chap. 52, pp. 421–22.

36. *DF*, chap. 15, p. 467.

37. *DF*, chap. 31, p. 249.

38. *DF*, chap. 56, p. 560.

39. *DF*, chap. 1, p. 1.

40. *DF*, chap. 40, p. 161.

41. *DF*, chap. 28, p. 146.

42. *DF*, chap. 23, p. 373.

43. *DF*, chap. 38, p. 53.

44. *DF*, chap. 34, p. 362.

45. *DF*, chap. 51, p. 377.

46. *DF*, chap. 1, p. 27.

47. *DF*, chap. 21, p. 300.

48. *DF*, chap. 26, p. 3.

49. *DF*, chap. 23, p. 379.

50. *DF*, chap. 1, p. 11.

51. *DF*, chap. 47, p. 35.

52. *DF*, chap. 38, p. 86.

53. *DF*, chap. 2, p. 29.

54. *DF*, chap. 15, p. 467.

55. Ibid., p. 446.

56. Ibid.

57. Ibid., p. 483.

58. *DF*, chap. 38, p. 60.

59. Ibid., pp. 103–12.

60. Ibid., p. 111. See Hugh R. Trevor-Roper, ed., *Gibbon: The Decline and Fall of the Roman Empire and Other Selections* (New York, 1963), p. xxix, for the suggestion that the interplay between the history of empires and the history of the sciences provides the constant theme of *The Decline and Fall*.

CARLYLE'S *FREDERICK THE GREAT*

1. For details, see Hugh R. Trevor-Roper, *The Last Days of Hitler* (New York, 1947), pp. 97–98, 231–32.

2. See Walter E. Houghton, *The Victorian Frame of Mind, 1830–1870* (New Haven, 1957), chap. 12.

3. David Masson, *Edinburgh Sketches,* cited in David Alec Wilson, *Carlyle Till Marriage, 1795–1826* (London, 1923), p. 147.

4. See René Wellek, "Carlyle and the Philosophy of History," *Philological Quarterly* 23 (1944), pp. 55–76; and Ernst Cassirer, *The Myth of the State* (New Haven, 1946), chap. 15.

5. Julian Symons, ed., *Carlyle: Selected Works, Reminiscences and Letters* (Cambridge, Mass., 1967), p. 50.

6. Ibid., p. 54.

7. Carlyle to John Sterling, June 4, 1835, cited in ibid., p. 738.

8. Ibid., pp. 282–83.

9. Ibid., p. 300.

10. Ibid., p. 415.

11. Carlyle to Varnhagen von Ense, October 29, 1851, cited in David Alec Wilson, *Carlyle at His Zenith, 1848–1853* (London, 1927), p. 388.

12. Carlyle to Ralph Waldo Emerson, June 25, 1852, cited in ibid., pp. 422–23.

13. Carlyle to Joseph Neuberg, October 8, 1854, cited in David Alec Wilson, *Carlyle to Threescore-and-Ten, 1853–1865* (London, 1929), p. 121.

14. Carlyle to his sister [1852], cited in Wilson, *Zenith*, p. 443.

15. Carlyle to Neuberg, May 9, 1864, cited in Wilson, *Threescore-and-Ten*, p. 543.

16. Symons, *Carlyle*, p. 655.

17. Carlyle to Emerson, January 27, 1867, *The Correspondence of Thomas Carlyle and Ralph Waldo Emerson* (Boston, 1883), vol. 2, p. 301.

18. Friedrich Meinecke, *Machiavellism: The Doctrine of Raison d'Etat and Its Place in Modern History,* translated by Douglas Scott from *Die Idee der Staatsraison* (London, 1957), pp. 272–342.

19. Richard C. Beatty, "Macaulay and Carlyle," *Philological Quarterly* 18 (1939): 32–33.

20. Cited in Herbert Butterfield, *Man on His Past: The Study of the History of Historical Scholarship* (Cambridge, 1955), p. 217.

21. Harold Laski to Justice Holmes, September 26, 1923, *Holmes-Laski Letters: The Correspondence of Mr. Justice Holmes and Harold J. Laski* (Cambridge, Mass., 1953), p. 544.

22. Thomas Carlyle, *History of Frederick the Great* (Chicago, 1969), pp. 24, 250.

23. Thomas Carlyle, *History of Friedrich II of Prussia Called Frederick the Great* (Centenary Edition, New York, 1900), vol. 6, pp. 304–5.

24. Carlyle, *Frederick* (1969 Chicago ed.), p. 31.

25. Carlyle, *Frederick* (1900 New York ed.), vol. 6, p. 61.

26. Ibid., p. 62.

27. Ibid., vol. 4, p. 25.

28. Carlyle, *Frederick* (1969 Chicago ed.), p. 234.

29. Ibid.

30. Carlyle to Emerson, April 8, 1854, cited in Wilson, *Threescore-and-Ten*, p. 92.

31. Carlyle, *Frederick* (1900 New York ed.), vol. 4, p. 206.

32. Ibid., pp. 215–16.

33. New Haven, 1968.

34. Emerson to Carlyle [May 1859], cited in Wilson, *Threescore-and-Ten*, p. 312.

35. Carlyle, *Frederick* (1969 Chicago ed.), p. 102.

36. Carlyle, *Frederick* (1900 New York ed.), vol. 2, p. 100.

37. Ibid., pp. 286–87.

38. Carlyle, *Frederick* (1969 Chicago ed.), p. 207.

39. Carlyle, *Frederick* (1900 New York ed.), vol. 4, p. 472.

THE SOCIAL BACKGROUND OF THE
SCOTTISH RENAISSANCE

1. Cf. T. C. Smout, *Scottish Trade on the Eve of Union, 1660–1707* (Edinburgh, 1963). Smout dates significant economic advancement from about 1730.

2. This bifurcation is strikingly illustrated by the Easy Club, in whose founding (1712) Allan Ramsay had a part. Its members "met in a Society By themselves in order that by a Mutual improvement in Conversation they may become more adapted for fellowship with the politer part of mankind and Learn also from one anothers happy observations." Originally the six founding members picked English literary pseudonyms such as "Bickerstaff," "Rochester," and "Newton." By 1713 all except "Newton" had assumed names connected with native literary history, Ramsay undergoing a metamorphosis from "Bickerstaff" to "Gavin Douglas." A. Gibson, *New Light on Allan Ramsay* (1927), pp. 42, 48.

3. D. Stewart, "Account of the Life and Writings of Adam Smith, LL.D.," in W. Hamilton, ed., *The Collected Works of Dugald Stewart* (1854–60), vol. 10, p. 82.

4. W. E. H. Lecky, *A History of England in the Eighteenth Century* (New York, 1878), vol. 2, p. 97.

5. [D. Stewart], *Account of the Life and Writing of William Robertson* (London, 1802), p. 4.

6. F. A. Pottle, ed., *Boswell's London Journal 1762–1763* (New York, 1950), p. 287.

7. H. W. Thompson, *A Scottish Man of Feeling* (New York, 1831), p. ix.

8. Cf. N. T. Phillipson, "The Scottish Whigs and the Reform of the Court of Session, 1785–1830" (Cambridge University Doctoral Thesis, 1967).

9. [E. Topham], *Letters from Edinburgh, 1774–1775* (Dublin, 1776), vol. 2, p. 121.

10. The list, dated October 17, 1759, is printed in Dugald Stewart's *Life of Robertson,* pp. 214–20. The Rev. Alexander Carlyle, who supplied Stewart with the list, notes in his *Autobiography* (1910), pp. 311–12, that it is incomplete. But he lists only two additional members, one of whom is a lawyer.

11. For a list of members (undated, but probably compiled in the 1720s) cf. A. F. Tytler, Lord Woodhouselee, *Memoirs of the Life and Writings of the Honourable Henry Home of Kames* (2nd ed., 1814), vol. 3, 75–76. It totaled nineteen.

12. J. Ramsay of Ochtertyre, *Scotland and Scotsmen in the Eighteenth Century* (1888), vol. 1, p. 39.

13. James, Viscount Stair, *Institutions of the Laws of Scotland* (3rd ed., 1749), p. ii.

14. Woodhouselee, *Kames,* vol. 1, p. 12.

15. W. Blackstone, *Commentaries on the Laws of England* (Chicago, 1876), p. 4.

16. D. B. Smith, "Roman Law," in *An Introductory Survey of the Sources and Literature of Scots Law* (Stair Society ed., 1936), p. 176.

17. Baron [David] Hume, *Lectures, 1786–1822* (Stair Society ed., 1939), pp. 1–2.

18. J. C. Gardner, "French and Dutch Influences," in *Survey of Scots Law*, p. 233. Utrecht and Bourges also attracted many Scottish law students throughout the century. Dr. Phillipson has found that the influence of Dutch law schools on Scotland began to decline by the beginning of the eighteenth century, at a time when sons of gentlemen were starting to desert the Bar for other forms of employment, and when Scottish law schools were beginning to grow in importance.

19. S. G. Kermack, "Natural Jurisprudence and Philosophy of Law," in *Survey of Scots Law*, p. 440.

20. Ibid., p. 441.

21. On the works of Grotius as the antithesis of rigorous Protestantism, cf. E. Troeltsch, *The Social Teaching of the Christian Churches* (New York, 1931), vol. 2, p. 636; and the same author's *Die Bedeutung des Protestantismus fuer die Entstehung der modernen Welt* (Munich and Berlin, 1911), p. 79.

22. Stair, *Institutions,* pp. 2, 5–6, 13.

23. P. G. Stein, "Legal Thought in Eighteenth-Century Scotland," *Juridical Review,* new series, 2 (1957): 1–20.

24. A. Lang, *Sir George Mackenzie: His Life and Times* (London, 1909), p. 299.

25. A. Grant, *The Story of the University of Edinburgh During Its First Three Hundred Years* (London, 1884), vol. 1, p. 202.

26. Ibid. p. 188.

27. A. Grant, *University of Edinburgh,* vol. 1, p. 188; and A. Bower, *The History of the University of Edinburgh* (1817), vol. 1, pp. 214–15.

28. R. H. Tawney, *Religion and the Rise of Capitalism* (Pelican ed., New York, 1947), pp. 99–100.

29. Curriculum proposed by King's College, Aberdeen, cited in A. Morgan, *Scottish University Studies* (London, 1933), p. 69.

30. A. Monro, *Presbyterian Inquisition,* quoted in "Letters of Alexander Munro, 1690–1698," in W. K. Dickson, ed., *Miscellany of the Scottish History Society,* 3rd Series, 5 (1933): 199.

31. A. Bower, *University of Edinburgh,* vol. 1, pp. 269–70.

32. R. K. Merton, "Puritanism, Pietism, and Science," in *Social Theory and Social Structure* (Glencoe, Ill., 1940), pp. 329–46. It is, however, worthy of note that some

Presbyterians perceived no dangers in Cartesianism because they took it to show God's rational plan. Cf. G. D. Henderson, *Religious Life in Seventeenth-Century Scotland* (Cambridge, 1937), p. 133. And by the 1720s the "Literary Reformers" among the clergy began to approve of science because it ennobled the soul, "leading it to contemplate and adore the Author of nature, in all his works and ways." Ramsay, *Scotland*, vol. 1, p. 222.

33. P. Hume Brown, *History of Scotland* (Cambridge, 1909), vol. 2, pp. 414–15.

34. G. D. Henderson, *Religious Life*, pp. 71–75. Hutcheson was thus not undertaking anything radically new when he conducted special classes on the *De Veritate* at Glasgow. Ibid., p. 260.

35. Ibid., p. 157.

36. A. Grant, *Story of University of Edinburgh*, vol. 1, pp. 228–30, 262–63. See also D. B. Horn, *A Short History of the University of Edinburgh 1556–1889* (1967), pp. 36–47.

37. L. W. Sharp, ed., "Early Letters of Robert Wo[o]drow, 1698–1709," *Publications of the Scottish History Society*, 3rd series, 24 (1937): xl, xliii.

38. R. Wodrow, *Analecta* (1842–43), vol. 3, pp. 170–72. These contemporary comments, by a Presbyterian minister who looked back nostalgically to Covenanting days, are invaluable for any study of Scottish culture in the early eighteenth century.

39. Ibid., vol. 3, p. 309.

40. Ibid., vol. 3, p. 175.

41. See above, p. 153. For a brief but very important essay about the significance of the Rankenian Club for Scottish intellectual history, see G. E. Davie, "Hume in His Contemporary Setting," *David Hume: University of Edinburgh 250th Anniversary of the Birth of David Hume 1711–1761. A record of the Commemoration Published as a Supplement to the University Gazette* (1961), pp. 11–15. Davie shows that members of the Rankenian Club introduced Berkeley into the Scottish curriculum, and that some of the problems raised by Berkeley's philosophy supplied important raw materials for Hume.

42. Cf. H. W. Meikle, *Some Aspects of Later Seventeenth-Century Scotland* (Glasgow, 1947), p. 6: "So in the later seventeenth century, beneath the surface of Scottish life, dominated by bitter religious strife and persecution, and by tyrannical government, there were currents of thought and even cultural achievement which made their own permanent contribution to Scottish national well-being."

43. P. Hume Brown, *History*, vol. 2, pp. 286–308.

44. Ibid., vol. 3, p. 4.

45. For evidence on this point, cf. Woodhouselee, *Kames*, vol. 1, pp. 161–62; Ramsay, *Scotland*, vol. 2, pp. 5–52; Wodrow, *Analecta*, vol. 4, pp. 84, 415. Trevelyan is more cautious and sees the gentry of the lowlands divided not unevenly into Presbyterians and Episcopalians. G. M. Trevelyan, *England under Queen Anne: Ramillies and the Union with Scotland* (London, 1932), p. 183. On the contribution of Scottish land-

owners to the development of a dynamic economy in the eighteenth century, see T. C. Smout, "Scottish Landowners and Economic Growth, 1650–1850," *Scottish Journal of Political Economy* 11 (1964): 218–34.

46. This statement, citing Episcopalianism in contrast to the ascetic aspects of Presbyterianism, may err on the side of simplification. The differences, certainly through 1688, did not turn on forms of worship. What *did* distinguish the two Confessions was a definite spirit of anti-dogmatism on the part of the Episcopalians who generally looked askance at what seemed to them narrow and fanatical in Presbyterianism; deriving, as they did, from a theological tradition still close enough to Catholicism to be naturally amenable to both rationalism and latitudinarianism. It should be noted that the cleavage between the two came to rest not only on political but to some extent on class lines. (Cf. Ramsay's statement that while in a few shires Presbyterians formed a great proportion of the gentlemen, they constituted the vast majority of burgesses and commonalty in Scotland as a whole, with the Episcopalians dominating the upper classes. Ramsay, *Scotland*, vol. 2, p. 55.) Many of the Episcopalian clergy were men of good family who had traveled and had acquired some formal culture. G. D. Henderson, *Religious Life*, pp. 257–58.

47. See the description of an Edinburgh musicale in the early eighteenth century, with the Laird of Newhall playing the viola da gamba, Sir Gilbert Elliot of Minto the flute, and Lord Colville the harpsichord, in H. G. Graham, *Scottish Men of Letters in the Eighteenth Century* (London, 1901), p. 22. On the poverty of the gentry and minor nobility in the early eighteenth century, see Sir Walter Scott, "General Account of Edinburgh," *Provincial Antiquities and Picturesque Scenery of Scotland with Descriptive Illustrations* (London, 1826), vol. 2, pp. 71–82.

48. H. Arnot, *The History of Edinburgh to 1780* (1816), p. 127.

49. Cf. J. Colville, "Social Life in Edinburgh after the Union," *The Union of 1707: A Survey of Events* (Glasgow, 1907), pp. 123–33.

50. D. Duncan, *Thomas Ruddiman: A Study in Scottish Scholarship of the Early Eighteenth Century* (1965), p. 21.

51. Wodrow, *Analecta*, vol. 1, p. 218. (December 5, 1709).

52. Ramsay, *Scotland*, vol. 1, p. 221.

53. *Boswell's London Journal*, p. 201.

54. Wodrow, *Early Letters*, p. xxxvii; Graham, *Men of Letters*, p. 10. On the importance of Watson, originally Roman Catholic, see W. Ferguson, *Scotland 1689 to the Present* (1968), pp. 98–100.

55. See D. Daiches, *The Paradox of Scottish Culture: The Eighteenth-Century Experience* (London, 1964), on the literary importance of the Jacobite movement. On Jacobite circles in Rome, significant in the diffusion to Scotland of Italianate tastes in art and architecture, see B. Skinner, *The Scots in Italy in the Eighteenth Century* (1966), and A. Smart, *The Life and Art of Allan Ramsay* (London, 1952).

56. A. Bower, *University of Edinburgh*, vol. 2, pp. 66–67.

57. Ramsay, *Scotland,* vol. 1, p. 85.

58. G. Chalmers, *The Life of Thomas Ruddiman* (London, 1794), pp. 83–84.

59. J. Chamberlayne, *Magnae Britanniae Notitia: or, the Present State of Great Britain* (London, 1708), p. iii.

60. Perry Miller, *The New England Mind: From Colony to Province* (Cambridge, Mass., 1953), p. 6.

61. Wodrow, *Analecta,* vol. 3, p. 515.

62. David Hume to John Clephane, April 20, 1756, quoted in J. Y. T. Greig, ed., *The Letters of David Hume* (Oxford, 1932), vol. 1, p. 229; Adam Smith to Lord Fitzmaurice, February 21, 1759, quoted in W. R. Scott, *Adam Smith as Student and Professor* (Glasgow, 1937), p. 241; George Dempster to Adam Fergusson, December 5, 1756, quoted in J. Fergusson, ed., *Letters of George Dempster to Sir Adam Fergusson, 1756–1813* (London, 1934), p. 15.

63. Ramsay, *Scotland,* vol. 1, p. 5.

64. William Robertson to Baron Mure, November 1761, Dugald Stewart, "Account of the Life and Writings of William Robertson, D.D.," in W. Hamilton, ed., *The Collected Works of Dugald Stewart* (1854–60), vol. 10, p. 136; David Hume to Adam Ferguson, November 9, 1763, in Greig, *Letters of Hume,* vol. 1, pp. 410–11.

65. William Tod to William Smellie, November 29, 1759, in R. Kerr, *Memoirs of the Life, Writings, and Correspondence of William Smellie* (1811), vol. 1, p. 46.

66. *Boswell's London Journal,* p. 71; F. A. Pottle, ed., *Boswell in Holland, 1763–1764* (New York, 1952), pp. 137, 260.

67. For the whole subject of provincialism, see John Clive and Bernard Bailyn, "England's Cultural Provinces: Scotland and America," *William and Mary Quarterly,* 3rd series, 11, No. 2 (April 1954): 200–213.

ENGLISH CLIOGRAPHERS

1. G. M. Trevelyan left instructions that no biography be written of him. But see Joseph M. Hernon, Jr., "The Last Whig Historian and Consensus History: George Macaulay Trevelyan, 1876–1962," *American Historical Review* 81 (1976): 66–97.

2. *Lord Acton: A Study in Conscience and Politics* (Chicago: University of Chicago Press, 1952).

3. Leslie Stephen, ed., *The Letters of John Richard Green* (London: Macmillan, 1902), p. 59.

4. Ibid., p. 427, Green to Freeman, February 26, 1867.

5. Isaiah Berlin, "L. B. Namier: A Personal Impression," *Encounter* 27 (1966): 32–42.

6. George Macaulay Trevelyan, *Sir George Otto Trevelyan: A Memoir* (London: Longmans, Green, 1932), p. 30.

7. James Anthony Froude, *Thomas Carlyle: A History of His Life in London* (New York, 1884), p. 31.

8. Ibid., p. 82.

9. Ibid., p. 281.

10. Ibid., p. 130.

11. Richard Ellmann, "Literary Biography," in *Golden Codgers: Biographical Speculations* (New York: Oxford University Press, 1973), p. 16.

12. L. B. Namier, "History," in *Avenues of History* (London: Hamilton, 1952), p. 4; Alan Bullock, "The Historian's Purpose: History and Metahistory," in Hans Meyerhoff, ed., *The Philosophy of History in Our Time* (New York: Doubleday, 1959), p. 298.

13. Julia Namier, *Lewis Namier: A Biography* (London: Oxford University Press, 1971), p. 264; Neil McKendrick, "J. H. Plumb: A Valedictory Tribute," in McKendrick, ed., *Historical Perspectives: Studies in English Thought and Society in Honour of J. H. Plumb* (London: Europa Publications, 1974), p. 5.

14. W. E. Gladstone, *Gleanings of Past Years: 1845–1876* (London, 1879), vol. 2, p. 274.

15. Lytton Strachey, "David Hume," in *Portraits in Miniature and Other Essays* (New York: Chatto and Windus, 1931), p. 145.

16. Julia Namier, *Namier*, p. 280.

17. Walter Bagehot, "Mr. Macaulay," in *Collected Works* (Cambridge: Harvard University Press, 1965), vol. 1, p. 397.

18. Ibid., p. 399.

19. Ibid., p. 402.

20. Ibid., p. 399.

21. Ibid., p. 415.

22. George Otto Trevelyan, *The Life and Letters of Lord Macaulay* (London: Longmans, Green, 1959), p. 130.

23. Ibid., p. 133. On Macaulay's historical imagination, see John Clive, "Macaulay's Historical Imagination," *Review of English Studies* 1 (1960): 20–27.

24. McKendrick, "Plumb," p. 16.

25. Bernard Bailyn, "History and the Literary Imagination," Carl L. Becker Lectures, Cornell University, 1975.

26. Quoted in Trygve R. Tholfsen, *Historical Thinking: An Introduction* (New York: Harper and Row, 1967), p. 252.

27. Ibid., pp. 249–50.

28. L. B. Namier, *Skyscrapers and Other Essays* (London: Macmillan, 1931).

29. Trevelyan, *Macaulay*, p. 503.

PETER AND THE WALLAH

1. S. Gopal, *British Policy in India 1858–1905* (Cambridge, 1965), p. 36.

2. G. M. Trevelyan, *Sir George Otto Trevelyan: A Memoir* (London, 1932), p. 66.

3. Francis R. Hart, *Lockhart as Romantic Biographer* (Edinburgh, 1971), p. 62.

4. Marion Lochhead, *John Gibson Lockhart* (London, 1954), p. 291.

5. Hart, *Lockhart*, p. 58.

6. W. L. Burn, *The Age of Equipoise: A Study of the Mid-Victorian Generation* (London, 1964), p. 84.

7. Albert O. Hirschman, *The Passions and the Interests* (Princeton, 1977), p. 132.

MORE OR LESS EMINENT VICTORIANS

1. The literature is large. The brief summaries of the "defense" and "prosecution" in this essay owe most, on the "defense" side, to Charles Richard Sanders, *Lytton Strachey: His Mind and Art* (New Haven, 1957), a full and conscientious survey of Strachey's work that, while it fails to match the sprightliness of its subject, conveys a good sense of his range and his scale of values, and to Noel Annan, "Lytton Strachey and His Critics," *Listener* 40 (1949): 848–49; and, on the "prosecution" side, to F. A. Simpson, "Methods of History," *Spectator* 172 (1944): 7–8, and James Pope-Hennessy, "Strachey's Way," *Spectator* 182 (1949): 264. Sanders supplies extensive references to the other relevant literature. See also Leon Edel, *Literary Biography* (London, 1957), pp. 88–89, and Hugh Trevor-Roper, "Strachey as Historian," *Historical Essays* (London, 1957), pp. 279–85.

2. Shane Leslie, *Manning* (London, 1953), p. 190. This book is a revised and condensed version of the author's earlier *Henry Edward Manning, His Life and Labours* (London, 1921).

3. Lionel Trilling, *Matthew Arnold* (New York, 1939), pp. 36–76; Basil Willey, *Nineteenth Century Studies* (London, 1949), pp. 51–72. Fully granting the deficiencies of Strachey's portrait of Arnold, it is well to recall that the dangers of the sort of continuous moral hypertension inculcated by him at Rugby were observed long before *Eminent Victorians*—by Clough, by Fitzjames and Leslie Stephen, and by Jowett, to name only a few. This is not to say that they were necessarily right. But some of Strachey's detractors give the misleading impression that he was the first to denigrate people whom their contemporaries had perforce regarded as virtual saints.

4. For another biography of Chadwick, see R. A. Lewis, *Edwin Chadwick and the Public Health Movement, 1832–1854* (London, 1952).

5. In this he was in accord with the late Humphry House, who observed that the search for the ego had led to the neglect of the superego; and that this limitation of vision was the great danger facing the contemporary biographer. "Biography is being strangled by art; and we have to unwind the silken scarf from its throat" (Humphry House, "The Present Art of Biography," *All in Due Time* [London, 1955], p. 264). Actually, these fears have proved groundless. In fact, judging by recent evidence, historical background is not unlikely soon to gain a victory over preoccupation with personality, "Lives and Times" over "Lives."

6. See Edel, *Literary Biography,* for a shrewd discussion of this special form of biography. The present essay was completed before the appearance of the second volume of Gordon N. Ray's definitive *Thackeray* biography, *The Uses of Adversity, 1811–1846* (New York, 1955), and *The Age of Wisdom, 1847–1863* (New York, 1958), which should certainly be added to any list of outstanding Victorian biographies.

7. "The Intellectual Aristocracy," in J. H. Plumb, ed., *Studies in Social History: A Tribute to G. M. Trevelyan* (London, 1955), pp. 243–87.

8. *More Nineteenth Century Studies: A Group of Honest Doubters* (London, 1956), pp. 179–84.

9. Norman Foerster, "The Critical Study of the Victorian Age," in Joseph E. Baker, ed., *The Reinterpretation of Victorian Literature* (Princeton, 1950), p. 64.

10. Sir Geoffrey Faber, *Jowett: A Portrait with Background* (London, 1957), p. 153. And see the same book, p. 345, where Sir Geoffrey, referring to the time just before Jowett's ship came in, comments that Destiny began to take a hand: "He must not be allowed to spoil her plan by speaking his mind too fully on dangerous topics."

11. G. S. R. Kitson Clark, "The Electorate and the Repeal of the Corn Laws," *Transactions of the Royal Historical Society,* 5th series, 1 (1951): 109–26; "The Repeal of the Corn Laws and the Politics of the Forties," *Economic History Review,* 2nd series, 4 (1951–1952): 1–13; and "Hunger and Politics in 1842," *Journal of Modern History* 25 (1953): 355–74.

12. See Asa Briggs' point in *Victorian People,* p. 153, that character must have been a scarce endowment in the fifties and sixties *just because* there was so much stress on it.

13. House, "Are the Victorians Coming Back?" *All in Due Time,* p. 79.

Index

Permissions
Acknowledgments

══ ∘∘ ══

Various essays included in this work were originally published in *The American Scholar*, *Harvard Magazine*, *Harvard English Studies*, *History Today*, *The Nation*, *The New York Review of Books*, *Proceedings of the Massachusetts Historical Society*, and *The Review of English Literature*.

"The Education of Alexis de Tocqueville" was originally published in *Partisan Review*, Vol. XVII, No. 7 (1950).

Grateful acknowledgment is made to the following for permission to reprint previously published material:

Australian Broadcasting Corporation: "The Use of the Past" by John Clive, from the series "The Use of History." Reprinted by permission of the Radio Drama and Features Department of the Australian Broadcasting Corporation.

Australian Historical Association Bulletin: "Transitions and Suspense: Some Practical Hints from the Great Historians" by John Clive, published March 1985. Reprinted by permission.

The Critical Review: "Looking over a Four-Leaf Clover" by John Clive, published in *The Critical Review*, No. 27 (1985). Reprinted by permission.

Daedalus: "Gibbon's Humor" by John Clive, published as "Edward Gibbon and the Decline and Fall of the Roman Empire" (Vol. 105, No. 3, Summer 1976). Reprinted by permission of *Daedalus*, Journal of the American Academy of Arts and Sciences, Cambridge, Massachusetts.

Gerald Duckworth & Co. Ltd.: "Peter and the Wallah" by John Clive, from *History and Imagination*, edited by Hugh Lloyd-Jones, Valerie Pearl, and Blair Warden. Reprinted by permission.

Edinburgh University Press: "The Social Background of the Scottish Renaissance" by John Clive, from *Scotland in the Age of Enlightenment*, edited by Phillipson and Mitchison. Reprinted by permission of Edinburgh University Press, 22 George Square, Edinburgh, EH8 9LF, Scotland.

History and Theory: "A Nephew's Tribute" by John Clive, originally published as an untitled review in *History and Theory* 1 (1961), 210–215. Copyright © 1961 by Wesleyan University. Reprinted by permission.

The New Republic: "Michelet" (10/26/87) and "The Prying Yorkshireman" (6/23/82) by John Clive, published in *The New Republic*. Reprinted by permission.

The New York Times Company: "Majestic Histories" (8/27/84) by John Clive. Copyright © 1984 by The New York Times Company. Reprinted by permission.

The Times Literary Supplement: "The Victorians from the Inside" (1/20/78), "Carlyle and His Vocation" (4/20/84), "An Odd Couple" (4/18/86), and "The Great Historians in the Age of Cliometrics" by John Clive, published in *The Times Literary Supplement*. Reprinted by permission.

The University of California Press: "Laura, A Stonemason's Daughter" by John Clive, published in *University Publishing*, Spring 1981. Reprinted by permission.

The University of Chicago Press: "Carlyle's *Frederick the Great*" by John Clive, published as the "Introduction" to Thomas Carlyle, *History of Friedrich II of Prussia Called Frederick the Great*, edited by John Clive (in the Classics of European History Series, ed. Krieger). Copyright © 1969 by The University of Chicago. All rights reserved. Reprinted by permission.

Victorian Studies: "More or Less Eminent Victorians" by John Clive, published in *Victorian Studies*, September 1958. Reprinted by permission of the Indiana University Board of Trustees.